Gender in the Middle Ages

Volume 8

MARRIED WOMEN AND THE LAW IN PREMODERN NORTHWEST EUROPE

Gender in the Middle Ages

ISSN 1742-870X

This series investigates the representation and construction of masculinity and femininity in the Middle Ages from a variety of disciplinary and interdisciplinary perspectives. It aims in particular to explore the diversity of medieval genders, and such interrelated contexts and issues as sexuality, social class, race and ethnicity, and orthodoxy and heterodoxy.

Proposals or queries should be sent in the first instance to the editors or to the publisher, at the addresses given below; all submissions will receive prompt and informed consideration.

Professor Jacqueline Murray, College of Arts, University of Guelph, Guelph, Ontario, H1G 2W1, Canada

Professor Diane Watt, School of English and Languages, AD Building, University of Surrey, Guildford, Surrey GU5 7XH

Boydell & Brewer Limited, PO Box 9, Woodbridge, Suffolk, IP12 3DF, UK

Also in this series:

I *Gender and Medieval Drama,* Katie Normington, 2004

II *Gender and Petty Crime in Late Medieval England: The Local Courts in Kent, 1460–1560,* Karen Jones, 2006

III *The Pastoral Care of Women in Late Medieval England,* Beth Allison Barr, 2008

IV *Gender, Nation and Conquest in the Works of William of Malmesbury,* Kirsten A. Fenton, 2008

V *Monsters, Gender and Sexuality in Medieval English Literature,* Dana M. Oswald, 2010

VI *Medieval Anchoritisms: Gender, Space and the Solitary Life,* Liz Herbert McAvoy, 2011

VII *Middle-Aged Women in the Middle Ages,* edited by Sue Niebrzydowski, 2011

MARRIED WOMEN AND THE LAW IN PREMODERN NORTHWEST EUROPE

edited by

Cordelia Beattie and Matthew Frank Stevens

THE BOYDELL PRESS

First published 2013
The Boydell Press, Woodbridge

ISBN 978-1-84383-833-3

The Boydell Press is an imprint of Boydell & Brewer Ltd
PO Box 9, Woodbridge, Suffolk IP12 3DF, UK
and of Boydell & Brewer Inc.
668 Mt Hope Avenue, Rochester, NY 14620-2731, USA
website: www.boydellandbrewer.co.uk

A CIP catalogue record for this book is available from the British Library

Papers used by Boydell & Brewer Ltd are natural, recyclable products made from wood grown in sustainable forests

MIX Paper from responsible sources FSC® C013604

Printed and bound by
CPI Group (UK) Ltd, Croydon, CR0 4YY

CONTENTS

FIGURES AND TABLES

Figures:

Tables:

CONTRIBUTORS

Cordelia Beattie is Senior Lecturer in Medieval History at the University of Edinburgh. She is author of *Medieval Single Women: The Politics of Social Classification in Late Medieval England* (Oxford, 2007) and various essays on women and gender in premodern Europe. She is also co-editor, with Anna Maslakovic and Sarah Rees Jones, of *The Medieval Household in Christian Europe, c. 850–c. 1550: Managing Power, Wealth and the Body* (Turnhout, 2003) and, with Kirsten A. Fenton, of *Intersections of Gender, Religion, and Ethnicity in the Middle Ages* (London, 2011).

Lars Ivar Hansen is Professor of Medieval and Early Modern History at the University of Tromsø, Norway. His main fields of research are economic and social history, focusing on the role of kinship networks and other networks of alliance, inheritance practices, and the inter-ethnic relations between the peoples of northern Fennoscandia. Together with Bjørnar Olsen he is the author of *Samenes historie fram til 1700* [The history of the Sámi until 1700] (Oslo, 2004).

Shennan Hutton received her Ph.D. in medieval history from the University of California, Davis, and teaches courses at various colleges in northern California. Her interests include medieval Flanders, urban history, medieval wool cloth production, and gender. She is the author of *Women and Economic Activities in Late Medieval Ghent* (New York, 2011).

Lizabeth Johnson earned her Ph.D. in medieval history from the University of Washington, Seattle in 2008. She is currently teaching for the University Honors Program at the University of New Mexico. Her research focuses on the transition from native Welsh law to English common law in fourteenth-century Welsh society. In particular, she focuses on the treatment of women, married and single, in these post-conquest courts and women's access to the court system.

Gillian Kenny teaches history in the Department of Adult Education in University College Dublin. She is the author of *Anglo-Irish and Gaelic Women in Ireland c. 1170–1540* (Dublin, 2007). Her interests centre on women's history in Ireland, Wales and Scotland, particularly focusing on the issues surrounding intermarriage and cultural exchange.

Mia Korpiola is Reader in Legal History at the University of Helsinki, where she currently works as a Research Fellow in the Helsinki Collegium for Advanced Studies. She is author of *Between Betrothal and Bedding: Marriage Formation in Sweden, 1200–1600* (Leiden, 2009) and editor of *Regional Variations in Matrimo-*

nial Law and Custom in Europe, 1150–1600 (Leiden, 2011). Her interests include sexual crime, family law, and the reception of learned law in medieval and Reformation Sweden. She is now working on women in the legal professions and the legal history of cars and bicycles in nineteenth- and twentieth-century Finland.

Miriam Müller is Lecturer in Medieval History at the University of Birmingham. She has published widely on the later medieval English peasantry. Her current research project explores how the position of women in peasant communities varied according to locality.

Sheilagh Ogilvie is Professor of Economic History at the University of Cambridge. Her research explores how institutional constraints on the decisions of ordinary people affected economic development and human well-being. She is the author of *State Corporatism and Proto-Industry: The Württemberg Black Forest, 1580–1797* (Cambridge, 1997), *A Bitter Living: Women, Markets, and Social Capital in Early Modern Germany* (Oxford, 2003), and *Institutions and European Trade: Merchant Guilds, 1000–1800* (Cambridge, 2011); and co-editor of *European Proto-Industrialization* (Cambridge, 1996) and *Germany: A New Social and Economic History* (3 vols, London, 1996–2003). She has published widely on women's position in early modern Germany and Bohemia.

Alexandra Shepard is Reader in Early Modern History at the University of Glasgow. She is author of *Meanings of Manhood in Early Modern England* (Oxford, 2003) and several essays on gender and social relations in early modern England. She is co-editor of *Communities in Early Modern England* (Manchester, 2000) and *Gender and Change: Agency, Chronology and Periodisation* (Oxford, 2009), and is currently finishing a book on worth, status and the language of self-description in England between 1550 and 1730.

Cathryn Spence is a Social Sciences and Humanities Research Council of Canada Post-Doctoral Research Fellow at the University of Guelph in Ontario, Canada. Her Ph.D., completed at the University of Edinburgh, explored the economic roles of women in early modern Scottish towns. Her research interests include urban and economic history, and the impact of gender and socioeconomic status when accessing credit in Western Europe.

Matthew Frank Stevens is Lecturer in Medieval History at Swansea University. His interests include urban history, the development of common law, and the position of marginalized groups (women, ethnic minorities) within local and national legal frameworks. He is author of *Urban Assimilation in Post-Conquest Wales: Ethnicity, Gender and Economy in Ruthin, 1282–1348* (Cardiff, 2010).

INTRODUCTION: UNCOVERING MARRIED WOMEN

Cordelia Beattie and Matthew Frank Stevens

Why Married Women?

As a number of our contributors comment, particularly those writing on pre-modern Britain, there has been a tendency in the historiography on women and the law to see married women as hidden from view, obscured by their husbands in the legal records. It is this tendency, which did not fit well with our own experiences of medieval legal material, that we were reacting against when we decided to put together this volume of essays. It is our intention that, by offering detailed studies of legal material from pre-modern England alongside those from other parts of northwest Europe (Wales, Scotland, Ireland, Ghent, Sweden, Norway and Germany), we will gain a better sense of how, when, and where the legal principle of coverture – which designated the husband as his wife's legal representative and in control of her property – was applied and what effect this had on the lives of married women. Key threads running through the book pertain to married women's rights regarding the possession of moveable and immovable property, marital property at the dissolution of marriage, married women's capacity to act as agents of their husbands and households in transacting business, and married women's interactions with the courts. In what follows, we will justify our focus on pre-modern northwest Europe with reference to existing scholarship, as well as highlighting some of the findings of this collection of essays.

The aforementioned view of married women's legal subjection can be, and has been, traced back to Sir William Blackstone's *Commentaries on the Laws of England* (1st edition, 1765), which became a standard legal textbook for nearly a century:

> By marriage, the husband and wife are one person in law; that is, the very being or legal existence of the woman is suspended during the marriage, or at least is incorporated and consolidated into that of the husband; under whose wing, protection, and *cover*, she performs everything; ... Upon this principle, of an union of person

> in husband and wife, depend almost all the legal rights, duties, and disabilities that either of them acquire by the marriage.[1]

However, as Mary Beard has pointed out, Blackstone was referring to the wife's position under *common* law;[2] customary law, canon law and equity had different positions.[3] But, even in the context of English common law, there is the need for further caution. Frederick William Maitland warned about the perils of relying on 'unity of person' as 'a consistently operative principle':

> If we look for any one thought which governs the whole of this province of law [that which concerns the husband and wife], we shall hardly find it. In particular we must be on our guard against the common belief that the ruling principle is that which sees an 'unity of person' between husband and wife. This is a principle which suggests itself from time to time; it has the warrant of holy writ; it will serve to round a paragraph, and may now and again lead us out of or into a difficulty; but a consistently operative principle it can not be.[4]

Maitland argues that 'the main idea which governs the law of husband and wife is not that of an "unity of person", but that of the guardianship, the *mund*, the profitable guardianship, which the husband has over the wife and over her property'.[5] By this he means that the husband controlled the property that the woman brought

1 7th edn (1775) as cited in M. R. Beard, *Woman as Force in History: A Study in Traditions and Realities* (New York, 1965), p. 89. For Blackstone's influence (and critiques), see ibid., esp. ch. 4; C. Cannon, 'The Rights of Medieval English Women: Crime and the Issue of Representation', *Medieval Crime and Social Control*, ed. B. A. Hanawalt and D. Wallace (Minneapolis, 1999), pp. 156–85, esp. pp. 158–60.

2 Beard, *Woman as Force in History*, p. 92.

3 On the married woman's position according to borough customs see, e.g., M. Bateson (ed.), *Borough Customs*, Selden Society 18 (London, 1904), pp. 222–8, many of which are discussed in B. W. Gastle, '"As if she were single": Working Wives and the Late Medieval English *Femme Sole*', *The Middle Ages at Work: Practicing Labor in Late Medieval England*, ed. K. Robertson and M. Uebel (New York, 2004), pp. 41–64. On ecclesiastical courts see, e.g., R. H. Helmholz, 'Married Women's Wills in Later Medieval England', *Wife and Widow in Medieval England*, ed. S. S. Walker (Ann Arbor, 1993); L. Gowing, *Domestic Dangers: Women, Words, and Sex in Early Modern London* (Oxford, 1996), esp. pp. 30–58; T. Meldrum, 'A Women's Court in London: Defamation at the Bishop of London's Consistory Court, 1700–1745', *London Journal* 19 (1994), 1–20. On equity see, e.g., E. Hawkes, '"[S]he will ... protect and defend her rights boldly by law and reason ...": Women's Knowledge of Common Law and Equity Courts in Late-Medieval England', *Medieval Women and the Law*, ed. N. J. Menuge (Woodbridge, 2000), pp. 145–61; M. L. Cioni, 'The Elizabethan Chancery and Women's Rights', *Tudor Rule and Revolution: Essays for G.R. Elton from His American Friends*, ed. D. J. Guth and J. W. McKenna (Cambridge, 1982), pp. 159–82; T. Stretton, *Women Waging Law in Elizabethan England* (Cambridge, 1998), esp. pp. 129–54, on the Court of Requests.

4 F. Pollock and F.W. Maitland, *The History of English Law before the Time of Edward I*, 2 vols, 2nd edn (Cambridge, 1911), II, pp. 405–6.

5 Pollock and Maitland, *History of English Law*, I, p. 485.

to the marriage but he did not own it ('*her* property') and so the common law position was that her assent for various acts was needed. She should, for example, appear in court alongside her husband for any litigation concerning her land and she retained certain rights over her dower.[6]

This picture does not apply to northwest Europe in general. Here *all* women, married or single, were under legal guardianship; in England single women of age and widows were legal individuals in their own right.[7] Beyond the English realm, upon marriage the husband would usually become a woman's legal representative.[8] He would thus control 'part or even all of the property that she brought to marriage, as well as the property that they jointly acquired after marriage'.[9] But again the husband did not own the property. The key difference here is the idea of a *community* of property between the husband and wife, whereas the English property pattern kept distinct what belonged to the wife as opposed to what belonged to the husband. A number of essays in this collection – Lars Hansen on medieval Norway, Mia Korpiola on late medieval Sweden, and Shennan Hutton on late medieval Ghent – will discuss further how this worked, but it is worth noting here the scholarship which has distinguished between the English system of marital property and that in the Franco-Belgian region (with which Korpiola aligns Sweden). Charles Donahue Junior was the first to follow up on Maitland's attempt to explain why France adopted communal marital property and England did not, although their conclusions differ.[10] More recent scholarship, by Donahue and others, distinguishes further between the north of France and the northern low countries – known as the *pays de droit coutumier*, the region of 'customary', unwritten law, but also described as the Franco-Belgian region – which allowed for communal marital property, and the south of France and the southern low countries (today a large part of Belgium) – known as the *pays de droit écrit*, the region of written law – where decisions about marital property regimes and succession were made in accordance with principles derived from Roman law, as they were in much of southern Europe.[11] Such differences, we feel, justify our concentration on northwest Europe.[12]

6 Pollock and Maitland, *History of English Law*, II, pp. 407–9, 422–5.

7 A. L. Erickson, 'Coverture and Capitalism', *History Workshop Journal* 59 (2005), 1–16, pp. 2–3. On the age of majority for women see K. M. Phillips, *Medieval Maidens: Young Women and Gender in England, 1270–1540* (Manchester, 2003), pp. 32–5.

8 For German examples of married women (or the courts on their behalf) appointing other males as their legal guardians see Ogilvie's essay in this volume.

9 Erickson, 'Coverture and Capitalism', p. 3.

10 C. Donahue Jr, 'What Causes Fundamental Legal Ideas? Marital Property in England and France in the Thirteenth Century', *Michigan Law Review* 78 (1979), 59–88; Pollock and Maitland, *History of English Law*, II, pp. 402–3.

11 E.g. see C. Donahue Jr, *Law, Marriage, and Society in the Later Middle Ages: Arguments About Marriage in Five Courts* (New York, 2007), pp. 598–613; M. Vleeschouwers-Van Melkebeek, 'Separation and Marital Property in Late Medieval England and the Franco-Belgian Region', *Regional Variations in Matrimonial Law and Custom in Europe, 1150–1600*, ed. M. Korpiola (Leiden, 2011), pp. 77–97; M. C. Howell, *The Marriage Exchange: Property, Social Place, and Gender in Cities of the Low Countries, 1300–1550* (Chicago, 1998), pp. 196–217.

12 See also T. De Moor and J. L. Van Zanden, 'Girl Power: The European Marriage Pattern and La-

Why Medieval *and* Early Modern?

A long view of this topic seems logical for a number of reasons. For example, as discussed, there has been a tendency to see nothing as substantially changing in terms of married women's position under English common law between the medieval period and the end of the eighteenth century when Blackstone was writing, with the key change coming with the Married Women's Property Acts in the late nineteenth century. Also, as Judith Bennett famously argued in 1992, the sense of a 'great divide' between medieval and early modern is not borne out by studies of women's lives.[13] Similar points have been made for European society ever since Joan Kelly's classic essay 'Did Women Have a Renaissance?'[14] Indeed, Bennett, in a substantial and still influential 1988 review article of seven volumes on late medieval and early modern European women, applied the French historian Emmanuel Le Roy Ladurie's phrase 'history that stands still' to pre-modern women's history.[15]

Of course, the legal framework within which married women lived in the pre-modern era was not a static one. But its evolution followed a chronology in which the tectonic shifts in married women's legal position did not necessarily occur along other social and political fault lines in pre-modern society. There are few social institutions that evolve with such conservative lethargy as the law and marriage. For example, while countless volumes and articles have now established, sometimes in minute detail, profound short- and long-term economic and political (in the broad sense) effects of the Black Death of 1347–51, the persistent debate regarding post-plague women has been to what extent and why women delayed marriage and motherhood.[16] While debate continues regarding the extent to which women's pre-marital economic opportunities and lifecycles were affected, relative consensus now suggests that any plague-induced effects were short-term, most significant for unmarried women and overwhelmingly not reflected in the law. Perhaps the only clear exception to the immunity of married women's legal position to the varied effects of the Black Death was the compulsory service clause of the English Statute of Labours of 1351 which required unemployed men and women, including wives, when offered work, to either accept employment or endure imprisonment.[17]

bour Markets in the North Sea Region in the Late Medieval and Early Modern Period', *Economic History Review* 63 (2010), 1–33, esp. pp. 7–11.

13 J. M. Bennett, 'Medieval Women, Modern Women: Across the Great Divide', *Culture and History 1350–1600: Essays on English Communities, Identities, and Writing*, ed. D. Aers (London, 1992), pp. 147–75.

14 J. Kelly-Gadol, 'Did Women Have a Renaissance?', *Becoming Visible: Women in European History*, ed. R. Bridenthal and C. Koonz (Boston, 1977), pp. 137–64. See also M. E. Wiesner, *Gender, Church and State in Early Modern Germany* (London, 1998), pp. 63–78, 84–93, which asks if women had a Reformation and if the concepts 'Renaissance' and 'Early Modern' apply to women's experiences.

15 J. M. Bennett, '"History that Stands Still": Women's Work in the European Past', *Feminist Studies* 14 (1988), 269–83.

16 E.g. see S. H. Rigby, 'Gendering the Black Death: Women in Later Medieval England', *Gender and History* 12 (2000), 745–54.

17 J. M. Bennett, 'Compulsory Service in Late Medieval England', *Past and Present* 209 (2010), 7–51.

The essays in this volume span the period c.1200–1800, although there is a clustering around the middle of this period. Generally speaking, northwest European peoples showed, certainly from the latter half of the twelfth century, an increasing tendency to codify, circulate and refine the law, inclusive of elements touching upon the rights and activities of married women. Within the British Isles, for example, the influential jurists Ranulf de Glanville (d. 1190) and Henry de Bracton (d. 1268) commented upon and profoundly influenced the formation of legal practice in England, commenting on the property rights of married women.[18] Similarly, the earliest surviving redaction of the Welsh laws of Hywell Dda (the Cyfnerth redaction), including the law of married women, is thought to have been compiled in the late twelfth century, and elaborated through the thirteenth century.[19] And, further afield, in Norway for example, old regional law codes gave way to the first national law code, of Magnus the lawmender, in 1274, which carefully defined women's rights to property (see Hansen's essay). From at least the thirteenth century it is generally possible to discuss married women and the law with reference to surviving local or national legal custumals or treatises.

As some of the essays in the volume will discuss, lawmakers, jurists and courts constantly renegotiated these same very elaborate – but sometimes impractical or simply ignored – systems of law with respect to married women. We therefore need to be wary of seeing the law as something that evolves in a single direction, whether to married women's benefit or detriment. Shennan Hutton, for example, argues that – while Ghent's unwritten custom was redacted in 1563, stating that married women could not legally enter into contracts without the express permission of their husbands – the mid-fourteenth-century records of actual practice (contracts and lawsuit adjudications recorded in the aldermen's annual registers) show that there was widespread acceptance of married women's public performance of property management, with or without their husbands. Cordelia Beattie finds late medieval legal evidence that married women could make valid contracts for necessities in England, as suggested by an eighteenth-century treatise which claimed this was still the case, but also found that this ability was restricted over the course of the fifteenth century. Thus the long view enables us to assess change over time with respect to married women's legal position.

What Do We Mean by The Law?

As Sheilagh Ogilvie comments in her essay, it is important to examine what is meant by concepts that have largely been taken for granted such as 'the law'. We do not just use the term to refer to law codes, legal treatises and statutes, their

18 Ranulph de Glanvill, *De Legibus et Consuetudinibus Regni Angliae*, ed. G. E. Woodbine (New Haven, 1932); Henry de Bracton, *De Legibus et Consuetudinibus Angliae*, ed. G. E. Woodbine (New Haven, 1915). For Bracton on the property rights of married women, in translation, see C. McCarthy, ed., *Love, Sex and Marriage in the Middle Ages: A Sourcebook* (Abingdon, 2004), source 31, pp. 115–21.

19 See D. Jenkins and M. E. Owen, eds, *The Welsh Law of Women* (Cardiff, 1980).

enforcement in law courts, and the legal personnel involved. We have adopted a broad approach, in common with the 'new legal history', which sees the law 'not simply as an external mechanism regulating daily life, but as an integral part of the way in which social relations were actually lived out and experienced'.[20] Ogilvie, for example, looks beyond the question of married women's legal autonomy (in the German-speaking world, the key issue here is that of *Geschlechtsvormundschaft* or 'gender guardianship') and argues that we must also examine other legal influences which circumscribed the economic options of married women, and thus their life chances and well-being in early modern Germany: the legal privileges of guilds and other occupational associations; and the legal powers of local communities, including local church courts' jurisdiction over the conduct of married life. Other essays presented here – those by Cathryn Spence and Alexandra Shepard – also use legal material (Scottish burgh court registers and English church court records respectively) to assess married women's economic activities.

'The law', then, is multi-dimensional. It is also possible to speak of many co-existing and competing systems of law. Little more can be done here than to sketch out a basic map of major spheres of law, highlighting areas where the treatment of married women was particularly distinctive, as a guide for the reader in exploring the following chapters.

The major divisions of law during the Middle Ages and much of the early modern period were different from those relative in modern society. In particular, in the pre-modern world, 'the law' was divided principally between secular law and ecclesiastical, or 'church', law. Secular law was concerned with one's temporal activities (such as trade), while ecclesiastical law was concerned with governing one's spiritual welfare (and thus with such matters as adultery). Generally speaking, transgressions of, or disputes under, secular and ecclesiastical law were dealt with in their respective courts, which had their own hierarchies. However, human activities were often governed by a combination of secular and ecclesiastical law. Particularly pertinent to this volume is the institution of marriage, which formed the basis of both a spiritual union and a union of property – moveable and immovable – between the families of the bride and groom, and was therefore carefully regulated under both secular and ecclesiastical law. Disputed marriages, or disputes within marriage – for example regarding consanguinity or adultery – might give rise to related litigation in both secular and ecclesiastical courts, with the judgments of each potentially resulting in equally potent financial, proprietary or corporal censure.[21] This is demonstrated in Korpiola's essay, which investigates the implications of marital dysfunction and breakdown for property possession.

The division between civil and criminal law, perhaps that which springs first to mind in the modern era, was less distinct in the pre-modern era, particularly

[20] A. Musson, *Medieval Law in Context: The Growth of Legal Consciousness from Magna Carta to the Peasants' Revolt* (Manchester, 2001), p. 2. On 'new legal history', see ibid., p. 3; D. Sugarman, 'Writing "Law and Society" Histories', *The Modern Law Review* 55 (1992), 292–308, esp. pp. 298–9.

[21] On marriage disputes in ecclesiastical courts in five regions of northwest Europe see Donahue Jr, *Law, Marriage, and Society*.

in the Middle Ages. Many of the systems of law in northwest Europe – such as the Celtic Brehon Law and Laws of Hywel Dda observed in Gaelic Ireland and native-controlled Wales respectively – relied overwhelming on complex systems of payments to wronged parties and their extended families, rather than punishments, to resolve disputes for both 'civil' misdeeds (such as breach of contract) and 'criminal' misdeeds (including homicide). These systems, by their very nature, had to gauge the worth of individuals so that compensation for misdeeds could be set accordingly, with both gender and condition (particularly freedom or servility) being key determinants of personal worth. Transgressions against women and serfs were consistently redeemable by lesser payments than those due for wronging men.[22] Within this context, the identity of the party wronged was of equal importance to the nature of the illegal act, be it what we would now consider 'civil' or 'criminal', in determining the magnitude of the breach of law.

While primarily compensatory legal systems were not dominant in northwest Europe c.1200–1800, the contemporary social relevance of their then 'common sense' approach to social differentiation, and in many areas their legacy, is deeply ingrained in the legal codes of virtually all northwest European societies. For example, while in later medieval England a free landowner might be sued for unjustly dispossessing or assaulting another free landowner, he was within his rights to arbitrarily redistribute lands occupied by his servile tenants and to punish them corporally if he felt it justified. With respect to gender, while a man might be sued for assaulting another man of similar condition, he might freely chastise his wife as a corrective to her behaviour. Likewise, just as an individual's social 'worth', or position, was gauged for the setting of compensation payments, the measure of legal authority accorded persons to act independently in society, to make their own contracts or to bear direct responsibility for their actions or the management of their estates, was also dependent on their gender and condition. With respect to married women, the French phrase *coverte de baron* was used in legal records in England as a general term to describe the legal state of married women, whose autonomy was eclipsed by their husband under the law and customs described in English as 'coverture', giving rise to the nomenclature of *femme couverte* (sometimes anglicized as 'feme covert'). Variations of coverture – if not always so called – existed throughout northwest Europe in the pre-modern era.

Coverture was expressed in national law codes and closely observed in judicial forums of primary importance, as provided for litigation between (and against) tenants in chief. For example, in England, a married woman could not sue or be sued without her husband in the national courts of Common Pleas and King's Bench. However, the customary law employed in local judicial forums, where the tenants of greater landowners or members of urban liberties with special judicial privileges ordinarily resolved their disputes, might apply coverture less strictly or consistently. Miriam Müller's essay argues that it was sometimes ignored entirely in late medieval English manor courts and that previous scholars have mistak-

22 Jenkins and Owen, eds, *The Welsh Law of Women*; R. Thurneysen *et al.*, *Studies in Early Irish Law* (Dublin and London, 1936). For Ireland, see G. Kenny's essay in this volume.

enly assumed it had more of an influence there than it did; while Spence's essay illustrates the commonality with which early modern Scottish wives contracted legitimate debts within the framework of local legal regimes. Lizabeth Johnson's essay highlights the inconsistency with which it was applied in similar Welsh courts, and Beattie's essay suggests that urban liberties such as Norwich or London strategically relaxed the strictures of coverture for the convenience of trade in the late medieval period. In Ireland and Wales, indigenous traditions co-existed alongside those imported from England.[23] As Kenny argues in her essay, while the Anglo-Irish legal system ensured that married women were under the rule of their husbands, this was not the case in the Brehon law according to which Gaelic Irish society functioned. In Wales and England, local customary law faded at the end of the Middle Ages, but where strong central legal systems and law codes failed to take root, as in early modern Germany, the result was the multiplicity of regional variations of gender guardianship addressed by Ogilvie. As discussed above, Hutton's essay on Ghent argues that it was when customary law was codified in 1563 that married women lost some of their legal capabilities.

Throughout the transition from medieval to early modern society, the emergent state, embodied to a greater or lesser extent by a feudal lord or monarch, took an increasingly prominent role in the codification and manipulation of the law. In parallel to this, a clearer distinction emerged between criminal acts, as transgressions of the law of the lord or monarch and prosecutable by the state, and civil wrongs done by one private party to another, for which the law provided a remedy and judiciary within which to prosecute it. During the same period, when distinctions between 'criminal' and 'civil' aspects of the law became sharper, the servile condition largely ceased to exist in northwest Europe, and the state came increasingly to treat men with greater equality. However, coverture remained a key feature of the law in northwest Europe. The special legal position of women, and in particular married women, regarding their legal abilities and disabilities was more closely enumerated rather than abolished. And, as illustrated by some of the essays in this volume (for example, those by Beattie and Hutton), the clearer articulation of women's legal rights in the later medieval and early modern periods was as likely to lead – in legal theory at least – to the further circumscription of wives' legal capacities as it was to secure their rights.

Key Themes

Some areas of married women's interactions with the law stand out as recurrent points of concern for the pre-modern peoples of northwest Europe and thus as recurrent foci of the research presented in this volume. These can, as noted at the outset, be summarized under the following four headings: married women's rights regarding the possession of moveable and immovable property; married women's

23 On Wales see L. B. Smith, 'Towards a History of Women in Late Medieval Wales', *Women and Gender in Early Modern Wales*, ed. M. Roberts and S. Clarke (Cardiff, 2000), pp. 14–49, esp. pp. 25–30.

capacity to act as agents of their husbands and households in transacting business; married women's interactions with the courts; and marital property at the dissolution of marriage. Each of these four topics – while not in themselves exhaustive of married women's interactions with the law – can be further divided into general areas of study, all of which contain some degree of ambiguity regarding the position of married women.

The law's regulation of married women's ability to possess moveable and immovable property was generally cognizant of the transference of property to the control of the husband, but this transference was not always absolute. Often new husbands could not lay claim to all of their wives' moveable property, such as debts, except in right of the wife (see Matthew Stevens' essay). A wife's personal effects, such as her clothing and jewellery, were often considered her own, giving rise to confusion if wives should be required to assess their own worth (see Shepard's essay), and disputes should the wife alienate or run away with personal effects of substantial value (see the essays by Johnson and Korpiola). And married women were not always wholly in possession of the immovable property they brought into marital unions, especially where – for example, in Ghent, Norway or Sweden – the woman's wider kin retained certain rights to the property restricting its free alienation (see the essays by Hutton, Hansen and Korpiola).

Married women's capacity to transact business as agents of their husband or household was fraught by a natural conflict between the appealing practical utility of wives acting on their husband's behalves, and the legal necessity that the husband alone be accountable for the household as an economic unit. In both England and Scotland there were legal provisions for wives to purchase household necessities (such as food, drink, clothing and medicine – see the essays by Beattie and Spence), and one would assume that there were similar provisions across northwest Europe. Further, dependent upon location, in some circumstances (for example, in war), when practising certain occupations (for example, mercery) or in urban environments (for example, London) it was acceptable for women to make some agreements either independently of their husbands or as their agents (see the essays by Korpiola and Beattie).[24] The extent of a wife's accepted modes of independent action also differed sharply both between local and competing legal jurisdictions and within jurisdictions as they evolved through the pre-modern era (see the essays by Kenny, Ogilvie and Beattie).

Women's interactions with the law, within the court, could be similarly inconsistent. Court records offer an especially valuable insight into contemporary interpretations of how the law, and in particular coverture, should be applied. For example, studies of local court records from medieval England and Wales highlight the remarkable frequency with which the conventions of coverture might simply be ignored, in contrast with national legal custom, should doing so be felt expedient (see the essays by Müller and Johnson). And on a more subtle level, Johnson's essay argues that even the form that the matter took in court (for exam-

[24] On the London mercers see A. F. Sutton, 'The Shop-floor of the London Mercery Trade, *c.* 1200 – *c.* 1500: The Marginalisation of the Artisan, the Itinerant Mercer and the Shopholder', *Nottingham Medieval Studies* 45 (2001), 12–50.

ple, presentment or interpersonal litigation) might affect the apparent autonomy of women before the court.

Finally, the distribution of marital property at the dissolution of a marriage – through judicial separation or death – could often be complex. For example, in cases of adultery or homicide, strong prohibitions against the retention or reception of property by the guilty party or his/her heirs could effectively impoverish or enrich a wife (see Korpiola's essay). Likewise, strict rules typically governed the extent to which a wife could transfer moveable and immovable property acquired through one marriage union to another (see Hansen's essay).

Collectively, these foci of research serve to illustrate both how fruitful the study of married women and the law can be, in contrast to the past historiographical tendency to see such women as hidden from view in legal materials, and the scale of the task awaiting future historians. It is hoped that this collection will inspire other scholars to add to our increasing knowledge about married women and the law in the premodern past. One of its key arguments is that there has been a tendency to overplay the extent to which coverture applied. The collection points up differences between the English common law position, which gave husbands guardianship over their wives and their wives' property, and the position elsewhere in northwest Europe, where wives' property became part of a community of property. However, it also argues that we need to be attuned to further nuances over time and space and in different legal jurisdictions.

1

INHERITANCE, PROPERTY AND MARRIAGE IN MEDIEVAL NORWAY

Lars Ivar Hansen

This essay will highlight the position, capabilities and options of married women, according to Norwegian medieval law, regarding their control of property. Women's control and disposal of property during marriage were conditioned and influenced by a long series of factors – pertaining not only to legal regulations of different kinds but also to a broad field of interests, involving several actors and relations, such as the relationship between spouses themselves, the relationship to direct, lineal descendants, and the relationship between the conjugal couple and their kin groups on both sides. In order to evaluate the capabilities of married women in controlling property, and the possible strategies they employed, this wider 'space of action' must be taken into consideration.

The position of married women in controlling property will be discussed on the basis of the legal situation drawn up by the first nation-wide law codex encompassing the whole medieval Norwegian monarchy, which was established by king Magnus the lawmender in 1274. In contrast to the former provincial laws, this National Law Code introduced new principles for women's access to inheritance, thus influencing greatly women's options for acquiring control over property. However, as many of the regulations in this law related to principles that had been introduced into the provincial laws during the two preceding centuries, a short overview of previous developments is needed. This concerns above all the principles and conditions for contracting a valid marriage, the introduction and successive curtailment of marriage prohibitions according to canon law, and the rules regulating property transactions and exchange of gifts by contracting marriage. The essay will then discuss the various practices that can be observed during the later Middle Ages, based upon a selection of preserved charters, as well as the later legislative developments.

The Development of Norwegian Marital Law During the Eleventh and Twelfth Centuries

The oldest layers of the provincial law codes seem to reflect a secularly defined marriage, practised before all the ecclesiastical demands and qualifications for a valid marriage had been adopted, and which was primarily conceived as an agreement between two families. The betrothal agreement was considered the legally binding arrangement, and the negotiations focused primarily on financial transactions and obligations and were conducted by the men of both families. However, some parts of the provincial laws, which may be later amendments to the parts specifically dedicated to ecclesiastical and religious matters (so-called 'Christian laws'), emphasized that the consent of the spouses – not least the woman – was also needed for contracting a valid marriage.[1] This may well reflect the greater emphasis on the demand for mutual consent between the spouses that was raised by the church during the later part of the twelfth century.[2] But at the same time, these later versions of the law upheld the focus on property transactions, as they contained explicit formulas that should be cited by the male spouse in the presence of witnesses, concerning the agreement about transactions of dowry and countergift.[3] The weight on reciprocal consent, and explicit references to 'God's law' and the holy church, were further elaborated in the new versions of these Christian laws that were issued during the middle of the thirteenth century.[4] These more outspoken prescriptions to an explicit stating of the couple's consent, as well as the references to the holy church, were most probably the result of more energetic measures taken by the church, partly after having consulted the Holy See during the 1170s.[5] The background was the clearer definition of marriage as a sacrament, and the canonists' increasing emphasis on the necessity of consent by the parties involved.[6]

1 The older Christian Law of Eidsivathing 22.7–8, E. Fjeld Halvorsen and M. Rindal, eds, *De eldste østlandske kristenrettene, Riksarkivet, Norrøne Tekster nr. 7* (Oslo, 2008), p. 23; the Frostathing's law III, 22, J. R. Hagland and J. Sandnes, eds, *Frostatingslova* (Oslo, 1994); cf. T. Iversen, 'Landskapslovene og kanonisk Rett', *Nordiske Middelalderlover: Tekst og Kontekst, Senter for Middelalder, Skrifter nr. 5*, ed. A. Dybdahl and J. Sandnes (Trondheim, 1997), pp. 69–86. Both the editorial sequence in the laws of Eidsivathing and Borgarthing, and the fact that the very phrasing of the regulation is close to that of Frostathing's law, indicate that it is a later amendment, for instance from the period of archbishop Eystein Erlendsson (1161–88), since he is supposed to have revised the Christian Law section of the Frostathing's law.

2 Cf. the response from Pope Alexander III, issued some time between 1161 and 1172, to questions presented by the archbishop Eystein Erlendsson: '1. Consent to marriage must in all cases be voluntary, in order to be valid': G. Storm *et al.*, *Regesta Norvegica*, 8 vols (Oslo, 1989–2006), I, no. 140; cf. E. Vandvik, ed., *Latinske dokument til norsk historie fram til år 1204* (Oslo, 1959), no. 12 (with translation); statute of archbishop Eirik of 1189 in R. Keyser, P. A. Munch *et al.*, *Norges gamle Love Indtil 1387*, 5 vols (Christiania, 1846–95), IV, p. 100; Storm *et al.*, *Regesta Norvegica*, I, no. 124; cf. Iversen, 'Landskapslovene og Kanonisk Rett'.

3 The older Christian Law of Borgarthing, Fjeld Halvorsen and Rindal, eds, *De eldste østlandske kristenrettene*, p. 217.

4 The newer Christian Law of Borgarthing, nos. I and II (Keyser, Munch *et al.*, *Norges gamle Love*, II, pp. 291–306, IV, pp. 172–81), as well as the newer Christian Law of Gulathing, nos. I and II (ibid., vol. II, pp. 306–38, vol. IV, pp. 160–72, 176, 181–2). For the dating of these laws, see A. I. Riisøy and Bj. Dale Spørck, 'Dateringen av nyere Borgartings Kristenretter', *Collegium Medievale: Interdisciplinary Journal of Medieval Research* 12 (1999), 57–74; and Bj. Dale Spørck, *Kong Magnus lagabøters kristenretter: Innhold, Språk og Overlevering* (Oslo, 2006).

5 See n. 2 above.

6 Cf. J. A. Brundage: *Law, Sex, and Christian Society in Medieval Europe* (Chicago and New York, 1987), pp. 187–203, pp. 260–88.

The canonical prohibitions against marriages within forbidden degrees of consanguinity and affinity were introduced in Norway at the establishment of a separate Norwegian arch-diocese in Nidaros (Trondheim) in 1152–3. At this event, however, a concession was granted to the new church province by the visiting papal legate, Cardinal Nikolaus Brekespear (later Pope Hadrian IV), in that the forbidden degrees of consanguinity were reduced from seven to six.[7] The subsequent reduction to four degrees after the Fourth Lateran Council in 1215 can also be observed in various parts of the provincial laws.[8]

According to the oldest provincial laws, women's right to inheritance was extremely limited or non-existent. The Gulathing's law, valid for the western part of Norway, stipulated that only the three closest female relatives of the deceased – daughter, sister and mother – could be entitled to inheritance as such, provided that there were no closer male relatives.[9] However, both the provincial laws and the later National Law Code of 1274 seem to indicate that the dowry transferred to married women by their families was to a certain degree regarded as their part of the property devolution from their parents, and a kind of parallel to inheritance. At least, the property shares allotted to the married sisters should stand in a fairly proportional relationship to the property that was left for the brothers to inherit.[10]

In general, the oldest provincial laws seem to reflect a basic tripartite property system as the economic foundation for the household of the newly wedded spouses. One part was conveyed by the bride's family as dowry. The second part was made up of the indirect dowry or countergift (so called '*þing*' or '*tilgjof*') transferred by the man to the bride at the marriage. The third part consisted of the husband's separate property, that is, what was left after his conveyance of the indirect dowry to the wife. These will each be discussed in turn.

Judging from what has been documented in charters from the fourteenth century, the dowry was most often comprised of transferences of landed estate, but clothes and various household equipment were also common.[11] However, the Na-

7 Cf. K. Robberstad, 'Hadrians-løyvet i ekteskapsretten', [Norwegian] *Historisk Tidsskrift* 41 (1962–4), 341–4.

8 E.g. the Frostathing's law XII, 4, Hagland and Sandnes, eds, *Frostatingslova*, p. 183; cf. the Gulathing's law 266, K. Robberstad, ed., *Gulatingslovi* (Oslo, 1969), pp. 241–2; cf. L. I. Hansen, 'Slektskap, eiendom og sosiale strategier i nordisk middelalder', *Collegium Medievale* 7 (1994, publ. 1996), 103–54.

9 The Gulathing's law 103, Robberstad, ed., *Gulatingslovi*, pp. 129–30.

10 The Gulathing's law 128, 129, ibid., p. 144; the Frostathing's law XI, 2, Hagland and Sandnes, eds, *Frostatingslova*, p. 170. Cf. R. Andersen, 'Kvinnas økonomiske rettsstode i norsk mellomalder', unpublished Major thesis, University of Bergen, 1977, p. 65; R. Andersen, 'Kvinnas økonomiske rettsstode i norsk mellomalder', *Kvinnans ekonomiska ställning under nordisk medeltid*, ed. H. Gunneng and B. Strand (Gothenburg, 1981), p. 84 (cf. E. Hertzberg, 'Glossarium til Norges gamle Love', *Norges gamle Love*, V, p. 665); K. Maurer, 'Verwandschafts- und Erbrecht samt Pfandrecht nach Altnordischem Rechte', *Vorlesungen über Altnordische Rechtsgeschichte* (Leipzig, 1908), III, p. 640; National Law Code of king Magnus the Lawmender V, 1, A. Taranger, ed., *Magnus Lagabøters Landslov* (Oslo and Bergen, 1915 [repr. 1979]), pp. 72–3.

11 R. Ormøy, 'Kvinner og eiendom i vestnorske bygder, ca. 1270–1350', unpublished Major thesis, University of Bergen, 1984, pp. 15, 23–4. Landed property and objects of precious metal were

tional Law Code set an upper limit to how great a proportion of the dowry could be given in the form of clothes, namely, one-third of the value.[12] The dowry was considered to be the wife's separate property, both during marriage and after her death. If no special settlement had been made, this part passed to her children at her death. And in cases where the couple did not have any children, it was returned to her kinfolk, that is, those of her relatives who were her closest heirs. It should pass on at the same value as it had been granted.[13]

The indirect dowry or countergift, transferred by the man to the bride at the marriage, was a sort of reciprocal yield for the endowment from the wife's family. The provincial laws contain various regulations as to what kind of proportion should be stipulated between the dowry and the countergift. While the Gulathing's law held that they should match each other, the Frostathing's law stated that the countergift should amount to only half of the dowry. Consequently, it was called '*þriðjungsauke*', or 'third's increase'.[14] The later National Law Code seems to have opted for a more realistic evaluation of the economic capabilities of the two families, and did not stipulate a certain proportion between the two.[15] Conspicuously enough, however, the man's family is nowhere mentioned explicitly in connection with the countergift in the same way as the woman's is in relation to the dowry. This may indicate that the lawmakers assumed that the male spouse might already control his inheritance, or that he may have been granted permission to make an offer within certain limits.[16] In addition to these two basic contributions, the wedding transactions could also include other more specific 'bridal gifts' from the husband to his wife-to-be, like the so-called 'bench gift', 'betrothal gift' and 'linen goods', of which the latter was specifically determined for virgins.[17] Within the total conjugal property, the countergift formed a sort of flexible property-in-between. In the case that one of the spouses died, it was disposed by the survivor, and might possibly be inherited by his or her heirs. At a possible divorce or annulment of the marriage, the destination of the indirect dowry was dependent on whose fault the dissolution was.[18]

Upon the death of one of the spouses the husband's separate property – what was left after his conveyance of the indirect dowry to the wife – was subject to sim-

probably conceived as more advantageous for the future property management of the couple, than clothes and household equipment, which were not renewable and might be perceived as less negotiable.

12 National Law Code V, 1, Taranger, ed., *Magnus Lagabøters Landslov*, pp. 72–3; Ormøy, 'Kvinner og eiendom', p. 11.

13 Ormøy, 'Kvinner og eiendom', p. 60.

14 The Gulathing's law 54, Robberstad, ed., *Gulatingslovi*, pp. 75–6; cf. Andersen, *Kvinnas økonomiske rettsstode*, pp. 89–90; the Frostathing's law XI, 8, 14–16, cf. III, 6, 17, Hagland and Sandnes, eds, *Frostatingslova*, pp. 135, 41 and 45.

15 National Law Code V, 1, Taranger, ed., *Magnus Lagabøters Landslov*, pp. 72–3; Ormøy, 'Kvinner og eiendom', pp. 29–32.

16 Andersen, 'Kvinnas økonomiske rettsstode i norsk mellomalder', *Kvinnans ekonomiska ställning*, p. 84.

17 Cf. R. Frimannslund, 'Benkegave', *Kulturhistorisk leksikon for nordisk middelalder* (Copenhagen, 1956), cols 461–2.

18 I. Øye, 'Kvinner, Kjønn og samfunn. Fra vikingtid til reformasjon', *Med kjønnsperspektiv på norsk historie. Fra vikingtid til 2000-årsskiftet*, ed. I. Blom and S. Sogner (Oslo, 1999), p. 66.

ilar procedures to those prescribed for the dowry. If the wife died, this part was kept by the husband. In the opposite situation, the husband's property was passed on to the children as direct descendants. If they were of minor age, the property would be taken care of by guardians from the husband's kin. If the husband did not have any legitimate children – neither from earlier marriages, nor from the recently ended one – his separate property was probably returned to other members of his kin group, according to the sequence of potential heirs.[19] These three parts – the separate property of the spouses and the indirect dowry – were not necessarily of equal size.

This picture must be understood as a default description, that is, as a summary of the prevailing conditions if the standard regulations laid down by inheritance and marriage law were being followed straightforwardly, without any modifications. But from an early date – even according to the oldest provincial laws – there existed the possibility of making special agreements about 'joint property' or 'property in community' between the spouses, in particular on the initiative of the husband. As this kind of explicit marital settlement made it possible to expand the joint property considerably, but also to define separate property in a more precise manner, such arrangements might have wide-ranging consequences for the disposal of conjugal property during marriage, for the control of property by the longest-living spouse, and for the property distribution among the heirs.[20]

The Development of Women's Inheritance Rights

In Nordic medieval law there was a basic division between two legal traditions regarding succession, in which the relatives of the deceased were ascribed the status of potential heirs. While the provincial law codes of Denmark and eastern Sweden predominantly followed the so-called 'parentela principle', the western Nordic laws applied the 'gradual principle'.[21] According to the parentela principle – which is the one applied by modern inheritance law – the children and grandchildren of the deceased make up a first class, or parentela, which is given priority. Thereafter follows a second class, consisting of the parents of the deceased, as well as their descendants (siblings and nephews/nieces of the deceased), and then a third class, defined as the grandparents together with their descendants (uncles, aunts and first cousins of the deceased). At each stage, the next parentela in the priority order only comes into consideration when it is ascertained that no living heir still exists within the preceding one. Thus, the existence of a living heir within any given parentela precludes that

19 Ormøy, 'Kvinner og eiendom', p. 60.

20 This will be discussed further below.

21 Thus the provincial laws of Norway and Iceland (Grágás), as well as the older Västgöta law, the Östgöta law, the Dala law and the Västmanna law on the Swedish side (see B. Sawyer, *Kvinnor och familj i det forn- och medeltida Skandinavien* (Skara, 1992), p. 54; B. Sawyer, *The Viking-Age Rune Stones: Custom and Commemoration in Early Medieval Scandinavia* (Oxford, 2000); L. I. Hansen, 'Slektskap, eiendom og sosiale strategier i nordisk middelalder', *Collegium Medievale* 7 (1994, publ. 1996), 124–8; and H. Vogt, *The Function of Kinship in Medieval Nordic Legislation* (Leiden, 2010).

any member of the next should inherit. According to this principle, both male and female kin of the same relative distance from the deceased hold inheritance rights.

The gradual system, for its part, was based on an individual calculation of kinship distance from the deceased, expressed in terms of degrees or links. However, this calculation might adopt certain special principles of priority. For instance, *descendants* might be given priority over *ascendants* that technically were equally distant, and a certain priority might also be adopted according to gender: male individuals could be preferred to females of same distance, and kin members whose relations were mediated through male links might be given priority over those whose connections were mediated through female links. The oldest Norwegian inheritance laws – those of the Gulathing's and Frostathing's laws – applied the gradual system in this way.

During the twelfth and early thirteenth centuries, there seem to have been several competing tendencies at work in Norwegian society, trying to influence inheritance law, and possibly reflecting various strategies. Among others, the traditional, landowning aristocracy may have reacted against the new policies of the monarchy and the church, and wished to strengthen those aspects of inheritance law that would serve to concentrate property within the patrilineage.[22] On the other hand, newer regulations incorporated both patrilineal and more bilateral, cognatic ways of enumerating possible heirs into the Gulathing's and Frostathing's law, and evidently sought to supplement the older regulations, which only enumerated male heirs, with corresponding lists of potential female heirs.[23]

Nevertheless, any profound change regarding women's inheritance rights did not occur until the introduction of the National Law Code established by Magnus the lawmender in 1274. In the inheritance section of this law, which was valid until 1687, a greater number of female relatives were acknowledged as potential heirs.[24] The specification of possible female inheritors went as far as the second canonical degree, including for instance the daughters of children, brothers and sisters to the deceased, as well as sisters of the mother of the deceased. In general, the specification of potential female heirs extended just as far as the enumerated male heirs. But in the detailed ranking of possible heirs, a certain priority was given to men. The daughters of brothers of the deceased and the sisters of his father were for instance listed among the seventh rank of inheritance succession, while the corresponding males (sons of brothers and father's brethren) were of the fourth rank. But among the heirs in the first rank – the children of the deceased

22 Cf. Hansen: 'Slektskap, eiendom og sosiale strategier'.

23 The Gulathing's law 105, Robberstad, ed., *Gulatingslovi*, p. 131. A corresponding amendment, about a fourteenth class of potential heirs, i.e. relating to female inheritors of corresponding distance to the male ones, has been added to the Frostathing's law (Ftl. VIII, 15), but without the same detailed enumeration (Hagland and Sandnes, eds, *Frostatingslova*, p. 135). However, the amendment is ascribed to the three co-reigning kings, Sigurd, Eystein and Olav, all sons of Magnus the Bareleg. This may serve as basis for a dating of the law revision to their co-regency, 1103–15.

24 National Law Code V, 7, Taranger, ed., *Magnus Lagabøters Landslov*, pp. 80–6.

– both daughters and sons were entitled to inheritance. However, the daughters were allotted shares only half as great as those of their brothers.[25] This principle of unequal sharing was made valid for all cases where male and female relatives appeared in the same rank of inheritance succession, such as the mother's brothers and sisters (fifth rank), and daughter's sons and daughters (second rank).

As a whole, the inheritance succession in the National Law Code seems to be structured according to a combination of calculation of distance (the gradual principle), gender, and lineal consideration. To a certain extent, male relatives were given priority before female ones, and patrilineal relatives before matrilineal ones. But compared to the provincial laws of Gulathing and Frostathing, descendants seem to have been given a clearer priority over ascendants. This might indicate some influence from the parentela system of kinship reckoning.

By including a wide number of female relatives in the ranked inheritance succession in a more integrated way, where some women had priority over some male relatives, the National Law Code of 1274 established a completely new situation for women's capacity to acquire property. Even if married women earlier had been allotted a dowry which was in proportion with the expected inheritance of their male coheirs, they were now regularly receiving both dowry and an inheritance share. But still women had to marry in accordance with the advice of their parents or relatives; otherwise they would be disinherited.[26] Nevertheless, the new inheritance rules had substantial consequences for the property that a woman might bring into the matrimonial cohabitation, and thus accentuated the question of what kind of property dispositions could be made during marriage.

Women's Control of Property During and After Marriage

Women's disposal and control over property during marriage were conditioned and influenced by a series of factors pertaining to legal regulations of different kinds, as well as various sets of interests, related to the relationship between the conjugal couple and their relatives on both sides. In the first place, there was the standard legislation which regulated the rights to disposal and inheritance of the dowry, the countergift (indirect dowry) and the man's separate property. Second-

25 Cf. M. Gelting, 'Odelsrett – Lovbydelse – Bördsrätt – Retrait Lignager: Kindred and Land in the Nordic Countries in the Twelfth and Thirteenth Centuries', *Family, Marriage and Property Devolution in the Middle Ages*, ed. L. I. Hansen (Tromsø, 2000), pp. 133–65.

26 National Law Code V, 2, Taranger, ed., *Magnus Lagabøters Landslov*, p. 73. The National Law Code also presumed that the unmarried children should have just as great a share of the residual property to be apportioned upon the final inheritance division as those who had already been endowed (V, 1, ibid., pp. 72–3). This would seem to be parallel to the 'egalitarian system' of property devolution, which according to Jack Goody was predominant in Normandy and western France during the Middle Ages. In these regions, all children who had been endowed with shares of their family's property at different occasions and points of time were obliged to return with their allotted shares upon their parents' death, for a final redistribution on an egalitarian basis: J. Goody, 'Inheritance, Property and Women: Some Comparative Considerations', *Family and Inheritance. Rural Society in Western Europe, 1200–1800*, ed. J. Goody *et al.* (Cambridge, 1979), pp. 17–18.

ly, both the older provincial laws and the later National Law Code established that it was the man who should be in charge of the total conjugal property during the marriage. But it is explicitly stated that he must act to the benefit of them both, and not jeopardize any of his wife's property. By no means was he allowed to take his wife's property abroad.[27] Thirdly, the special set of legislative measures concerning the options for establishing the 'community of property' or 'joint ownership' during marriage came to have ever greater importance during the later medieval and early modern periods. The conditions for making such specific marriage contracts, and the following consequences, changed considerably throughout the period due to altered legislation.[28] In all, these terms reflected both divergent interests as to how property should be managed during the lifetime of the couple, and – not least – how property should be transferred to the next generation upon the death of one or both of the spouses. At the same time, they formed the framework or 'field' within which the divergent interests and strategies were played out against each other. And the new legislative measures laid down new conditions to be taken into consideration.

Most of the issues at stake became clearly manifest and accentuated at the end of marriage, in connection with inheritance procedures and the division of property among the heirs. A certain tension and potential conflict of interests existed between the conjugal couple as such – with their common children as directly descendant heirs – and their kin relatives on both sides who might come under consideration as heirs in special circumstances. The two spouses had their origins in two different kin lines, and were to a great extent dependent on them in many matters, but at the same time they formed a new, amalgamated union of the two lines, which could represent a continuation of both lines. Nevertheless, the kin relatives on each side had their interests to take care of, through various measures, in case the couple did not produce any children or in case the children died before either of the parents. Of central importance were such questions as, in the case that one of the spouses died before the other: what inheritance procedures must be undertaken immediately, and what should be postponed until after the other spouse's death? How much of the property and what parts of it could be kept by the surviving spouse for her or his lifetime? And how should the property of the spouse who died first be divided? Should it pass on to the children in its entirety, in the case that the couple had legitimate progeny? Or might other members of the deceased's kindred come into consideration, even if the couple had legitimate children? In the case that the children who were entitled to inherit were of minor age, who should be their guardian(s) and in charge of the property management? These were some of the questions the legislation had to deal with.

Matters were further complicated and accentuated by the institution of 'allodial property', or *odelsjord*, which entitled certain members of a kin group

27 The Gulathing's law 52, Robberstad, ed., *Gulatingslovi*, p. 74; National Law Code V, 3, Taranger, ed., *Magnus Lagabøters Landslov*, p. 74.

28 Cf. A. S. Arnórsdóttir, *Property and Virginity: The Christianization of Marriage in Medieval Iceland, 1200–1600* (Århus, 2010).

to the right of pre-emption and redemption of inherited lands, similar to the French *retrait lignager.*[29] Such rights were known in all the Nordic countries (except Iceland) during medieval times, but had different names. In Swedish, it was called *bördsrätt*, or 'birth's right', while the Danish term *lovbydelse*, or 'offer by law', referred to the obligation resting upon a person wishing to sell allodial land to offer it to the next of kin at the same price as strangers would pay.[30] To qualify as 'allodium', landed property had to have been owned by members of the same kindred for a specified number of generations, or – according to later legislation – for a minimum amount of time. The Gulathing's law laid down six generations as a minimum, while that of Frostathing prescribed four generations. According to the National Law Code of 1274, the minimum time required was only sixty years.[31] Allodial estates which had come into the possession of non-kin (by sale, mortgaging or inheritance) could be redeemed by lineal relatives of the last allodial possessor, according to detailed provisions. The National Law Code extended the period during which a prospective redeemer could postpone the take-over, provided that he repeatedly declared at the public assembly that he was the right 'odal heir', but that he temporarily lacked money. As we shall see, the special legal position of allodial estate led to even further considerations regarding the tactics and planning of property devolution between the generations, among other things through the conscious application of marriage contracts concerning property matters. The legitimate children of a couple represented a continuation of the two kin lines in question and were, as such, entitled to inherit allodial land. Nevertheless, special precautions were taken in many marriage contracts, in order to secure the allodial property for other members of the kin line, in the case that the couple's common children died before either of the parents.

The legal situation of married women regarding control and disposal of property was heavily influenced by this legislation concerning allodial property and the various measures taken by different actors who were able to influence the terms of the marriage agreement. We shall, therefore, take a look at the legislative developments, and at the same time draw attention to some of the marriage contracts and court cases which may highlight to what extent the various regulations were followed in practice, and to which outcome disputes about these matters led.

29 S. D. White, *Custom, Kinship, and Gifts to Saints: The Laudatio Parentum in Western France, 1050–1150* (Chapel Hill, 1988).

30 Gelting, 'Odelsrett – Lovbydelse – Bördsrätt – Retrait Lignager'; P. G. Norseng, 'Odelsrett – the Norwegian Retrait Lignager', *Land, Lords and Peasants: Peasants' Right to Control Land in the Middle Ages and the Early Modern Period – Norway, Scandinavia and the Alpine Region*, ed. T. Iversen and J. R. Myking (Trondheim, 2005), pp. 201–27.

31 The Gulathing's law 266, Robberstad, ed., *Gulatingslovi*, pp. 240–5; the Frostathing's law XII, 4, Hagland and Sandnes, eds, *Frostatingslova*, pp. 182–3; National Law Code VI, 2.1, Taranger, ed., *Magnus Lagabøters Landslov*, p. 98. It is noteworthy that the minimum number of generations prescribed by the Gulathing's law corresponded to the definition of incestuous, consanguinal relationships that was established at the foundation of the Norwegian church province in 1152–3, while the four generations prescribed by the Frostathing's law corresponded to the reduced number of forbidden degrees adopted by the Fourth Lateran Council in 1215.

Notwithstanding the provision that the husband should be in charge of the spouses' total property, women seem to have had a fair degree of control over the dowry and countergift during marriage.[32] The National Law Code repeated the regulation prescribing that the husband should be in charge of the whole conjugal property during marriage, but that he should make his disposals to the benefit of both.[33] However, practice may have revealed that this formulation was not adequate, since two successive amendments (of 1280 and 1313) underline that the husband needed to have his wife's consent if he sold any of her estates or the property which they owned together. In case a dispute arose, he or his heirs had to be able to produce two witnesses who could confirm that the sale had taken place with the consent of the wife.[34] Otherwise, the wife could announce that it had been contrary to her will, within a time limit of five years after being informed about the sale. According to the later charters, these regulations also seem to have been followed.[35] Apparently, the clause about the wife's consent being necessary for the husband's dispositions over his wife's property was no empty phrase.

Many late medieval charters testify that wives actually were questioned in advance of transactions and even played an active role by being present and expressing their views. According to a charter of 1345, a certain Gunnbjørn acknowledged that he had sold a share of a farm belonging to the dowry of his wife, Rannveig Gunnarsdaughter, to the canons of the chapter in Stavanger. Rannveig had been present at the transaction, had agreed to the sale, and confirmed that she and her husband had received full payment.[36] Negligence in acquiring the wife's consent might also have later judicial consequences. By a verdict issued some time between 1280 and 1299, lady Gudrun, who was the widow of the magnate Ivar Lodinsson, was awarded one-third of their total conjugal property, while Ivar's sister Ingegerd, who acted as his heir, got two-thirds. Gudrun's third included some landed property which Ivar – without her knowledge – had sold to the Munkeliv monastery in Bergen. This property was therefore to be returned to the widow, and the monastery had to be compensated with some other property of corresponding value among the two-thirds that had been allotted to Ivar's heir.[37] Further, the indirect dowry (countergift) could not be freely disposed by husbands. A sales letter from 1342 documents that Sigurd Brynjulvsson and his wife, Gyda, two years earlier had sold a share in the middle part of the farm, Kvåle, in the Valdres valley, which originally had been given to her as indirect dowry. At the sale, she publicly renounced her rights to the property share, and both husband and wife acted as sellers.[38]

32 The Gulathing's law 52, Robberstad, ed., *Gulatingslovi*, p. 74; the Frostathing's law XI, 5 and 8, Hagland and Sandnes, eds, *Frostatingslova*, pp. 171–3.

33 National Law Code V, 3, Taranger, ed., *Magnus Lagabøters Landslov*, p. 74.

34 Great general amendment by king Erik Magnusson 1280 and great general amendment by king Håkon V Magnusson 1313; Keyser, Munch *et al.*, *Norges gamle Love*, III, pp. 8, 101; cf. Ormøy, 'Kvinner og eiendom', pp. 66–8.

35 *Diplomatarium Norvegicum* (hereafter, *DN*), vol. XII, no. 141 – 1303; *DN* V, no. 336 – 1340; and *DN* IV, no. 336 – 1348.

36 *DN* XIV, no. 6 – 1345.

37 *DN* XII, no. 33 – 1303.

38 *DN* II, no. 251 – 1342.

This general framework of property distribution was, however, made even more complicated, due to the specific rights and provisions concerning allodial property. By inheritance, male heirs had a certain priority to allodial property. In case a deceased man left both allodial and other property to be inherited by his children of both sexes, the National Law Code of 1274 prescribed that the sons should be assigned the allodial lands while the daughters should get 'out-lands' (landed property without specific allodial status) and moveables.[39] Nevertheless, if the deceased did not have any sons or grandsons, some of the women who were nearest in kin were entitled to take over the allodial property. Both the Gulathing's provincial law and the National Law Code specified further a group of female relatives who could receive allodial estates after the deceased: his daughter, his sister, his father's sister, his brother's daughter and his son's daughter. There also existed specific provisions as to how women in possession of inherited allodial land should offer it for sale to relatives (male or female) having rights of pre-emption.[40]

As far as allodial lands inherited directly from a father without any closer male heirs were concerned, women therefore had quite strong rights to possession. The same went for allodial property that was part of a wife's dowry. But the case with allodial lands conveyed as part of the indirect dowry was quite different. The National Law Code stated explicitly that allodial land that had come into the possession of a woman as part of her countergift, or by being inherited backwards from dead children, could not acquire allodial status by prescription (*hevd*) through the woman's line. That is, the widow might keep it for some limited time, but as soon as the nearest one of the deceased husband's male relatives raised an interest in it, he could sue her, and redeem the property after a closer value assessment.[41] The Gulathing's law contains quite elaborate provisions for the value assessment and payments, and concludes laconically: 'So he shall take care of his allodium, and she of the money.'[42]

A royal amendment of 1313 reinforced the regulations of the National Law Code concerning 'backward' inheritance by one of the parents from children who already had inherited from the other parent but had then died without leaving any direct heirs of their own. In such cases, the longest-living parent should only dispose of moveables which the children had inherited. Landed property could only be kept by the longest-living parent for his or her lifetime and should then be returned to the kin group from which it had originated.[43] A charter from 1317 gives

39 'But if a father leaves allodial estate, then the sons shall go to the allodial lands, and the daughters to the out-lands and moveables, if there are not any separate lands, and should the oldest [son] take over the main residence, and leave the other allodial lots on their part, so that they are equal, according to legal assessment.' National Law Code V, 7, 3, Taranger, ed., *Magnus Lagabøters Landslov*, pp. 80–1.

40 The Gulathing's law 275, Robberstad, ed., *Gulatingslovi*, p. 253; Ftl. XII, 5, Hagland and Sandnes, eds, *Frostatingslova*, p. 184; National Law Code VI, 7, Taranger, ed., *Magnus Lagabøters Landslov*, p. 101.

41 National Law Code VI, 7, 14 & 15, Taranger, ed., *Magnus Lagabøters Landslov*, pp. 101, 106–7; cf. Ormøy, 'Kvinner og eiendom', pp. 74–7.

42 The Gulathing's law 274, Robberstad, ed., *Gulatingslovi*, p. 252.

43 Keyser, Munch *et al.*, *Norges gamle Love*, III, pp. 99–100.

an example of this practice. A share of allodial land in the farm Rogne, assessed at a value of 140 marks of silver, was then redeemed from the widow Gudrid Audfinnsdaughter by the brother and sister of her deceased husband, on behalf of the couple's sons who were of minor age.[44] The purchase price was to make up for the claims Gudrid had in Rogne, corresponding to her indirect dowry, some debt of her dead husband that she had paid, as well as some other gift. From two charters of 1339, concerning landed property in Voss, we learn that a property share in the farm Hylle, which made up half of the indirect dowry of Ingegerd Torgautsdaughter, widow after Orm Kavle, was redeemed by her two stepsons.[45]

The Role of Joint Ownership

This picture of general conditions, which was drawn up by the standard or 'default' legislation governing inheritance succession and the division of property in the aftermath of an ended marriage, was further influenced by the option of combining the property of the two spouses into 'joint ownership' or 'community of property'. In Norwegian medieval law this institution was called *félag*, a compound term made up by combining '*fé*' (n.), which could mean 'cattle', 'goods' or 'property', and '*lag*' (n.), meaning 'community' or 'in common'. Thus the term *félag* refers to 'property held in common' or 'joint ownership'.[46]

The institution of matrimonial *félag* was mentioned in the oldest provincial laws, but only referring to the basic content and conditions for establishing such a combination of the spouses' property. However, from the National Law Code of 1274 and onwards, the legislation became more concerned with detailed prescriptions – evidently in response to many doubts and questions as to what were the correct procedures and conclusions to be drawn. The legislators of the monarchy were also probably influenced by the church's conception of marriage. Between 1280 and 1348, four royal amendments gave more detailed instructions concerning how joint property between spouses should be understood and practised. The last comprehensive legislative measure came with a decree issued in 1557 by a meeting of members of the Council of the Realm and noblemen in Bergen.[47]

In the first place, such joint ownership arrangements regulated the range of dispositive capabilities which were available to the spouses during marriage, regarding the various gifts and property that had been exchanged at the contraction of marriage. At the same time, the joint property practice also had repercussions for inheritance procedures and the way the conjugal property should be divided upon the end of the marriage, and led, in part, to other solutions than those prescribed in the standard legislation. One of the main features was that it guaranteed

44 *DN* I, no. 151 – 1317.

45 *DN* II, nos. 231, 232 – 1339.

46 In general, the term *félag* referred to cases of partnership in which people pooled their values or goods together and embarked on joint ventures, such as trading expeditions.

47 Rettertingsrecess 1557, H. Winge, ed., *Lover og forordninger 1537–1605, Norsk lovstoff i sammendrag* (Oslo, 1988), pp. 59–60.

the longest-living spouse the right to dispose of a certain share of the common property for her or his lifetime, so that the preliminary inheritance procedure only concerned the remaining share. Thus, the joint property arrangement might serve to guarantee a subsistence basis of support for the longest-living spouse, in a way that transgressed what would have been the case if the customary dividing principles concerning dowry, indirect dowry and separate property of the husband had been followed.

Still, there were several significant distinctions as to how joint property should be established, which parties had the decisive authority and could conclude settlements about community of property and which proportional division should be applied at the end of marriage. All these points were subject to changes, according to new developments in legislation. Both the provincial laws and the National Law Code distinguished between a *félag* by law and an arranged *félag*. Joint ownership 'by law' was established automatically, after the spouses had been married for a certain number of years, while the arranged *félag* was established by an actual agreement or marriage contract. However, the oldest provincial laws set various conditions for a joint ownership to be established automatically, concerning the duration of marriage. The Frostathing's law required only one year of marital cohabitation, while the Gulathing's law required twenty years, and the older Borgarthing's law thirty years.[48]

Secondly, there was the question of who could claim the property to be joined by a so-called arranged *félag*, and whose consent was necessary. The old provincial laws seem to recognize the husband as the prime initiator of arranged forms of joint property. Both the Gulathing's law and the National Law Code contain clauses stating that the wife cannot deny her husband *félag*, but the Gulathing's law required the consent of the wife's nearest heirs, unless the couple had common children:

> The wife cannot deny her husband *félag*. When a man marries a girl, they cannot join their property without the consent of their closest heirs. But if they have children to inherit them, they may join their property (make *félag*) as they want. (The Gulathing's law 53)[49]

This tension, between the interests of potential heirs on both sides and the interests of the couple in question, became an ever-recurring topic in the successive legislation. The National Law Code stated that the spouses should have the capability of joining their properties themselves, according to their own will – without any other consent being necessary – provided that they followed certain prescribed rules. Attention was given, in particular, to the relative size and value

[48] The Frostathing's law XI, 8, Hagland and Sandnes, eds, *Frostatingslova*, pp. 172–3; the Gulathing's law 53, 125, Robberstad, ed., *Gulatingslovi*, pp. 74–5, 143; the older Christian Law of Borgarthing, Version 2, Fjeld Halvorsen and Rindal, *De eldste østlandske kristenrettene*, pp. 187, 220; National Law Code V, 4, 3. Taranger, ed., *Magnus Lagabøters Landslov*, p. 77.

[49] Robberstad, ed., *Gulatingslovi*, pp. 74–5

of the separate portions of property that had been joined together at the making of the marriage, and the consequences of a possible differential increase or loss in the value of those portions during marriage. However, later royal amendments strengthened the position of kin relatives to some extent, and underlined that the consent or advice of 'legal heirs and relatives' was necessary. Without any further reservations, this was ascertained in two amendments from c.1297 and 1358, issued respectively by Håkon V Magnusson acting as a duke, and by the later king Håkon VI Magnusson. But some time between 1299 and 1306, when Håkon V Magnusson was reigning king, he issued an amendment with some more specific qualifications. Provided that the wife had been married with the consent of her relatives, and on the condition that she had received an indirect dowry from her husband, the couple should be free to join property, as soon as they had children of their own. But if the spouses had children from earlier marriages, who were of minor age, consent was needed from the nearest kin relatives, that is, those who were nearest in line to inherit. In other words, consent from relatives was now restricted to those cases where at least one of the spouses had children from before.

A third distinction concerned the theoretical shares that husband and wife were supposed to own in the joint property and the way the property should be divided upon the death of one of the spouses. Here, there existed two forms: the so-called *þriðjungsfélag*, or 'one-third-joint-property', and the *helmingsfélag*, that is, 'half-share-' or 'bipartite joint property'. These notions specified how the joint property was held and how it should be split up when one of the spouses died. With a *þriðjungsfélag*, all that was not held aside as separate estate should be divided according to 'thirds', with two thirds going to the husband or his heirs and one third passing to the wife or her heirs. With the *helmingsfélag*, everything that was put into the joint property should be divided equally between the surviving spouse and the other heirs, either their children or other relatives. The oldest provincial laws knew only the 'one-third-joint-property', which was used as a standard for both the automatically established *félag* by law, and the arranged forms of *félag*:

> If the couple has been together for twenty years or more, the law joins their estates, if it was not done before [...] then she owns one third of the estate and he two thirds of it. If they had made a *félag*, but not made it public before twenty years had gone, it is like it was never done. (The Gulathing's law 53)[50]

> But if the wife looses her husband and they have been living together for at least twelve months, the wife owns a third of the estate and all moveables, and her clothes in addition. (The Frostathing's law XI, 6)[51]

50 Ibid., pp. 174–5.

51 The Frostathing's law XI, 6, cf. XI, 8: 'If a man marries a widow or a girl with her own property, he does not own anything in her estate before twelve months has passed; then the law puts their

The National Law Code, for its part, introduced the concept of 'bipartite joint property', but prescribed a combined application of property division into halves and thirds. In so far as the amount and value of property at the end of marriage corresponded to what had been put into the joint ownership, a bipartite division should take place, between the surviving spouse and the heirs of the deceased spouse. The only exception was in the case where one of the spouses had put in more than the other at the conclusion of the *félag* settlement. Then a corresponding surplus part should be taken out first. But if the amount of property had increased during marriage, this increase should be divided according to thirds. The husband or his heirs should have two thirds, while the wife and her heirs were entitled to one third of the property increase.

> 1. His wife's estate shall no man take out of the country, unless she wants. He is to govern for all of their estates, to their benefit ... 2. No wife shall deny her husband *félag* ... And this is the way they shall make *félag* between themselves: Each of them shall put into the *félag* what they own and what they are going to own, either by inheritance or by other means ... But the one of the spouses who put the most into the *félag*, shall take most out of it, or alternatively his or her heirs, (only) then shall the estate be divided in two halves, even if the value has been reduced. But if the value of the estate has grown, the husband or his heirs should have two thirds of the profit, the wife or her heirs should have one third. They do not have to ask anyone of permission to make this kind of *félag*.[52]

The position of the 'bipartite jointure' was further strengthened through later royal amendments. In the great amendment given by king Håkon V Magnusson some time between 1299 and 1306 ('About joint property between spouses'), it was explicitly stated that the kind of joint ownership which the spouses were entitled to conclude by themselves should be a bipartite one. The amendment of the later king, Håkon VI, can be read as a confirmation of this principle. The final, decisive step in favour of this principle of bipartite division came with the above-mentioned decree from the 'nobility assembly' in Bergen in 1557.[53] Here the bipartite form of joint property was established as standard legislation, which should govern all divisions of property taking place after the death of one or both spouses, without any exceptions. In other words, bipartite jointure was established as the default form by law. But, in addition, the decree repeated certain procedures

estate together.' Hagland and Sandnes, eds, *Frostatingslova*, pp. 172–3.

52 National Law Code V, 3, 1, Keyser, Munch *et al.*, *Norges gamle Love*, II, p. 76, Taranger, ed., *Magnus Lagabøters Landslov*, p. 74.

53 Winge, ed., *Lover og forordninger*, pp. 59–60; A. Taranger, *Udsigt over Den norske rets historie, vol. IV: Privatrettens historie* (Christiania, 1907), pp. 330–1, 396. After the establishment of the union between Denmark and Norway, and after the abolition of the separate Norwegian Council of the Realm in 1536, selected members of the Danish Council of the Realm acted periodically as a High Court commission in Norway, also having legislative and administrative functions.

to be followed at the division of inheritance – about the paying of debts, et cetera – partly coinciding with the instructions in the National Law Code.

The gradually more dominant position of the bipartite form of joint ownership and the greater capabilities of the spouses to make agreements about joint property by themselves, without having to seek the advice or consent of their relatives, seem to have laid down new conditions for property devolution between the generations and, consequently, also for property strategies among the landowning segments of society. In particular the new law regulations must have had implications for the transference of allodial estate. As we have seen, the National Law Code contained quite elaborate instructions about the procedures that should be followed, in the cases where 'that land comes under a woman, which men have the right to redeem from her'.[54] But the institution of joint property influenced these matters, so they got more complicated than in the 'default' cases, where no settlements had been made, and the total marital property was divided into the three clear-cut parts of dowry, indirect dowry and the husband's separate property.

The varying use of different kinds of marital property arrangements throughout late medieval times has been studied by Kathrine Græsdal, on the basis of 103 preserved charters from the period 1300–1565. The charter material comprises testimonies about marriage contracts, actual marriage contracts, letters specifically referring to earlier concluded contracts and letters concerning inheritance procedures which seem to reflect that such agreements or contracts must have existed.[55] On the basis of this evidence, the following tendencies can be observed (see Figure 1.1). Although keeping the property of the spouses separate may have been standard procedure earlier, the use of marriage contracts explicitly establishing this kind of property relationship seems to decrease substantially, and almost vanish. Documentary evidence of contracts establishing separate property decreases from ten during the first half of the fourteenth century, to four in the following fifty-year period. While separate property agreements are no longer used, the contracts establishing joint property become completely dominating, though one has to take into consideration that a certain number of the referred marriage settlements are of an uncertain kind, which cannot be determined precisely. What is more, of the two possible forms of joint ownership, the bipartite jointure is the prevailing one, while the 'one-third-jointure' (*þriðjungsfelag*) is also discarded. In all, only four cases of this latter kind of contractual agreement are found, all stemming from the first two fifty-year intervals. The last known jointure of this kind was documented in 1398. In general, the number of bipartite jointure contracts rises markedly during the fourteenth century and reaches a maximum during the fifteenth century, but then drops to an insignificant number throughout the first half of the sixteenth century. A possible explanation for the last development may be that the practice of joint property arrangements was by then so established that it did not cause the same number of conflicts, and therefore is less liable to be reflected in the documentary evidence.[56]

54 National Law Code VI, 14, Taranger, ed., *Magnus Lagabøters Landslov*, p. 106.

55 K. Græsdal, '... Legge i felaget alt det som de da eier og kommer til å eie ..., om kvinner, eiendom og ekteskap i norsk middelalder', unpublished Major thesis, University of Tromsø, 2002.

56 Ibid., pp. 53, 77.

Figure 1.1 Norwegian Marriage Contracts, 1300–1565

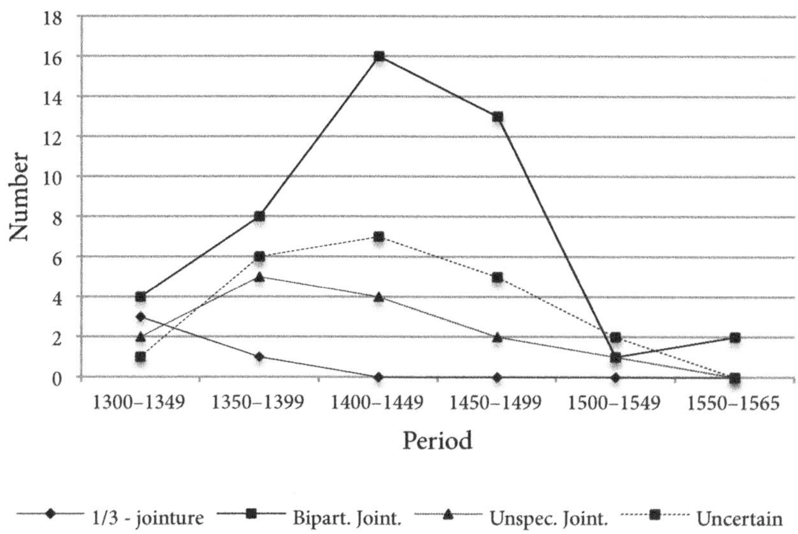

Source: Græsdal, '...Legge i felaget alt det som de da eier og kommer til å eie'.

A peculiar feature which should be noticed, however, is that the bipartite jointure, to an increasing degree, is combined with separate property in such a way that the agreements stipulate that some parts of the spouses' property should be included in the joint ownership, while other parts should remain separate property. About one-third of the contracts covering bipartite jointure in the period 1330–1430 were made up of combined contracts which also stipulated separate ownership for some parts of the property. In a Nordic context, this kind of combined contract appears rather particular to Norway. In contrast, the landowning elite in Iceland – who also applied both bipartite jointure and separate ownership – did so at different times and presumably with different strategic aims depending on the socio-economic situation. Such combined contracts are not known from Iceland.[57]

The respective roles played by joint and separate ownership in combined marriage settlements could be defined in different ways. One way was to let the property which each spouse owned at the making of the marriage be defined as separate property, while the property they acquired together, during wedlock, should be subject to joint ownership.[58] Another way of dividing the property was to include the disposal of moveables in the joint property, while the landed property possessed by each spouse at the time of the wedding should remain separate property.[59] But there were even more elaborate ways of dealing with

57 Arnórsdóttir, *Property and Virginity*.

58 E.g. *DN* III, no. 191 from 1337.

59 *DN* XVIII, no. 39 from 1400; *DN* X, no. 100 from 1403; *DN* III, no. 576 from 1405; *DN* II, no. 646 from 1418; and *DN* V, no. 605 from 1431.

the division, such as having the allodial estates from each kin group defined as separate property, while other forms of landed property which had recently been bought or taken by mortgage became the subject of joint ownership. All in all, the fairly new procedure with bipartite jointure, combined with reservations of separate property, opened up a new flexibility and diverse adaptations.

According to a charter of 1337, the two sons of Ingebjørg, the surviving widow of Reidar Ogmundsson, sued the woman Arnbjørg, heir of Reidar, claiming that their mother had not got what she was entitled to concerning her dowry and the previous agreement between her and her deceased husband. They presented witnesses who could testify that an arrangement had been made at the wedding, according to which each spouse should preserve what they owned at the betrothal as separate property, but that property acquired later should be held in jointure. During their marriage, Reidar had inherited the whole farm Spikdalen from his father, Ogmund, and it was now decided that Ingebjørg was entitled to half of the farm.[60]

Settlements combining jointure and separate property seem also to have made it easier to safeguard women's allodial property. A charter from 1366 is a testimony of two witnesses who were present at the making of a joint ownership agreement between Jon Torleivsson and his wife, Gjertrud. At this event, she excluded from the jointure shares in the following farms: Tveit, Oppsal, Holdhus, Haugen and Gjøn (situated in Fusa county in the western part of Norway), as well as some textiles, some silver buckles and a brooch. But, thereafter, they made a joint property agreement, encompassing the remaining property.[61] In a similar document from 1400, two witnesses testified under oath that they had been present when Andres Pálsson and his wife, Ingegjerd Arnfinnsdaughter, made a jointure agreement. But Ingegjerd had insisted that her property in the farms Hisøy, Halse and Ime in Mandal (in the county of East Agder) should be kept outside of it. At the same time, she gave the farm Halse, as a token of appreciation, to her relative and sole legitimate heir, Eiliv Brynjolvsson, because he had consented to the joint property agreement. Two other witnesses testified to the fact that Eiliv, after the death of Ingegjerd, also had received the farm Hisøy and considerable other property.[62] According to a testifying charter of 1401, from the region east of the Oslofjord, three witnesses gave proof in a case concerning the property relationships of the late Tord Gautesson and his wife, Åsa. They all swore that they had been present at the deathbed of Tord and had heard him declare, in his full senses, that the farm Voll was not included in the joint property settlement between him and his wife. Åsa confirmed this, and added that Voll was her allodial property.[63]

60 *DN* III, no. 191 – 1337.

61 *DN* XVI, no. 27 – 1366.

62 *DN* XVIII, no. 39 – 1400.

63 *DN* II, no. 568 – 1401.

Conclusion

Thus, the institution of joint ownership – and in particular the bipartite jointure which prevailed throughout the late Middle Ages in Norway – created a new 'space of action', compared to the old, established 'standard' inheritance system. New options were laid down for the unfolding of more flexible property strategies on the part of the kin groups, on the part of the married couples, and on the part of individuals, including women.[64] As we have seen, the position of the spouses in relation to that of the kin relatives on both sides was strengthened, at least in cases where they had their own children. This gave them a greater freedom for establishing agreements about joint ownership at their own will, offering several possible options as to what kind of property should be included in the jointure, and what might be excluded, as separate property, for each of them. It is highly probable that this increased focus on the decisions of the spouses themselves was due to the monarchy becoming ever more influenced by the ecclesiastical view of marriage as an independent, binding union between the spouses, in the presence of God.[65]

Nevertheless, the continued influence of the kin groups should not be underestimated, and the legislation from the early years of the fourteenth century displays a certain variation in how far it went in strengthening the rights of the couple. The spouses were still dependent on their kin relatives for many matters, and could – certainly in relation to the management of property – have common interests with them. Nor do the kin groups seem to have been too closely attached to the standard procedures of property transference, as defined by the laws, with a priority for men and male links. If it might serve the interests of the kin group in the long run, and ensure that property stemming from one kin line might, in the future, be transferred to heirs that were acceptable, they seem to have been willing to let property pass through an intermediary female link.

Relative freedom in defining what kind of property might, or might not, be included in the joint ownership seems to have opened up complex strategies. The jointure institution was predominantly used by those segments of society which disposed landed property in some quantity. A fair hypothesis might be that the kin groups of these strata primarily saw the bipartite jointure as a suitable mechanism for getting a better hold on landed property that had been acquired successively and recently – through buying, mortgage loans and exchange – and which did not yet qualify as allodial lands in their line. One possibility is, therefore, that the practice of combining jointure and separate property in marriage contracts reflected a double objective: to ensure that well-defined allodial property should be inherited primarily by lineal descendants of the original kin line through which it had been established – possibly by the new couple's children, who represented

64 Cf. Ormøy, 'Kvinner og eiendom', p. 87.

65 It is interesting to note that an explicit reference to 'God's and man's law' is made in the section concerning joint property in the great royal amendment for the counties Ringerike and Hadeland, issued by duke Håkon Magnusson in 1297 (Keyser, Munch *et al.*, *Norges gamle Love*, III, p. 28).

a new, affinally united line – but otherwise by other lineal kin members. Property acquired by the individual spouses through their lifetime could also preferably be passed on through the same direct descendants so that it, in time, would acquire allodial status. This would represent a combination of thinking in terms of lineally defined kin groups, and consideration of the affinal connections established through the institution of marriage. Both concerns would probably serve as incentives for strategically contracting marriages with a conscious deliberation of which other (bilaterally defined) kin groups would offer the best conditions for the establishment of a new, common line of descendants who, in turn, could take care of the allodial property in the best way. In some cases, such strategies appear to have been followed for several generations.

2

SPOUSAL DISPUTES, THE MARITAL PROPERTY SYSTEM AND THE LAW IN LATER MEDIEVAL SWEDEN

Mia Korpiola

Recent research has emphasized the nexus of separation customs and marital property systems in medieval Europe.[1] Indeed, the practice of marital separation across the late-medieval Franco-Belgian region may have been influenced by its communal property system. Charles Donahue Jr has observed that 'a system of marital community property, which existed all over the Franco-Belgian region, virtually requires that a separating couple obtain a public declaration that they have separated', whereas the English 'separate marital property system' more markedly fostered informal 'do-it-yourself' separations.[2] Donahue's observations have been corroborated by a recent article by Monique Vleeschouwers-Van Melkebeek, focusing on separation and the division of property in the late-medieval southern Low Countries. There, the 'customary property system in the Franco-Belgian region spurred the couples on in their demand for a judicial separation', in contrast to England. From the Franco-Belgian region, hundreds of preserved divisions of marital property can also be found in secular court records as a material consequence of judicial separations, granted by ecclesiastical courts.[3]

In my previous research, I have observed some resemblance between Swedish marriage patterns and those of the Franco-Belgian region. Parental consent was important in Swedish law and practice. The decision to marry, as well as the process of marriage formation, remained a very collective undertaking in Swe-

[1] See, e.g., L. I. Hansen's essay in this volume. I would like to extend my warm thanks to the editors of this volume for their invaluable comments on previous versions of this essay.

[2] C. Donahue, Jr, 'Conclusion: Comparative Approaches to Marriage in the Later Middle Ages', *Regional Variations in Matrimonial Law and Custom in Europe, 1150–1600*, ed. M. Korpiola (Leiden, 2011), p. 306. See also C. Donahue, Jr, *Law, Marriage, and Society in the Later Middle Ages: Arguments About Marriage in Five Courts* (New York, 2007), pp. 604–13; and C. Donahue, Jr, 'English and French Marriage Cases in the Later Middle Ages: Might the Differences Be Explained by Differences in the Property Systems?', *Marriage, Property, and Succession*, ed. L. Bonfield (Berlin, 1992), pp. 339–66.

[3] M. Vleeschouwers-Van Melkebeek, 'Separation and Marital Property in Late Medieval England and the Franco-Belgian Region', *Regional Variations in Matrimonial Law and Custom in Europe, 1150–1600*, ed. M. Korpiola (Leiden, 2011), pp. 77–97.

den throughout the Middle Ages.[4] From the little we know of the Swedish medieval church courts, separation-related causes formed a substantial part of their matrimonial legal activity.[5] In addition, the medieval Swedish marital property system was based on a communal pool of property, in addition to separate and lineal inherited land. The Swedish system was a variant of the northern European, 'Germanic' one. It 'did not entail a separation of property but rather a merger ... The wife [and her property] was thus incorporated into her husband's household and assigned to his care.'[6] These similarities between the Franco-Belgian region and Sweden invite a closer exploration of the connection between spousal disputes and the marital property system in later medieval Swedish law and practice.[7] When dealing with spousal difficulties and marital breakdown, communities had to take property issues into consideration in various ways. Material interests could trigger quarrels and litigation. Crimes against one's spouse could have property consequences, as did informal or judicial separations.

As will be discussed below, Swedish law authorized husbands to administer both communal property and their wives' inherited property during marriage. Nevertheless, their managerial rights were limited both by law and in practice. In this context we might ask: did marital disputes affect these powers to manage property? How did the law regulate marital problems and separation? What kind of property consequences did marital difficulties and breakdowns have according to the law? These are some of the questions that I will address in this essay. However, before analysing these issues, Sweden's two marital property systems have to be presented; one applied to the countryside and the other to towns. Both marital property systems were basically governed by separate, though partly similar, laws enacted in the mid-fourteenth century.

The Marital Property System in Medieval Swedish Law: Protecting Inherited Land

The Swedish marital property system was partly separate and partly communal. In the countryside, where over 95 per cent of the Swedish population resided, sharp distinctions were drawn between inherited land and other property (chattels and acquired land). Inherited land always remained in the kin group (maternal or

4 M. Korpiola, *Between Betrothal and Bedding: Marriage Formation in Sweden, 1200–1600* (Leiden, 2009), esp. chs 1, 3–4.

5 M. Korpiola, 'Marriage Causes in Late Medieval Sweden: The Evidence of Bishop Hans Brask's Register (1522–1527)', *Regional Variations in Matrimonial Law and Custom in Europe, 1150–1600*, ed. M. Korpiola (Leiden, 2011), pp. 220, 226–35, 247–9.

6 M. C. Howell, 'Marital Property Law as Socio-Cultural Text: The Case of Late-Medieval Douai', *To Have and To Hold: Marrying and Its Documentation in Western Christendom, 400–1600*, ed. P. L. Reynolds and J. Witte (Cambridge, 2007), p. 426.

7 My focus will be on the period 1350–1530, from the laws of King Magnus Eriksson (r. 1319–64) until, roughly, the onset of the Reformation. The essay relies heavily on secular sources from certain late-medieval Swedish towns – mainly Stockholm (after 1474), Arboga (after 1451) and Jönköping (after 1456) – but ecclesiastical sources and other documents are also used.

paternal line), and spouses could neither have rights to that property nor inherit it. Only a tenth of inherited land could be willed to the church for pious purposes. Otherwise, it could not be alienated outside the kin group without the consent of the next heirs.[8] Even in towns, inherited land had first to be offered to one's nearest relatives in the maternal or paternal line, depending on its provenance. Closest relatives had the right to redeem land (*byrdh*) that had been bartered or alienated outside the family without their consent.[9]

Sweden practised partible inheritance; both daughters and sons inherited. While daughters and sons had equal inheritance shares in Swedish towns, in the countryside a son inherited double the amount that his sister inherited.[10] Any property given by parents as dowry (*hemfylghþ*) or advanced inheritance to sons or daughters would revert to the parental estate after the death of the benefactor for a new and final division between the heirs.[11] Thus, daughters inherited along with their brothers and, unlike in many other European countries, they were not separated from the parental estate in advance through their dowry. Women regularly inherited land in Sweden – not only women in towns, but also among the nobility and the large landowning peasantry.

Unlike elsewhere on the Continent, where written marriage contracts were customary, Swedish dowry arrangements hardly ever left traces in the existing sources. However, hundreds of medieval morning gift letters and documents have been preserved. In the countryside, the morning gift consisted of land, chattels or money, given by the husband to the wife on the morning of the second wedding day for her maintenance in widowhood. In towns, the morning gift was given on the first wedding day.[12] Among the wealthy, the morning gift was usually specified land, being one or several manors or farms. After the husband's death, his widow became the absolute possessor of this property. Unlike her inherited land, she could freely alienate her morning gift property if she so wished.[13] Swedish medieval law had established maximum values for the morning gift depending on the groom's status, so that knights in the highest category could give property worth forty marks, compared to the three-mark morning gift of the peasant or the one-mark morning gift of the non-landowner.[14] Nevertheless, the size of morning gifts was subject to inflation as they became

8 E.g., *Naimiskaari* [Chapter on Marriage] 5:1, *Maakaari* [Chapter on Land] 2 and 9, M. Ulkuniemi, ed., *Kuningas Kristoferin maanlaki 1442* [hereafter *KrL*] (Helsinki, 1978), pp. 45, 59–61.

9 *Jordabalken* [Chapter on Land] 1–2, Å. Holmbäck and E. Wessén, eds, *Magnus Erikssons stadslag i nusvensk tolkning* [hereafter *MESL*] (Lund, 1966), pp. 70–1.

10 *Ärvdabalken* [Chapter on Inheritance] 1–2, *MESL*, p. 56; *Ärvdabalken* 1–2, Å. Holmbäck and E. Wessén, eds, *Magnus Erikssons landslag i nusvensk tolkning* [hereafter *MEL*] (Lund, 1962), p. 58; *Perintökaari* [Chapter on Inheritance] 1–2, *KrL*, pp. 50–1. See also, A. L. Erickson, 'The Marital Economy in Comparative Perspective', *The Marital Economy in Scandinavia and Britain 1400–1900*, ed. M. Ågren and A. L. Erickson (Aldershot, 2005), pp. 7–8.

11 *Giftermålsbalken* [Chapter on Marriage] 12, *MEL*, p. 44; *G* 12, *KrL*, p. 48.

12 *Giftermålsbalken* 6:2, *MESL*, p. 41; *Giftermålsbalken* 10, *MEL*, p. 43; *Giftermålsbalken* 9–10, *KrL*, p. 47; Korpiola, *Between Betrothal and Bedding*, pp. 78–85.

13 E.g., H. Petersson, *Morgongåvoinstitutet i Sverige under tiden fram till omkring 1734 års lag* (Lund, 1973), pp. 29–32.

14 *Giftermålsbalken* 10, *KrL*, p. 47.

important status symbols. The maximum values were totally and universally disregarded, especially among the nobility.[15]

The legal subjection of married women to their husbands was sanctioned by most legal authorities of the time, based upon the Bible. As the man was the head of his wife (*vir est caput mulieris*),[16] she was to obey him. Her legal subjection also largely applied to property concerns as men managed the marital economy, including the property of their wives, both separate and communal, during marriage. As the law stated, 'after man and wife are married and have lain a night together in the same bed, he is her *målsman* [*mals maþer*] and has the right to represent her in court'.[17] *Målsman* has often been translated as legal guardian, which meant that the husband became manager of his wife's property and, by law, her representative in legal affairs.

Both in the countryside and in towns, the authority of the husband to manage the wife's affairs was assumed after the couple had spent the wedding night together. After this, all other property – except inherited land – was pooled together. According to the mid-fourteenth-century laws, this communal property was divided in the countryside so that two-thirds went to the husband and one-third to the wife. In towns, the joint estate would be split into equal halves.[18] The husband managed his wife's property during the marriage, including her inherited land. For example, in 1478, Arvid Olofsson appeared at the Arboga town court explaining that he wished to redeem some land to which his wife had kin-rights. Arvid could act as his wife's representative, as only the closest heirs to the land could use the kin-right of redemption (*byrdh*) to the land.[19] In town law, married men and widows could be gaoled for debt as married men represented the household in financial affairs, but the wife's property – unlike her person – was not necessarily similarly immune from confiscation for debt.[20]

Legal guardianship did not mean that the wife was treated as a minor in all respects, but her capacity to conduct business transactions independently with outsiders, without the knowledge of the husband – and his tacit authorization by non-opposition – was restricted. In the countryside, husbands could annul all transactions made by their wives without their knowledge if the interest was higher than one *öre*, a relatively small sum. In addition, the person who had conducted

15 Petersson, *Morgongåvoinstitutet*, pp. 65–87; H. Ylikangas, *Valta ja väkivalta keski- ja uudenajan taitteessa Suomessa* (Porvoo / Helsinki / Juva, 1988), pp. 89–96.

16 Eph. 5:22–4 (Vulgate version): '*Mulieres viris suis subditæ sint, sicut Domino: quoniam vir caput est mulieris, sicut Christus caput est Ecclesiæ: ipse, salvator corporis ejus. Sed sicut Ecclesia subjecta est Christo, ita et mulieres viris suis in omnibus*.'

17 *Giftermålsbalken* 9, *MEL*, p. 43; *Giftermålsbalken* 8, *MESL*, p. 42; *Naimiskaari* 6:1, *Naimiskaari* 9, *KrL*, pp. 46–7; Erickson, 'The Marital Economy', pp. 10–11. See also L. Carlsson, 'Jag giver dig min dotter', *Trolovning och äktenskap i den svenska kvinnans äldre historia, I* (Lund, 1965), esp. pp. 148–51, 172–4, 181–7.

18 E.g., *Jordabalken* 28:1-29, *KrL*, pp. 66–7.

19 26 January 1478, E. Noreen and T. Wennström, eds, *Arboga stads tänkebok* [I–IV, hereafter *AST*] II (Uppsala, 1935–50), p. 104: Arvid also empowered the town bailiff to represent him in the case. See also 3 November 1477(?), *AST* II, p. 98.

20 *Rättegångsbalken* [Chapter on Procedure] 18:1, *MESL*, p. 178. This applied to persons living in the country but coming to town.

business with the wife was liable for a three-mark fine. Conducting business with a man's servants or children without his knowledge was altogether forbidden and similarly punishable by a three-mark fine.[21] This hardly encouraged people to engage in business with married women, although the situation may have been more fluid than the law suggests. By contrast, in Swedish towns, wives were expected to play a more active role in their husbands' businesses or trades – as was the case elsewhere in northwest Europe.[22] King Magnus Eriksson's town law did not limit a wife's authority to conduct sales. The husband's knowledge or authorization was immaterial. However, purchases from a man's children or employees were forbidden and punishable by a three-mark fine unless they had expressly been made sales assistants.[23]

Despite the rules of guardianship, very occasionally some married women appear in documents acting as their husbands' representatives or conducting their land transactions themselves, with their husbands' consent. For example, in 1499, Claus the Tailor of Stockholm authorized his wife Katarina, daughter of Danneberg, to collect his debts in Lübeck and other places.[24] It is possible that married women could act in person more freely in town courts than in the countryside. Yet, even in the countryside, pragmatic reasons probably caused the relatively rigid legal rules to be interpreted flexibly. Late medieval and Reformation correspondence between spouses shows how Swedish noblewomen – as mistresses of the household – made acquisitions, managed estates, collected revenues, wielded power and so on during the absence of their husbands.[25] Once widowed, women had full and extensive rights to act for themselves. For example, burgher Olof Nilsson of Stockholm tried to have the property sale made by his new wife Katarina Jakobsdotter, daughter of town councillor Jacob Moyse, revoked. However, this was denied as the sale had been lawfully made during Katarina's widowhood, when she was free to make such transactions.[26]

Although wives were under the authority of their husbands, they had legitimate authority both over members of the household and over property as mistresses of their household. The keys of wives were visible cultural symbols of this authority over the household, and taking them away from a wife was a serious insult to her status and family.[27] For example, Klemit the Pouch-Maker's wife complained that her husband disliked (*vanelzkar*) her, drove her away from their home, and was

21 *Köpmålabalken* [Chapter on Sale] 3:1, *MEL*, p. 153; *Kauppakaari* [Chapter on Sale] 4, *KrL*, p. 104.

22 E.g., see B. A. Hanawalt, *The Wealth of Wives: Women, Law, and Economy in Late Medieval London* (Oxford, 2007), pp. 120–5. See also the essays by Spence, Shepard and Ogilvie in this volume.

23 *Köpmålabalken* 3:1, *MESL*, p. 115.

24 E.g., 2 September 1499, G. Carlsson, ed., *Stockholms stads tänkeböcker* [I–V, hereafter *SST*] III (Stockholm, 1921–44), p. 452.

25 T. Hockman, *Kolmen polven perilliset. Ingeborg Aakentytär (Tott) ja hänen sukunsa (n. 1460–1507)* (Helsinki, 2006), esp. pp. 90–2; A. Lahtinen, *Anpassning, förhandling, motstånd. Kvinnliga aktörer i släkten Fleming 1470–1620*, trans. C. Frostell (Helsinki/Stockholm, 2009), esp. pp. 39–61.

26 23 January 1497, *SST* III, p. 321; M. Lamberg, *Dannemännen i stadens råd. Rådmanskretsen i nordiska köpstäder under senmedeltiden* (Stockholm, 2001), p. 128.

27 E.g., *Naimiskaari* 5, *KrL*, p. 45; D. Gaunt, *Familjeliv i Norden* (Södertälje, 1983), pp. 45, 47–8.

always in the company of the maid-servant.[28] Ousting the wife from the home and replacing her with the maid turned the domestic roles and hierarchies upside down, as wives had disciplinary power over servants in the household as the secondary co-manager in household affairs.

As has been discussed, Swedish law gave married men substantial power to manage the household and the property of their wives during marriage. The morning gift property received by the wife from her husband was considerable among the nobility. Women also received property from their natal family as dowry and inheritance, regularly inheriting land. A woman's closest relatives, as potential heirs to her inherited lands, had vested interests in assuring that they were neither mismanaged nor alienated without their consent. This brings us to the Swedish legal provisions safeguarding property from negligence.

Safeguarding Property from Spousal Mismanagement and Elopement

Property, moveable as much as immovable, and its management have always been potential sources of marital conflict. We get two vivid descriptions of such instances of spousal tension because of property loss in the miracles associated with Saint Katarina [Ulfsdotter, 1331–81] of Vadstena, daughter of Saint Birgitta [Birgersdotter, 1303–73] of Sweden.[29] Peter Petersson of Vadstena and his wife had been blessed with thirteen children but, because of his wife's lack of milk, she could not nurse any of them herself. Thus, they had been forced to hire a string of wet nurses, causing extra expenditure and an obvious burden on the family economy. Peter felt great indignation towards his wife, reviling and verbally abusing her because of her inability to nurse the infants herself.[30] In 1470, another married Vadstena woman was returning home from church carrying her small son in her arms. The child started to cry and she put a silver spoon into the baby's hand in order to calm him. But, the infant dropped the spoon on the ground. When the mother later realized this, she was distraught, fearing the wrath of her husband after losing the valuable silver item.[31]

However, these were minor troubles concerning matrimonial funds. The authority of the husband to represent his wife in court and to administer her property during marriage was potentially far more problematic. Maria Ågren has observed that medieval Swedish law 'implicitly depicted husbands as the ones against whom [married] women might need protection, and the law consequently provided means by which the power of husbands was circumscribed'.[32] The means

[28] 18 June 1488 and 23 June 1488, *STT* II, pp. 277, 279.

[29] The miracles are part of the canonization records printed in Stockholm in 1487 as *Processus seu negocium canonizacionis b. Katerine de Vadstenis*, T. Lundén, ed., 'Den heliga Katarinas av Vadstena liv och underverk efter medeltida urkunder översatta', *Credo* 31:2 (1950), p. 67.

[30] Lundén, ed., 'Den heliga', 31, p. 121.

[31] Lundén, ed., 'Den heliga', 70, pp. 138–9.

[32] M. Ågren, *Domestic Secrets: Women and Property in Sweden, 1600–1850* (Chapel Hill, 2009), p. 39.

of curtailing the power of their husbands were granted to wives' male relatives, though, rather than to the married women themselves.

The threat posed to a married woman's property by her husband's mismanagement was countered by various means. The law required that people managing the possessions of others, as curators or guardians, could not alienate property belonging to their wards or charges either by barter or sale unless this was beneficial for the ward or charge. If not, the transaction was revocable.[33] Regarding husbands managing the property of their wives in particular, the law expressly specified that regardless of whether the couple had children together or not, the husband could only barter his wife's lands with her consent and that of her heirs. Even if this consent was given, the exchange had to be 'for better land, not worse'.[34] This is what Katarina Larsdotter claimed when her husband bartered away her inherited land. According to her, he had not exchanged her land for better land, as the law stated, but for worse. The court found in her favour and annulled the transaction because of her lack of consent.[35]

Although claiming a wife's lack of consent could be a strategic pretext for annulling land transactions later discovered to be disadvantageous, it is also probable that some such cases resulted from real disputes between the spouses or a husband's mismanagement of his wife's property. The interests of a wife's natal family in her land, which they potentially stood to inherit from her, ensured that she would have their support if the alienation was unlawful or disadvantageous.[36] Women occasionally complained in court that their husbands had sold their land without authorization. In the countryside, as a general rule, husbands could not alienate their wives' property without their consent unless there were extraordinary circumstances. If foreign troops invaded the country, taking one spouse into captivity of war, the other spouse – even if it was the wife – was allowed to sell the captive's land in order to redeem them. If there was famine and dire necessity, the husband had a limited right to sell his wife's land, provided he also sold double the amount of his own lands. In such a case, the sale had to be made at the assizes (district courts in the countryside) and the selling spouse had to define the necessity that drove them to sell the other's land.[37]

Even in towns, where livelihood was less dependent on landed property, and the exigencies of the market economy were better taken into account, husbands could not freely dispose of their wives' inherited land. Her consent and that of her closest relatives were needed. Nevertheless, under exceptional circumstances, either spouse could again unilaterally sell the other's land in order to redeem him/her from foreign captivity of war. Town law mentioned famine but added poverty in general as another acceptable reason for selling land. However, it was expressly

33 *Maakaari* 16, *KrL*, pp. 62–3.

34 E.g., *Naimiskaari* 19, *KrL*, pp. 62–3.

35 K. H. Karlsson, ed., *Upplands lagmansdombok, 1490–1494 efter en Uppsala-handskrift* [hereafter *ULD*] (Stockholm, 1907), p. 30; Giftomålsbalken 20, *MEL*, p. 46.

36 Ågren, *Domestic Secrets*, pp. 30–40.

37 *Jordabalken* 32, *MEL*, pp. 80–1; *Maakaari* 27, *KrL*, p. 66. If the husband owned neither realty nor chattels, he could only sell lands worth six marks per annum in case of famine.

stipulated that the poverty was not to be caused by wastefulness such as gambling if a spouse's inherited land was to be sold.[38] In 1397, Helga Anundsdotter, widow of lord Valdemar Eriksson, complained how her – probably former – husband Joar Königsmark had violently forced her (*med store nödh, at jac var slaghin oc trughat oc illa haldnat ther til*) to cede her seal. Then he had used it against her will for alienating her estate of Bro without her consent.[39] Luckily for lady Helga, unlawfully ceded lands would be returned, even if much later, to the rightful owner if no acute emergency had driven the husband to alienate the land (*vtan besynderlig nöd driffuer han thär til*), as she claimed.[40]

A wife's interests were protected, as her inherited lands could never become the property of her husband without the consent of her kinsmen. She could not validly alienate her inherited land without their consent, but neither could her husband. If a married woman received her inheritance in the form of land, this provided her the best protection against her husband's mismanagement. The legal capacity of the owner of inherited land was curtailed by the law as 'legally he [or she] was only holding it on behalf of his family, as a trustee'.[41] Therefore, not only sentimental reasons, but also property-related self-interest, ensured that a wife's natal kinsmen would come to her aid if her husband proved incompetent and wasteful.

Occasionally, when women sought aid from their male relatives, their marital difficulties had probably also caused other disputes between their kin and husbands. For example, in 1458, Olof Jonsson and his son-in-law (*magh*) Mårten first appeared at the town court of Arboga in connection with a dispute concerning some barrels of malt and grain, but the court then moved on to consider the state of Mårten's marriage. This reflected the connection between two disputes. At Mårten's request, two men had gone to Olof demanding the return of Mårten's wife. Olof had replied that Mårten would neither have his wife back that day nor the next day, and she had remained with Olof for two nights. The court sentenced Olof Jonsson to an extremely high eighty-mark fine for taking away Mårten's wife, but, in reality, he only paid a small fine for the offence.[42]

Hiding or smuggling away communal property from the marital estate was a sign of a failing marriage. The hidden property would form a nest egg for life after separation. As men managed the household assets, they were better positioned to liquidate the property and abscond with valuables. Their power to manage chattels was uncontested, while only the wife's inherited land was especially protected. Peder Kopman from Stockholm secretly made off to Germany with his own property, that of his wife Kristina, widow of Evert the Goldsmith, and that of his stepchildren, leaving them to cope with his debts. However, the Councils of the Realm and town freed them of all Peder's debts, observing that 'he had trans-

38 *Jordabalken* 16, *MESL*, p. 76.

39 P. Wieselgren, ed., *DelaGardieska Archivet, eller Handlingar ur Grefl. DelaGardiska Bibliotheket på Löberöd, II* (Lund, 1832), pp. 5–7, 169–70. See also Hansen's essay in this volume.

40 E.g., *ULD*, pp. 13, 24.

41 Ågren, *Domestic Secrets*, p. 20.

42 22 November 1458, *AST* I, p. 96.

gressed against them by his own neglect and crime' (*hans egin forsyn och brot*).[43] Margaretha, wife of the Danzig barber Jacob Blumenstein, chose to write to the bishop of Turku explaining how the woman staying with Jacob in Turku was, in fact, a common woman (*gemen wiff*), not his lawful wife (*getrude wyff*). Jacob had taken Margaretha's property with him to Turku, and she now wanted him punished for his adultery.[44]

Such disloyal and dishonest behaviour could also frustrate attempts at reconciliation. In Stockholm, rumours circulated of a matrimonial fracas between Kristina Kuste and her husband Klaus Grabow, both from the patrician elite. She was accused of adultery. Sten Sture, regent of Sweden (1470–97 and 1501–3), and the Council of the Realm had probably been informally called to the rescue by persons in social circles close to the parties. Both the two mayors of Stockholm were required to demand an oath from Grabow that he would not desert his wife and sail away – probably to Lübeck where he had relatives – or send his possessions overseas.[45]

Spousal elopement raised several property issues, partly related to the eloping spouse (for example, bigamous new marriages), and partly related to the remaining spouse (for example, management of the estate). The reasons for spousal desertion could be financial, such as those of the above-mentioned Peder Kopman. Alternatively, crime could lead to desertion. In Arboga, in 1546, Karin's husband committed homicide and deserted her because of that.[46] Knight Krister Nilsson, governor of Viborg castle, wrote in 1429 to Tallinn complaining of Cort, a gunner (*bussenschutte*), who after having committed misdeeds and causing injuries (*grote bosheit hevet bodreven unde my groten drepeliken schaden hevet gedan*) had run away, deserting both wife and children.[47]

Runaway husbands could try to contract another, bigamous, marriage with unsuspecting women if the officiating clerics were lax and failed to enquire into the potential impediments to the marriage. Swedish late-medieval synodal statutes demonstrate that unknown couples asking for solemnization without presenting proper evidence of their freedom to marry were perceived as a major problem. To remedy this, synods insisted that priests demand proof from unknown couples wishing to get married, 'for many come running with wives of others'.[48] Conscientious clerics required evidence, especially if there were rumours that another spouse was still alive.[49]

43 7 September 1489, *SST* II, pp. 378–9; M. Lamberg, 'Säädyllisyyden vartijat: Tukholman valtaporvariston sukupuolimoraali myöhäiskeskiajalla', *Jyväskylän historiallinen arkisto* 3 (1997), 68–70; Lamberg, *Dannemännen*, p. 134.

44 20 October 1509, R. Hausen, ed., *Finlands medeltidsurkunder* [I–VIII, hereafter *FMU*] VII (Helsingfors, 1910–53), doc. 1655, pp. 272–3.

45 1 August 1487, *SST* II, p. 207; Lamberg, 'Säädyllisyyden vartijat', 68–70; Lamberg, *Dannemännen*, pp. 132–7.

46 8 March 1546, *AST* IV, pp. 59–60.

47 25 June 1429, *FMU* II, 1891, p. 409.

48 E.g., Statutes of Archbishop Jöns Håkansson, 14 February 1425 and 4 March 1425, H. Reuterdahl, ed., *Statuta synodalia veteris ecclesiæ sveogothicæ* (Lund, 1841), p. 40.

49 2 December 1522, H. Gunneng, ed., *Biskop Hans Brasks registratur. Textutgåva med inledning*

Swedish secular medieval law, considering bigamy one of the most serious sexual crimes, penalized male bigamists by beheading and female bigamists by stoning or burning if the second marriage had been consummated.[50] The bigamists prosecuted and executed in medieval Swedish towns tended to be male.[51] Because of the heinousness of the crime, secular authorities tried to trace deserters before they could actually do their wicked deed. Knight Niklis Kurck, in around 1420, warned the Tallinn town council that the daughter of a local woman, Margeret Laisghe, was getting married to an unworthy (*unwerdich*) man with a wife still living in Sweden. The council was requested to prevent the union and the injustice it would cause.[52] Namely, the wedding would have given the man access to the property of Margeret's daughter, and he could have wasted it under the pretence of being her lawful husband and legal guardian.

For bigamists, wealth acquired by second marriages compensated for the possible loss of property left behind when absconding. Runaway spouses usually had to leave some of their property behind, especially if they owned real estate. Deserting wives, most particularly, carried off property from the communal home to compensate for the financial difficulties likely to threaten them later. Occasionally, circumstances suggest a premeditated elopement with a lover.[53] For example, in 1506 Olof Skroma complained that David Kolstok had absconded with his wife, taking two rugs (*ryghor*) and a pot (*gritto*) with her.[54] Bengt of Skövlingsryd, in 1480, accused Jon of Beth of taking away his wife and some property from his house. The list of items taken largely concerns women's clothes: four kirtles, three chemises (*særkia*), two hats or outer garments (*kappa*), one sheet, and a conical hat (*strwthætta*).[55] In a letter in an ecclesiastical model letter collection from the early fifteenth century in which the exact names of the parties and dates are omitted, it was alleged that the wife of N., burgher of Linköping, had gone even further. Not only had she deserted her husband at the instigation (*ipso machinante*) of the newly-appointed vicar in Skänninge, but she also had taken with her almost all of her husband's chattels (*omnibus quasi rebus suppellectilis sue distractis*).[56] The court records fail to mention explicitly whether or not the property carried off by eloping wives was part of their dowries but, irrespective of this, it was managed by their husbands as communal property.

When husbands eloped, in addition to the wives' potential loss of property, the restrictions on married women's ability to make legal transactions hindered

[hereafter *BHBR*] (Uppsala, 2003), no. 46, p. 138; Korpiola, *Between Betrothal and Bedding*, pp. 213–23.

50 *Högmålsbalken* [Chapter on Heinous Crime] 3, *MESL*, pp. 231–2; *Högmålsbalken* 4, *MEL*, p. 214; *Törkeitten asiain kaari* [Chapter on Heinous Crime] 5, *KrL*, pp. 132–3.

51 E.g., 17 June 1476, *SST* I, p. 60; 18 February 1505, *SST* IV, p. 103.

52 Circa 1420, *FMU* II, 1655, pp. 272–3.

53 Cf. Johnson's essay in this volume.

54 27 July 1506, *SST* IV, p. 123.

55 Year 1480, C. M. Kjellberg, ed., *Jönköpings stads tänkebok, 1456–1548* [hereafter *JST*] (Jönköping, 1918), p. 149.

56 P. Ståhl, ed., *Johannes Hildebrandi, Liber epistularis (Cod. Upsal. C 6). 1. Lettres nos 1 à 109 (fol. 1r à 16r). Édition critique avec des analyses et une introduction* (Stockholm, 1998), no. 73, p. 106.

property management. To remedy this, Swedish law contained specific provisions for alienating property in the case of a spousal desertion or a husband's pilgrimage. The remaining spouse had the right to sell any chattels belonging to the other if necessary for her/his livelihood or that of their children, provided he/she also sold an appointed fraction of his/her own property. Under these circumstances, wives could make valid transactions without husbands.[57] For manager-husbands, the situation was less complicated. In a property case from the 1420s, the town court of Kalmar investigated the ownership of a house. Sven the Smith argued against Störge the Smith, Sven's brother- or father-in-law (*swagh*), that a part of the house had been his wife's dowry. As she had 'behaved badly and run away from her husband', Sven was allowed to keep the dowry and administer it until his wife should die. Then, the property would go to her lawful heirs 'in accordance with the chapter [of law] on inheritance'.[58] Swedish law had explicit, separate provisions for adultery.

Wages of Sin: Punishing Adultery

God had constituted marriage to save people from sexual sin and fornication. As St Paul said, 'It is better to marry than burn.' Marriage being a remedy of sexual sin, the Church had introduced the notion of conjugal debt obliging each spouse to have sex with the other on demand.[59] Otherwise, the threat of adultery loomed. Even with this legitimate outlet for sexuality, the devil could ensnare married men and women. The canonization records of Saint Katarina of Vadstena tell how the wife of Andor was secretly pestered by Satan's temptations and the impure thoughts in her heart. Luckily, the saint intervened and helped her.[60] Others, less fortunate, acted on their impulses and broke the Sixth and Ninth Commandments ('Thou shalt not commit adultery' and 'Thou shalt not covet thy neighbour's wife'). As a corollary of the avoidance of sin, the couple had to live together. Long absences by one spouse required the permission of the other so that paying the conjugal debt was not jeopardized. Separate residences were, in effect, unacceptable for the Church unless a judicial separation had been pronounced by the local bishop.[61]

Adultery had connotations of theft, a property crime. These were emphasized in the text of King Christopher's Law of the Realm of 1442, which sharpened the penalties for adulterous elopement by equating elopement with theft. Although the law did not consider married women as chattels, it stated that 'the best thing the man has in his household is his lawful wife. He who steals [her] from him is the worst and greatest thief.' Consequently, men caught in the act would be

57 *Jordabalken* 19, *MEL*, p. 77; *Maakaari* 28, *KrL*, p. 66.

58 Circa 10 August 1427, I. Modéer and S. Engström, eds, *Kalmar stads tänkebok* (Uppsala, 1945–9), p. 58.

59 E.g., 1 Corinthians 7; E. M. Makowski, 'The Conjugal Debt and Medieval Canon Law', *Journal of Medieval History* 3 (1977), pp. 99–114.

60 Lundén, ed., 'Den heliga', 67.

61 J. A. Brundage, *Law, Sex, and Christian Society in Medieval Europe* (Chicago, 1987), pp. 358–60, 453.

hanged – like thieves were – whereas the fate of the women, facing a maximum penalty of burial alive, depended on their husbands. Alternatively, if the eloping couple had not been taken in the act, paying a high fine was required.[62] Although the 1442 law was hardly applied during the Middle Ages, it still demonstrates a hardening of attitudes towards adultery.[63]

While the medieval Church largely insisted on equal treatment for both sexes for similar crimes, secular society fostered a double standard, partially related to women's reproductive role.[64] The legal presumption that matrimony determined paternity (*pater est quem nuptiae demonstrant*) was widely accepted in medieval Europe. Unless there was proof to the contrary, children born to married women were presumed to be their husbands'.[65] In Swedish law, a child born within ten months after the husband's demise was considered his legitimate descendant and heir.[66] If the wife had been forcefully taken from her husband, the presumption of paternity extended to forty weeks calculated from when 'she last shared his bed'.[67] Through clandestine and treacherous female infidelity, a husband and his family could be defrauded of their property by a bastard. According to the Church, a woman had to perform penance for concealing the true paternity of her child and deceiving her in-laws.[68]

In medieval Swedish secular law the penalty for adultery, a forty-mark fine, was divided between the injured party, king and community. An additional fine to the church was over thirteen marks.[69] In practice, the size of the fines depended on the wealth, or poverty, of the offender and whether or not he or she was married. Records of the medieval town court of Stockholm usually fail to mention explicitly whether the adultery was single or double, that is, whether one or both parties were married. Exceptionally, Eskil, a married man, was sentenced to pay both a forty-mark fine for violating a virgin (compensation for the virginity of Anna, daughter of Olof the Carpenter) and another forty-mark fine for the adultery.[70]

Adulterous men were regularly punished with fines.[71] A few male adulterers were executed but the circumstances were unusual. In two cases, theft was

62 *Varkaankaari* [Chapter on Theft] 1, *KrML*, p. 157. See also R. Hemmer, 'Kristofers landslag Tjuvabalken 1', *Kyrkohistorisk Årsskrift* 58 (1958), 154–5; L. Carlsson, 'Tolkningen av Tjuvabalken 1 i Kristofers landslag', *Kyrkohistorisk Årsskrift* 58 (1958), 156–61; R. Hemmer, 'Ännu i frågan om Kristoffers landslag Tjuvabalken 1', *Juridisk Tidskrift för Finland* 95 (1959), 154–5.

63 M. Korpiola, 'Rethinking Incest and Heinous Sexual Crime: Changing Boundaries of Secular and Ecclesiastical Jurisdiction in Late Medieval Sweden', *Boundaries of the Law: Geography, Gender and Jurisdiction in Medieval and Early Modern Europe*, ed. A. Musson (Aldershot, 2005), pp. 108–13.

64 E.g., Brundage, *Law, Sex, and Christian Society*, pp. 462–3; R. M. Karras, *Sexuality in Medieval Europe: Doing unto Others* (New York, 2005), pp. 87–9, 120–4.

65 Brundage, *Law, Sex, and Christian Society*, pp. 543–4.

66 *Giftermålsbalken* 23, *MEL*, p. 46; *Giftermålsbalken* 17, *MESL*, pp. 45–6; *Naimiskaari* 22, *KrL*, p. 50.

67 *Ärvdabalken* 5, *MEL*, p. 59; *Ärvdabalken* 5, *MESL*, p. 57; *Perintökaari* 6, *KrL*, p. 52.

68 Penitential regulations, diocese of Skara, J. Gummerus, ed., *Beiträge zur Geschichte des Buss- und Beichtwesens in der Schwedischen Kirche des Mittelalters* (Uppsala, 1900), p. xvi.

69 E.g., *Giftermålsbalken* 10, *MESL*, p. 43; Korpiola, 'Rethinking Incest', pp. 110–11.

70 16 July 1485, *STT* II, p. 102.

71 E.g., *JST*, pp. 39, 112; 9 June 1507, *AST* III, p. 205; 21 January 1478, *SST* I, pp. 142–3; 1 December 1473, *AST* II, p. 23; 12 May 1483, *AST* II, p. 209.

also involved, which alone warranted death by hanging.[72] Usually husbands were not vindictive enough to insist on the lives of their unfaithful wives, who could generally expect fines instead.[73] As men living in the countryside received bigger inheritances than women, such men were usually wealthier and better able to afford to pay fines, while women more often had to undergo shaming penalties and banishment. For adulteresses living in towns, this could involve carrying publicly the heavy 'stones of the town', two stones linked with an iron chain and weighing more than twenty-five kilos in total. In towns, adulterers could theoretically be put on parade, with a rope around the penis by which their lover would lead them around the town.[74] The threat of this penalty probably motivated the parties to pay the fines. Part of the population in Swedish towns was German and – through the Hanseatic league and German immigration – Swedish town law had, to some extent, been influenced by northern German town laws, as these two penalties show.[75] A spell in the pillory or carrying the town's stones was usually the prologue to permanent banishment from the town.[76]

According to Swedish law, only the personal property of a criminal could be forfeited or used for paying a fine.[77] One might assume that male criminals in particular would use household funds, regardless of whether these were derived from communal or inherited property, for fines. In 1504, Cecilia, Bertil Michelsson's wife, bought a house in Stockholm using inherited funds. She then energetically denied that her property could be used to cover any fines her husband might be sentenced to pay. According to her, 'on no account could he pay fines using her property as she had had enough of his beatings and blows due to his ale-drinking and drunkenness and his madness (*yrgalinheet*)'.[78]

Paying fines for crimes such as adultery could cause problems regarding the ownership of inherited land. According to medieval Swedish law, only the property of a criminal spouse was to be confiscated, while the lands and chattels of the innocent spouse were to be separated before confiscation.[79] Thus, the property of the innocent party was not wasted because of the spouse's crime. In 1558, when the rights to a farm were disputed, it was proven that the land had been lawfully sold by Lasse of Gärdsby's maternal grandmother, who needed the money in order to pay a fine for adultery.[80] A more problematic case arose in the town

72 E.g., *JST*, pp. 97–8; 27 July 1506, *SST* IV, p. 123; 18 December 1484, 17 January 1485, 14 March 1485, *STT* II, pp. 74–5, 81–2.

73 8 October 1477, *AST* II, p. 92; 21 January 1478, *SST* I, pp. 142–3; Year 1483, *AST* II, pp. 216–17.

74 *Giftermålsbalken* 10, *MESL*, p. 43; G. Hedberg, 'En skamprocession', *Rig* (1971), 89–91; Lamberg, *Dannemännen*, p. 130; Lamberg, 'Säädyllisyyden vartijat', pp. 57–8.

75 Hedberg, 'En skamprocession', pp. 89–91.

76 E.g., 26 October 1504, *AST* III, p. 159; 2 December 1504, *AST* III, p. 159; *JST*, pp. 97–8; 3 June 1477, *SST* I, p. 107.

77 *Edsörebalken* [Chapter on Peace Legislation] 24:1, *MEL*, p. 194; *Rauhavalan kaari* [Chapter on Peace Legislation] 21:2, *KrL*, p. 125.

78 3 June 1504, *SST* IV, pp. 4–5.

79 *Rättegångsbalken* 20:2, *MEL*, p. 166; *Käräjäkaari* [Chapter on Procedure] 27:2, *KrL*, p. 116.

80 31 January 1558, N. Edling and O. Svenonius, eds, *Långhundra härads dombok, 1545–1570* (Uppsala, 1946), p. 102.

court of Jönköping in 1547. Ingerd, wife of Måns Öbo, complained that Måns had mortgaged their jointly-owned house (*gård*) to Bengt Larsson for forty-five marks. With the money, Måns had paid his fine for adultery after a relationship with a certain Esbjörn's wife. The court ruled that as Måns had personally wasted the money, he had to pay his fine out of his own half of the house and not her share. Therefore – and because she had no other domicile – Ingerd was granted her half.[81] Nevertheless, the innocent spouse occasionally consented to pay the fine of the adulterous spouse. In 1544, the Stockholm burgher Henrik Finne accused Jon Månsson of adultery with his wife, whom he wanted to be rid of, but not by insisting on the death penalty. He even wanted to pay her fine to enable her to leave the town unhumiliated (*oskamfærath aff by*), as she was to be banished from the city for life.[82] Undergoing public shaming penalties, such as the pillory or carrying the stones, made reintegration into society more difficult.

In addition to punishments in secular or ecclesiastical courts, adulterers – and particularly adulteresses – faced property penalties. Adulteresses lost their morning gifts, regardless of whether they lived in town or countryside. In the countryside, they also lost their third of the communal marital property.[83] Occasionally, the wife's previous behaviour was commented upon in court, in connection to inheritances and distributions of estates; 'the wife had behaved badly towards her husband, stolen and run away from him', thus forfeiting her rights to the husband's estate.[84] Loss of property and/or property rights was the typical penalty for adulteresses: morning gift property, dowry and/or dower rights. Similarly, research has shown that medieval English abduction legislation was largely used, in practice, to publicize adultery and elopement, and thereby to deprive adulteresses of their dower rights.[85]

Medieval Swedish society demonstrated its sexual double standard by allowing adulterers living in the countryside to retain their property rights while, in towns, adulterous husbands suffered somewhat by losing their right to take certain privileged personal property from the joint estate (*fordel*) after the wife's death. This privileged property of a husband lost consisted of the best bed in the household, his best outfit, his saddle, weapons and chest.[86] The estranged spouses could freely be reconciled, but what happened then with the forfeited property rights? In 1488, Ragnar and his wife appeared at the court of Arboga because she was guilty of an unnamed offence, possibly adultery. He declared himself ready to take back his wife and pardon all the wrongdoings she had done to offend him. Nevertheless,

81 *JST*, p. 149.

82 6 October 1544, J. A. Almquist, ed., *Stockholms stads tänkebok 1544–1548* (Stockholm, 1936), pp. 26–7.

83 *Giftermålsbalken* 8, *MESL*, p. 42; *Giftermålsbalken* 6, *MEL*, p. 41; *Naimiskaari* 11, *KrL*, p. 48.

84 2 October 1514, *SST* V, p. 13.

85 Brundage, *Law, Sex, and Christian Society*, pp. 388–9, 480; P. Brand, '"Deserving" and "Undeserving" Wives: Earning and Forfeiting Dower in Medieval England', *Journal of Legal History* 22 (2001), 8–15; C. Dunn, 'Forfeiting the Marriage Portion: Punishing Female Adultery in the Secular Courts of England and Italy', *Regional Variations in Matrimonial Law and Custom in Europe, 1150–1600*, ed. M. Korpiola (Leiden, 2011), pp. 164–5, 174–87.

86 *Giftermålsbalken* 9–10, *MESL*, pp. 42–3.

should she transgress again, she would be punished for all her deeds – even the past ones.[87] At the town court of Stockholm, in 1504, Jakob Walske of the town of Nyköping swore publicly that he had never learned of any dishonour in his wife since he last took her back.[88] But, it is not completely clear whether or not forgiveness and resumed cohabitation also re-established the spouse's property rights that had been lost by the adulterous act, as was the case in England.[89]

The loss of property rights provided incentives for rapacious relatives to accuse a woman, after her husband's death, of adultery. When Kettil Jonsson, brother-in-law of the noble widow Arfrith Knutsdotter, accused her of adultery during her husband's lifetime, the court observed that her own husband had never accused her of the deed, there was no adulterine child, nor could Kettil produce proper witnesses to the deed. Therefore, her innocence was proclaimed.[90] As will be discussed below in more detail, the prolonged case between Kettil Jonsson and Arfrith Knutsdotter indicates that the property rights of widows also motivated some accusations of adultery and murder.

Sleeping with the Enemy: Spousal Violence, Homicide and Property

Swedish law reinforced a traditional gender hierarchy, but not domestic tyranny, by observing that God had given the husband his wife to assist him and to be subjected to him, 'but not for a slave and footstool' (*til hielp oc wnderdan, tho ey til træl eller fota trodh*).[91] Because of this, mutual love was expected: 'the wife was to love him as [her] head, and the husband her as [his] limb' (*elska, hon han som howd, oc han hona som lim*).[92] As head of the household, the husband's esteem and honour partly depended on the kind of house he ran. He was expected to control it and its mistress, his wife. As elsewhere in Europe, the husband, as head of his wife, was authorized by both ecclesiastical and secular law to correct her improper or bad behaviour with moderate physical violence.[93] Medieval Swedish law limited the husband's authority to chastise his wife with respect to the

87 28 April 1488, *AST* II, p. 330.

88 14 October 1504, *SST* IV, p. 26.

89 Brand, '"Deserving" and "Undeserving" Wives', pp. 8, 12–15.

90 31 December 1453, diocese of Skara, *Fotostatkopior av medeltida pergamentsbrev i Riksarkivet* [hereafter *FMPR*]. For the restrictions on making accusations of adultery, see M. Korpiola, 'On Ecclesiastical Jurisdiction and the Reception of Canon Law in the Swedish Provincial Laws', *How Nordic Are the Nordic Medieval Laws?*, ed. D. Tamm and H. Vogt (Copenhagen, 2011), pp. 229–31. See also *Giftermålsbalken* 10, *MESL*, p. 42; *JST*, p. 112; 3 June 1477, *SST* I, p. 107; 11 December 1475, *AST* II, pp. 64–5.

91 *Tahallisen haavoittamisen kaari* [Chapter on Intentional Wounding] 19, *KrL*, p. 154. Citation from *Konung Christoffers Landslag*, ed. C. J. Schlyter. Corpus iuris Sueo-Gotorum antiqui, 12 (Lund, 1869), p. 361.

92 *Tahallisen haavoittamisen kaari* 19, *KrL*, p. 154. Citation: *Konung Christoffers Landslag*, ed. Schlyter, p. 361.

93 E.g., J. A. Brundage, 'Domestic Violence in Classical Canon Law', *Violence in Medieval Society*, ed. R. Kaeuper (Woodbridge, 2000), pp. 186–7; S. M. Butler, *The Language of Abuse: Marital Violence in Later Medieval England* (Leiden, 2007), esp. pp. 2–3, 25–9, 41–65, 144–50, 183, 230–6, 262–3.

amount of violence used and the motivation for that violence. Chastisement was permitted, intentional homicide was not. If the husband's disciplining was excessive and the wife died thereof, he had to pay fines and compensation but he did not atone for the crime with his life.[94] The law of 1442 held that if the husband caused wounds, bruises or even worse injuries to his wife, he was to pay a sum that was double the usual fine for such an injury. He was not authorized to beat his wife 'out of hatred, wickedness, drunkenness, or love towards another woman'.[95] Sharp-edged weapons, like swords or knifes, were not considered permissible for such 'chastisement'.[96]

If one spouse caused the death of the other, whether intentionally or accidentally, the surviving party lost his or her rights to the communal estate. Even here, a husband forfeited less than a wife because, in addition to her share of the communal property, a widow would also lose her morning gift, both in towns and in the countryside.[97] If either spouse was fined for causing the death of the other – depending on whether the death was accidental or intentional – a third of the fine went to the relatives of the deceased spouse and could not be inherited by the culprit (that is, the killer). In instances where the couple had children, after the death of the spouse, the fines went to the relatives of the deceased spouse. This confirmed the principle that one was not allowed to inherit from a person whom one had killed, nor could the killer's relatives (*ätlinger*).[98]

If one spouse died at home under unclear circumstances, the other tended to be the prime suspect. In Stockholm, in 1516, Olof the Goldsmith managed to clear himself of suspicion of killing his wife after a doctor had investigated the corpse and concluded that Olof had not caused her death.[99] Therefore, Olof did not lose his marital property rights. In another case from Stockholm, in 1507, the wife of Rolof – who had probably belonged to the castle garrison – had behaved suspiciously when her husband was killed. She had 'walked or run' to the monastery in order to seek asylum there. Consequently, she had to take an oath, together with eleven compurgators, that she had not been a party to her husband's death. Unless she did this, Roleff's heirs were to be granted her property share.[100]

The property interests involved explain, in part, why the dead spouse's relatives might accuse the widow of murder. For example, Erik and his sons Ingemund and Lars Eriksson, father and brothers of Anders Eriksson, accused Anders's widow Cecilia of murdering her husband. Cecilia had cleared herself of the accusation by producing twenty-four compurgators, and when the case was heard again in 1490, the jury was also ready to confirm this sentence, acquitting her of the homicide.[101] In contrast to this, in 1417, Sven Lax had felt compelled to deny at court that he

94 *Edsörebalken* 19, *MESL*, pp. 218–19; *Edsörebalken* 33, *MEL*, p. 196.

95 *Tahallisen haavoittamisen kaari* 19, *KrL*, p. 154.

96 E.g., Year 1545, *JST*, p. 149.

97 *Edsörebalken* 33, *MEL*, p. 196; *Edsörebalken* 19, *MESL*, pp. 218–19; *Perintökaari* 11, *KrL*, p. 54.

98 *Edsörebalken* 33, *MEL*, p. 196; *Edsörebalken* 19, *MESL*, pp. 218–19; *Perintökaari* 11, *KrL*, p. 54.

99 2 June 1516, *SST* V, p. 106.

100 31 October 1507, *SST* IV, p. 175. See also 11 March 1555, J. A. Almquist, ed., *Konung Gustaf den förstes registratur 25* (Stockholm, 1910), pp. 74–8.

101 *ULD*, p. 22.

had ever accused his son Lasse Svensson's widow Birgitta, daughter of the lesser nobleman (*knape*) Brynolf Magnusson, of having murdered her husband.[102]

Nobleman Kettil Jonsson obviously wished to play it safe when he accused his sister-in-law, Arfrith Knutsdotter, niece of superior judge (*lagman*) Bengt Gylta, of both adultery and killing her husband (Kettil's brother), Torsten Jonsson. Kettil seems to have been motivated by the morning gift property that came into Arfrith's possession as a widow. When the case first came before the court, in 1442, she managed to free herself from the charge of homicide but was ordered to free herself from the adultery charge by compurgation in the ecclesiastical court. Failing this, she would forfeit her morning gift.[103] However, Kettil Jonsson seems to have been unhappy that Arfrith managed to prove her innocence, as the case came up again eleven years later. Arfrith's innocence, in relation to both accusations, was reconfirmed, as Kettil only found one witness to her supposed adultery. The jury observed that Kettil had not proven his allegation by witnesses or by the birth of an illegitimate child. Moreover, Torsten had never accused Arfrith of the crime when he was alive. But the long dispute regarding the morning gift was only settled some days later by eight arbitrators, who confirmed Arfrith's morning gift, consisting of several estates and a mill. Some of the farms Kettil or his heirs could redeem after twenty years, but the rest remained Arfrith's for life.[104] Obviously Torsten Jonsson had given what his relatives considered an over-generous morning gift, which then triggered long litigation on various pretexts after his death.

Although malice or greed explains some accusations of viricide or uxoricide, gruesome murders did occasionally take place. For example, Katerin Pedersdotter of Estuna was condemned to the stake for murdering her husband by hitting him on the head with an axe. However, the execution was postponed until she had given birth to the child she was carrying.[105] The community had no understanding for such cruel and premeditated murders, and the culprits had to atone for them with their lives without mercy.

Severe cases of spousal violence were certainly monitored, and unclear circumstances in a spouse's death sent the widow(er) to the dock immediately. As we have seen, the spouse who caused the other's death forfeited matrimonial property rights, which may have spurred some relatives of the deceased to make accusations of murder. And at least some cases suggest that litigation was motivated by an attempt to deny the widow her property rights.

Separation and Division of Property

Medieval Swedish secular law did not discuss the possibility of judicial or voluntary separation but left it to the ecclesiastical jurisdiction. In addition to in-

102 25 June 1417, C. Silfverstolpe, ed., *Svensk diplomatarium III* (Stockholm, 1879–87), no. 2386, pp. 256–7.

103 11 June 1442, Lödöse, *FMPR*.

104 31 December 1453, Skara, and 4 January 1454, Skara, *FMPR*.

105 4 August 1477, *SST* I, pp. 116–17. See also 26 May 1523, *BHBR*, no. 65, pp. 156–7.

formal ways of separating, adultery, heresy and cruelty (serious physical abuse) constituted grounds for judicial separation in church courts, according to later medieval canon law.[106] Unlike some church courts in the Franco-Belgian region, wastefulness and mismanagement of communal property seem not to have been accepted as grounds for judicial separation in medieval Sweden, despite the relatively liberal practice of separation.[107] The Swedish episcopal courts worried about the conjugal bond, not marital property. Based on the little we know of Swedish medieval episcopal courts, ecclesiastical sentences of separation also seem to have failed to mention post-separation property provisions or divisions. For example, a sentence between Lars Johansson and Katarina Staffansdotter, pronounced by Bishop Hans Brask of Linköping in 1525, noted the grounds for the separation (her adultery) and forbade both parties to remarry, but did not refer to their property.[108] Nor did secular law regulate property divisions of separated couples. The existing records of secular courts are nearly completely silent on spousal agreements regarding the division of property.

The Swedes did not normally use written contracts when marrying, nor did they register agreements of division of goods when separating. Property divisions were made privately by the parties and their friends. In an exceptional case, Katarina Jakobsdotter, daughter of the late Stockholm town councillor Jakob Moyse, and Katarina's husband, Olof Nilsson, had their property divided when separating in 1499. Eleven men, including several town councillors and noble councillors of the Realm, made the division in Stockholm. Katarina and Olof had 'on both sides completely given themselves to [the appointed noblemen and burghers] from their own hands'.[109] The separation agreement was written down in the court records and it divided the townhouses and some chattels of the couple. Katarina was freed from any debts in the town, while both were liable to half of possible non-Stockholm debts. The couple had only been married for a few years but they had obviously had serious marital difficulties of an unspecified kind, as both spouses had been forced to find sureties for not angering the other spouse 'with words, acts, counsel or deeds'.[110] In a Stockholm inheritance dispute from 1596, it was recorded that a married couple had separated – probably informally – decades ago because of the noble husband's adultery. The couple had agreed on a division of property between themselves.[111]

Another late sixteenth-century property dispute involved the consequences of divorce. The main legal issues in the case between Anders Jonsson and the heirs of Arvid Bosson, including Anders's ex-wife Elin Arvidsdotter, revolved around whether Anders and Elin Arvidsdotter had been separated by the bishop. It also

106 E.g., R. H. Helmholz, *Marriage Litigation in Medieval England* (Cambridge, 1974), pp. 100–7; Brundage, 'Domestic Violence', pp. 187–95.

107 Korpiola, 'Marriage Causes', pp. 226–8.

108 28 May 1525, *BHBR*, p. 396.

109 4 May 1499, *SST* III, pp. 426–7.

110 30 June 1498, *SST* III, p. 384; Lamberg, *Dannemännen*, p. 128.

111 21 February 1596, D. Almqvist, ed., *Stockholms stads tänkeböcker från år 1592, II* (Stockholm, 1951), pp. 64–6.

mattered who was the guilty party because this determined how the property of the couple was to be lawfully divided. Already, some years before, Anders had received on these grounds a considerable, listed amount of property belonging to his wife, including her clothes and the domestic utensils that had then been in the house. The same inventory indicated that the wife had received very little or near to nothing. Anders had to provide the court with a letter from the bishop proving that he had indeed been granted a lawful divorce from his wife and specifying who was to blame for the divorce; the town council had already tried to find out which of the two was the guilty party. It would then be calculated what Anders Jonsson and his wife had each received, and a lawful division of property would then be made between the spouses.[112] Elin – who still lived in the same town – and some of her relatives, had to return gifts (spoons, a pot, a bearskin, and a hat) to Anders. Anders also wanted back all the money he had spent on his wife and her family concerning the wedding, gifts, clothes, and shoes.[113] Guilt thus mattered, and mattered largely for reasons of property.

Swedish wives, when separated, usually received their third or half of the communal estate, and their heritable lands (unless guilty of adultery, in which case they lost their morning gifts and the right to communal property). Thus, specific maintenance payments seem to have been unnecessary. By contrast, English ecclesiastical courts dealt with claims of alimony in connection to separation causes, and they were ready to grant maintenance even to adulterous or abusive separated wives (although common law courts stripped adulteresses of dower rights).[114]

Although a separation *de jure* put an end to cohabitation and the conjugal debt, as well as giving cause to a division of property, it left the marriage bond intact. This settlement was sometimes not enough. In one instance, in 1513, the wife's family helped to rid her permanently of her husband. Jon of Starbäck and his sons accused Jon Pedersson, the son-in-law and brother-in-law of the Starbäck men, respectively, of theft. Here, the supposed larceny probably was the final straw in a longer conflict. Namely, Jon Pedersson had been living in adultery with a woman called Gunnil, slighting his own wife, Jon of Starbäck's daughter. Not content with this, adding injury to insult, Jon Pedersson had stolen silver items from his in-laws. One of these, a silver hair decoration, could have been intended for his mistress. Intra-family thefts were hardly ever taken to court and, even more surprisingly, Jon Pedersson's in-laws insisted on having him hanged for his deed. As Jon had confessed to the crime and the injured parties demanded the death penalty, the court reluctantly condemned Jon to the gallows.[115] Probably he had managed to permanently and fatally alienate his wife and in-laws by his brazen behaviour.

112 22 September 1590, 24 September 1590, 27 October 1590, 21 August 1591, S. Grauers, ed., *Nya Lödöse tänkeböcker (1586–1621)* (Gothenburg, 1923), pp. 209–10, 217–18, 245.

113 21 October 1590, 25 November 1590, 21 August 1591, Grauers, ed., *Nya Lödöse tänkeböcker*, pp. 215, 223, 245.

114 S. M. Butler, 'Maintenance Agreements and Male Responsibility in Late Medieval England', *Boundaries of the Law: Geography, Gender and Jurisdiction in Medieval and Early Modern Europe*, ed. A. Musson (Aldershot, 2005), pp. 78–80.

115 1513, *JST*, pp. 97–8.

His wife could have been judicially separated from him on the grounds of his adultery by the bishop of Linköping, but this outcome seems not to have been felt sufficient. Starbäck's daughter and her family probably considered Jon Pedersson's death the best, and permanent, solution to her domestic predicament, protecting her spousal property, widowing her, and thus enabling her to remarry.

Conclusions

In Sweden, the marital property system was largely based on communal possession, so that all the property of the spouses was managed by the husband during marriage and could be freely alienated by him. Nevertheless, inherited land was to remain within the paternal or maternal line and formed an exception to the husband's managerial powers as both the consent of the wife and that of her closest heirs – possessing rights of redemption – were required for its alienation. Without their consent, land transactions could be revoked. Only in extraordinary circumstances (war captivity, famine and elopement) were husbands allowed to sell their wives' inherited land, or wives allowed to sell property in the absence of their husbands. In these circumstances, Swedish law took into account the possible impasse caused by the long absence of the wife, or of the husband who managed the communal marital estate. In these exceptional circumstances, wives had the same power as husbands to administer and alienate property.

In cases of gross neglect of the duties of conjugal loyalty (that is, in cases of adultery or elopement), a spouse could have his/her marital property rights curtailed or lost in Swedish secular law and practice. However, in accordance with a prevailing sexual double standard, the law penalized adulteresses with a more thorough loss of property rights (that is, their morning gift and rights to communal property) than was experienced by men, especially if the wife's property did not include inherited land. This encouraged eloping spouses – wives in particular – to take property with them, as they risked losing everything when leaving their marital home. Moreover, as women in the countryside inherited only half as much as their brothers, when adulteresses lost their matrimonial property rights those in the countryside could not afford to pay their fines as often as men. Consequently, women had to undergo shaming penalties and banishment more often than men, which contributed to their pauperization and could drive them to crime and prostitution. If one spouse killed the other, either accidentally or intentionally, the culprit lost his or her marital property rights (that is, their share of the communal property and, for widows, their morning gift), which went to the heirs of the deceased. Accusations of adultery and homicide were occasionally made by a dead husband's relatives, intent upon stripping the widow of her property rights, thereby acquiring property for themselves.

Swedish law mentions neither judicial separations nor the division of property between spouses after such a separation. The first was left to canon law and the second to the married couple and their trusted friends. Consequently, it was not customary to record information of such divisions after separation in either ecclesiastical or secular medieval courts. There are some similarities with the

Franco-Belgian region, concerning the relatively high frequency of separation causes in ecclesiastical courts and a similar communal marital property system. Nevertheless, in medieval Sweden, wastefulness or mismanagement of property as such never became accepted as grounds for separation in ecclesiastical courts. Spousal property divisions were not regularly registered in Swedish court records, but rather left to be privately negotiated. The publicizing of separations, necessary for practical reasons, was usually achieved more informally in the relatively small communities of Sweden. Unlike the Low Countries, Sweden did not use written marriage contracts, which probably partly accounts for the difference.

Severe spousal discord was certainly taken seriously in medieval Swedish society because it disturbed the peace of the community, but also because marriage breakdown could be caused by property mismanagement or because marital property and its management could be affected by the conjugal difficulties. The scarce Swedish medieval sources do not divulge to us how often property issues were behind spousal disputes or separation. However, analyses of the relatively rare English ecclesiastical separation causes have suggested that property issues or economic concerns may, in many cases, have acted as the ultimate trigger to initiate litigation.[116] This study can only suggest directions for further research, but certainly the interplay between matrimonial property systems and spousal disputes, in a general sense, merits more attention in the future.

116 Butler, *The Language of Abuse*, pp. 176–7.

3

WHEN TWO WORLDS COLLIDE: MARRIAGE AND THE LAW IN MEDIEVAL IRELAND

Gillian Kenny

After the Anglo-Norman invasion of 1169 two entirely different legal systems concerning women and their rights upon marriage co-existed within Ireland. One system was based on the principles and tenets of the English common law which the invaders brought with them in the later twelfth century. This legal system enforced coverture, that is, the basic premise that, legally, married women were under the rule of their husbands. In contrast to this, Gaelic Irish society functioned according to its own ancient legal code, commonly called the Brehon law, which had reached its apogee and received codification in the seventh and eighth centuries but which was still in use in the later medieval period. Under this system women's rights after marriage were often very different from those provided for under the imported English common law. Because the two co-existing legal systems and societies were so different, women's experiences after marriage varied greatly within Ireland. These systems flourished and evolved separately but did not integrate or amalgamate in any way successfully. Of course certain habits and practices were adopted by both sides, but not to a significant extent. Indeed there was no overwhelming desire on either side to accommodate the traditions of the other, and thus these two societies grew ever more separate and alien to each other. Problems also occurred when intermarriage took place, as often both the married couple and those around them were confused as to which legal system to follow when it came to the woman's rights at marriage.

Initially, however, there is a certain shared experience for women of both societies. When a single woman became a wife in late medieval Ireland, in both Gaelic and Anglo-Irish society, she experienced many changes in her life. She passed from her own family into that of her husband, and entered into a new life with a new set of experiences and expectations, most notably to be a mother. This change in circumstance was a shared life-experience for the women of both societies. In both cases the woman's status changed upon marriage, as did her title and affiliation, and she had to become accustomed to new rules of social conduct. However, after that initial change, there were profound differences in how women from Gaelic Ireland and Anglo-Ireland were permitted to conduct their lives as married women. The existence of a church *inter Hibernicos* as well as a church *inter Anglicos*, in addition to the pervasive influence of the Gaelic secular code concerning marriage, made for very different marital experiences for Gaelic and Anglo-Irish women.[1] In general, the rights of a wife at marriage, and her behaviour and freedoms within marriage, varied enormously between the Gaelic and Anglo-Irish worlds.

Marriage Amongst the Anglo-Irish

Anglo-Irish marriage law took its cues, and indeed its entire legal basis, from English legal attitudes to marriage. The colonization of the later twelfth century, and beyond, brought English legal concepts concerning marriage into Ireland for the first time. This, allied with the rise of the English-influenced church, ensured that the Anglo-Irish model of marriage would have been recognizable to most other citizens of later medieval Europe. In English Ireland, as in the rest of Europe, people married in two main ways: in public and clandestinely.[2] The church accepted clandestine marriages as valid but always tried to encourage marriage in church. Medieval canon law with its acceptance of words of consent as binding vows 'made the marital bond strikingly easy to create but very difficult to break'.[3] Predictably, therefore, the church courts in Ireland were often busy dealing with the fall-out from clandestine marriages. A church-sanctioned marriage was increasingly preferred, for a number of reasons. A public ceremony was an important way to be sure of witnesses to the ceremony, who were often crucial, especially if any questions were later raised over the validity of the marriage. A church ceremony was a vital public way of affirming a connection between families, as well as a means of transmitting wealth from one generation to another. It was also a very public way of transferring guardianship of the new wife to her husband, and thus control over any lands or goods she might bring to the marriage. Therefore, the wealthier the families, the more important a public marriage ceremony was.[4] A public marriage was also a means of proving mutual consent, and of guaranteeing the legitimacy of both the union and its offspring.[5] Furthermore, a public marriage made the abandonment of wives harder to accomplish and clarified arrangements like dowers and jointures, which were to the benefit of the woman involved. However, many couples continued to engage in clandestine marriages, probably due in the main to a deep-rooted belief in Anglo-Irish communities that, despite what the clergy had to say, marriage was a private rather than a public affair.[6]

1 The ethnic divisions are outlined in J. Watt, 'Ecclesia *inter Anglicos et inter Hibernicos*: Confrontation and Coexistence in the Medieval Diocese and Province of Armagh', *The English in Medieval Ireland*, ed. J. Lydon (Dublin, 1984), pp. 46–64.

2 M. M. Sheehan, 'The Formation and Stability of Marriage in Fourteenth-Century England: Evidence of an Ely Register', *Mediaeval Studies* 33 (1971), 235.

3 S. McSheffrey, *Marriage, Sex and Civic Culture in Late Medieval London* (Philadelphia, 2006), p. 33.

4 G. Duby, *The Knight, the Lady and the Priest: The Making of Modern Marriage in Medieval France* (London, 1984), p. 30.

5 A. Cosgrove, 'Marriage in Medieval Ireland', *Marriage in Ireland*, ed. A. Cosgrove (Dublin, 1985), p. 26.

6 Ibid., p. 40.

Once they were married, Anglo-Irish women were legally subject to their husbands, who, upon marriage, controlled all their property and moveables but could not alienate them without their permission.[7] The legal restrictions placed upon wives in Ireland also included an inability to make a will without their husbands' permission.[8] Land grants within Anglo-Irish areas concerning lands held by married women take the form of documents made by husbands with the consent of their wives. The extent, if any, to which married women consented to the alienation of their lands, or were even concerned with the repercussions of such actions, remains unknown. It is impossible to ascertain from formulaic legal documents concerning land transactions whether or not wives did actually consent to their husbands' land deals regarding lands brought to the marriage by the wife. No matter who initiated such deals, or who approved of them or not, what is not in doubt is that in the minds of many husbands and wives the husband was pre-eminent – even without legal sanction – and his authority was paramount.

Marriage Amongst the Gaelic Irish

This view of the marital contract wherein the husband's legal authority was paramount was not reflected in the contemporary Gaelic world or at least not to the same extent. In Gaelic Ireland, marriage was an overwhelmingly secular affair. The body of Gaelic laws dealing with marriage was written and codified in or around the eighth century and, after this period, it is very difficult to ascertain the types of changes and developments which evolved in Gaelic society concerning women and marriage, in particular.[9] However, it does appear that these early laws concerning marriage to a large extent continued to be utilized throughout the later Middle Ages in Ireland, especially amongst the aristocracy.

When a Gaelic Irish woman married, guardianship of her was also transferred to her husband, but, unlike in the Anglo-Irish tradition, he was not her sole guardian and the wealth she brought into the marriage did not pass into his hands. In Gaelic Irish society marriage did not sever the tie between a woman and her original family, and so her own kin never relinquished all their rights over and interest in her.[10] This link may have aided her if she had to deal with an unpleasant husband or marital situation, but it could also limit the woman, who could sometimes find her actions controlled by her native kin, because of the mesh of

7 P. Fleming, *Family and Household in Medieval England* (Basingstoke, 2001), p. 38.

8 F. Pollock and F. W. Maitland, *The History of English Law before the time of Edward I*, 2 vols, 2nd edn (Cambridge, 1911), I, pp. 409, 428.

9 Most of the following on early Irish law and marriage is taken from B. Jaski, 'Marriage Laws in Ireland and in the Continent in the Early Middle Ages', *The Fragility of Her Sex? Medieval Irishwomen in Their European Context*, ed. C. Meek and K. Simms (Dublin, 1996), pp. 16–42.

10 R. Thurneysen *et al.*, *Studies in Early Irish Law* (Dublin, 1936) pp. 180–1. This included a right to a proportion of her goods at death and also of the wergild if a stranger had killed her, and they were also partly liable for any wrongdoing she might commit. The mother-kin also had certain limited rights in regard to her children.

obligations between them that a marriage did not completely sever.[11] However, if a woman produced sons whilst married then the ties of her parental family became less binding.[12]

Gaelic Irish marriage was a complex and layered affair. According to the early law tracts a woman held differing legal status depending on whether she was a primary wife of equal status to her husband (known as a *cetmuintir*), a wife of lower status, a concubine or involved in a more casual union, and that status also depended on whether she had sons or not. The differences in rights accorded to women based on the perceived legitimacy or not of their sexual unions with men could lead to intriguing situations. For instance, whereas, legally, a wife of equal status was, to a certain extent, under her husband's rule, the concubine, in contrast, was not. This meant that a concubine could choose whether to put herself under the rule of her husband, her own family or her sons.[13] Within a marriage contract the status of each partner depended on the amount of property he or she brought into the marriage. The law tracts advocated that marital relationships be made up of men and women of equal status so that the wife would then enjoy the same contractual capacity as her husband.[14] By the later Middle Ages many married couples are likely to have consisted of a man and woman of equal status, meaning that both were of equal property and family.[15] It is worth pointing out that the property consisted of moveables in general. Amongst the higher orders, cattle and horses in large amounts changed hands at marriage.

Within Gaelic areas the secular attitude towards marriage and the begetting of children meant that official separation was not always a prerequisite to multiple relationships. Because Irish law made a distinction between formal marriage, informal relationships and illegitimate relationships, different rights accrued to the children of the differing relationships.[16] Adding to the wide array of possible relationships, men and women of the Gaelic Irish also frequently entered into formal contracts of concubinage throughout this period. It was not uncommon for a high-status man to have more than one concubine, which could lead to dozens of offspring. To give just one example – and there are many more – Turlough *an fhiona* O' Donnell, lord of Tirconnel, who died in 1423, had eighteen sons by ten different women, and fifty-nine grandsons in the male line. This was an activity that the church wished to stamp out. For example, a regulation issued from the diocese of Armagh in the mid-fourteenth century stated that, 'no subject of the province of Armagh, lay or clerical, may hold women or concubines under the name of *Cayf* otherwise *Choghir* [*Choghie*?] *for* obtaining their concubinage'. The document went on to promise excommunication to those who would give or

11 K. Simms, 'The Legal Position of Irishwomen in the Later Middle Ages', *Irish Jurist New Series* 10 (1975), p. 110.

12 B. Jaski, *Early Irish Kingship and Succession* (Dublin, 2000), p. 146.

13 Marriage was the subject of a special legal text, the *Cáin Lánamna*, and nine forms of sexual union were distinguished: see F. Kelly, *A Guide to Early Irish Law* (Dublin, 1988), pp. 70–1.

14 Jaski, *Early Irish Kingship*, p. 144.

15 K. M. O' Meara, 'Under the Heel of Church and State? Women in Late Medieval Ireland', unpublished M.Phil. thesis, University of Dublin, 1996, p. 42.

16 Jaski, *Early Irish Kingship*, p. 143.

promise a woman anything in return for her becoming their concubine and entering into a contract with her.[17] Generally amongst the Gaelic Irish, concubines were not viewed as negatively as they were in Anglo-Ireland.[18] In Anglo-Irish areas these legally irregular relationships presented serious problems when it came to issues such as land ownership and inheritance, and property rights.[19]

Amongst the Gaelic Irish, however, illegitimacy was not a stigma nor was it necessarily a bar to inheritance (as it was in areas subject to the common law in Ireland) and so concubinage was not necessarily disparaged. Irish law permitted the affiliation of children by their mother's declaration provided that the alleged father formally accepted this declaration. Only this acceptance could make the declaration legally valid.[20] This was important because, according to Irish law, a son born due to an extra-marital relationship who was acknowledged by the father could claim a right to part of the inheritance, although any claims he had were difficult to enforce if his mother was of a low status.[21] He could not succeed to any kind of power at all, for example, if his mother was a serf, a slave or a female satirist. The preferred heir was the son of a lawful wife, according to the law tracts, and it may have been difficult for any other sons to gain power unless they had strong political allies.[22] In terms of succession, the son of a primary wife was preferred above younger candidates or the son of a concubine, unless the latter was better qualified than the former.[23] If a father refused to acknowledge a son, for example, then the woman had to produce witnesses to attest to her relationship with the father. If doubt still persisted, she could pay an adoption fee which was set at a price equivalent to the honour-price of a king, a sum which lower-class women would have found impossible to raise. According to Jaski, this rule was probably designed to halt the unwanted illegitimate sons of lower-class mothers becoming the responsibility of noble families. Intriguingly, the woman's reputation (regarding her sexual history) was also crucial to any chance of the child being accepted by the father and his kin.[24] The woman's sexual history was subject to scrutiny and her claims were found to be lacking should she be judged promiscuous and, therefore, untrustworthy.

This is all in direct contrast to the legal proscriptions concerning the succession of non-legitimate children within Anglo-Irish society. It is worth pointing out that, in Anglo-Irish areas too, people did not always adhere to the teachings of the church regarding sexuality. Marriages, clandestine marriages and relationships not sanctioned by any kind of formal ritual were not uncommon

17 Cosgrove, 'Marriage in Medieval Ireland', p. 29; Simms, 'Legal Position of Irishwomen', pp. 101–2.

18 Jaski, 'Marriage Laws', p. 33.

19 For the source of most of this information on clandestine marriages and concubinage see James A. Brundage, 'Concubinage and Marriage in Medieval Canon Law', *Journal of Medieval History* 1 (1975), 5–6.

20 For more on the various chieftains' offspring see K. Nicholls, *Gaelic and Gaelicised Ireland* (Dublin, 1972), p. 11.

21 Jaski, *Early Irish Kingship*, p. 143.

22 Ibid., pp. 150–1, 155.

23 Ibid., pp. 155–6.

24 Ibid., pp. 149–50.

outside Gaelic Ireland.[25] Nevertheless, the church's hold on marriage was always far stronger in Anglo-Irish-controlled areas than in Gaelic ones. As the Middle Ages wore on in Ireland the church did exert increasing influence on Gaelic areas. Gaelic Irish wives, especially, increasingly began to use church courts to redress marital wrongs such as being repudiated by their husbands. Gaelic Irish men and women also applied, in increasing numbers, to the Holy See for dispensations to marry during the fifteenth century, a period of intense religious fervour amongst the Gaelic Irish.

Marriage Contracts

Once marriage was agreed upon, the first step for the families of couples who were to be married, in both cultures, was often the drawing-up of a marriage contract. In these documents, reciprocal arrangements were made, usually by the respective fathers of the bride and groom, for such necessities as dowry and marriage grants. In all societies, including medieval Ireland, marriage was fundamentally 'a time of bargaining'.[26] In Anglo-Irish areas, the bride's parents/guardians negotiated her dowry (*maritagium*), while the groom's family may have had to decide on what kind of reasonable dower and/or jointure to award her, if the naming of it was insisted upon at the ceremony. Dowry and other financial arrangements at marriage were primarily exchanges, not between individuals but between families.[27] Detailed dowries were a staple of life in parts of Ireland from the earliest days of the Anglo-Norman colonization. For example, a grant made by Richard de Burgh to Theobald Walter and his wife, Richard's daughter Margery, on the occasion of their marriage, sometime before 1242, was probably Margery's dowry. In this grant, it was specified that only the heirs of Margery should inherit.[28] In areas subject to the common law a dowry given to a woman by her family upon her marriage was (conditionally) a permanent grant. If the woman had no heirs of her body, or if her line failed in the third generation of heirs, her dowry was to revert to the donor's heirs.[29] The dowry could be given as moveables, but generally came in the form of a land grant. This land grant remained entirely with the wife after her husband's death, but she could not control it during her marriage as it was vested in her husband. It remained, however, the wife's property during this time.[30]

The two societies' laws concerning marriage were very different but they did not exist entirely independently from each other. In some cases it can be seen

25 Cosgrove, 'Marriage in Medieval Ireland', p. 30.

26 R. C. Palmer, 'Contexts of Marriage in Medieval England: Evidence from the King's Court circa 1300', *Speculum* 59 (1984), 43.

27 R. M. Karras, *Common Women: Prostitution and Sexuality in Medieval England* (New York, 1996), p. 88.

28 *Ormond Deeds, i*, no. 100.

29 E. Searle, 'Seigneurial Control of Women's Marriage: The Antecedents and Function of Merchet in England', *Past and Present* 82 (1979), esp. pp. 8–14.

30 For much of the following on grant limitations see Palmer, 'Contexts of Marriage in Medieval England', esp. pp. 46–65.

that certain aspects of the opposing culture's traditions concerning marriage were adopted. A marriage contract made in 1401, detailing how the earl of Ormond granted to Theobald de Burgh his illegitimate daughter Elizabeth in marriage, gives an interesting insight into the extent to which certain Gaelic customs concerning marriage had been adopted by the Anglo-Irish.[31] Theobald had to pay 240 cows to the earl for the marriage, 120 up front and 120 to follow.[32] (The value ascribed to cattle and the use of such moveables in a marital contract is more associated with Gaelic Ireland than with Anglo-Ireland.) He also had to give forty stud horses, and undertook (with his kinsmen) to aid the earl in his wars and disputes. Ormond, in turn, granted to his daughter as her dowry his manor of Coraneyer Owenagh [*sic*] for the term of her life, and free passage for all merchants, carriers and tradesmen going as far as Limerick, a privilege that he held. On the day this document was drawn up, those listed as being present to receive and witness the oaths of the de Burghs and their followers were recorded as being the earl of Ormond and Katherine of Desmond, who was the earl's concubine (and a member of one of the most powerful of Anglo-Irish families) as well as being Elizabeth's mother.[33] The marriage appears to have gone ahead for, in 1402, the MacWilliam Burkes, of which Theobald was the leader, came to the aid of the earl of Ormond in his war with the earl of Desmond, which indicates that he was keeping his side of the bargain.[34]

Gaelic Women and their Property

In Gaelic areas the bargaining over marriage was similar in some ways to the Anglo-Irish system, in that both families were expected to contribute to the match. Marriages of the more formal type were probably arranged by the families of the bride and groom, and the betrothal was a contract sustained by the sureties of both families.[35] It was the custom for a husband to pay a bride-price (*coibche*) to the bride's family upon marriage. The bride was entitled to a portion of that *coibche* and if the marriage broke up due to a fault on the husband's part then the *coibche* was retained by the wife's father, but, if the fault lay with the bride, then the *coibche* was to be returned to the husband.[36] This bride-price may have gradually lessened in importance in legitimate marriages, as the dowry appears to have risen in importance within such relationships. The meaning of the gift itself gradually changed, and it began to signify property contributed by the father of the bride, thus becoming neutral marriage goods.[37] This change seems to have been primarily due to ecclesiastical pressure to enforce the dowry, as its payment was

31 *Ormond Deeds, ii*, no. 353.

32 This appears to be similar to the Gaelic Irish *coibche* or bride-price paid to the bride's family.

33 T. Blake Butler, 'Seneschals in the Liberty of Tipperary', *Irish Genealogist* 2:12 (1955), 369.

34 A. J. Otway-Ruthven, *A History of Medieval Ireland*, 3rd edn (New York, 1993), p. 342

35 Kelly, *Early Irish Law*, p. 71.

36 Ibid., p. 72.

37 Simms, 'Legal Position of Irishwomen', p. 110.

demanded by the canon law.[38] However, the *coibche* payment continued into the sixteenth century as a vital part of the concubinage contract. The *spréidh* (stock) which the woman had been accustomed to receive from her own family on setting up home duly seems to have been converted into a dowry paid to the husband (by the woman or her family). Because of the Gaelic Irish system of fosterage, sometimes the bride's marriage-portion could be provided by her foster family.[39] However, the husband still remained liable for its repayment in case of divorce, and it would also be repaid if he died.[40]

The Gaelic wife's continuing control over her own property could have interesting repercussions, especially if, as could sometimes be the case, part of that property consisted of soldiers. The Annals of Loch Cé, for example, refer to the marriage of Aedh O Conor and Ailin, the daughter of Dubhgall MacSomhairle, upon which the young wife brought as her dowry 160 galloglass.[41] Dowries in Gaelic Ireland are not very well documented before the sixteenth century but, in general, they probably consisted of moveables, which could include soldiers as well as the more usual cattle and horses. Gaelic married women appear to have had the right to hold and administer these dowries independently of their husbands, which was completely opposite to the English common law (as it was interpreted in Ireland) regarding the rights of married women. The ability to control their own property after marriage was the crucial difference between the lives of Gaelic wives and those of their Anglo-Irish counterparts.

According to Gaelic law, married women of equal status to their husbands had extensive legal powers regarding their own property and the couple's joint property. A Gaelic Irish wife had the freedom to administer her own goods, which she brought with her to the marriage, as well as any marriage-portion settled on her by her husband. She was to be consulted in every case involving their joint land and property, and had veto rights, just as her husband had those same rights to any contract she made on her own. If her husband made a bad decision concerning joint property, then his wife had the right to rescind it.[42] Regarding property which the wife may have held separately, she was allowed to sell or let it independently.[43] A married woman was regarded, under Gaelic law, as having wide powers of independent contract, almost as wide as her husband's . However, if a woman brought property which she had inherited to her marriage, there were limitations to her enjoyment of it. A female heir (*banchomarbae*) could inherit

38 K. Nicholls, 'Irishwomen and Property', *Women in Early Modern Ireland*, ed. M. MacCurtain and M. O'Dowd (Edinburgh, 1991), p. 20.

39 The type of fosterage is referred to as 'milk nurse fostering' and seems to have occurred in cases of fostering when the child was taken at a very early age into a family and raised by that foster family to whom it gave its primary emotional loyalty: see F. FitzSimons, 'Fosterage and Gossipred in Late Medieval Ireland: Some New Evidence', *Gaelic Ireland, c. 1250–1650*, ed. P. J. Duffy *et al.* (Dublin, 2001), p. 142.

40 Nicholls, *Gaelic and Gaelicised Ireland*, p. 76.

41 W. M. Hennessy, ed., *The Annals of Loch Cé: A Chronicle of Irish Affairs, 1014–1590* (London, 1871), p. 1259.

42 Thurneysen *et al.*, *Studies*, p. 228.

43 Ibid., p. 227.

a lifetime interest in her father's land, assuming she had no brothers. However, upon her death, the property would not be inherited by her husband or sons but would revert to her own kin, unless she was married to a foreigner who held no land, in which case, she could pass on a limited amount of her family land to her own heir.[44] This was opposite to the status and rights of female heiresses under the common law who could freely transmit their inheritance to their heirs. It also meant that, in Gaelic society, there was no prospect of acquiring lands or title by marrying a female heir, which again was in opposition to the Anglo-Irish system regarding female heirs.[45]

There were other limitations on female power within Gaelic Ireland. Women, for example, were not allowed formally to wield political power. The right of Gaelic Irish women to retain control over their own property or moveables was, however, a crucial factor in how their personal power was exerted during marriage. The wife of a Gaelic chieftain, for example, was independently wealthy and was also, by virtue of her marriage, entitled to some share of the chief's authority over his territories. This may have led to some wives wielding a certain amount of political power within Gaelic Ireland. Gaelic Irish wives of chieftains sometimes became very involved in the political concerns of their husbands' families through their active involvement in the warfare that was habitual in Ireland.[46] Thanks to their activities, some Gaelic wives were acknowledged by the authorities as being troublesome and dangerous to both church and state. In 1315, Donal O' Neill, his wife Gormlaith and their son, John, issued *Letters Patent* in which they promised the harassed archbishop, dean and chapter of Armagh that they would no longer make any demands upon ecclesiastically-owned lands and tenants for themselves or their allies' troops. They also promised to restore all church lands which they had seized, and to deliver pledges for good behaviour.[47]

Other Gaelic Irish wives were used as bargaining pieces by an administration desperate to keep order. In 1316 the royal justiciar was ordered to ascertain whether the release from prison of Mór, the wife of Hanlon, who was being held in Drogheda, would be prejudicial to the keeping of the peace or injurious to the interests of the king.[48] There are other instances of Gaelic Irish wives being involved in the conduct of war. In 1471, Sile, the daughter of Niall Garbh O' Donnell and wife of Niall, the son of Art O' Neill, defended the castle of Omagh against O'

44 Kelly, *Early Irish Law*, p. 104.

45 Jaski, *Early Irish Kingship*, pp. 144–5.

46 R. R. Davies, 'Frontier Arrangements in Fragmented Societies: Ireland and Wales', *Medieval Frontier Societies*, ed. R. Bartlett and A. MacKay (Oxford, 1989), p. 83.

47 H. J. Lawlor, ed., 'Calendar of the Register of Archbishop Fleming', *Proceedings of the Royal Irish Academy* 30 C (1912–13), 170, Gormlaith was not the only O' Neill woman to make life difficult for the church. During the mid-fifteenth century the O' Neills were repeatedly excommunicated for continuing to make exactions on church lands. One of the worst offenders on that account was the then chief's wife, Evelina Baret (an Anglo-Irish woman): see the Register of Archbishop John Prene (Trinity College Dublin, MS 557/6/385), as cited in Simms, 'Legal Position of Irishwomen', p. 108.

48 B. Smith, 'The Medieval Border', *The Borderlands; Essays on the History of the Ulster-Leinster Border*, ed. R. Gillespie and H. O'Sullivan (Belfast, 1989), p. 50

Neill and his sons. Her husband and his brothers had been defeated by O' Neill and his sons, and had fled to O' Donnell. Sile remained in the castle and defended it until the family feud was resolved.[49] Other wives seem to have pursued a more diplomatic course in dealing with their husband's enemies. In 1392–3, a safe conduct pass was issued to Una, the wife of Niall Óg O' Neill, who was going to and from Drogheda, accompanied by twelve men and women, to meet with the Lord Justice and Council.[50]

A wife acting as an intermediary is not, perhaps, very unusual, but a wife concluding a formal peace with her husband's enemies can be judged as more remarkable. This appears to have happened in 1433 when Fionnuala, the wife of O' Donnell and daughter of O' Connor Faly, along with Nachtan O' Donnell and the sons of the chieftains of Tirconnell, made peace with the O' Neills who had been attacking them. This was without the consent of her husband as he was absent.[51] Her father was so powerful that her husband's opinion may not have mattered much to her.[52] In these instances high-ranking Gaelic wives are involved in political and military affairs at the highest levels. It is possible that their ability to maintain control over the marriage-portions, which they brought with them into marriage, as well as the continuing influence of their natal family, granted them a freedom of action and a right to join in with and aid their husband's political and military plans. It also enabled them to control and unify their husband's family if he was taken captive. For example, in 1422, Owen O' Neill was ransomed by his wife and family after capture, by giving his captor cattle, horses and 'other gifts'.[53] Certainly, at the higher levels of Gaelic society, the independent action of wives was tolerated and their continuing control over their own property could also come to their family's aid in times of trouble.

As well as retaining control of her own property, in Gaelic areas the wife of a chieftain was often entitled to various other taxes on her husband's lands such as *cáin bheag* and *cíos Bantighearna* (lady's rent).[54] Married Gaelic Irish women – at least those married to chieftains – seem to have enjoyed greater wealth and power during their husband's lifetime than at any other stage of their lives. Again this is in direct contrast to the experiences of their Anglo-Irish contemporaries whose lives were very severely curtailed once they married and became subject to the rule of their husbands. Gaelic Irish wives appear to have been well provided for by husbands who may have been nervous of a powerful wife taking her soldiers or cattle away with her should she wish to end the marriage. The Irish rental of MacNamara listed certain of his lands which owed *cíos Baintighearna* in addition

49 J. O' Donovan, ed. and trans., *Annala Rioghachta Eireann: Annals of the Kingdom of Ireland from the Earliest Period to the Year 1616 by the Four Masters*, 7 vols (Dublin, 1854), p. 1471.

50 J. Graves, ed., *A Roll of the Proceedings of the King's Council in Ireland for a Portion of the 16th Year of the Reign of Richard II, a.d. 1392–3* (London, 1877), no. 161.

51 O' Donovan, ed. and trans., *Annala Rioghachta Eireann*, p. 1433.

52 C. Ó Cléirigh, 'The O' Connor Faly Lordship of Offaly 1395–1513', *Proceedings of the Royal Irish Academy* 96 C (1996), 87–102.

53 O' Donovan, ed. and trans., *Annala Rioghachta Eireann*, p. 1422.

54 R. McCauley, 'Female Patrons of Bardic Poetry', unpublished M.Phil. thesis, University of Dublin, 2000, p. 25.

to their normal services to the chief.[55] As part of McCarthy's rights as lord of Desmond, for instance, he was entitled to '*rout*'. This was a cess (tax) for horsemeat for either his horses or those of his wife, which was charged on the barony of Maguinhy. The wife of MacCarthy Mór had 'a small spending ... out of divers quarters of the country, called *canebeg* [*cáin beag*]'.[56]

Anglo-Irish Women: Land and Power

Such arrangements may also have had an influence on areas subject to the common law. In great Anglo-Irish lordships there was also sometimes an endowment assigned to the lady, like the tax on Gaelic lands given to Gaelic Irish wives, which she was able to use for her lifetime. Thomas, earl of Desmond (1529–34), granted to his second wife, Katherine, 'besides the manor of Inchiquin, County Cork, an annual rent of 33 marks (£22) in Kerry 'as fully as Evlina Roche [wife of Maurice, earl 1487–1520] and other countesses had been accustomed to receive the same'.[57] Again this is an instance of an Anglo-Irish family (admittedly the Desmonds who were quite extensively Gaelicized) aping Gaelic custom.

Despite the fact that the rights of Anglo-Irish women, once married, were severely curtailed, some wives may have actively joined with their husbands, or even led them, in pursuing power and influence through the disposal and acquisition of land. Some of these women, who actively aided their husbands in both the pursuit and consolidation of political power, have been both lauded and demonized because of their actions. One such woman was Margaret, the wife of Piers Butler, sixteenth-century earl of Ormond (1537). Her active support of her husband during the many years he had to wait for the earldom of Ormond, as well as in his schemes to deprive his elder brothers of their rights, earned his wife both opprobrium and respect.[58] Margaret Butler was regarded by Stanihurst as 'a lady of such a port, that all estates of the Realme crouched unto hir: so politique, that nothing was thought substantially debated withput hir advice: manlike and tall of stature: very liberall and bountiful'.[59] She was known popularly as Mairéad Gearóid and various wild stories are attached to her. The castles of Ballyragget and Balleen in the lordship of Ormond had stone benches in the watchtowers that were called Mairéad's Chairs because Margaret is supposed to have hung prisoners from them.[60] She was also said to have hung

55 Hardiman, *Ancient Deeds*, pp. 93–5, as cited in Simms, 'Legal Position of Irishwomen, p. 108.

56 W. F. Butler, 'The Lordship of MacCarthy Mór', *Journal of the Royal Society of Antiquaries of Ireland* 36 (1906), 354 and 365.

57 Nicholls, 'Irishwomen and Property', pp. 19–20.

58 For an examination of Margaret's political actions on behalf of her husband, see E. MacKenna, 'Was There a Political Role for Women in Medieval Ireland? Lady Margaret Butler and Lady Eleanor MacCarthy', *Fragility of Her Sex*, ed. Meek and Simms, pp. 163–74.

59 Richard Stanihurst as quoted in L. Miller and E. Power, eds, *Holinshed's Irish Chronicle* (Dublin, 1979), p. 328.

60 I. Kehoe, 'Margaret FitzGerald, Wife of Piers Butler 8th Earl of Ormond and 1st Earl of Ossory', *Old Kilkenny Review* 4 (1991), 827.

people on a tree known as '*sceach na Cuntaoise*' or the Countess's Bush.[61] Her impact on local folklore and myth was deep and testament to the strength of her rule with her husband. The extreme reactions that she appears to have inspired are also testament to the fact that Margaret was a very unusual woman. Her activities, though, are not representative, and most Anglo-Irish women had to wait until the death of their husbands to display any kind of sovereignty of action. They could do this because of the extensive provisions made for widows in the common law, in particular their dower and jointure rights. These allowances made by the common law for the widow's rights were not matched within Gaelic Ireland. The ability of married women resident in Anglo-Irish-controlled areas to hold lands jointly with their husbands gave them an added element of financial security, particularly if their husbands died before them. To accomplish the holding of lands as a jointure, a man conveyed his estate to named trustees or feoffees, to the joint use of himself and his wife for life. Until the introduction of the Statute of Uses in Ireland, in 1634, a married woman was able to claim both dower and jointure, but after that date, where provision was made for a jointure, she had to elect for one or the other, but could not claim both.[62]

Before this legislation was enacted, however, married women took advantage of both jointure and dower, and pressed their claims to them after their husband's death. The process of enfeoffing a third party (or parties) and having them re-enfeoff the grantor and his wife meant that several documents attested to these transactions, certain of which can sometimes be traced in the records. For example, in 1329, the first earl of Ormond requested permission from the king to enfeoff James Lawless with all of the earl's land, rents, advowsons and fees in England, and all reversions pertaining to the earl and his wife, so that Lawless might re-enfeoff the earl and Eleanor his wife and the heirs of their bodies.[63] The earl also seems to have been busy doing the same for his lands in Ireland. The Pipe Roll of 1342, regarding the manors of Turvey and Cloncurry, stated that there was nothing to answer for them since the earl's death as he was jointly enfeoffed in them along with his wife Eleanor, a close relative of the king, and so the manors were delivered to her.[64]

Gaelic widows had no such explicit and legally protected provisions made for them from their husband's property after his death. However, although they were not entitled to a dower, Gaelic widows could retain their *spréidh* (dowry), which then probably became the responsibility of their male guardian after the death of their husband. Thus the measure of independence afforded Anglo-Irish widows through their economic independence was not reflected in the Gaelic tradition.

61 D. O' hÓgain, *Myth, Legend and Romance: An Encyclopaedia of the Irish Folk Tradition* (London, 1990), p. 65.

62 H. O' Sullivan, 'Women in County Louth in the Seventeenth Century', *Journal of the County Louth Archaeological Society* 23 (1995), 346.

63 P. Connolly, 'Irish Material in the Class of Chancery Warrants Series I (c. 81) in the PRO, London', *Analecta Hibernica* 36 (1995), 149.

64 *Report of the Deputy Keeper of the Public Records in Ireland* 44 (1912), no. 64, p. 39.

At all stages in a Gaelic woman's life she had a legal guardian, who could be her father or another male relative as an unmarried woman, or her husband when married.[65] As a widow the identity of her legal guardian depended on whether or not she had adult male children. Early Irish law regarded a widow as being under the tutelage of her grown-up sons, if she had any, failing which her own kin took responsibility for her.[66] It often became an imperative for widows to quickly re-marry and so gain some sort of agency concerning their affairs again. As a result Gaelic widows are very hard to trace in remaining records, as they either re-married or disappeared, legally speaking. However, it is possible that over the hundreds of years since those laws were first committed to writing the realities of life for widows in Gaelic Ireland may have changed somewhat. Intermarriage with the colonists and the establishment of family networks with them, as well as interaction with Anglo-Irish widows and observation of their circumstances, may have served to make life less proscriptive for Gaelic Irish women after the death of their husbands.

Intermarriage

The two legal traditions concerning women's rights during and after marriage were very different in many ways but it was impossible for them not to become a little mixed as intermarriage between Gaelic and Anglo-Irish was a fairly common occurrence during the later Middle Ages. Members of Gaelic and Anglo-Irish societies seem to have regularly enjoyed concubinous or casual sexual relations, but when people from the two traditions married, legal problems could emerge, particularly concerning the rights of the Gaelic wives of Anglo-Irish men. Under the law of the colony, common law was not extended to the Irish and this could cause problems for a Gaelic wife if she ever wished to claim her dower from her Anglo-Irish husband's estate, for example, as legally she was not entitled to such benefits. This deficit in law was highlighted by the Irish in their request for an extension of English law made in 1277.[67] The children of such unions were also at risk of failing to get their inheritance. To avoid this occurrence, Irish wives had to apply for an official grant of English law to safeguard both themselves and their children.

In the pockets of colonized areas in Ireland, away from the Anglicizing influence of Dublin and the surrounding areas, the Gaelicization of English families through intermarriage with Irish women could have very serious political consequences.[68] The children of such unions were comfortable in both worlds and

65 Thurneysen *et al.*, *Studies*, p. 180.

66 Ibid., p. 80.

67 A. J. Otway-Ruthven, 'Select Documents VI: The Request of the Irish for English Law 1277–80', *Irish Historical Studies* 6 (1949), 261–70.

68 Gaelicization was also evident in Dublin from early on after the Anglo-Norman colonization; an early civic ordinance of Dublin ordered the fining of women if they wore kerchiefs dyed in saffron, in the style of Gaelic Irish women: see J. McMorrow, 'Women in Medieval Dublin: An Introduction', *Medieval Dublin II*, ed. S. Duffy (Dublin, 2000), p. 205, n. 1.

the influence of their Gaelic mother was no doubt significant, as well as that of her family. Many of the descendants of the settlers belonged by birth to the Gaelic Irish traditions, as well as to the Anglo-Irish.[69] The 'degeneracy' of those Anglo-Irish who were becoming more like the Gaelic Irish began to worsen towards the end of the thirteenth century especially, and was legislated against. The parliament of 1297 forbade the English to wear their hair in a *cúlán* (a traditional Gaelic hairstyle), for example, which indicates an increasing assimilation of Irish modes of dress and behaviour amongst the settlers. The government also began to try to restrict the colonists' choice of marriage partner through prohibitions that forbade marriage between the colonists and any enemy of the king, whether they were Gaelic or Anglo-Irish.[70] These worries continued and statutes of the Kilkenny parliament of 1366 indicate that, by that stage, 'degeneracy' was viewed as almost being out of control.[71] Successive statutes imposed a ban on marriage or any relationship (i.e. concubinage) between Gaelic and Anglo-Irish.[72] Marriage may have been a contributing factor in 'degeneracy', but such influences run both ways and it could be argued that intermarriage could also lead to increasing Anglicization, especially for women. Gaelic women in particular increasingly began to use church courts to enforce their marriages, thus indicating a growing awareness of church law and teaching on marriage and their legal entitlements under both canon and common law as opposed to Gaelic law.[73] Ireland, in the fifteenth century, did see a substantial rise in applications to dispense and enforce marriages amongst the Gaelic Irish. Abandoned wives from Gaelic areas began to utilize the church courts in attempts to force husbands to return. Granted, these developments occurred at a time of increasing and obvious religious devotion amongst the Gaelic Irish, but the influence of ongoing contacts with settlers on this behaviour should not be discounted.

Therefore, throughout the history of the colony in Ireland (except perhaps in its very early stages), intermarriage with Irish women and the adoption of Irish customs met with disapproval and attempts to outlaw it by the government. The prevalence of intermarriage between the Gaelic Irish and Anglo-Irish, or English, was always seen as a weakness in the stability of the colony. It was repeatedly prohibited by the government and equally repeatedly ignored.[74] For many Anglo-Irish families, living near areas of predominantly Gaelic ethos and influence, intermarriages were a crucial means both of gaining acceptance and of building up alliances that could be achieved in no other way. The dictates of the government on the matter were thus comprehensively ignored throughout the later Middle

69 Nicholls, *Gaelic and Gaelicised Ireland*, p. 17.

70 H. F. Berry, ed., *Statutes, Ordinances and Acts of Parliament of Ireland King John to Henry V* (Dublin, 1907), pp. 386–7.

71 J. F. Lydon, 'Nation and Race in Medieval Ireland', *Concepts of National Identity in the Middle Ages*, ed. S. Forde *et al.* (Leeds, 1995), pp. 103–5.

72 Berry, *Stat. Ire. John to Henry V*, pp. 432–3.

73 S. Duffy, 'The Problem of Degeneracy', *Law and Disorder in Thirteenth Century Ireland: The Parliament of 1297*, ed. J. Lydon (Dublin, 1997), pp. 88–9.

74 M. O' Dowd, 'Women and the Law in Early Modern Ireland', *Women in Renaissance and Early Modern Europe*, ed. C. Meek (Dublin, 2000), pp. 100–1.

Ages in Ireland, as the government had no means of enforcing their strictures against this matter. Amongst the Gaelic Irish the links between their culture and that of the 'foreigners' were generally more accepted.[75]

Every stratum of Gaelic Irish and Anglo-Irish society was familiar with intermarriage. From the highest levels of society, where intermarriage was often a way of securing a family's position in the face of local Gaelic opposition, to lower down the scale, where the stakes were not as high, people from the two cultures met and married. The cross-fertilization of cultural attitudes and traditions, as well as implications for the legal status of the women involved in these marriages, are of interest. It is possible that, depending on where and to whom she was married, a wife would follow the customs of the tradition she had married into. Gaelic wives of Anglo-Irish men can be found applying for grants of English law so they would be eligible for benefits such as jointures and dowers, if and when their husbands died. For example, grants of English law to Irish women such as Mariota, the wife of Ralph Burges, and Artesia, who may have been the daughter of Primate Mac Maolisa and who was married to Peter de Repentenny in 1285, safeguarded their rights in an Anglo-Irish world.[76] In 1289 Primate Mac Maoiliosa also petitioned for a grant of English law to be given to Ismaya, the wife of Bertram de Repenteneye, in order that she might have her dower after her husband's death. It was explained that she was Irish and the custom in Ireland was that Irish women did not have that right.[77] She was the daughter of O' Rahilly.[78]

However, not all marriages were between Gaelic women and Anglo-Irish or English men. Gaelic Irish men also married Anglo-Irish women. For example, a series of deeds from the early fifteenth century relates to grants of lands made by William O' Dowyr and his wife Isabella, the daughter and heiress of David Wodstok. In such a situation a Gaelic man's right to administer his wife's land could be brought into question simply because he was Gaelic, and the onus was likely to have been on him to have himself admitted to English law in order to safeguard his rights in relation to his wife and their property. The necessity for Gaelic Irish men, living in areas subject to the common law, who were married to Anglo-Irish women, to have themselves admitted to English law can be seen in a case dating from 1384. In that year allegations over Adam Nores's background and descent led a jury to conclude that he was not of the Irish nation but 'of descent of the mere English' and was, therefore, entitled to hold land in right of his wife.[79] When an Anglo-Irish woman married a Gaelic Irish man in a Gaelic area, her status was likely to have been that accorded to a Gaelic Irish wife under Gaelic law. However, it is likely that only women making political marriages entered into such agreements regularly, and that, in such cases, they were entitled to all the many benefits of life as the wife of a chieftain. For example, in 1269 the earl of Ulster insisted that

75 The acceptance of links between the Gaelic Irish and Gaelicized Anglo-Irish families was perhaps easier the further away from the Pale one travelled.

76 McNeill, ed., *Harris*, '"Collectanea"', p. 318.

77 D. MacÍomhair, 'Primate MacMaoiliosa and County Louth', *Seanchas Ardmhacha* 6:1 (1971), 90.

78 B. Smith, *Conquest and Colonisation in Medieval Ireland* (Cambridge, 1999), p. 82.

79 *Dowdall Deeds*, no. 290.

Aedh Bui O' Neill grant his Anglo-Irish wife Eleanor (a cousin of the earl) the full rights of a Gaelic Irish married woman. This was in response to the fact that Aedh had previously neglected her, and the earl forced him to accord to Eleanor all the rights that she was entitled to according to the 'custom' of his land.[80]

Intermarriage was also often seen in Ireland as a means of procuring truces through alliances which would then end periods of warfare. The prevalence of these requests can be discerned in the applications made to the Vatican for marriage dispensations in order to guarantee peace. In such an instance it was argued that providing a dispensation was performing a public service, in that it kept the peace. This could be a persuasive argument in a war-torn country such as Ireland. In 1426, for instance, it was advised that the Pope remove the impediments delaying the marriage of the 'noble and puissant' Roger Mccmahuna (*sic*) of Clogher diocese and Alice White of the Armagh diocese. These impediments were that they were closely related on several levels, but the marriage was advised for several reasons. These included the legitimization of the children who had already been born as well as the peace that their union brought to the warring English and Irish.[81] It may be that in a country exhausted by feuds and warfare this excuse was found to be a powerful and effective way for the families involved to gain a political or military advantage, by dint of an honourable reason for marriage.

Conclusions

The move into marriage for the women of both Gaelic Ireland and Anglo-Ireland saw them affected by new rights and restrictions according to the secular and ecclesiastical laws by which they lived their lives. With regard to the preparation and organization of marriage, the two societies were similar in that a marriage was often controlled by families as an act of political, social or economic aggrandizement, and both families expected to profit in some way from the match. Fundamentally, within Gaelic and Gaelicized society, marriage was a secular act and the definition of a wife was somewhat looser than in the Anglo-Irish areas. As wives, Anglo-Irish women were legally subject to their husbands and lost the legal abilities they enjoyed as single women. Similarly, Gaelic Irish women were always under the legal sway of a man throughout their lives, but, despite this, as wives they enjoyed extensive rights regarding the administration of their own property, which Anglo-Irish women effectively lost when they became wives. Gaelic wives' continuing control over their property led to the emergence of some women as powerful agents in political matters.

In both societies the church's strictures concerning the proper rituals for the making and breaking of marriages were often ignored as members of both socie-

80 *Report on the Manuscripts of Lord De L'Isle and Dudley, I* (Historical Manuscripts Commission, London, 1925), p. 32, as quoted in Simms, 'Women in Norman Ireland', *Women in Irish Society: The Historical Dimension*, ed. M. MacCurtain and D. O'Corráin (Dublin reprint, 1979), pp. 17–18.

81 D. A. Chart, ed., *The Register of John Swayne Archbishop of Armagh and Primate of All Ireland, 1418–1439* (Belfast, 1935), pp. 45–6.

ties strayed from the orthodox path. In Gaelic society, in particular, the widespread nature of more casual sexual unions and the effect these had on the legal rights and status of the women involved and of their children, exist in contrast to the prevailing situation in Anglo-Irish society. However, the rise of Gaelicization may have led to more acceptance of casual sexual relations amongst the Anglo-Irish as well. Meanwhile, the rise in religious adherence in both the Gaelic and Anglo-Irish worlds, from the fifteenth century onwards, witnessed a concomitant increase in applications to the Holy See to regularize existing unions or gain dispensations for planned ones that erred in the matters of consanguinity or affinity. The need for politically advantageous marriages saw ongoing intermarriage between the Gaelic and Anglo-Irish, a situation that could lead to legal confusion concerning the rights of the wives involved. Intermarriage was also conducive to the exposure of members of both societies to the ideas, laws and traditions of the other concerning women.

It should be clear therefore that two worlds co-existed when it came to women and marriage in later medieval Ireland. When these worlds collided for women, as they sometimes did, it was during love affairs, concubinous relationships and when the marriage bond was entered into. These two worlds were fundamentally very different in terms of how they viewed what a wife was, how a wife ought to behave and how marriages should begin and end. Yet they were both subject to change as increasing communication between them was established through links such as intermarriage. Over time cultural influences spread, traditions were copied and soon members of opposing societies began to manifest socio-cultural habits that were previously thought to be alien. Great Anglo-Irish lords took concubines and treated their offspring as well as if they had been legitimate, thus reflecting Gaelic practice. Gaelic women went to court like their Anglo-Irish counterparts to punish errant husbands and try to rectify the calamitous consequences of abandonment. Divorce at will was allowed in Gaelic tradition, but the social and economic effects on discarded women and children could be disastrous.

These cross-cultural exchanges of ideas and traditions are examples of what societies in tense opposition do to survive: they adapt and appropriate. It was not a process free of problems, as the issues surrounding the need for Gaelic wives of Anglo-Irish men to be admitted to English law attest. Officially intermarriage was not promoted; unofficially it was a necessary aid for survival for many Anglo-Irish families. It was also a catalyst of Gaelicization, which successive governments acknowledged and feared.

Indeed the greatest instance of where these cultures collided is in the many examples of intermarriage that appear in the records. Here one can see at first hand the processes inherent in adapting to a new culture for women (for it was mainly women who had to adapt to their husband's culture). Their new husbands treated them, it seems, according to their own law codes, so Anglo-Irish women were accorded rights under Gaelic law and vice versa. The changes required of these women to shift their world-view to a new outlook must have been tremendous and life-altering, not only for them but also for those closest to them, most notably their children. The effect of a Gaelic mother on children brought up in an Anglo-Irish tradition, for example, must have been hugely important in shaping those children's views of the 'other' culture, and vice versa (though, it appears, less common). Wives and mothers were practical promoters and facilitators of cultural exchange between two hostile societies and yet the gulf between the English and Gaelic worlds remained throughout the later Middle Ages.

The volume of marriages and other sexual relationships so far uncovered from the paltry surviving Irish sources testifies to an island where the two societies did, indeed, exist independently of each other, but also where, increasingly, collision in the form of complex human relationships was becoming a habit rather than a rarity. It appears that the worlds collided very often indeed but never enough for one cultural tradition to take precedence over the other on the island. That would take place at a later date, but during the Middle Ages, at least, the two societies on the island of Ireland presented a complex web of interpersonal relationships with women as wives and mothers at the heart of any collisions that took place.

4

MARRIED WOMEN, CRIME AND THE COURTS IN LATE MEDIEVAL WALES

Lizabeth Johnson

For the pre-conquest period of medieval Welsh history, historians interested in the activities of married women – their rights within marriage, their responsibilities within the household, or the work they performed – are severely limited by a lack of sources. Welsh chronicles have little to say about married women. Law texts provide theoretical information about married women, including information about marriage practices, the various fees that accompanied marriage negotiations, and the circumstances in which divorce was acceptable.[1] However, the laws do not provide any specific examples of marriages being contracted or ended, fees that were exchanged between those contracting a marriage and the lord of a specific Welsh territory, or the extent to which a married woman's legal voice was muted by her husband. In short, Welsh chronicles and law texts leave much to be desired as sources for the historian attempting to reconstruct women's history in pre-conquest Welsh society.

After the English conquest of Wales in 1282–3, however, the historian suddenly finds him or herself with court roll evidence that sheds light on the issues of marriage, property ownership and work. Court rolls survive from various Welsh courts, both from the principality of Wales and from the Marcher lordships. The entries on these court rolls, although often brief in their wording, provide indicative information regarding the activities of women in Welsh communities, describing marital practices and domestic relations, as well as women's occupations. In addition, the court rolls provide information on women's involvement in legal disputes, whether civil or criminal, and – even more importantly – the legal status of women in courts of law, namely, whether women represented themselves at court or were represented by male relatives, as was often the case in other medieval societies.[2] In all, court rolls from the post-con-

1 For information on marital practices described in the laws, see T. M. Charles-Edwards, 'Nau Kynywedi Teithiauc', *The Welsh Law of Women*, ed. D. Jenkins and M. E. Owen (Cardiff, 1980), pp. 23–39. See also R. R. Davies, 'The Status of Women and the Practice of Marriage in Late-Medieval Wales', *The Welsh Law of Women*, ed. Jenkins and Owen, pp. 93–114.

2 Studies of women's activities in late medieval Welsh communities include Ll. B. Smith, 'Towards a History of Women in Late Medieval Wales', *Women and Gender in Early Modern Wales*, ed. M.

quest period of Welsh society are an extremely valuable resource for the study of women's history because they provide practical information about the lives of women and because they reveal the various legal actions women were involved in as both plaintiffs and defendants.

The purpose of this essay is to examine the scope of married women's involvement in litigation regarding abduction, assault and defamation in the post-conquest Marcher lordship of Dyffryn Clwyd, with respect to the legal doctrine of coverture, that is, a wife's legal subordination to her husband. The Marcher lordships comprised territory in Wales that had been conquered in the centuries after the Normans arrived in England in 1066. Marcher lordships were under the direct rule of various Anglo-Norman families, rather than the king, and this rule extended to the court system in each individual lordship. The reason for focusing on Dyffryn Clwyd in particular is the large number of post-conquest court rolls which survive from the lordship. Additionally, the Dyffryn Clwyd court rolls were the subject of a preservation, transcription and translation project in the mid-1990s, which resulted in the *Dyffryn Clwyd Court Roll Database*, a collection of more than 100,000 court roll entries from that lordship during the period 1294–1422.[3] This resource makes it possible to reconstruct the lives of married women in the lordship of Dyffryn Clwyd.

With regard to the Dyffryn Clwyd evidence, this essay will highlight married women's legal activities in cases involving abduction, assault and defamation. Abduction was a crime in which married women, unmarried women and even men might all appear as victims. However, married women sometimes exhibited a degree of agency in abduction cases. And the convention of coverture was evident in the claims husbands made regarding property taken in conjunction with the abduction of their wives. Likewise, assault and defamation cases involved married women, unmarried women, and men as both plaintiffs and defendants, and can provide further evidence regarding the operation of coverture in fourteenth-century Dyffryn Clwyd. By examining married women's roles as plaintiffs and defendants in these cases, particularly when compared to their unmarried and male

Roberts and S. Clarke (Cardiff, 2000), pp. 14–49; M. F. Stevens, *Urban Assimilation in Post-Conquest Wales: Ethnicity, Gender and Economy in Ruthin, 1282–1348* (Cardiff, 2010); and D. Hutton, 'Women in Fourteenth-Century Shrewsbury', *Women and Work in Pre-Industrial England*, ed. L. Charles and L. Duffin (London, 1985), pp. 83–99. These studies focus largely on female property ownership and occupation. However, Stevens's work also discusses the frequency with which women appeared in Welsh courts; see Stevens, *Urban Assimilation*, pp. 123–7.

3 The Dyffryn Clwyd Court Rolls are deposited in The National Archives (TNA) SC 2/215/64 to SC 2/226/16. They were calendared in a computerized database at the University of Wales, Aberystwyth with Economic and Social Research Council support (ESRC award numbers R000234070 and R000232548) as R. R. Davies and Ll. B. Smith, eds, *The Dyffryn Clwyd Court Roll Database, 1294–1422*, electronic resource (Aberystwyth, 1995), hereafter *Dyffryn Clwyd Database*. A user's guide for the database has been published as A. D. M. Barrell, *The Dyffryn Clwyd Court Roll Database, 1294–1422: A Manual for Users* (Colchester, 1997). The database and user's guide are available in digital format from the Economic and Social Data Service, http://www.esds.ac.uk/ (accessed 28 June 2012). I owe Dr Frederick Suppe and the History Department of Ball State University a debt of gratitude for making a licensed copy of the database available to me. A recent study of these court rolls is Stevens, *Urban Assimilation*.

counterparts, it can be shown that although married women were occasionally represented at court by their husbands, they also actively engaged in court cases – both civil and criminal – on their own behalf. Thus the practice of coverture, seen in many medieval northwest European cultures, was not consistently observed in medieval Dyffryn Clwyd. Instead, married women in Wales were often active in pursuing their own legal interests.

The court rolls from Dyffryn Clwyd provide glimpses of the lives of many women from the period 1294–1422, allowing scholars to gain a general sense of the legal activities of married women in the lordship. However, it must be noted that there are some limitations in using this evidence. First, as is the case with all medieval court roll evidence, the Dyffryn Clwyd material provides only an incomplete picture of a select group of medieval communities. It is next to impossible to track the movements, actions and experiences of any one person throughout his or her lifetime merely through court records. Second, while the court rolls from the lordship of Dyffryn Clwyd are relatively well preserved, they do not represent all the conflicts which arose within the lordship. Many conflicts may never have been brought to court, and yet others, after being initiated, were settled out of court. Further, not all of the lordship's court records have survived, nor are all surviving court rolls still legible. Nonetheless, the Dyffryn Clwyd court rolls provide important information regarding the litigation in which married women engaged and the application of coverture in the courts.

The lordship's officials oversaw two Great Courts, one representing the borough of Ruthin and the other representing Dyffryn Clwyd as a whole; three commotal (or hundred) courts, held for the commotes of Llannerch, Colion and Dogfeiling; the lesser borough court of Ruthin; and proceedings of gaol delivery, fines and bails. The Great Courts were each held twice yearly, at Easter and Michaelmas, and the lesser borough court and commotal courts were held roughly fifteen times a year.[4] This essay draws on the surviving and legible court roll entries regarding cases of abduction, assault and defamation from these courts.[5] Evidence from abduction and defamation cases, which appear in the court records relatively infrequently, has been gathered from all records calendared in the *Dyffryn Clwyd Database* for the period 1294–1422, while evidence from much more frequently occurring cases of assault has been gathered from two calendared sample periods, 1340–52 and 1390–9. The detail of these court roll entries is normally limited to the names of plaintiffs and defendants, the type of lawsuit or infraction of local

4 Barrell, *Dyffryn Clwyd: A Manual*, pp. 1, 7. A. D. M. Barrell *et al.*, 'The Dyffryn Clwyd Court Roll Project, 1340–1352 and 1389–1399: A Methodology and Some Preliminary Findings', *Medieval Society and the Manor Court*, ed. Z. Razi and R. Smith (Oxford, 1996), pp. 266–7.

5 The section on abduction draws evidence from various court rolls throughout the period 1294–1422, as published in the *Dyffryn Clwyd Database*. For the periods 1294–1339, 1353–64, 1364–76, 1376–90 and 1408–22 the records on abduction come from the two Great Courts of Ruthin and Dyffryn Clwyd, fines and bails rolls and the rolls from the commote of Llannerch, representing, for these date ranges, 6,580, 5,039, 5,042, 4,109 and 3,367 cases respectively. For the periods 1340–52 and 1390–9 the records on abduction come from the court rolls of all courts in the lordship, representing 21,106 and 17,419 cases respectively. Consequently, more cases are evidenced from the periods 1340–52 and 1390–9 than the others.

regulation concerned, and whether or not the court's involvement resulted in a judgment or amercement. The names used in these cases present certain challenges. Married women are normally indicated by the phrase 'X *uxor* Y', or 'X wife of Y'. In other cases, the scribes used the Latin abbreviation *qfu* for *que fuit uxor*, or 'X who was the wife of Y'. Despite the implication in the Latin phrasing, that women designated in this way were widows, there are cases where the scribes used the abbreviation *qfu* while the woman had a living spouse. For this reason, cases in which the woman is identified as *qfu* have here been grouped with cases in which the woman is identified as 'wife of'. The Latin term *relict*, however, is consistently used to designate widows.[6] Other women, who are listed in the court rolls with descriptive names, rather than marital or familial names, have also been treated as unmarried. The incomplete survival of court rolls and the occasional scribal error must be borne in mind when examining the Dyffryn Clwyd material, but despite these limitations the evidence is illuminating with regard to the legal activities of married women.

Abduction

Although abduction and rape were crimes that affected both married and unmarried women – and occasionally men – in medieval society, related issues that arose with regard to married women were their agency in such abductions and the operation of coverture, evidenced by husbands' claims to property taken by or with their wives.[7] The majority of the cases describing the abduction of married women also describe the property that disappeared with them, along with the value of that property. The cases involving unmarried women and men, on the other hand, typically do not include such information. Additionally, those cases describing the abduction of unmarried women often describe the rape of the woman in question, a situation that does not occur as commonly in cases involving married women.[8] For these reasons, litigation over abduction and rape operated differently depending on whether the victim was a married woman, an unmarried woman or a man. Furthermore, the majority of abduction cases were

6 For the use of the terms *qfu* and *relict* in the Dyffryn Clwyd database, see Barrell, *Dyffryn Clwyd: A Manual*, p. 21.

7 For a discussion of women's agency in abduction cases, see G. Walker, '"Strange Kind of Stealing": Abduction in Early Modern Wales', *Women and Gender in Early Modern Wales*, ed. Roberts and Clarke, pp. 50–74; and S. M. Butler, 'Runaway Wives: Husband Desertion in Medieval England', *Journal of Social History* 40 (2006), 337–59. Butler's article also discusses the issue of 'ravishment' of goods in such cases. For discussion of abduction in medieval Ruthin, see Stevens, *Urban Assimilation*, pp. 208–13.

8 The court scribes described the sexual violation of a woman through the verbs *abducere*, *rapere*, *concumbere* and *deflorare*, translated here as 'abduction', 'snatch', 'violate' and 'ravish'. Barrell, *Dyffryn Clwyd: A Manual*, pp. 91, 104. On the complexities of the use of this terminology in fourteenth-century English court rolls, see C. Cannon, '*Raptus* in the Chaumpaigne Release and a Newly Discovered Document Concerning the Life of Geoffrey Chaucer', *Speculum* 68 (1993), 74–94.

pursued by husbands or other male relatives. Relatively few of these cases involved women representing themselves.

The earliest records of abduction involving married women speak to both the issue of women's agency and the issue of coverture. Out of twenty-two cases of abduction of married women appearing in the calendared Dyffryn Clwyd materials between 1294 and 1422, fourteen of them also involved the abduction of property. One entry from 1296 describes a husband's plaint that his wife was abducted and that the abductor lived with her after the crime had been committed.[9] In a second case, from 1313, the husband of the abducted woman claimed that the perpetrator had 'seduced' her by night, taking both the plaintiff's wife and his goods.[10] A third entry, from 1329, states that a married woman had been abducted 'by the free wish of the said woman', again with the husband's goods.[11] In two of these cases, those from 1296 and 1329, the women in question left their husbands of their own volition. The wife's agency in the 1313 case is suggested by the fact that the husband was found guilty of making a false claim and fined. In fact, out of the twenty-two cases from the Dyffryn Clwyd court rolls, only two state that the abduction was against the woman's wishes.[12] That these women, and no doubt others, chose to leave their husbands should not be surprising, as scholars, such as Sara Butler, have demonstrated a variety of reasons why a medieval wife – despite the legal complications that could ensue – might choose to leave her husband (including abuse, the husband's impotence or her own general dissatisfaction with the marriage).[13] Additionally, until the English conquest of 1282–3, divorce had been allowed under native Welsh law, and Welsh women may have continued to embrace that custom despite subsequent changes to the legal system in the early post-conquest period.[14]

In those cases involving the taking of property together with the abduction of a married woman, it is often unclear whether it was the wife who took the property with her or her abductor, or whether the wife felt the goods to be her own. Regardless, the property is always stated as belonging to the husband, although this can be interpreted as either the husband's claim or the court's assumption based on the legal concept of coverture. In one such case, from 1296, a husband came to court to report the abduction of his wife and '7s. 6d. in money and corn', a case which was later resolved through concord.[15] In a 1341 case, which was lodged both in the Great Court of Ruthin and in the Great Court of Dyffryn Clwyd, a priest was accused of having abducted a woman and her husband's goods, valued at 10s., only to deliver both to the house of yet another man, where the woman remained for a

9 TNA, SC 2/215/66 m.1.

10 TNA, SC 2/215/72 m.11.

11 TNA, SC 2/216/9 m.12.

12 The two cases in which the crime was committed against the wishes of the woman are TNA, SC 2/218/1 m.1 and SC 2/221/1 m.15B.

13 Butler, 'Runaway Wives', pp. 345–8.

14 On divorce in pre-conquest Welsh society, see R. Chapman Stacey, 'Divorce, Medieval Welsh Style', *Speculum* 77 (2002), 1107–27. See also Huw Pryce, *Native Law and the Church in Medieval Wales* (Oxford, 1993), pp. 89–95.

15 TNA, SC 2/215/60 m.1.

month.[16] Another case, from 1396, describes a married woman, whose abductor had 'bodily violated her against [the] wish of [her husband]', giving her husband's goods to the man who had abducted her, including a pair of shoes and a brooch, all together valuing 8½d.[17] An even clearer example of abduction of a husband's goods, along with his wife, appears in a case from 1395, in which a woman and one of her female associates took goods from the woman's husband against his wishes. Compounding this crime was the fact that two clerics assisted the woman in leaving the lordship with her husband's goods, taking a horse from the prior of Ruthin in order to help the woman flee to Chester. The assistance that this woman and the one described in the example above from 1341 received from clerics may indicate that these women were trapped in abusive marriages and the members of the local clergy saw it as their duty to help them escape those marriages. Marital advice manuals written by clerics in the late medieval period urged husbands to be firm but not excessively violent toward their wives, but this was not always the reality of medieval marriages.[18] Alternatively, in the 1395 instance, the woman may have sought sanctuary in Ruthin priory and received assistance because of a sense of social and spiritual responsibility on the part of the clerics. The court rolls indicate that the woman was outlawed, but later pardoned by the lord of Dyffryn Clwyd.[19] Cases such as these, where the husband's goods were reported as taken or given willingly by the wife into the hands of her abductor, provide evidence of the interpretation of coverture in Dyffryn Clwyd. Because coverture legally placed a woman and the goods that she brought into the marriage, or subsequently produced during her time in the household, in her husband's hands, if a woman left her husband and took goods from the home without his consent the husband had the right to regain that property in court. As Butler notes, even in cases where a woman took refuge with family members to escape a marriage, those family members could be brought to court for the seizure of the husband's property.[20] This typically English system of assessing property ownership as resting strictly with the husband, as is evident in the court rolls of post-conquest Dyffryn Clwyd, is contrary to native Welsh law, which allowed wives to separate from their husbands and to take some property with them.[21]

Cases of abduction involving unmarried women and men, on the other hand, do not as commonly indicate volition on the part of the abductees. Nor do these cases typically entail litigation to recover lost property. Additionally, as noted above, many of the cases involving the abduction of unmarried women also involved the rape of those women. Of the forty-three cases of abduction involving unmarried women identified for this essay, eighteen specifically mention that the women were raped,

16 TNA, SC 2/217/6 m.1, SC 2/217/6 m.3 and SC 2/217/6 m.11. On the role that clerics may have played in the abduction of wives, see Butler, 'Runaway Wives', p. 350.

17 TNA, SC 2/220/9 m.51.

18 B. A. Hanawalt, 'Violence in the Domestic Milieu of Late Medieval England', *Violence in Medieval Society*, ed. R. Kaeuper (Woodbridge, 2000), pp. 204–7.

19 TNA, SC 2/220/9 m.39b.

20 Butler, 'Runaway Wives', p. 342.

21 D. Jenkins, trans. and ed., *The Law of Hywel Dda* (Llandysul, 1986), pp. 45–7. See n. 14 above.

sometimes violently. In one such case, the perpetrator was granted a pardon by the lord of Ruthin, Reginald de Grey, for the crime of 'ravishing' Gladys, daughter of Ednyfed le Cook. The court scribe wrote that the defendant was 'not to be molested or annoyed, but [was] to give surety for his good behaviour toward Gladys and all others in Ruthin'.[22] In some cases, the perpetrators went even further than abduction and physical violation, as in the case of one unnamed woman who was abducted and then sold to another man for 10s. in 1349.[23] Only one case out of forty-three involving unmarried women specified goods taken along with the woman, a clear contrast to the fourteen out of twenty-two cases involving married women which specified goods taken.[24] However, unlike those cases involving married women, there are two cases in which unmarried women represented themselves at court against their abductors, who they claimed had raped them. In both cases, the accusations were found to be false, and the women were imprisoned briefly and fined.[25] These cases, affirming that unmarried women might represent themselves at court in cases of abduction and rape, may stand as testament to the difficulty of prosecuting such accusations in late medieval society. But, alternatively, if these were false accusations, they could hint that single women too may sometimes have left their homes willingly but contrary to social convention, later feeling the need to cover up their agency in such actions.[26] Nevertheless, in either case, unmarried women were less likely than married women to abscond with goods from their homes, whether familial or otherwise.

There are eleven cases recorded in the Dyffryn Clwyd material in which the abducted party was a man, including several bondsmen and servants, in some cases along with goods, as well as one young male heir abducted from the household of the man who had paid relief for his lands.[27] In these cases, it is difficult to assess whether the men left willingly due to difficult conditions they faced as servants, bondsmen or wards, or whether they were truly victims. But it is entirely possible that they sought the same kind of escape that married women sought from life *covert de baron* and, because of the nature of their service, condition or wardship, they were viewed in a very similar manner by the court.

Assault

The evidence from Dyffryn Clwyd's courts concerning assault indicates that what determined whether married women were regarded as legally culpable individuals in such cases was whether the case appeared in court as an interpersonal lawsuit or as a criminal presentment. In interpersonal suits of assault, married women most commonly appeared alongside their husbands. In contrast, in crimi-

22 TNA, SC 2/220/9 mm.18A, 18B.
23 TNA, SC 2/218/1 mm.1d, 5, 5d, 6, 6d, 7. Ultimately, the perpetrator was outlawed.
24 TNA, SC 2/220/3 mm.12 and 25.
25 TNA, SC 2/216/3 m.19 and SC 2/215/71 m.10.
26 M. Prestwick, *Edward I* (London, 1988), pp. 281–3.
27 The case involving the male heir is TNA, SC 2/218/2 m.10.

nal presentments for assault, married women most commonly appeared independently in court. Consequently, records of assault demonstrate different patterns with regard to coverture, with interpersonal suits adhering more consistently to the practice of coverture than criminal presentments.[28]

Interpersonal suits of assault were brought in response to incidences of personal harm which amounted to 'battery' under English common law.[29] These pleas were, most likely, initiated orally, following which the named defendant was required to appear to answer the charge. A plea of battery could be brought by and against men, married or unmarried women, and married couples jointly. When the altercation was mutual, the Welsh phrase *brwdyr gyfaddef* (to 'confess battle') occasionally appears in the court record.[30] In interpersonal suits of assault brought before the courts of Dyffryn Clwyd in two sample periods, 1340–52 and 1390–9, unmarried women and men represented themselves before the court individually and, where liability was determined, the responsibility for fines or amercements did not extend to a litigant's wider family or the community (even in the case of never-married women). Married women, however, typically appeared alongside their husbands in these suits, even when the women themselves were responsible for the assault. In fact, in both 1340–52 and the 1390s, the majority of lawsuits involving married women named both the women and their husbands as either plaintiffs or defendants, in 91 per cent and 76 per cent of suits respectively (see Table 4.1). That married women rarely appeared without their husbands indicates that these women were not normally regarded as legally liable individuals in interpersonal suits of assault, and that coverture was observed in this litigation.

Table 4.1. Interpersonal Suits of Assault

	Men	Unmarried Women	Wives appearing with husbands	Wives appearing without husbands	Total Cases
1340–52	364	122	116	11	613
1390–99	153	41	19	6	219

Source: Dyffryn Clwyd Database; TNA, SC 2/217/6 to SC 2/220/10.

28 Karen Jones has argued that the late medieval Kent courts prosecuted some married women independently of their husbands in criminal cases involving property but that it is unclear whether this principle was upheld in all criminal cases involving married women, making any effort to compare married women's legal position to that of men 'highly problematic'. See K. Jones, *Gender and Petty Crime in Late Medieval England: The Local Courts in Kent, 1460–1560* (Woodbridge, 2006), pp. 37–8. According to Barbara Hanawalt, medieval officials were reluctant to arrest women or to indict them for crimes, making a study of women's criminal behaviour difficult. See B. A. Hanawalt, 'The Female Felon in Fourteenth-Century England', *Viator* 5 (1974), 253–68, at p. 256.

29 On the use of pleas of battery in English courts, see J. H. Baker, *An Introduction to English Legal History*, 4th edn (London, 2002), pp. 403–5. On pleading in native Welsh law, see R. Chapman Stacey, 'Learning to Plead in Medieval Welsh Law', *Studia Celtica* 38 (2004), 107–23; and S. E. Roberts, 'Plaints in Mediaeval Welsh law', *The Journal of Celtic Studies* 4 (2004), 219–61.

30 For a discussion of *brwdyr gyfaddef*, see Barrell, *Dyffryn Clwyd: A Manual*, p. 86.

Examples of interpersonal suits for assault involving married women amply demonstrate the application of coverture in the courts of Dyffryn Clwyd. In one suit, from 1342, the plaintiff, Madog ap Gruffudd, stated that the married female defendant, Lleucu wife of Cyn ap Einion, had 'unjustly assaulted him' and 'in breach of the peace beat him'; both Lleucu and her husband denied the charges.[31] In another suit, from 1346, Iorwerth ap Ieuan ap Heilyn and his unnamed wife appeared in court as defendants for assaulting Madog ap Gronwy Bach, although the court record indicates that it was Iorwerth's wife who had drawn blood from Madog and not the husband.[32] A suit from 1389 demonstrates the same pattern, when Dafydd ap Madog ap Llywelyn and his wife Lleucu were ordered to appear as defendants against Margaret ferch (Welsh, 'daughter of') Dafydd.[33] Married women appeared without their husbands in only a few instances, whether as plaintiffs or as defendants, such as in a 1342 lawsuit in which Alice wife of Richard son of William le Tailor appeared alone as a plaintiff against Hugh le Mon, who did not appear but was to be forced to do so at the next court.[34] In suits such as this one, no indication is given as to why the husband was absent from the court. Similarly, no indication is given regarding whether the independent prosecution of lawsuits by married women was viewed as unusual or inappropriate behaviour. However, the fact that married women most commonly appeared with their husbands suggests that they had only limited legal independence in interpersonal suits of assault, regardless of whether they were plaintiffs or defendants, as coverture was usually – if not strictly – observed. Even in those instances where the wife was very clearly indicated as the victim of the violence, rather than her husband, both were normally named in such suits.[35]

Options for resolving interpersonal lawsuits for assault included the plaintiff or defendant requesting concord (licence to settle out of court), for which a small fine was paid, the plaintiff withdrawing the accusation and paying a more substantial fine, the court's decision that the suit was an unjust plaint (a 'false claim'), similarly resulting in a fine, or – where the defendant was found liable – a fine and an order that compensation be paid.[36] The settlements listed in the court rolls further reaffirm

31 TNA, SC 2/217/7 mm.34d and 35. The name Cyn may be a shortened version of several different male Welsh names. See Barrell, *Dyffryn Clwyd: A Manual*, pp. 26–7.

32 TNA, SC 2/217/11 m.18d. The drawing of blood in this instance led to the original fine doubling. The shedding of blood as an exacerbating circumstance in physical assault has been demonstrated in cases of spousal violence in the courts of Dyffryn Clwyd. See L. Johnson, 'Attitudes Toward Spousal Violence in Medieval Wales', *Welsh History Review* 24 (2009), 81–115.

33 TNA, SC 2/220/7 m.16d.

34 TNA, SC 2/217/7 m.19. There were seven other suits in the 1340s and two in the 1390s. See TNA, SC 2/217/7 m.19, SC 2/217/7 m. 29, SC 2/217/8 m.11, SC 2/217/8 m.12d, SC 2/217/9 m.22, SC 2/217/10 m.11, SC 2/217/14 m.35, SC 2/220/9 m.69 and SC 2/220/10 m.29d.

35 TNA, SC 2/217/7 mm.32 and 32d.

36 The range of outcomes in assault cases remained unchanged between the 1340s and 1390s, the sample periods used here. But, while in the 1340s individual cases usually occasioned only a single court roll entry, recording the outcome of the lawsuit (e.g. Gronwy ap Ieuan v. Dafydd ap Gwyn, TNA, SC 2/217/6 m.31d.), in the 1390s individual lawsuits often occasioned entries on the rolls of several courts before an outcome was recorded (e.g. Ieuan Goch v. Dafydd ap Cyn, TNA, SC 2/220/7 mm.6, 6d, 7, 7d, 8).

that coverture was usually observed in interpersonal suits for assault. The majority of the settlements in lawsuits involving married women name both spouses as responsible for any fines or compensation arising, regardless of whether the wife alone was responsible for the dispute. In the 1346 lawsuit discussed above, for example, Iorwerth ap Ieuan ap Heilyn and his wife were originally ordered to pay 6d. for concord, which amount was later raised to 12d. when it was discovered that the wife had drawn blood from the plaintiff. In two instances, however, a wife who appeared as the sole plaintiff or defendant paid the fine herself. In one of these instances, from 1344, the married woman, Gwenllian wife of Iorwerth ap Gronwy, paid a fine of 6d. for concord with an unmarried woman, Elen ferch Gronwy.[37] In the other instance, from 1345, the married woman, Gladys wife of Madog Myn, was fined 40d. for withdrawing a lawsuit; no defendant was listed.[38] It may be worth speculating that in the first of these cases at least (and possibly the second as well) coverture was not enforced as the dispute was between two women. Two additional lawsuits also stand out as unusual. In the first of these lawsuits, from 1341, the fine was levied against Isabel wife of John le Plommer alone, although both she and her husband were named as co-defendants.[39] In the second, from 1344, both Einion Crach and his wife Gwenllian appeared as defendants, but only Einion was fined.[40] The fine recorded for Isabel alone cannot readily be explained, as no clear indication is given as to why Isabel was fined independently of her husband. The suit against Einion and Gwenllian is less surprising, in that the doctrine of coverture would dictate that Einion, as husband and head of the household, ought to pay the fine even if his wife had incurred it. That husbands and wives were, in the majority of lawsuits, listed as paying for concords or making other fines jointly, indicates a general, but nevertheless incomplete, application of coverture in interpersonal cases of assault.

In contrast, assault lawsuits involving unmarried women and men show litigants of each sex appearing on their own behalf, as plaintiffs and defendants, with lawsuits involving only men accounting for well over half of those cases examined here, from both 1340–52 and the 1390s. Typical of lawsuits involving single women, in 1342, Gwenhwyfar ferch Iorwerth appeared in court alone – without a male relative to represent her – accused of assault by Elias de Holond and his wife, who ultimately chose not to prosecute her.[41] In a suit from 1395, Gwenllian ferch Madog appeared alone as a plaintiff, and successfully prosecuted a suit against Maredudd ap Ieuan ap Dafydd ap Ieuan.[42] Hence, unmarried women, even when identified by reference to their fathers – that is, 'X ferch Y', or the English equivalent – seem to have initiated and responded to litigation with similar legal independence to men. Likewise, when found liable in suits of assault, unmarried women were recorded as responsible for paying their own fines or compensation. And the records of some of these suits list pledges for payment, who were not

37 TNA, SC 2/217/9 m.22.

38 TNA, SC 2/217/10 m.11.

39 TNA, SC 2/217/7 mm.29, 30.

40 TNA, SC 2/217/9 m.9d.

41 TNA, SC 2/217/8 m.2d.

42 TNA, SC 2/220/12 m.19d. In this suit, a jury decided that Maredudd had to pay damages of 15s.

normally related to the liable party. For example, one such suit from 1347 states that Tege ferch Iorwerth was involved in mutual assault, or *brwdyr gyfaddef*, with a man simply named Llywelyn and his wife Malkin, for which she was fined 6d., and her pledge for payment was an apparently unrelated man.[43] This suggests a relatively broad and consistent recognition of the legal autonomy of unmarried women in interpersonal suits of assault.

When taken all together, the majority of the evidence of interpersonal litigation concerning assault depicts wives as dependent on the legal presence of their husbands in these lawsuits, in accordance with the doctrine of coverture. Nevertheless, in a small minority of lawsuits married women do seem to have appeared on their own behalf, and to have paid their own fines, contrary to the strict application of coverture.

Criminal presentments for assault differed from interpersonal lawsuits in that they were not usually initiated by an individual entering a plea. Instead, a community jury – appointed either for a fixed period of time (six months, for the Great Courts of Ruthin and Dyffryn Clwyd) or to hold an inquest regarding a single incident (in the commotal courts and lesser borough court of Ruthin) – presented evidence of criminal assaults, normally those occurring since the previous sitting of the court, and determined the penalty to be levied against the person or persons responsible.[44] Such presentments commonly named the wronged party – who presumably had had some agency in bringing the incident to the jury's attention – and the defendant, who was fined. Either party could be a married woman, an unmarried woman, a man, or a married couple. In certain occasional circumstances, such as when a defendant in an interpersonal suit of assault denied all wrongdoing and requested a decision by inquest jury, a related criminal presentment for assault might later appear in the court rolls. Unlike in strictly interpersonal suits for assault, however, in criminal presentments for assault, married women – like unmarried women and men – were usually recorded in the court rolls as individually liable for fines. In both 1340–52 and the 1390s, the majority of presentments involving married women fined those women alone, without their husbands: 75 per cent and 65 per cent of presentments respectively (see Table 4.2).

Table 4.2 Criminal Presentments for Assault

	Men	Unmarried Women	Wives appearing with husbands	Wives appearing without husbands	Total Cases
1340–52	95	52	13	38	198
1390–99	131	32	11	20	194

Source: Dyffryn Clwyd Database; TNA, SC 2/217/6 to SC 2/220/10.

43 The suit involving Tege ferch Iorwerth is given in TNA, SC 2/217/12 m.10. Other examples of settlements can be found in TNA, SC 2/217/8 m.5, SC 2/220/9 m.78 and SC 2/220/7 m.16d.

44 Stevens, *Urban Assimilation*, pp. 60–71 (the lordship's hierarchy of courts), 117–38 (women in Ruthin's courts).

Criminal presentments for assault that named married women alone, as victims or defendants, emphasize the greater independent legal standing of women in criminal presentments, relative to interpersonal litigation. Examples from both 1340–52 and the 1390s serve to illustrate this point. For instance, in a presentment of 1341, Alice the wife of Adam le Muleward was fined for having committed 'hamesucken' (that is, home invasion) and assault on Emma the daughter of Alice de Newton, while Alice's husband Adam was not himself cited to pay any fine.[45] The fact that Alice alone was fined does not seem to have been related to her victim's sex because, in 1341, it was presented that Felicia wife of Richard de Pres assaulted William Lloyd and 'tore his hood' and Felicia too was fined for her actions independently of her husband.[46] Similarly, in a presentment from 1395, Tangwystl wife of Ieuan Goch Saer was presented and fined, without any recorded mention of her husband, for an assault on Iorwerth ap Ieuan ap Llywelyn, during which she 'took him violently by [the] neck'.[47] Criminal presentments for assault in which married women were the victims, and not the perpetrators, also adhere to this pattern. For example, in 1340, Hwfa ap William ap Ithel de Yale was presented, and later incarcerated, for having beaten Gladys wife of Gronwy ap Ithel in her home, with no mention of any wrong done directly or indirectly to Gladys's husband, for example, as householder or owner of the goods in his wife's keeping.[48] Presentments from the 1390s similarly fail to note the interests of husbands, as in 1399, when it was presented that Beatrice daughter of John Fairchild had beaten Joan the wife of John Bach, making no direct mention of Joan's husband.[49] In all of these presentments, married women were recorded as either assailants or victims independently, which, in any local 'court of record', would seem to suggest that coverture was not observed in these criminal presentments as it was in the majority of married women's interpersonal lawsuits.

The settlements in criminal presentments also differ slightly from those in interpersonal suits in that the settlements were determined by juries – either standing presentment juries or special inquest juries – which simply rendered a presentment of an individual's guilt (or occasionally, in the case of inquest juries, innocence) and set a fine, ordered an arrest, or both a fine and arrest. Some presentments were never acted upon because the defendants simply could not be found.[50] However, the presentments recorded in the court rolls demonstrate that married women could both expect to be awarded damages and to pay fines for criminal behaviour, independently of their husbands, reaffirming that coverture was not enforced in these presentments. For example, in 1341, it was presented that Efa wife of Carwed ap Moylagan had been beaten by Ma-

45 TNA, SC 2/217/6 m.24.

46 TNA, SC 2/217/6 m.28.

47 TNA, SC 2/220/8 m.17.

48 E.g. consider husbands' claims to property taken in cases of abduction, as discussed above, and potential damage to their goods during assaults, such as the 'torn hood' resulting from the assault on William Lloyd (TNA, SC 2/217/6 m.2).

49 TNA, SC 2/220/9 m.77d.

50 E.g. see TNA, SC 2/220/9 m.23d, from 13 May 1393, in which instance the bailiffs were unable to locate any of the ten people summoned to court.

dog Purkas, for which he was fined and she – without mention of her husband – was to receive 6d. in damages.[51] Another presentment, from 1348, indicates that defendant Alice wife of Dafydd ap Hopkin, named alone, was to pay compensation to Alice daughter of Richard Agas, whom she had beaten.[52] Similarly, a presentment from 1393 lists Angharad wife of Griffri le Werkmon as having assaulted and drawn blood from Gladys daughter of Ednyfed le Cook, for which Angharad, again cited alone, was to be fined.[53] These examples, in which married women either were awarded damages or were fined independently of their husbands, demonstrate that marriage, as observed in Dyffryn Clwyd, neither removed all of a married women's rights to compensation nor shielded her from all legal liability. Instead, in making criminal presentments and awarding compensation for assaults, the courts treated married women overwhelmingly as independent victims or perpetrators.

There is little in the court records of presentments for assault that indicates unmarried women and men were dealt with any differently, either from one another or from married women. However, it is noteworthy that assaults perpetrated by women, whether married or unmarried, differed from those perpetrated by men in so far as they tended not to involve weapons other than the women's hands or fists.[54] Whereas presentments involving men, which represent close to half the examples from 1340–52 and well over half those examined from the 1390s, often involved weapons, such as swords or staffs, or damage to physical property, including one case in which a man was said to have broken down a mill door.[55] It is perhaps worth speculating, in the absence of evidence of wives perpetrating such significant property damage or considerable physical injury, how great a fine the lordship's courts might have issued a married woman, or even an adolescent daughter, before invoking the doctrine of coverture to ensure a husband's or father's assistance in paying that fine. Given the eagerness of the husbands of at least some 'abducted' wives to assert claims to property in their wives' keeping, which was taken in conjunction with those abductions, the regular absence of husbands in the recording of criminal presentments and fines for assault, no doubt to be paid from the household purse, is conspicuous.

While the court rolls do not provide a clear indication why married women were treated as independent when they had been the perpetrators or victims of assaults, it is probable that the courts viewed married women as subject to direct legal oversight – beyond the competence of a husband – when they were involved in a crime. Civil or interpersonal suits might still fall within the realm of the husband, as the head of the family and legal representative of his wife, but criminal

51 TNA, SC 2/217/6 m.14.

52 TNA, SC 2/217/13 m.8.

53 TNA, SC 2/220/8 m.10d. Angharad did not make her subsequent appearance at court, and the order was given for bailiffs to arrest her. TNA, SC 2/220/9 m.23d.

54 Examples of presentments involving unmarried women include TNA, SC 2/217/8 m.9d, SC 2/217/10 m.3d., SC 2/220/9 m.37d, SC 2/220/9 m.38B and SC 2/220/9 m.77d.

55 See TNA, SC 2/217/7 m.30 for a presentment in which a man was said to have assaulted another man with his sword; SC 2/217/10 m.3 for a presentment that lists assault with a staff; and SC 2/220/7 m.16d for the presentment which lists the breaking of a mill door.

presentments clearly fell within the realm of the lord of Dyffryn Clwyd, whose peace had been violated during the assault. As a subject of that lord, the married female perpetrator had to answer for her actions directly to the lord's legal representatives. Similarly, as a subject of the lord, the married female victim could look to the lord's courts for the protection and compensation that neither she nor her husband could obtain on their own.

Defamation

Cases of defamation in the Dyffryn Clwyd court rolls, from across the period 1294 to 1422, demonstrate a mixture of interpersonal and criminal legal aspects. In the early part of the fourteenth century, defamation was most commonly presented at court as an interpersonal suit. By the early fifteenth century defamation appeared less frequently in the secular courts of Dyffryn Clwyd, and when records of defamation do appear they were prosecuted as criminal presentments. Sandy Bardsley has demonstrated that this transition from interpersonal lawsuits to criminal presentments in defamation litigation also occurred in English manorial courts after the Black Death, in parallel to which early fourteenth-century ecclesiastical courts increasingly prosecuted defamation, leading to its gradual removal from the secular courts.[56] Furthermore, Bardsley has argued that while men accounted for the majority of defendants in defamation cases in pre-plague manorial courts, women – both married and unmarried – were the most common defendants when defamation litigation shifted from secular to ecclesiastical courts. Bardsley states that this transition resulted from church authorities coming to view women's speech as increasingly problematic from the mid-fourteenth century onward.[57]

In the courts of Dyffryn Clwyd, litigation for defamation, whether involving married women, unmarried women or men, is most commonly denoted by one or more of the following terms: *vilificare* (to abuse), *litigare* (to quarrel), *dispersonare* (to insult), and *defamare* (to defame). In those instances where an individual repeatedly used abusive language against others, that individual appeared in the court rolls as a *litigator* (male, common quarreller), *litigatrix* (female, scold), *obiurgatrix* (female, shrew), or *garrulatrix* (female, gossip).[58] That three of these four common terms have feminine endings may be indicative of the perception that women's verbal abuse took more diverse forms than did men's. As the terms suggest, men who engaged in defamation were perceived to be quarrelsome. Women, however, were not only accused of quarrelsome behaviour, but also of rebuking or scolding others and simply talking too much. While the majority of litigation for defamation in Dyffryn Clwyd from the period 1294 to 1422 involved men as lone defendants or perpetrators, litigation involving married women likewise

56 See S. Bardsley, *Venomous Tongues: Speech and Gender in Late Medieval England* (Philadelphia, 2006), pp. 34–41, 77–82.

57 Bardsley, *Venomous Tongues*, pp. 78–80.

58 See Barrell, *Dyffryn Clwyd: A Manual*, p. 104. For a discussion of these terms in medieval English courts, see Bardsley, *Venomous Tongues*, pp. 82–9, 90–5.

most commonly resulted in wives being held personally responsible for their verbal violence; married women appeared alone in 79 per cent (23 of 29) of their defamation cases (see Table 4.3). Married women thus stand out as independently liable in defamation cases, as only their names appear next to the fines indicated in the court rolls, suggesting that coverture did not protect married women who engaged in verbally abusive behaviour.

Table 4.3 Interpersonal Suits and Criminal Presentments for Defamation

	Men	Unmarried Women	Wives appearing with husbands	Wives appearing without husbands	Total Cases
1294–1422	42	19	6	23	90

Source: Dyffryn Clwyd Database; TNA, SC 2/215/64 to SC 2/221/11.

Of the twenty-three instances of defamation that list married women as acting without their husbands, nine indicate that the women had committed verbal abuse but the women are not specifically labelled 'scolds' or 'shrews'. In the other fourteen instances, the women are called either 'scolds' or 'shrews'. The earliest example of defamation involving a married woman in the calendared Dyffryn Clwyd materials, from 1307, states that Elen wife of Richard *sutor*, and Thomas *pelliparius*, had each slandered (*maledixit*) the other.[59] Elen's husband was not himself fined in the case, and while both Elen and Thomas were fined and compelled to secure pledges for payment, Elen's husband was not her pledge. From the language used, it is unclear whether the litigation was begun as an interpersonal suit or as a criminal presentment, but it is significant that Elen's husband did not make an appearance on behalf of his wife. The first clear example of criminal presentment for defamation involving a married woman found in the calendared Dyffryn Clwyd materials was recorded in 1311, when Christine wife of John le Tailor was convicted, by inquisition, of having defamed Henry le Messager.[60] As in the case from 1307, the wife appeared without her husband. After 1341, the terms 'scold' and 'shrew' appeared increasingly in the court rolls, for example in the 1394 case of Efa wife of Gruffudd Fawr, who was described as 'a common shrew and disturber of the peace [*obiurgatrix et pacis perturbatrix*] within ... [Ruthin] town at times for a long time past'.[61] This entry suggests that Efa's behaviour had been considered problematic for some time. The court roll entry suggests that she appeared on her own in court, and she alone was fined, with neither her husband nor another pledge for payment recorded. Further presentments also suggest the fining of persistent defamers who were, it would seem, beyond the control of their husbands. An entry from 1419 describes Emery wife of Richard Dogyn as 'a common scold [*litigatrix*] and gossip [*garrilatrix*] between neighbours [who] will not

59 TNA, SC 2/215/69 m.4.

60 TNA, SC 2/215/71 m.13.

61 TNA, SC 2/220/8 m.14Bd.

be corrected'.[62] In 1420, Emery appeared in court again for abusing people of the town with 'insulting words'.[63] Emery's husband did not appear either time his wife was called to court and, in both incidences, Emery alone seems to have been fined. Hence, as was the case with criminal presentments for assault, married women were usually treated as independently liable for their defamatory speech and any consequent fines; coverture did not play a significant role.

Regarding settlements, the majority of both defamation lawsuits and presentments ended with a fine levied on the perpetrator of the verbal abuse. Many court roll entries also record damages awarded to the plaintiff or victim. While the records of most litigation involving married women name the wives alone, followed by fines for their own actions, many such court roll entries also list male pledges for those fines. However, only two entries name a woman's husband as either paying the fine or acting as a pledge. In 1352, Henry Libyn was named as the pledge for his wife, who was fined after being presented as a 'common scold'.[64] And, in 1359, Ieuan ap Ithel paid the fine for his wife Gladys, similarly presented as a 'common scold'.[65] In just one instance in which a married woman was a victim of verbal abuse, in 1314, was a woman's husband specified as the individual who should receive damages, rather than the woman herself, suggesting a strict application of coverture.[66] In this case, an inquest jury presented that Richard Pecok was to receive damages for the defamation made against his wife by Emma la Walker. These three instances, in which husbands either paid – or pledged to secure payment of – their wives' fines, or received damages for injuries sustained by their wives, were unusual among cases which came before the courts of Dyffryn Clwyd. Instead, married women were usually treated as individually liable in cases of defamation. For women like Emery wife of Richard Dogyn, who appeared in the courts twice in the space of a year and a half, and paid the fine herself each time, an inability or refusal to keep the peace verbally must have had a high personal cost.

Unmarried women and men were also liable for their verbal abuses. While more men than unmarried women were fined as perpetrators of verbal abuse (Table 4.3), only two court roll entries name men as 'common quarrellers'.[67] In contrast, while entries recording fines for unmarried women were fewer in num-

62 TNA, SC 2/221/11 m.12.

63 TNA, SC 2/221/11 m.15.

64 TNA, SC 2/218/3 m.2.

65 TNA, SC 2/218/7 m.30.

66 TNA, SC 2/215/73 m.27.

67 TNA, SC 2/217/10 m.29 and SC 2/218/7 mm.26 and 30. In one entry from 1294, the male defendant, Thomas ap Gilth Crist, was accused of having 'of his evil wish, abused the constable's beard' (TNA, SC 2/215/64 m.2). Native Welsh law clearly indicates that shaming a man's beard was a serious offence against that man's honour. See Jenkins, ed., *The Law of Hywel Dda*, p. 53. On the concept of insults to honour in medieval Welsh society, see N. Patterson, 'Honour and Shame in Medieval Welsh Society: A Study of the Role of Burlesque in the Welsh Laws', *Studia Celtica* 16/17 (1981–2), 73–103; T. M. Charles-Edwards, 'Honour and Status in Some Irish and Welsh Prose Tales', *Eriu* 29 (1978), 123–41; M. Staveley Chicon, 'Shame on Thy Beard! A Study of Insult, Redress and the Process of Law in Two "Owein" Romances', unpublished Ph.D. thesis, Centre for Medieval Studies, University of Toronto, 2002.

ber than those citing men, unmarried women – like their married counterparts – were more commonly labelled as 'scolds' or 'shrews', suggesting perceived persistent wrongdoing, in eleven of nineteen instances.[68] Settlements in defamation cases involving unmarried women and male defendants, like those of married women, resulted in fines, and sometimes damages to be paid by the guilty party alone – without formal familial assistance.[69]

Overall, the prosecution of defamation in Dyffryn Clwyd, whether involving married women, unmarried women or men as defendants, followed the same patterns identified by Bardsley. The number of defamation cases decreased over time, such that this study identified only seven cases (out of ninety, 1294–1422; Table 4.3) prosecuted in the fifty-two year period from 1370 to 1422, while a disproportionate six of these seven post-1370 cases name married women as defendants. This latter statistic, in particular, correlates with Bardsley's argument that women's speech was increasingly viewed as problematic by late medieval authorities, leading more women to be punished for that speech. Similarly, the evidence from Dyffryn Clwyd lists twenty-five 'scolds' or 'shrews' versus just two 'common quarrellers', with more than half of those 'scolds' or 'shrews' being married women. This again indicates that women were more likely to be penalized for outspoken or insulting language than were men. It is difficult to discern how tenants and local officials in the lordship reconciled the courts' increasing tendency to make presentments and levy fines against married women for defamation, independently of their husbands, with prevailing concepts of coverture and male domestic authority. The cases against the wives of Henry Libyn and Ieuan ap Ithel discussed above, in which the husbands pledged for and paid their fines respectively, suggest that not all men in the community were comfortable with this. As was the case with the presentment of wives for assault, it is probable that the lordship's courts viewed married women as subject to their direct legal oversight where those women had broken the lord's peace, due at least in part to the husband's inability to manage his wife's activities.

Conclusions

Several conclusions regarding the position of married women in the late medieval Welsh March emerge from the evidence presented in this essay. Perhaps the most important of these conclusions is that coverture was applied in Dyffryn Clwyd only in certain situations. Married women were typically regarded as personally

68 For example, TNA, SC 2/217/6 m.1.

69 In instances where an official of the lordship had been abused, the fines were higher. See TNA, SC 2/217/11 m.26d and SC 2/215/71 m.9d. In two entries, unmarried women paid their fines to avoid the 'judgment called le Thew'; SC 2/217/11 m.1 records both instances. 'Le Thew', also known as a ducking stool, was a common punishment for female 'scolds' in late medieval and early modern England. According to Bardsley, although towns were required to use ducking stools to punish those guilty of verbal abuse, many courts levied fines instead: Bardsley, *Venomous Tongues*, pp. 142–3.

liable in criminal presentments for assault and defamation in the lordship's courts. Contrary to coverture, they were expected to pay the fines and damages set by the court in these cases, and could be called upon to find pledges to ensure that they did so. In only a few cases of assault or defamation were married women represented by their husbands at court. For the purposes of criminal presentments, then, married women were treated much the same as their male and unmarried female counterparts. Coverture did not protect married women who had committed physical or verbal wrongs in late medieval Dyffryn Clwyd from responsibility for paying the courts' pecuniary judgments against them. But also coverture did not restrict the right of those married women who had been victims of physical or verbal crimes to bring such events to the attention of the courts, independently of their husbands.

In litigation for abduction and interpersonal suits for assault it was much more common for husbands to represent their wives at court. The records of such cases demonstrate that the concept of coverture was often applied in the courts of Dyffryn Clwyd when a crime had been committed against a married woman, but especially if it was to her husband's material loss. In litigation for abduction, even in those instances where married women exhibited agency by choosing to leave their husbands, a husband still had the right to go to court to seek the return of – or compensation for – goods that had been taken when his wife had been abducted. Records of abduction involving unmarried women and men do not tend to describe the property taken with the victim. Thus, although any abducted man or woman was viewed as a victim from the perspective of the court, spouse or victim's family, only the records of those cases involving married women focused closely on the issue of property. In interpersonal lawsuits for assault, where married women could be either plaintiffs or defendants, wives were most commonly accompanied at court by their husbands. In this type of litigation, husbands and wives were held jointly responsible for the behaviour, even if the wife had actually committed the assault, and husbands normally paid the fines and the damages to those individuals whom either they and their wives, or their wives alone, had injured.

The evidence from the courts of late medieval Dyffryn Clwyd indicates that coverture was observed in some legal cases but that the point at which coverture ceased to protect married women, or to restrict their independence, was when their actions were regarded as criminal. In criminal presentments, married women were normally recorded alone, both as victims awarded compensation and as perpetrators who were issued fines and orders to make compensation, for which they alone were ultimately responsible. This distinctive treatment seems to arise from the premise that married women involved in civil suits were still under the jurisdiction of their husbands, who both represented them as plaintiffs and were responsible for them as defendants in court. In criminal presentments, however, it was the lord's law that had been violated, and – as subjects of the lord – married women could expect both the lord's protection and to be held personally liable for the consequences of their actions. In this way, the lord's authority – as exercised by the courts – may have superseded that of the husband, as dictated by coverture, offering wives a certain type of legal equality with unmarried women and men in criminal presentments. Therefore, in the process of resolving complaints of assault and defamation, which were sometimes prosecuted as interpersonal litigation in the early fourteenth century but increasingly as presentments thereafter, the limits of coverture are highly visible.

5

PEASANT WOMEN, AGENCY AND STATUS IN MID-THIRTEENTH- TO LATE FOURTEENTH-CENTURY ENGLAND: SOME RECONSIDERATIONS

Miriam Müller

There are many things we will never know about Agnes de Schonedon. We will never be able to find out how old she was when she first started to appear in manorial court rolls in December 1276. We will also never know what she looked like, nor what her likes or dislikes were. However, we can reconstruct quite a lot of other information about her from the surviving court records of the coastal manor of Heacham, located on the Norfolk Wash, and under the lordship of the Priory and Convent of Lewes in Sussex. These records paint a picture of a woman with a determined nature and, at least to some degree, her own economic means. In December 1276 Agnes was involved in four separate lawsuits against four men: Stephen Berre, John de Redham, Radulf de Redham and John Elnoth. Agnes claimed that Stephen, John Elnoth and John de Redham were indebted to her, while a court inquiry had just proven that Radulf did owe Agnes a total of 11d.[1] In January 1277 it emerged that the debt Agnes claimed from John de Redham involved 22d. for ale purchased from Agnes.[2] Indeed, the records for the next few years reveal that Agnes was an occasional brewer. However, Agnes's brewing activities were not her only source of income, as is clear from the year of 1277, throughout which Agnes brought various suits of debt against a variety of individuals. In February she claimed 8d. from John Elnoth, in November she claimed an unknown debt from Roger Payn, and while one may suspect by now that Agnes was involved in money-lending, this was finally confirmed in December 1277, when Roger Payn was found guilty of 'unjustly withholding 7s.' from Agnes, which he owed her 'from a loan'.[3]

1 Heacham court rolls, held at the Norfolk Record Office, sourced from microfilm [hereafter NRO], DA1 MF/RO 206, December 1276. I am very grateful for all the helpful comments and criticisms from Chris Wickham, Jean Birrel, Richard Goddard and Chris Dyer, who kindly read and commented on earlier drafts of this chapter, and to the editors of this volume, who helped to hammer it into shape. I am also grateful to the participants of the Birmingham Medieval Seminar for their suggestions and thoughts on an earlier version of this chapter. Finally, a big thank you must go to my students: it was because of countless discussions with them about peasant women that I decided to write this.

2 NRO DA1 MF/RO 206, 25 January 1277.

3 NRO DA1 MF/RO 206, February 1277; NRO DA1 MF/RO 206, December 1277.

At first glance, Agnes might appear to be unusual, and, considering her prominent visibility in the court records in her own name, almost certainly not married. However, she was neither particularly unusual in her economic activities nor in her visibility in the manorial court rolls, and nor was Agnes single. Instead Agnes de Schonedon was married to Richard de Schonedon, even though much of the time she appeared in her own name, without the familiar adage of 'wife of'.

The case of Agnes highlights the potential problems and difficulties inherent in the interpretation of court roll data, on the one hand, as well as those of imposing the preconceptions and assumptions of the historian on the past, on the other hand. Considering our knowledge of the legal implications of coverture, whereby the husband was ultimately legally responsible for his wife's activities, economic and otherwise, it has been readily assumed that a woman appearing in court records in her own name was not married. This, however, assumes that the concept of coverture can not only be used to understand the position of women in medieval society, but also that women's position in peasant society can be extrapolated from common law and used to explain the private jurisdiction of the manor, as expressed in manorial custom and the manor court.

The historiography of peasant women, on the one hand, reflects the sometimes contradictory and complex evidence of the status of women and their ability to exercise agency in the manorial court. On the other hand, it provides a looking-glass reflecting the debates and concerns regarding the status of women in the societies of the historians writing about them. While there is a general agreement that women and men were far from equal in medieval society, much as there is inequality between the sexes today, explanations as to why such inequalities exist or existed depend partially upon one's conception of the past as well as one's conceptualization of the future. A Whiggish approach to history, which tends to see a general narrative of progress, will stress the important advances in gender equality over time. Others have reacted against such interpretations and pointed to greater freedoms among the women of the labouring class in medieval society when compared to women in industrial society.[4] Some have even seen a 'rough and ready equality' between men and women in peasant communities, which was not in evidence among the more noble echelons of society.[5] Barbara Hanawalt, in examining the economic basis on which peasant households were organized, argued for an understanding of them as economic units, which may have fostered a higher status for women in peasant society than for women among the nobility.[6] Thus, a number of writers have found important distinguishing features in the nature of female status, and hence women's ability to exercise agency rooted in class structures, which to some degree overrode, but certainly did not eliminate, concerns of gender.[7]

4 See further B. Hanawalt, 'Golden Ages for the History of Medieval English Women', *Women in Medieval History and Historiography*, ed. S. Mosher Stuart (Philadelphia, 1987), pp. 1–24.

5 See E. Power, 'The Position of Women', *The Legacy of the Middle Ages*, ed. C. G. Crump and E. F. Jacob (Oxford, 1926), p. 410.

6 B. A. Hanawalt, *The Ties that Bound: Peasant Families in Medieval England* (Oxford, 1986), esp. pp. 107–23.

7 E.g. R. H. Hilton, 'Women in the Village', *The English Peasantry in the Later Middle Ages*, ed. R.

The concept of greater equality among the labouring class has been criticized by some historians, such as Judith Bennett, who has attacked it as an 'appealing image of a golden age', the proponents of which look back longingly to a pre-industrial world, before the relentless advance of capitalism which, along with its various other associated evils, could also be blamed for sexual inequality.[8] Instead, Bennett has argued that the status of women in medieval villages was severely restricted in ways not too dissimilar to those affecting rich women.[9] In reacting against what she regards as various hues of the golden age theory, Bennett has also stressed, more recently, the continuities evident in the oppression of women and their inequality in relation to men.[10]

Despite such very valid criticisms of the concept of a golden age of working women in pre-industrial society, it has proven difficult to discard class completely. No matter how unequal the sexes may have been, an aristocratic woman would never have been perceived as subordinate to a peasant man.[11] Even those who have argued for a conceptualization of women as a separate estate in medieval society, like Shulamith Shahar, still acknowledge that socio-economic status was important in the understanding and categorization of women.[12]

Aside from considerations of class, most commentators have argued that the status of women in medieval peasant communities was also greatly, if not crucially, dependent upon their marital status.[13] While it is generally accepted that widows and other single women had a great deal of autonomy in peasant communities, upon marriage or re-marriage such freedoms vanished, as the woman's independence and indeed her ability to act as an autonomous being in her own right largely came to an end due to her legal identity being subsumed under that of her husband.[14] Shahar went so far as to argue that a married woman 'partially reverted to the status of minor with restricted legal rights'.[15]

H. Hilton (Oxford, 1975), esp. pp. 96–105; P. J. P. Goldberg, *Medieval England: A Social History, 1250–1550* (London, 2004), p. 3.

8 J. M. Bennett, *Women in the Medieval English Countryside* (Oxford, 1987), pp. 4–5. For a critique of the prevailing acceptance of the deterioration in female status and the restrictions early capitalism placed on women's work, see C. Middleton, 'Women's Labour and the Transition to Pre-industrial Capitalism', *Women and Work in Pre-Industrial England*, ed. L. Charles and L. Duffin (London, 1985), pp. 181–206.

9 Bennett, *Women in the Medieval English Countryside*, p. 6.

10 J. M. Bennett, *History Matters: Patriarchy and the Challenge of Feminism* (Philadelphia, 2006), pp. 84–6. On this theme see also M. F. Stevens, 'London Women, the Courts and the "Golden Age": A Quantitative Analysis of Female Litigants in the Fourteenth and Fifteenth Centuries', *London Journal* 37 (2012), 67–88. I am very grateful to Matthew Stevens for sharing this article with me prior to publication.

11 E.g. see K. M. Phillips, *Medieval Maidens: Young Women and Gender in England, 1270–1540* (Manchester, 2003), p. 12; Goldberg, *Medieval England*, p. 3.

12 S. Shahar, *The Fourth Estate: A History of Women in the Middle Ages*, rev. edn (London, 1996), p. 2.

13 Bennett, *Women in the Medieval English Countryside*, p. 28; R. M. Smith, 'Women's Property Rights under Customary Law: Some Developments in the Thirteenth and Fourteenth Centuries', *Transactions of the Royal Historical Society*, 5th series, 36 (1986), 180.

14 E.g. see P. Skinner, 'Gender and Poverty in the Medieval Community', *Medieval Women in their Communities*, ed. D. Watt (Cardiff, 1997), p. 204.

15 Shahar, *The Fourth Estate*, p. 92.

The concept generally used to explain this legal phenomenon, which is also invariably blamed for an alleged low visibility of women in various legal records, including the records of the manorial court, is that of coverture. Under medieval common law, married women were theoretically disadvantaged as they were 'deprived of a separate legal capacity' from their husbands.[16] The married woman was not able to enter contracts or loan money, as all her chattels ultimately belonged to her husband, with whom she became, effectively, one person under his guardianship.[17] And yet, the concept of coverture itself is beset with problems. The married woman retained certain rights over her dower and was supposed to give her consent in land transfers. And where does it leave individuals like the aforementioned Agnes? It seems unsatisfactory to explain such individuals away as 'unusual' or even 'aberrations' from the norm.[18] Therefore, this essay seeks to revisit the question of the status and agency of women in the medieval English village, with three main aims in mind. First, it aims to position female status and agency within the contexts of the feudal framework and class. Second, it seeks to re-examine the usefulness of the concept of coverture to explain female subordination in the medieval village. And third, it seeks to contextualize these findings within a comparative framework, taking account of local variations.

The problems associated with the concept of coverture originate partly from the understandable desire of the historian to categorize and compartmentalize human behaviour and the laws applying to such various human interactions. One of the key questions here concerns the applicability of the legal concept, namely to what extent common law can be applied in the context of the private jurisdiction of the manor and manorial custom. To what extent did lordship itself play a formative role in determining female status or circumscribing female agency? How did the two interrelate, if at all? Such considerations have potential wide-ranging consequences. Has our assumption of the applicability of coverture blinded us to the real active agency of married women in village society by making us see single women where there were in fact married women?

This essay therefore also strives to move away from assertions of rough and ready equality between male and female villagers, legal coverture or indeed Whiggish notions of progress. Instead it is an attempt to position an analysis of female status within the specifics of feudal modes of production more broadly, while calling for an examination of gender and the status of women in medieval rural society in relation to particular local or regional factors.

16 A. Musson, *Medieval Law in Context: The Growth of Legal Consciousness from Magna Carta to the Peasants' Revolt* (Manchester, 2001), p. 87

17 Bennett, *Women in the Medieval English Countryside*, p. 28; C. Briggs, 'Empowered or Marginalised? Rural Women and Credit in Later Thirteenth and Fourteenth Century England', *Continuity and Change* 19 (2004), 21; F. Pollock and F. W. Maitland, *The History of English Law Before the Time of Edward I* (Cambridge, 1898), p. 485.

18 E.g. see Bennett's comments regarding Hilton's discovery of female officers in the manorial court: Bennett, *Women in the Medieval English Countryside*, p. 5.

Problematizing the Public/Private Dichotomy: Lordship, Tenure and Married Women

The concept of the public/private dichotomy has been used to explain and analyse sexual inequalities both today and in past societies. A now classic text, exploring the issues of public and private spheres, is Rosaldo and Lamphere's *Women, Culture and Society* (1974).[19] In this collection of anthropological essays the authors explored the nature of gendered roles relating to the public and private spheres, and the nature of women and men as actors within their designated spheres. These roles were reflected in a division of labour between men and women, whereby women were predominantly associated with caring and domestic roles and men with political and public roles. The division between the public and private, it was argued, itself contributes to and re-enforces gender inequality. If superimposed upon medieval peasant society it appears that peasant women were trapped in gendered divisions between the public and private, a trap which was, especially for married women, re-enforced by the common law of coverture, whereby married women were denied autonomy.[20]

It has often been pointed out that the manorial court, the most public, political and, from the lord's point of view, economic hub of village life, was in the public sphere and very much a male domain.[21] The jurors were exclusively male, and local officialdom was usually exclusively in male hands. Women were therefore, if we take our records at face value, barred from occupying positions of local importance. They could not be reeves, haywards or any other manorial official who did a great deal of the direct governing of local village affairs as the intermediaries between the demands of lordship and the peasant community.

The tithing system was also in male hands. This was the official system of local policing whereby all young men in the village were sworn into a tithing upon reaching the age of twelve. It was the duty of the tithing to report and, if necessary, to bring to court offenders against local custom and law. This encompassed a wide range of issues, stretching from seigniorial customs relating to the running of the manor, the breaking of boundaries, or destruction (wilful or otherwise) of the lord's property, to offences concerning breaches of the peace, such as bloodshed, violent assault and theft.

Such official structures, maintained by the private jurisdiction of the manor, do not tell us the whole story though. We know that the local homage, that is the

19 M. Rosaldo and L. Lamphere, eds, *Woman, Culture and Society* (Stanford, 1974).

20 This assumption has also been supported by, for example, Hanawalt's studies based on coroners' rolls. She found that women, and the girls copying them, died more frequently around domestic environments, while men tended to die in the fields, that is, in the public sphere. B. Hanawalt, 'Childrearing among the Lower Classes of Late Medieval England', *Journal of Interdisciplinary History* 8 (1977), 1–22. See also her *The Ties that Bound*, p. 113. In a more recent analysis of coroners' rolls, P. J. P. Goldberg did not find such gendered associations with the locations of the deaths of children: see his 'Childhood and Gender in Later Medieval England', *Viator* 39 (2008), 257.

21 E.g. see Hilton, 'Women in the Village', p. 105; Bennett, *Women in the Medieval English Countryside*, pp. 5–6.

tenants bound to attend the court of a manor, usually with notions of custom and law quite separate from lord and state, imprinted their own agenda on local court proceedings.[22] Similarly, court rolls occasionally allow one to glimpse the local legal pathways which women, whether married or not, inhabited with full responsibility. While women were not sworn into tithings, they certainly had a role to play in the tithing system. This was because it was also the responsibility of women to report any offences to the tithing, through, for example, the raising of the hue and cry, a formal communal self-policing mechanism in which women played a full part.[23] Courts also occasionally ordered inquiries to be conducted to resolve disputes, either between tenants or between the lord and tenants. These were often initiated by one of the affected parties. One may assume that women, as well as men, were questioned regarding the rights and wrongs of particular matters, since women were also able to call for inquiries. Those constituting the official inquiry were always sworn men, but they came to their conclusions by interviewing and questioning villagers and neighbours of the opposing parties, listening to gossip and hearsay, as well as looking for legal precedents, lodged in collective or individual village memories or noted down in previous court rolls.

In considering the visibility of women in court records, it is also important to remember who manorial court records were written for and what they represented. While local peasants actively used the courts to their own ends in a variety of ways, first and foremost the courts were there for the benefit of the lord. For every case of debt, trespass and assault which appeared in the manor court, the lord received amercements. And seigniorial incomes from manorial court proceedings, alongside other incomes from the tenantry, could represent a substantial proportion of the overall income from individual manors. At the Glastonbury manor of Badbury in Wiltshire, according to manorial accounts between 1301 and 1334, seigniorial income from the tenantry ranged from 35 per cent of all sources of income from the manor in 1314–15 to as much as 78 per cent in 1301–2. At the Ely manor of Brandon in Suffolk, fourteenth-century accounts reveal lower, but still substantial, incomes from the peasantry, ranging from 25 per cent to 36 per cent of the total seigniorial incomes from the manor's various assets.[24]

The visibility of women in the court records is partly dependent on what type of manorial court is being considered, partly on their position *vis-à-vis* lordship and partly on other locally specific factors. These factors could include the style of individual lordship and patterns of local customs, or regional peculiarities, which

22 E.g. see P. R. Schofield, 'Peasants and the Manor Court: Gossip and Litigation in a Suffolk Village at the Close of the Thirteenth Century', *Past and Present* 159 (1989), 3–42; L. Bonfield, 'The Nature of Customary Law in the Manor Courts of Medieval England', *Comparative Studies in Society and History* 31 (1989), esp. 528–9.

23 M. Müller, 'Social Control and the Hue and Cry in Two Fourteenth-Century Villages', *Journal of Medieval History* 31 (2005), 29–53. Cf. S. Bardsley, *Venomous Tongues: Speech and Gender in Late Medieval England* (Philadelphia, 2006), esp. pp. 69–89.

24 M. Müller, 'Peasant Mentalities and Cultures in Two Contrasting Communities in the Fourteenth Century; Brandon in Suffolk and Badbury in Wiltshire', unpublished Ph.D. thesis, University of Birmingham, 2001, pp. 44, 58.

were also influenced by the local peasantry.[25] Married women who had committed an offence against other tenants were usually held responsible for that offence in their own right in manorial courts. However, cases which impinged directly on the rights of the lord, such as labour services, where the lord tended to hold the male head of the household responsible for the failings of his co-householders, tend to hide women. This is quite logical, as it was the legal tenant who had to satisfy the lord for any services and customs demanded from the household occupying a peasant holding.

For this reason, female agency may be found more frequently in leet courts rather than halimot courts in manors where such clear delineations exist.[26] In leet courts female agency can be quite prominent. This is because the legal remit of leet courts was considerably wider than that of the typical halimot court. At leet courts cases including assaults, thefts, break-ins and brawls were presented. In leet courts, or courts including leet-type business, women emerge as peacekeepers among brawling men, and they can be found suing other women and men for incidents such as thefts, various types of trespasses, assaults and defamation. The halimot courts, less concerned with the fractious behaviour of the local peasantry, reflected the more administrative manorial business concerning landholding and seigniorial demands. Therefore, in the space of the halimot court, female visibility and, to some degree, agency were circumscribed due to tenurial structures which ensured that men were more likely than women to be tenants, especially where the dominant mode of inheritance was male primogeniture.[27] To see the manorial court, the public forum of local regulation and the enforcement of custom and seigniorial demands, as part of a public/male sphere is therefore difficult.

The application of analytical frameworks like the public/private dichotomy to medieval society assumes that the public and private spheres carried the same or very similar connotations then, as those in modern or capitalist society do now. This involves, rather crucially, the assumption that the public sphere, meaning the political, cultural and economically productive sphere, is located outside of the domestic sphere, and is one from which women were mainly disassociated, hence cementing gendered inequalities. This form of presentism is, however, very problematic.

25 It is sometimes very difficult, or indeed impossible, to discern to what degree local variations depended either upon the local peasantry or upon lordship. More research in this area is clearly needed.

26 Many manors did not seem to distinguish between different types of court, and occasionally headings on manorial court rolls will simply proclaim that a 'court' was held, rather than which type of court it was.

27 In the nature of inheritance practices and gender hierarchies within peasant holdings it has been argued that patriarchal relationships among the peasantry clearly overlapped with factors of lordship. See C. Middleton, 'Peasants, Patriarchy, and the Feudal Mode of Production in England: A Marxist Appraisal: I, Property and Patriarchal Relations within the Peasantry', *Sociological Review* 29 (1981), 105–33. It remains to be seen whether women were more prominent in manorial court proceedings where freehold alongside partible inheritance ensured that sisters, in the absence of sons, inherited equally; or in manors where liberal seigniorial policies permitted a land market to take place which allowed parents to endow non-inheriting daughters with some land through *inter-vivos* transfers.

The nature of pre-capitalist peasant production was centred around the household. Crucially different from capitalist society in which the domestic is primarily associated with the reproduction of the workforce, that is, bringing up the next generation of workers, in feudal villages the household was not merely the core of reproduction, but also represented the cornerstone of the lord–tenant relationship through which lords collected rents and services.[28] This relationship made the peasant household the centre of productivity as far as the lord, the peasant family and the local community were concerned.

This has consequences for our analysis of the position of peasant women, especially married women, because the status of women was related both to the household's productive relationship to lordship and to production (and reproduction) within the household itself. Because of the overlap between domestic and non-domestic production of a surplus, which was then forcibly extracted by lords, the concept of a dichotomized public-private sphere reflected in labour has only limited, if any, applicability.[29] In other words, due to the specific relations of production in feudal society, there was no clear division between the public and private spheres in the village, even if there were certain gendered associations attached to individual spaces such as fields or houses.[30]

The people who were answerable to the lord for rendering various customary dues (for example, payments of rents in cash or kind), servile dues (such as involuntary labour services), and carrying services, were almost always the tenants of holdings, vetted and approved by the lord. As such, peasant households were answerable to the lord via the head of the household, the tenant, who was usually, but not always, a man. This subordinated many women to their male head of household. However, in a similar way, the system also subordinated all other males residing in that household, such as sons, elderly retired relatives or servants, to the head of that household. Such subordinated men and women in a household similarly did not wield the authority of a tenant. The important relationship between the household and the lord was therefore that between the lord and the tenant. Gender did play a role, particularly in the structures of inheritance customs which discriminated against women, but gender was not the only, and perhaps not even the main, factor. Therefore, in this particular relationship, it is not as men that communities of political influence were primarily forged, but as heads of households and tenants.

The nature of peasant production ensured that female labour, alongside male labour, was crucial both to the subsistence, and therefore the survival, of the household itself, and to the fulfilment of the various rent obligations to the lord.[31]

28 See also C. Middleton, 'The Sexual Division of Labour in Feudal England', *New Left Review* 113–14 (1979), 1–9; and C. Middleton, 'Peasants, Patriarchy', esp. pp. 108–10.

29 Surplus, or surplus labour, is here understood in the Marxist sense, as what is forcibly extracted from the peasant holding by the lord. K. Marx, *Capital*, vol. 3 (London, 1981), esp. pp. 925–7. See also Middleton, 'The Sexual Division', pp. 2, 4–5.

30 For gendered spaces see B. Hanawalt, 'Childrearing among the Lower Classes of Late Medieval England', *Journal of Interdisciplinary History* 8 (1977), 1–22.

31 Middleton, 'Peasants, Patriarchy', pp. 108–9.

This was the case both in free and unfree holdings, although in unfree holdings more was at stake for the lord as the rents due were higher and of much greater variety than those which fell on free holdings.

Some manorial customs implicitly recognized the integral role of female labour to the peasant holding. In the late thirteenth-century customs of the Glastonbury manors of Longbridge and Monkton Deverill, for example, virgaters (tenants holding about forty acres of land) had to render among other rents a 'churchscot' to their lord. Three measures of this had to be brought to the hall of the lord, alternating between wheat one year and rye the next. This was to be rendered only if the tenant had 'a wife, [but] if he has none' he was expected to pay only 'half the churchscot'.[32] Other tenants, like Alvred the Miller, had to provide four chickens 'and if he has no wife he gives two chickens like his ancestors'. The same principle held for women, in reverse. Hodeherne de la Srodd was told that 'if she has a husband' she had to render four chickens, and if she had none, only two.[33] Marriage was therefore recognized as a partnership which elevated the economic value of a peasant holding to which female labour was integral.

Occasionally individual cases in manorial court rolls also indicate an understanding of the economic assets of the peasant holding to have belonged to both husband and wife. At the Norfolk manor of Heacham in 1280 the court ordered the distraint of half a quarter of barley from Ranulf Taliser and his wife in order to put them under pressure to appear before the next court, 'until they have come to answer Reginald Baker' in his suit against them.[34]

In assessing the ability of married women to exercise active agency, including resisting the demands of lordship, and to consider their status in the medieval village, it is important to appreciate the integral role female labour played on the peasant holding and to the lord's income. The nature of female labour should be examined in order to assess the viability of a conceptualization of separate, gendered spheres, as an explanatory tool for female oppression. In order for the concept to be usefully applied it requires a degree of specialization of labour along gendered lines, alongside, as Middleton pointed out, a 'distinction between domestic and non-domestic labour'.[35]

Ultimately, lords cared little about the sex of the tenant responsible for rendering various dues and services, as long as they were duly delivered to a satisfactory standard. Manorial customs from the later thirteenth century onwards go to great lengths in detailing the nature of labour services and rents which could be demanded of tenants for particular holdings. These typically make it quite clear that there was no division of labour according to sex. At the manor of Laughton in Sussex in 1292, for example, Alice atte Hamme held a medium-sized holding containing a messuage, fourteen acres of land and some meadow. She was expected to

32 C. J. Elton, ed., *Rentalia et Customaria Michaelis de Ambresbury, 1235–1252 et Rogeri de Ford, 1252–1261*, Somerset Record Society, vol. 5 (1891), p. 135.

33 Elton, ed., *Rentalia et Customaria*, pp. 138, 142.

34 NRO DA2 MF/RO 206, November 1280.

35 Middleton, 'The Sexual Division', p. 2.

'draw out dung with her cart', as well as to 'harrow with her horse for three days'. She was also expected to perform hoeing service for one day, together with one man, as well as to cart wood to the lord's hall. She could also be called on to carry hay and reap during the harvest for three days with one man, and to be fed by the lord for this service.[36] Four male tenants were recorded alongside her, holding land under identical conditions.

At the manor of Taunton, Hawis de Staplegrove held half a virgate of land in the later thirteenth century, and, alongside an annual cash rent of 5s., she was expected to perform various services including the heavy work of ploughing, namely 'one acre in winter and one acre in Lent'. She was also expected to sow, thresh and harrow those same acres. Additionally, if she was in possession of a full plough team, she was expected to 'plough for two days in Lent as ploughing boonwork from morning until evening'. She was also called upon to harrow, to mow the meadow, to make hay, to 'reap and carry the corn', and to be a 'worker for one day every week of the year, except three at Christmas, Easter and Pentecost'.[37]

Customs never seem to have made allowances in the works demanded on the basis of sex, but they did make occasional allowances if the tenant was not married, again recognizing the economic value of peasant marriage. At the manor of Brandon in Suffolk a survey dating from 1251 set down that tenants described as 'toft tenants' could be called upon to fulfil a long list of work obligations, which included the obligation to carry their lord, the bishop, if required, or the Seneschal if he visited the manor. Works included digging ditches, reaping, binding and stacking rye and wheat, and finding additional men to help out at the harvest boons. However, if the tenant was an unmarried widow, she only had to perform half the number of works demanded.[38]

It is true that customs only tell us about works and dues which could theoretically be demanded, and not all of these had to be rendered by each tenant every year. And it is feasible to assume that some tenants, both men and women, actually hired others to perform some of these works. However, since female tenants were theoretically as liable to render such works as men, it would be wrong to assume that such customs were in practice never demanded of women, or that women never performed them, and we have no evidence to the contrary. This has led some historians to comment that divisions of labour, where they did exist, were neither very advanced nor consistent, as it has been frequently observed that women appear to have participated in all manner of agricultural tasks, even if there is increasing evidence that women were paid less than men where they participated in waged labour.[39] However, some have still found it difficult to be-

36 A. E. Wilson, ed., *Custumals of the Manors of Laughton, Willingdon and Goring*, Sussex Record Society, vol. 60 (1961), p. 11.

37 T. J. Hunt, ed., *The Medieval Customs of the Manors of Taunton and Bradford on Tone*, Somerset Record Society, vol. 66 (1962), pp. 65–6.

38 MS 485/489 Gonville & Caius fols 354–5.

39 Middleton, 'The Sexual Division', esp. pp. 4–5; Hilton, 'Women in the Village', p. 102; S. V. Smith, 'Women and Power in the Late Medieval Village: A Reconsideration', *Women's History Review* 16

lieve that women were actually capable of doing all these tasks. It has therefore occasionally been asserted that it is doubtful that women were actually asked to perform such backbreaking tasks as ploughing.[40]

Most recently, in attempting to explain the lower wages women received for the same work as men, it has been argued that differences in pay may have been due to the lower productivity of female as against male labour.[41] Such lower productivity could be explained by, so Hatcher contends, greater strength and physical stature which 'are attributes possessed in greater abundance by men'.[42] Anthropological research indicates, however, that the amount of difference between the physiques of men and women is at least in part culturally determined.[43] It is therefore problematic to extrapolate either divisions of labour or other gendered patterns of work from our own gendered culture, which, in discouraging physical activity in girls, while encouraging it in boys, may well contribute to women being generally physically weaker than men. It is certainly doubtful that the otherwise rather canny abbot of Glastonbury, with a shrewd eye on profit, would have made the mistake of hiring an unprofitable or slow worker when he hired Alienor la Gauntes to be one of his three full-time 'ploughmen' in the manor of Longbridge Deverill in 1328.[44]

Women's economic activities in town and countryside were wide-ranging and typically encompassed various by-industries, such as brewing, baking or making malt.[45] Legislation recognized the breadth and the flexibility of female economic activities. The Statute of Labourers of 1351 forbade individuals from practising more than one craft, in order to help lock workers into individual contracts, in an attempt to stem the tide of socio-economic change resulting from the drastically changed land–labour ratio after the Black Death. However, an explicit exception was made for women. In 1363 it was announced that it was the 'intent of the king and his council', while bearing in mind the decree that workers were to hold to merely 'one mystery', 'that women, that is to say, brewers, bakers, carders, spinners and workers as well of wool, as of Linen cloth, and of Silk, brawdsters and breakers

(2007), esp. 312–13. For female wages see S. Bardsley, 'Women's Work Reconsidered: Gender and Wage Differentiation in Late Medieval England', *Past and Present* 165 (1999), 3–29; Bennett, *History Matters*, pp. 82–3.

40 See, e.g., E. Power, *Medieval Women* (Cambridge, 1975), p. 71.

41 J. Hatcher, 'Debate: Women's Work Reconsidered: Gender and Wage Differentiation in Late Medieval England', *Past and Present* 173 (2001), 193. He was replying to the article by Bardsley, 'Women's Work Reconsidered'.

42 Hatcher, 'Debate', p. 193.

43 A. Oakley, *Sex, Gender and Society* (London, 1972), pp. 27–8.

44 Glastonbury Abbey Document at Longleat, hereafter GADL MS 8085 Skin no. 3v.

45 This has been commented on quite frequently: see Power, *Medieval Women*, pp. 61–71; Hilton, 'Women in the Village', pp. 102–5; H. Graham, '"A Woman's Work ...": Labour and Gender in the Late Medieval Countryside', *Woman is a Worthy Wight: Women in English Society c. 1200–1500*, ed. P. J. P. Goldberg (Stroud, 1992), pp. 136–44; P. J. P. Goldberg, ed., *Women in England c. 1275–1525* (Manchester, 1995), pp. 24–5; R. Goddard, 'Female Apprenticeship in the West Midlands in the Later Middle Ages', *Midlands History* 27 (2002), esp. 168–70; M. K. McIntosh, *Working Women in English Society, 1300–1620* (Cambridge, 2005) – her discussions are extensive: see esp. Parts II and III.

of wool, and all other that do use and work all handy works, may freely use and work as they have done before without any impeachment, or being restrained by the Ordinance.'[46]

Women still fell afoul of the Statute of Labourers, however, and while there is still lively debate regarding the remuneration of women *vis-à-vis* men, women did try to gain from the changed economic climate after the first arrival of the Black Death.[47] Women can be found engaged in all sorts of works, some single, some married and some alongside their husbands. The Assize Rolls of Wiltshire dealing with offenders against the Statute of Labourers in 1349 often recorded married female offenders alongside their husbands. So, for example: 'Walter Cook of Thornhull (fine 2s.) and Agnes his wife, Thomas Averil of the same (fine 12d.) and Alice his wife, and John London of the same (fine 12d.) and Agnes his wife took excessively from divers men for reaping corn in the autumn last past.'[48]

Such insights into female engagement in physical labour can be more difficult to locate in manor court records. As lords only held the head of the household responsible for failings which impinged on his customary rights, including the performance of labour services, married women – as well as any other dependants in the household – under such circumstances are hidden from the view of the historian. In such cases it was often the husband who was held responsible for the failure to perform certain duties pertaining to the customary holding. However, this absence of their names from the records should not be taken to imply that their labour was not expected to be performed. Also, it does not make the agency of these women less important to the lord, or indeed her household; but it makes their agency wholly or partly invisible to us. This is an important distinction to make.

Women who were tenants in their own right were of course held responsible for failures to perform certain services. For example, Agnes Qualm of Walsham le Willows was, in 1390, accused of having withheld one and a half day's work from the lord at harvest time.[49] Rarely, however, do cases presented in the manorial court indicate that wives could at least sometimes be expected to work on the lord's lands as part of a holding's labour obligations. In 1353, John Spilman of Walsham le Willows was amerced 3d. 'because he withheld Christina Springold from reaping service in the autumn.' Despite their separate surnames, Christina and John were married. In the same court it had been presented previously that Christina had given birth to an illegitimate child by John, for which she had had to pay a childwyte of 32d. to the lord. The lord had further ordered John 'not to cohabit with Christina in the future, under penalty of 40s.'. Instead, the couple had decided to get married and Christina had paid a hefty marriage licence of 10s.[50]

46 *Statutes of the Realm*, 12 vols (London, 1810–28), vol. 1, Henry III to Edward III 1235–1377, pp. 379–80.

47 On women and the labour legislation see also J. M. Bennett, 'Compulsory Service in Late Medieval England', *Past and Present* 209 (2010), 7–51.

48 E. M. Thompson, 'Offenders against the Statute of Labourers in Wiltshire A.D. 1349', *The Wiltshire Archaeological and Natural History Magazine* 33 (1903–4), 407.

49 R. Lock, ed., *The Court Rolls of Walsham le Willows, 1351–1399* (2002), p. 170.

50 Ibid., p. 40.

The fact that lords at least sometimes expected the wives of their male tenants to perform labour services further indicates that the fields of the manorial community were not purely a male preserve. Women also occasionally refused to perform labour services: in Walsham le Willows, in 1353, five out of ten individuals who were presented for labour refusals were women. Some women, like Alice Galyon and Christina Lene, had been employed by the lord to work during the harvest for cash wages but refused to do so, with Alice at least having gone to 'reap for other men' instead, thus breaking the law as set out in the Statute of Labourers.[51]

If certain duties only fell on the head of the household, such as the annual payments of cash rents, a wife's ability to participate in the resistance to rendering those duties was limited to background support, away from the direct gaze of the lord and, at least in some cases, the manorial court. Therefore, while female members of the household might have actively participated, or colluded with others, in the withholding of rents, services or certain dues, it is often only the husband's agency which becomes visible to us through the court, which need not imply an absence of female agency.

Female Peasants in their Communities: Agency, the Manor Court and Locality

Under the private jurisdiction of manorial custom, which encompassed jurisdictional parameters over free as well as unfree individuals, common law rules often appear to have fallen by the wayside, and coverture – as a legal concept to explain or categorize the position of married women – becomes far less useful. A close, comparative investigation of the activities of peasant women in manorial communities highlights some important local differences which can only be explained by different styles of lordship and regional socio-economic factors.

The manor of Longbridge Deverill in Wiltshire was held by the abbots of Glastonbury. The predominant tenure on the numerous Glastonbury manors was customary tenure, which was servile in nature. In the records of a single hundred court held at Longbridge Deverill in 1301 a total of fifty-six cases are recorded, reflecting various offences committed by individual tenants. In these cases, eleven women are mentioned as having been involved in offences in one way or another, representing nearly 20 per cent of the total number of presented cases.[52] While the representation of women in these courts is thus less than that of men, it is sizeable enough for us to question the idea of the relative absence of women from such courts. At a halimot court of the same manor in 1301 the representation of women in court business is lower: of sixty-one presented cases only seven concerned a woman, representing just over 11 per cent of all cases.[53] At the neighbouring Glastonbury manor of Monkton Deverill a similar picture emerges when, in a Halimot court in 1301, only about 4 per cent of those involved in court proceedings were

51 Ibid., pp. 40–1.

52 GADL MS 9629, no. 5.

53 GADL MS 9629, no. 5v.

female.[54] By contrast, in a typical Monkton Deverill hundred-type court held in 1328, female involvement in the court was again higher, at 19 per cent, due to the wider range of jurisdictional issues encompassed by the court.[55]

Differences were not only due to the type of business recorded in the courts. If we compare the relatively low direct visibility of women at such typical Glastonbury manor courts to female participation in the perhaps less conservative manor of Heacham in Norfolk, some interesting differences emerge. Here, in a typical court recorded in January 1278, a total of 38 per cent of presented cases involved women, including the purchase of marriage licences, a case of debt, cases of trespass, a case of broken contract, sales of land and a dispute over dower land.[56] In the previous January, in 1277, the participation of women in the manor court had been even higher, at 40 per cent, while in a court held on 16 March 1280 female participation was lower, but still substantial, at 33 per cent.[57] Heacham's very detailed Leet court records added the names of brewers and bakers, which were predominantly female, but as the boundary beaters were also recorded, who were all men, female involvement in these courts is comparable to the 'other' courts. In a Leet court held in September 1277, for example, 116 men are recorded, including fifty-one boundary beaters and five other officials, alongside forty-six women representing only 28 per cent of the total number of individuals appearing in this court.[58] If, however, the essentially administrative lists of court officials and boundary beaters are taken out of the total, then female involvement in the remaining court affairs stands again at a very high level of 43 per cent of the total.

A key problem when examining manorial court roll evidence is the correct identification of female status. Following the logic of coverture, it has sometimes been assumed that named women without the adage of 'wife of' to identify them as married must be understood as single.[59] However, such assumptions cannot be made without serious risk of misidentifying the status of individuals.[60] We have already met the brewer and money-lender Agnes de Schonedon from the Norfolk manor of Heacham, whose example illustrated the problem of identifying individual status by taking scribal habits at face value. Agnes's example is by no means unusual.

54 GADL MS 9629, no. 4v.

55 GADL MS 8085, no. 4.

56 NRO DA1 MF/RO 206, January 1278. This was not a specific Leet-type court.

57 NRO DA1 MF/RO 206, January 1277; NRO DA2 MF/RO 206, March 1280.

58 NRO DA1 MF/RO 206, September 1277. Of those 116 men fifty-one were merely noted down as boundary beaters, another one was noted as reeve and four as ale-tasters. If these officials are excluded from our calculation then female participation in active cases, including presentments under the assize of bread and ale, was 76.7 per cent.

59 E.g. C. Briggs, 'Empowered or Marginalized? Rural Women and Credit in Later Thirteenth- and Fourteenth-Century England', *Continuity and Change* 19 (2004), 28–9.

60 See the discussions of this problem, especially in the context of brewsters, in Graham, '"A Woman's Work ..."', pp. 141–4; J. M. Bennett, *Ale, Beer and Brewsters in England: Women's Work in a Changing World, 1300–1600* (New York, 1996), pp. 166–70. See also E. McGibbon Smith, 'The Participation of Women in the Fourteenth-Century Manor Court of Sutton-in-the-Isle', *Marginalia* 1 (2005), 3–4.

At the manor of Brandon in Suffolk, held by the bishop of Ely, female brewers, for example, were presented in one of three ways in the fourteenth century. They were presented in their own name, they remained anonymous while only being noted by their marital status as 'the wife of' a man, or they were identified by their first name and their marital status, such as 'Isabella, wife of Ranulf Smith'. The latter two options made it clear that the woman concerned was in fact married. However, there were also a number of instances in which women brewers were presented in their own right, under their own names, but where it is possible to establish through family reconstructions or otherwise that they were in fact married.

In 1353 Agnes Smith was presented as having broken the assize of ale, apparently as a single woman.[61] But, in 1355, an 'Agnes wife of Robert le Smith' was likewise presented, and the fact that this was the same Agnes as in the previous presentment can be confirmed by the pattern of the presentment of Robert Smith, her husband.[62] Robert was a regular brewer, and was presented early in 1353 for breaking the assize of ale. In the following court Agnes Smith was presented for the same offence without mention of her marital status. The next year Robert Smith was again presented, while it was the turn of 'Agnes wife of Robert le Smith' in 1355.[63]

Family reconstruction reveals similar patterns in the records of the Glastonbury Abbey manor of Longbridge Deverill in Wiltshire. For example, Alice Palmer was married to Henry Palmer, who died and left her a widow at some point in the year 1332: Alice is noted as a widow of Henry le Palmer for the first time in November of that year.[64] However, in December 1331, Alice Palmer had been recorded by her own name and amerced 12d. for breaking the assize of ale, while her still very much alive husband was amerced 3d. in the same court for having broken a boundary.[65] And in August 1331 Henry le Palmer, instead of his wife, had been recorded for having broken the assize of ale and amerced 12d.[66] In some instances it may indeed have been the case that the wife was recorded for brewing offences if her husband was not in court, as has been suggested by Helena Graham, but this does not account for cases where wives were recorded by their own names while their husbands were also in court.[67] It may have been the case that such recording was considerably more *ad hoc* than we would like to believe.[68]

Recording conventions appear to have been at least in part due to local custom, and some variation can be observed. At the manor of Badbury, also held by Glas-

61 Bacon Collection, Brandon, at the University of Chicago Library, sourced from microfilm, hereafter BCUC, MS 291, no. 31

62 BCUC MS 291, no. 36.

63 BCUC MS 291, no. 29v; BCUC MS 291, no. 31; BCUC MS 291, no. 36.

64 GADL MS 11237, no. 3.

65 GADL MS 6367, no. 5.

66 GADL MS 6367, no. 6v.

67 Graham, '"A Woman's Work"', pp. 143–4.

68 A similar point has also been made by McGibbon Smith, who noted that changes in recorded numbers of women and men presented for brewing offences at Sutton-in-the-Isle may have been due to 'changes in scribal convenience': McGibbon Smith, 'The Participation of Women', pp. 3–4.

tonbury Abbey and located in Wiltshire, it seems that only unattached women were presented for breaking the assize of ale, and most of these were widows, in the fourteenth century. Thus, tracing the brewing activities of women over a number of years, it seems that they ceased to brew commercially upon marriage. In fact, their husbands had quite literally taken over the responsibility to the court for these brewing activities from their wives. So, for example, Edith Wynsom, who was the younger of two sisters at the manor, was presented for her brewing activities in 1348. She then married and thereafter it was her husband's name which appeared in the court rolls for breaking the assize of ale.[69]

Problems of correctly identifying marital status can also be encountered when attempting to identify whether women recorded in court records were widows or not. At the Norfolk manor of Heacham in the later years of the thirteenth century, Matilda Herre was a widow, usually referred to in her own name. But she had previously been married to Adam Herre, as was noted in a case presented to the manor court in November 1277.[70] Matilda Thorp was similarly a widow, and quite active in a number of different lawsuits in the manorial court rolls of Heacham throughout the 1270s, but she was only recorded once, in March of 1277, as 'Matilda, widow of William de Thorp'.[71] Therefore, the shorthand assumption of the applicability of coverture to the records of manorial court proceedings can lead to methodological problems, which in turn can mislead the historian concerning the true extent of female agency in the medieval village.

Women only rarely acted as pledges in the manorial court, but it is not at all clear why they sometimes did and mostly did not. Margery Puttock of Heacham must have possessed sufficient economic and social clout in the village to have been accepted to act as a pledge on at least two occasions. The first such occasion was in a land transaction, which involved both her and a tenant called Godfrey Wydie, in April 1277; the second occasion was in a deal concerning the sale of land from Alex Holiday to Margery, when she acted as his pledge in January 1278.[72] While the court's insistence on pledges in some cases was to the advantage of tenants, it should be stressed that it was usually the lord or his agents – rather than other tenants – who demanded the application of pledges to act as sureties for various amercements or licence payments to be rendered to the lord. In the case of the land transaction between Margery and Alex, Margery pledged as surety that Alex would pay 8d. he owed to the lord as a licence to allow him to sell the land in question to Margery. It is therefore difficult to assess why women acted as pledges so rarely, that is, whether the stimulus for keeping the pledging system mainly in male hands came from the lord, from the tenantry, or from both.

While a woman's access to and ability to affect any agency in court were curtailed under common law, such restrictions did not apply to manorial courts in the same way. Wives were often held accountable for their own actions in the court. In December of 1331, Christina, the wife of Henry Spylman, of the manor

69 GADL MS 11179, no. 30; GADL MS 11223, no. 37.

70 NRO DA1 MF/RO 206, November 1277.

71 NRO DA1 MF/RO 206, March 1277.

72 NRO DA 1 MF/RO 206, January 1278; NRO DA 1 MF/RO 206, April 1277.

of Monkton Deverill in Wiltshire, was amerced 6d. because she took a cow from the lord's pinfold.[73] In the same court Robert Popedy was amerced 6d. because he trespassed in some unspecified way against the very same Christina Spylman, although in this instance her name appeared without the adage of 'wife of', who was then awarded damages of 5s. by the court.[74] In other words, the injury of the trespass was perceived to have been committed against Christina, not against her husband or even against Christina with her husband, and damages were specifically awarded to her alone.

A similar case can be found in the manor court rolls of Longbridge Deverill, the neighbouring village to Monkton Deverill under the same lordship of Glastonbury Abbey. Here, in 1329, John Horloc came to court and gave 'Alice wife of Stephen' 12d., again, 'for a trespass made against the same'.[75] Once more, the damages were awarded to the wife, not to the husband or to the wife with her husband, which one might expect had they been perceived by the court to constitute one legal entity.

I have argued elsewhere that women played an integral role in communal policing by, for example, raising the hue and cry against an offender, whereupon it was up to the tithing to investigate the matter. Accordingly, a hue and cry was always presented in court as having either been raised justly or unjustly against the alleged offender.[76] At Longbridge Deverill, typically, such an entry would read: 'Christina wife of John le Man justly raised the hue against William Popedy....'[77] Christina took the initiative in this example and drew attention to whatever misdemeanour William had been involved in. It was Christina's actions which were investigated as either justified or unjustified, and the fact that she was married seems to have been added to the entry to identify her rather than to draw attention to any legal or extralegal dependence on her husband. Conversely, if the hue had been found to have been raised unjustly, as in the case of Alice, wife of Stephen Jurdon, who raised the hue against John Horlock of Longbridge Deverill in 1329, it was she who had raised the hue who was held responsible for 'the injury' done to 'the same John', and she was placed in mercy and amerced 3d.[78]

Husbands and their wives could be held answerable together for certain wrongs done if they were both implicated in the offence. At Heacham, Joscelyn Rus and his wife Christina were together amerced 6d., 'because they directed insulting words against Elvina Christmass', before proceeding to make off with her manure.[79] As both husband and wife insulted Elvina and carried off her manure, they were both held responsible for their actions, but only one amercement was entered. It is difficult to ascertain why this was. The typical amercement for single people for such offences was either 3d. or 6d. Therefore it is possible that

73 GADL MS 6367, no. 5.
74 GADL MS 6367, no. 5.
75 GADL MS 6366, no. 3.
76 Müller, 'Social Control', pp. 34–5.
77 GADL MS 11237, no. 3.
78 GADL MS 6366, no. 3.
79 NRO DA1 MF/RO 206, 1277

the court felt that they should either be amerced 3d. each or 6d. together, as one legal or economic unit. Alternatively, it is possible that the scribe simply did not wish to note down 3d. twice and, saving himself some time, merely entered 6d. Wives were also sometimes called to court to answer certain charges in their own right. This happened in June 1277 when the wife of Thomas Loellebulle, whose name was not recorded, was called to the court of Heacham for an unrecorded reason, and she refused to attend. Her default made her liable to pay an amercement of 6d.[80]

Land represented the cornerstone of medieval village life. It cemented the villagers' residence in the manor, rooted them within the village community and defined their relationship to lordship. Land determined, to a degree, a person's wealth or poverty, social status in the community and status as a tenant of the lord. The land determined the type of tenure the peasant enjoyed, whether it was free or of unfree status and required the rendering of survives and other servile dues. It is not surprising, therefore, that it is through an investigation of the relationship of women with land that some interesting patterns and regional variations emerge.

At the Wiltshire manor of Badbury an interesting custom can be found, which implicitly acknowledged propertied women. At this manor, upon marriage to a propertied bride, a husband often adopted her surname. Joan Jones, for instance, was a propertied widow when she married Richard Austin in 1358. Thereafter her new husband was referred to as Richard Jones.[81] Thus, while at this manor husbands took over the legal responsibilities for their household's brewing activities, as we saw earlier, it was the landed status of wives which was acknowledged in the surname conventions of the manor. The implication is that the propertied bride had a high social status, in some cases higher than that of the husband, which was implicitly recognized in his change of surname. This also suggests that legal status should not always be equated automatically with social status.

Apart from such local conventions, the nature of the local peasant land market and tenurial structure had the potential to impact significantly upon a woman's status and agency both in her community and *vis-à-vis* her lord. It is interesting, therefore, to compare the participation of women in the peasant land market at manors of different locations, lordships and varying socio-economic structures. At manors located in East Anglia very active land markets have been observed. The region was defined by a high degree of commercialization, high population density alongside rather fragmented holdings, and a sizeable free population.

A snapshot of the land market at the manor of Heacham, between September 1276 and September 1280, confirms this picture of busy courts dominated by transfers of often only tiny pieces of land. Across this short period, no fewer than 263 land transfers were recorded at the manor, and, of those, 41 per cent involved women in some way. Women were active here in almost all aspects of land exchange, be it inheritance, gifts of land or surrenders to the lord – usually for the benefit of another tenant – and 25 per cent of purchases of land involved

80 NRO DA1 MF/RO 206, June 1277.

81 GADL MS 11224, no. 18; GADL MS 10634, no. 11; GADL MS 11225, no. 20; GADL MS 11225, no. 45; GADL MS 11181, no. 47; GADL MS 10636, no. 5.

women. Women were also active litigants over land at the manor; no less than 76 per cent of presented cases of litigation over land involved women. Some of these disputes over land involved women attempting to reclaim dowers after the deaths of their husbands, but these concerned only 17 per cent of the disputes recorded in that period.[82]

An important aspect of the widespread involvement of women in Heacham's land market was joint tenure, whereby both husband and wife held their land jointly.[83] The system bestowed considerable rights on married women, whose husbands were not allowed to alienate land – at least in theory – without their wives' approval. However, at Heacham wives also traded separately from their husbands in land, acting in their own name. In 1280, Alice, 'the wife of Radulf de Brecham', for example, went to the manor court seeking a licence from the lord to purchase some land together with a house from Radulf Carleton and his wife Christina. She was granted the licence by the lord for 6d.[84]

Another interesting case involves a surrender of land by Myriel, who in 1278 surrendered one rood of land with a house to Luke, son of Reymond Lex. Moreover, she explicitly rescinded all her right in the land which she had inherited after the death of her father Peter. In the following entry of the same court it is noted that 'the same Luke and Myriel' paid the lord 18d. 'for a licence to marry'.[85] Quite in contrast to common law, Luke clearly would not have enjoyed an automatic right over Myriel's inheritance, and the land transfer looks like a pre-nuptial gift from Myriel to Luke. Similarly, in 1278 Alan Grile paid the lord 12d. for a licence to marry Elena Hot and to 'enter two and a half acres of land as a gift from Elena his wife'.[86] Strictly speaking, gifts between husband and wife were not valid under common law, according to Bracton, and such a gift should not have been necessary if the husband really did have automatic rights over his wife's real property.[87]

In May 1280, Alice, the wife of Richard Hammond, was involved in a land dispute with Alex Chaunceler. Alice, so it was claimed, had been Alex's guardian until he reached maturity and was alleged to be in possession of charters leading to the deforcement of lands which, so Alex claimed, rightfully belonged to him. Alice replied to the court that she was 'not able to answer without Richard her husband'.[88] A number of months later the court took up the case again, this time asking Richard Hammond, Alice's husband, to defend himself against a charge by Alex Chaunceler that he had deforced Alex of half an acre of land for a total of sixteen years. Richard's reply was that the land came to him through his wife Alice, who was rightfully essoined from the court, 'and that he is not able nor al-

82 NRO DA1 MF/RO 206, September 1276 to (and including) NRO DA1 MF/RO 206, 29 August 1280.

83 See Smith's discussion of the issue in his 'Women's Property Rights', pp. 165–94.

84 NRO DA2 MF/RO 206, June 1280.

85 NRO DA1 MF/RO 206, September 1278.

86 NRO DA1 MF/RO 206, February 1278.

87 S. E. Thorne, trans., *Bracton on the Laws and Customs of England*, vol. 2 (Cambridge, MA, 1968), p. 97.

88 NRO DA2 MF/RO 206, May 1280.

lowed to answer without his wife'.[89] The court accepted Richard's reply. We might sympathize with Alex's frustration over the delaying tactics of his opponents, but it is also clear that it was acknowledged that Richard had no right to answer for his wife concerning the land, and that although she was married, she had been expected to attend the court and was essoined.[90] It was similarly accepted that she was not able to answer without her husband, and, at least in theory, both parties would have to answer the case together.

Not every manor entertained such liberal policies regarding the land market or female involvement in it. In stark contrast to Heacham, the manors under the conservative lordship of Glastonbury Abbey saw very little activity in the land market and joint tenure was rare. This had a profound effect on the ability of women to actively participate in court proceedings and may well have impacted on their status in their communities. At Longbridge and Monkton Deverill the land market between 1276 and 1329 was decidedly flat with only thirty-six transfers of land recorded across the period. Women were involved in a very large proportion of these, that is, just over 52 per cent. But this figure becomes less impressive if the types of land transfers are looked at in more detail. There were no purchases, leases, exchanges or even disputes over land recorded at all, and 78 per cent of transfers of land concerned inheritance and widows taking over the holdings of their deceased husbands. At the Glastonbury manor of Badbury a similar picture emerges. Here only ninety transfers of land were recorded across the whole period between 1307 and 1403, over 83 per cent of which concerned whole tenements containing half a virgate of land or more, which usually moved straightforwardly from one tenant to the next, typically due to inheritance, surrender for another's benefit or sale. Due to the lord's intolerance of sublets, they were virtually non-existent, with only one licit sublet recorded across the period.[91] Women primarily surfaced in the land market in the absence of male heirs, when they took over their husband's holdings upon his death.

In his hostility to inter-peasant land transfers and peasant subletting, the fourteenth-century abbot of Glastonbury also put his tenants under pressure to marry and to re-marry quickly when widowed. Widows have often been noted as active in the leasing market, as they were likely to be in a position where they might wish to shrink their arable acreages due to want of labour power, especially when younger children were as yet unable to contribute sufficiently to tilling the land, and yet unwilling to alienate their land permanently.[92] Unless they could find informal ways to cohabit with others in a similar position, barred from subletting, widows and widowers would have had few options open to them for farming larger acreages other than to re-marry so as to reconstitute a viable economic

89 NRO DA2 MF/RO 206, October 1280.

90 What is not so clear is why her essoin, as her proxy, was not empowered to answer for her.

91 GADL MS 10654, no. 20 or 20v. On the Glastonbury land market, see also: H. S. A. Fox, 'Exploitation of the Landless by Lords and Tenants in Early Medieval England', *Medieval Society and the Manor Court*, ed. Z. Razi and R. Smith (Oxford, 1996), p. 535.

92 R. H. Hilton, *A Medieval Society: The West Midlands at the End of the Thirteenth Century* (Cambridge, 1983), p. 163.

unit. From the lord's point of view, the maintenance of large single-unit holdings was integral to the preservation of the rendering of labour services and other rents from these holdings. He wanted his tenements preserved in such a way as to avoid his rights over them being jeopardized.

This carefully exercised control over his assets impacted profoundly, therefore, on the ability of women, and to some degree men, to exercise full agency over the land they held from the Abbey. It also led to a policy, not seen for example at the manor of Heacham, whereby propertied women surrendered their land into the hands of the lord upon their marriage, who then proceeded to hand the land over to the woman's husband. For example, in 1328, Elena la Gauntes of Longbridge Deverill returned one messuage and one ferdell of land to the lord, and in the same entry it was noted that John Judon took it for the term of his life, and paid the lord a fine of 40s. for the land and to take Elena as his wife.[93] In this way the previously propertied wife was effectively dispossessed.

It was not only in such indirect ways that lords could encourage marriage and re-marriage among their propertied tenants and exercise their control over land. Sometimes the abbot put tenants under direct pressure to marry. That this was not always welcome is shown in a rare example at Longbridge Deverill in 1329, where a tenant, Edward Skylk, paid the lord 40d. in order to have 'neither the lands of Matilda Uppehulle nor to have Matilda Uppehulle in marriage'.[94]

Differences in styles of individual lordship were therefore important to the status of women in their communities, and access to land and the ability to participate in an open land market considerably widened the scope of female involvement in village affairs and participation in the public forum of the manorial court. However, it was not only style of lordship which affected such female public engagement. If we turn our attention back to manorial customs, there seems to be a correlation between the number of female tenants and the prominence of freehold at individual manors.

On all Glastonbury Abbey manors freehold was a rare luxury, and according to the thirteenth-century customs, so were tenements in female hands. By comparison, if we examine manors with a sizeable proportion of freeholders, like the Suffolk manor of Brandon held by the bishopric of Ely, the ancient demesne manor of Laughton in Sussex, or the archbishop of Canterbury's manor of Loventon, also in Sussex, a slightly different picture emerges (see Table 5.1). It seems to be the case that a greater degree of personal freedom fostered a larger number of female tenants holding land in their own right. The reality that female free tenants were completely absent from the selected Glastonbury manors, even if an element of free tenure was present, is interesting, but considering the very low numbers of free tenants involved (five at High Ham, two at Winterbourne, six at Damerham, four at Badbury, and four at East Pennard), the free tenantry was statistically insignificant. It is also striking that, at Brandon and Laughton at least, female tenants were still rarer among the unfree population than among the free population.

93 GADL MS 8085, no. 7.

94 GADL MS 6366, no. 5v.

Table 5.1. Free and Unfree Tenants at Selected Manors, in the Later Thirteenth Century.

	All Tenants		Female Tenants	
	Unfree as a %	Free as a %	Unfree as a % of all tenants	Free as a % of all tenants
Badbury, Wiltshire	89.8	10.2	20	0
Damerham, Wiltshire	96.7	3.3	12.6	0
High Ham, Somerset	90	10	6.8	0
Winterbourne, Wiltshire	94.5	5.5	11.8	0
Grittleton, Wiltshire*	100	0	5.7	0
Nettleton, Wiltshire	100	0	12.3	0
East Pennard, Somerset	89.2	10.8	16.2	0
Brandon, Suffolk	56.7	43.3	16.4	23.8
Laughton, Sussex	78.1	21.9	6.2	25.9
Loventon, Sussex	59.2	40.8	27.5	25

Sources: C. J. Elton ed., *Rentalia et Customaria Michaelis de Ambresbury, 1235-1252 et Rogeri de Ford, 1252–1261*, Somerset Record Society, vol. 5 (1891)*; Custumals of the Manors of Laughton*, Sussex Record Society, pp. 1–22; B.C. Redwood and A.E. Wilson, eds, *Custumals of the Sussex Manors of the Archbishop of Canterbury*, Sussex Record Society, vol. 57 (1958), pp. 16–20; Gonville and Caius, MS 485/489.
* Only two female tenants were recorded at Grittleton, one was a widow.

Again it is notable that an apparent relationship between freedom and a concomitant ability of women to effect agency in the local village sits uneasily with coverture. This is because, if we believe legal commentators of this period, coverture should have applied to free women, who therefore should have been less visible in court records than their unfree counterparts.[95]

Some Conclusions

Female peasant status was complex and multifaceted, and dependent upon a number of interrelated factors. Styles of individual lordship could have profound effects on the ability of women to hold on to their land and thereby exercise agency in their communities. Regional differences to do with factors such as the level of local commercialization and the proportion of personal freedom also seem to have affected the status of women, and require a great deal more investigation to help us understand these dynamics more fully.

In light of these complexities, concepts such as the public/private dichotomy or the legal concept of coverture are inadequate and unhelpful in our attempts to

95 These issues deserve much more study and detailed comparative examination, in order to help us understand better exactly how individual lordship, serfdom, freedom or indeed regional factors impacted on the lives of peasant women.

explain gender relationships and female subordination to men in the medieval countryside. Instead, the question of female status needs to be explored within the context of the feudal mode of production. We need to try to understand the likes of women such as Agnes de Schonedon in their own contexts, in their own world, with respect to the restrictions and opportunities offered them by the peasant community, by lordship and by the way production was organized in the countryside. Thus, taking account of seigniorial demands and jurisdiction over the local tenantry, we need to be less wedded to our understanding of medieval common law and we need to try to understand gendered relationships within their specific local and manorial contexts, which in turn varied considerably across the country. To acknowledge that the nature of the subjection of women in medieval peasant society was different from that experienced in other societies, including capitalist society, does not imply that pre-industrial peasant women experienced a golden age. But it does mean that the structures underpinning oppression and inequalities change, and it is these structures which need to be understood.

6

LONDON'S MARRIED WOMEN, DEBT LITIGATION AND COVERTURE IN THE COURT OF COMMON PLEAS

Matthew Frank Stevens

Introduction: the Court of Common Pleas and the London Evidence

In the weeks after the feast of St Hilary (13 January) in 1403 a plea brought on a writ of debt, between plaintiffs Margaret le Toller of Smithfield, London, and her husband John le Toller, and defendant Richard Barbour of Wycombe, Buckinghamshire, was heard before the justices of the royal Court of Common Pleas at Westminster.[1] In this case, Margaret and her husband claimed that nearly two decades before, on 8 August 1384, while Margaret was a single woman, an accounting was held between herself and Richard Barbour in the London parish of St Bride Fleet Street before two London tradesmen appointed by Margaret as auditors. Margaret pleaded that this accounting found Barbour to owe her £10 arrears and clear debt concerning diverse monies and receipts, which 'although often requested' he had not yet paid, neither 'to Margaret as a single woman, nor to John le Toller and Margaret since their marriage'.[2] Barbour responded, not denying the alleged accounting nor debt, by pleading that just over three years before, on 6 October 1399, he, John and Margaret had submitted to arbitration before certain men, at Wycombe, concerning all debts and disputes between them from the creation of the world until that day. And further, Barbour pleaded that this arbitration had decided that he ought to pay John and Margaret 18d. to settle all disputes between them, which he duly paid, thereby acquitting himself of all obligations to the couple. Margaret and John, denying all of what Richard Barbour alleged, then pleaded that they had never submitted to arbitration before the men specified by Barbour and sought an inquest

1 The National Archives (TNA), CP 40/668, rot. 479. I would like to thank Professor Ralph Griffiths for his very helpful comments on an earlier draft of this essay. All errors are, of course, my own.

2 Ibid.: '... prefate Margarete adtunc accrevit predictus Ricardus Barbour licet sepius requisitus predictas decem marcas [elsewhere 'decem libri', an obvious scribal error] prefato Margarete dum sola fuit nec etiam predictas John le Toller et Margarete post desponsalia inter eos celebrata nondum soluit set illas ei hucusque solile contradixit'.

by jury to decide the matter. Three writs were subsequently sent to the sheriff of Buckinghamshire, ordering him to raise a jury, but none was returned and the record of the case concluded without judgment.

In the fifteenth century the Court of Common Pleas was the principal national venue for civil litigation in the English realm, hearing several times as many cases as the realm's second busiest central common law court, the Court of King's Bench, which heard a mixture of civil and criminal pleas.[3] Additionally, Chancery, which increasingly exercised jurisdiction in conscience (and eventually equity) towards the close of the Middle Ages, later to be strongly associated with disadvantaged female petitioners in the early modern period, handled only a small volume of business in the fifteenth century, probably less than two hundred cases per year, as opposed to the roughly four to nine thousand cases in progress at Common Pleas in any given law term.[4] The Court of Common Pleas had four main sorts of jurisdiction: real actions, in land; personal actions, including actions of account, covenant and debt over 40s.; mixed real/personal actions such as ejection from lands held for a term of years; and trespass, both against an individual and in breach of a statute of the realm, which jurisdiction was shared with King's Bench.[5]

The case of *Toller and Toller v. Barbour* is somewhat exceptional with respect to both the long interval between the initial accounting of 1384 and the dispute's pleading before the court, and, as suggested by the fifteen years between the accounting and the alleged joint arbitration of Margaret and her husband, Margaret's likely late age of marriage.[6] But, in so far as it reflects a married couple's attempt to collect a debt owed to the bride from a time before her present marriage, it is wholly unremarkable among the records of Common Pleas. In fact, even a brief survey of cases involving female litigants before the fifteenth-century Court of Common Pleas makes it apparent that recently married, or re-married, women routinely came, or were summoned to come, before the court concerning disputes stemming from a time when they were single. And, most commonly, these mar-

3 For details of sampling, see M. Stevens, 'Introduction to the Edition', J. Mackman and M. F. Stevens, eds, *Court of Common Pleas: The National Archives, CP 40: 1399–1500* (2010), British History Online, http://www.british-history.ac.uk/source.aspx?pubid=1272 (accessed 25 July 2011). For the volume of business at Common Pleas in perspective, see M. Hastings, *The Court of Common Pleas in Fifteenth Century England: A Study of Legal Administration and Procedure* (Ithaca, 1947), pp. 16–27; regarding London, see M. F. Stevens, 'Londoners and the Court of Common Pleas', *London and Beyond: Essays in Honour of Derek Keene*, ed. M. Davies and J. Galloway (London, 2012), pp. 217–37, esp. table 12.1.

4 T. S. Haskett, 'The Medieval English Court of Chancery', *Law and History Review* 14 (1996), 282, n. 131; Stevens, 'Londoners and the Court of Common Pleas', table 12.1. For Chancery as a women's court see M. K. McIntosh, *Working Women in English Society, 1300–1620* (Cambridge, 2005), pp. 14–28. The court is also discussed further in Beattie's essay in this volume.

5 Hastings, *The Court of Common Pleas*, p. 16.

6 If one assumes Margaret was of legal majority (variously interpreted under common and customary law as roughly fourteen to twenty-one years of age) at the time of the 1384 accounting, and recently married around the time of the alleged 1399 arbitration, she is likely to have married at around thirty. For a discussion of female legal majority see K. M. Phillips, *Medieval Maidens: Young Women and Gender in England, 1270–1540* (Manchester, 2003), pp. 32–4.

ried women came to claim, or to answer litigation claiming, monies owed from a time before their (most) recent nuptials.

A systematic investigation of fifteenth-century Common Pleas cases either laid in London, that is revolving around disputed events alleged to have taken place in London, or involving a litigant described as 'of London', reveals that female litigants appeared in just under a fifth of cases reaching the stage of pleading before the king's justices. Further, roughly three-quarters of women's cases pleaded at Common Pleas were economically-orientated actions of debt, detinue or account, in 43 per cent of which a female co-plaintiff or co-defendant was a married woman (see Table 6.1).[7] Put plainly, more than one in twenty London-related lawsuits pleaded before the fifteenth-century Court of Common Pleas involved a married woman as plaintiff or defendant in an economically-orientated dispute. This is despite the limitations of coverture, which severely curtailed the roles of women, and particularly of married women, in litigation in the king's common law courts.

Table 6.1. London-related Cases Before the Fifteenth-century Court of Common Pleas

Writ type	All cases		Cases with female litigants		Cases with married female litigants	
		Percent of total		Percent of all cases by writ type		Percent of cases with female litigants
Debt, detinue and account	5039	80%	810	16%	352	43%
Trespass (inc. breach of statute)	1134	18%	218	19%	120	55%
Disseisin	69	1%	41	60%	29	71%
Other	79	1%	14	18%	10	71%
Total	6321		1083	17%	511	47%

Source: Mackman and Stevens, eds., *Court of Common Pleas*, years sampled, 1399–1409, 1420–1429, 1445–1450, 1460–1468, 1480 and 1500, all dates inclusive.

The Legal Context of Married Women at Law

Confusion over the frequency with which married women were party to legal actions, and particularly legal actions not involving real property, relates to the

7 Actions of debt, detinue and account have been grouped together as 'economically-orientated' lawsuits for ease of expression, as these are actions most commonly arising from commercial or other economic contracts. Unlike actions seeking seisin of land or compensation for personal injury alone, these actions typically revolve around agreements, with clear economic elements or implications, which have gone wrong.

persistent, but erroneous, suggestion that women would not naturally have been party to litigation in economically-orientated actions 'because ... control over the chattels they brought to marriages passed to their husbands'.[8] Critically, this view does not acknowledge the importance of unpaid debts and other outstanding obligations owed to, or owed by, women at the time of their marriage. A single woman, or *femme sole*, that is a woman recognized as representing her own legal affairs as a never-married woman of legal majority (roughly fourteen to twenty-one years of age) or as a widow, could bring any form of action at common law in her own right.[9] Equally, a widowed or never-married woman in her legal majority named as an executor or administrator could initiate or respond, jointly or independently, to litigation regarding the debts or chattels of her testator or intestator. When a woman married, the common law principle of unity of person, or coverture, dictated that, as a married woman was under her husband's coercion in all aspects of her life, in the words of Blackstone, 'all deeds executed, and acts done, by her, during her coverture, are void' and 'if the wife be injured in her person or her property, she can bring no action for redress without her husband's concurrence, and in his name'.[10] But, at one and the same time, 'if the wife be indebted before the marriage, the husband is bound afterwards to pay the debt; for he has adopted her and her circumstances together'.[11]

Although Blackstone was writing in the early eighteenth century, the legal principle on which his latter commentary reflects is self-evident in a fifteenth-century tendency of recently married husbands to attempt to collect outstanding debts owed to their new wives, as demonstrated by the alleged arbitration in the case of *Toller and Toller v. Barbour* cited above. Equally, the reality that a husband adopted a wife and her circumstances is represented by the many lawsuits which came before Common Pleas in which a recent bride and her husband were sued for debts owed, by way of the bride, from a time when she was a single woman, and sometimes contracted many years previously. For example, early in 1424 the justices heard a plea of debt brought by William Yorke, citizen and skinner of London, against John Bedell of Southwark and his wife Rose, formerly Rose Power of London, for a series of bonds totalling £4, contracted in 1418 between William and Rose, then a single woman, and allegedly in default since Easter 1419.[12] Recent brides, as co-litigants with their respective

8 E. Hawkes, '"[S]he Will ... Protect and Defend Her Rights Boldly by Law and Reason ...": Women's Knowledge of Common Law and Equity Courts in Late-Medieval England', *Medieval Women and the Law*, ed. N. J. Menuge (Woodbridge, 2000), pp. 149–50.

9 Also, under the customary law of some urban liberties, such as London, a married woman acknowledged before the court as operating a business independently of her spouse could prosecute lawsuits as a '*femme sole*'. F. Pollock and F. W. Maitland, *The History of English Law before the Time of Edward I*, 2 vols, 2nd edn (Cambridge, 1911), I, p. 482; P. Hogrefe, 'Legal Rights of Tudor Women and the Circumvention by Men and Women', *The Sixteenth Century Journal* 3 (1972), 97–105, p. 98. Regarding legal majority see n. 6 above.

10 W. Blackstone, *Commentaries on the Laws of England*, 4 vols, ed. W. Morrison (London, 2001), I, no. 442, pp. 340–1.

11 Ibid., p. 340.

12 TNA, CP 40/652, rot. 495.

husbands, sued and were sued in a variety of economically-orientated disputes similar to those involving single women and men more generally (Table 6.1). Typical disputes revolved around the detention of chattels, unpaid bonds, unpaid purchases on credit and similar matters.

Legally and practically speaking, the same transfer of legal control was also true of the real property which women brought to marriage unions. Whether a woman had, upon marriage, a right to an unpaid debt or a right to real property, the process by which the couple, once married, brought disputes before the court concerning either debts outstanding or real estate of which they had been disseised (that is, wrongly dispossessed) was by means of a husband's claim in right of his wife, made via an original writ naming both husband and wife as co-litigants. A woman did retain some limited rights over lands which she brought into a marriage union, such as the right to veto attempts by her husband to alienate her dower lands, but these were, under most circumstances, unenforceable during the husband's lifetime and could not result in intra-domestic litigation as a married women and her husband were, in the eyes of the common law, one person.[13] However, concerns over securing the rights to lands which might be subject to dower acted as a natural inducement to the laying of lawsuits by and against husband and wife as co-litigants. This situation was further complicated by the rise of the custom of 'jointure', so called from at least 1451, which held that upon marriage the husband and wife would be joint tenants of specified lands, to be remaindered to the longer-lived party.[14] Like dower, this custom did not allow for intra-domestic litigation but rather emphasized the need for man and wife to appear as co-litigants at common law in actions concerning jointure lands, which actions might arise at any point during their married life. In turn, this led to a high visibility of female litigants in the records of Common Pleas concerning disseisin when compared with other types of lawsuit.

Notable in Table 6.1 is the high proportion (60 per cent) of London-related disseisin cases involving female litigants, and in particular married women (71 per cent of such cases), which reached the stage of pleading in the fifteenth century. Women acted in about 15 to 20 per cent of pleaded cases, excepting in actions of disseisin, which actions contained a disproportionate concentration of female litigants.[15] Equally notable, however, in absolute numbers, is the roughly three economically-orientated London-related cases involving female litigants pleaded before Common Pleas for each disseisin or trespass case heard there. Among lawsuits brought under these forms of action, the economically-orientated actions of debt, detinue and account are the most common, amount-

13 J. H. Baker, *An Introduction to English Legal History*, 3rd edn (London, 1990), pp. 550–7; for a broader European perspective see S. Bardsley, *Women's Roles in the Middle Ages* (London, 2007), pp. 147–54.

14 A. L. Erickson, *Women and Property in Early Modern England* (London, 1995), pp. 25–6. See also Hogrefe, 'Legal Rights of Tudor Women'.

15 The overall proportion of cases at Common Pleas involving women declined sharply from the fourteenth to the fifteenth century. M. F. Stevens, 'London Women, the Courts and the "Golden Age": A Quantitative Analysis of Female Litigants in the Fourteenth and Fifteenth Centuries', *London Journal* 37 (2012), 67–88, esp. p. 84. Also, see below.

ing to 80 per cent of the London-related cases identified as the basis of this study and 75 per cent of cases involving female litigants, nearly half of whom were married.

Reassessing the Historiography of Married Women and the Common Law

The frequency with which London's married women appeared as co-litigants with husbands in economically-orientated disputes before the court of Common Pleas is counterintuitive in light of the current historiography of Englishwomen and the law. This historiography is strongly influenced by the persistent, if incorrect, assumption that married women subject to coverture normally could have no legal interest in economically-orientated lawsuits. On the one hand, great emphasis has been placed on the relative independence of women who were *femme sole*. For medievalists, the legal rights and experiences of unmarried women, especially when related to real estate, upon entering into or exiting from marital unions, or long after such unions, have received a disproportionate amount of attention;[16] while, on the other hand, equally great emphasis has been placed by pre-modern jurists and modern historians alike on the pervasive nature of the pre-modern doctrine of *coverture*, and the theoretical limits it placed on married women. In legal history, married women have been viewed largely as a conduit through which men disputed land rights gained through marriage.[17] And so the experiences of married women, their relationship with the law – especially in non-land disputes – and the practical realities of life *covert de baron* have remained largely unexplored. A tacit, if inaccurate, understanding persists that the near-universal application of coverture in most courts has rendered medieval married Englishwomen all but invisible to modern legal historians. Moreover, within this historiographical framework false expectations are raised: that we might expect to see women most often in land disputes, and for those female litigants in non-land disputes to be unmarried. However, as is shown in Table 6.1, women in London-related lawsuits were involved in some twenty times more economically-orientated cases than land disputes, and 43 per cent of the women in those actions of debt, detinue and account were married, as exemplified by the case of *Toller and Toller v. Barbour*.

16 For example, seven of eight essays in *Wife and Widow in Medieval England*, ed. S. S. Walker (Ann Arbor, 1993), focus on the experiences of widows or, in one instance, litigation to enforce or dissolve a marriage. For a historiographical overview see J. S. Loengard, 'Legal History and the Medieval Englishwoman: A Fragmented View', *Law and History Review* 4 (1986), 161–78; revised as '"Legal History and the Medieval Englishwoman" Revisited: Some New Directions', *Medieval Women and the Sources of Medieval History*, ed. J. T. Rosenthal (London, 1990), pp. 210–36.

17 S. S. Walker, 'Introduction', *Wife and Widow in Medieval England*, ed. Walker, p. 3. On unity of person see Baker, *Introduction*, pp. 550–7; and Blackstone, *Commentaries on the Laws of England*, I, no. 442, pp. 339–42. For a modern historical perspective on the views of pre-modern jurists, and references to the related historiography, see J. Bailey, 'Favoured or Oppressed? Married Women, Property and "Coverture" in England, 1660–1800', *Continuity and Change* 17 (2002), 351–72.

This divergence between the historiography of married women at common law and the experiences of women in pleaded cases relating to fifteenth-century London may not come as a surprise to historians who have looked at the records of manorial and borough courts where coverture was often simply not observed, even to the extent of allowing married women to initiate and answer litigation independently.[18] Moreover, John Baker long ago noted that even where coverture was strictly observed, as in the king's common law courts, 'the husband could ... [sue or] be sued for ante-nuptial debts' by way of claims made in right of a wife.[19] This essay maintains that married women's debt litigation in London-related cases – and doubtless litigation in other localities – is far in excess of all women's land litigation; and yet women's debt litigation at Common Pleas relating to London and elsewhere has not been subject to careful research. The reasons for the current underestimate of married women's economic interests under coverture are twofold. First, the records of the national common law courts are still virtually unexplored. Secondly, and of equal importance, a series of narrowly informed observations drawn from the records of the Court of Common Pleas have supported the erroneous conclusion that, as a result of coverture, women at common law were involved overwhelmingly in land disputes.

In reconsidering these assertions, it is necessary to consider, first, why there has not been more research on the records of the Court of Common Pleas, given that the records of this principal and busiest national court survive *en masse* from the late thirteenth century onwards. The evidence of London-related cases suggests that English legal records, and particularly court records, contain an abundance rather than a paucity of information regarding married women. Indeed, Ruth Kittel, in 1979, pointed out that 'legal records may be one of the best sources for studying medieval women ... with whole classes of documents virtually untouched'.[20]

The main impediments to the collection and interpretation of evidence from court records, now as in the past, are the large volume of material which the historian must examine in order to collect sufficient evidence on which to build an understanding of married women's activities, and the need to apply at least basic quantitative methods. Charles Donahue, in 1993, employed quantitative methods to analyse litigation before the medieval York Consistory Court, commenting 'that legal history ... has traditionally avoided even the simplest forms of statistics'.[21] Since the appearance of Donahue's essay, the use of quantitative methods to explore married women's legal actions has remained sporadic. But a growing interest in women's economic activities as well as a sustained interest in real-prop-

18 See Müller's essay in this volume; and Stevens, 'London Women, the Courts and the "Golden Age"'. For non-English examples, see the essays by Johnson, Hutton and Spence in this volume.

19 Baker, *Introduction*, p. 555, n. 51.

20 R. Kittel, 'Women under the Law in Medieval England: 1066–1485', *The Women of Medieval England from Anglo-Saxon Times to the Present*, ed. B. Kanner (Hamden, CT, 1979), pp. 132–3.

21 C. Donahue, 'Female Plaintiffs in Marriage Cases in the Court of York in the Later Middle Ages: What Can We Learn from the Numbers?', *Wife and Widow in Medieval England*, ed. Walker, p. 183.

erty litigation has produced a small but important body of quantitative research, which this present volume complements.[22]

What remains problematic is the challenge of accessing sufficiently robust series of legal documents in a location or form that makes feasible their systematic investigation and quantitative analysis. As Kittel lamented in 1979, despite the potential of legal records for the writing of medieval women's history, 'only two percent' of the common law records of the thirteenth century had been published.[23] Likewise, substantially less than 2 per cent of fourteenth- and fifteenth-century common law records, including only a handful of records from the Court of Common Pleas, had been published. This is now rapidly changing.

In 2006 the National Archives of the United Kingdom licensed the University of Houston, O'Quinn Law Library, to preserve digitally, publish online and distribute freely digital facsimiles of the records of the common law courts, 1272–1650.[24] Additionally, between 2006 and 2010, two major research projects were undertaken at the Institute of Historical Research, University of London, surveying London-related lawsuits at Common Pleas which reached the stage of pleading: that is, the stage at which the plaintiff(s) and defendant(s) appeared before the justices, in their own persons or by attorneys, to argue their case.[25] These two latter projects have resulted in the publication of an English language calendar of fifteenth-century pleaded cases, either laid in London or involving a London litigant, prosecuted at the Court of Common Pleas.[26] It is this calendar which contains details of the 6,321 pleaded cases analysed for this essay, drawn from the years 1399–1409, 1420–9, 1445–50, 1460–8, 1480 and 1500 (all dates inclusive).[27] It enables quantitative analysis, for the first time, of a substantial body of the records of later medieval England's principal and busiest court for interpersonal, or 'civil', litigation. The greater accessibility of these and similar records of the royal common law courts has the potential to prompt a reconsideration of current as-

22 See the essays by Johnson, Hutton, Spence, Shepard and Ogilvie in this volume. See also, for example, J. M. Bennett, *Women in the Medieval English Countryside: Gender and Household in Brigstock before the Plague* (Oxford, 1987), esp. ch. 5; Hawkes, '"[S]he Will ... Protect and Defend"', pp. 145–61; C. Briggs, 'Empowered or Marginalized? Rural Women and Credit in Later Thirteenth- and Fourteenth-Century England', *Continuity and Change* 19 (2004), 13–43; E. McGibbon Smith, 'The Participation of Women in the Fourteenth-Century Manor Court of Sutton-in-the-Isle', *Marginalia* 1 (2005), online journal, http://www.marginalia.co.uk/journal/05margins/smith.php (accessed 14 September 2011); Stevens, 'London Women, the Courts and the "Golden Age"', 67–88.

23 Kittel, 'Women under the Law', pp. 132–3, cited in Loengard, 'Legal History ... A Fragmented View', p. 164.

24 This project has been under the directorship of Professor Robert Palmer. The majority of these records, plus other document classes similarly under licence, are now available for viewing or download from the O'Quinn Law Library at http://aalt.law.uh.edu/ (accessed 14 September 2011).

25 Arts and Humanities Research Council project, 'Londoners and the Law: Pleadings in the Court of Common Pleas, 1399–1509' (award ref. AR119247), and the Economic and Social Research Council funded project 'London Women and the Economy before and after the Black Death' (award ref. RES-000-22-3343).

26 Mackman and Stevens, eds, *Court of Common Pleas*.

27 Stevens, 'Introduction to the Edition', for details of sampling.

sumptions regarding the interactions of married women and the common law.

The second reason why the present historiography of women's experiences at common law neglects women's economically-orientated litigation arises from a misconception: namely, that women's litigation at common law 'was mostly concerned with claims to land' and, further, that 'women were even more likely than men to be involved in cases concerned with land'.[28] These views reflect the general legal doctrine and belief that all of a woman's chattels were transferred to the control of her husband immediately upon marriage, and they overlook the reality that women were often creditors or debtors at the time of marriage. Single women both actively extended and received credit before marriage, as exemplified by the already noted cases of *Toller and Toller v. Barbour* and *Yorke v. Bedell and Bedell (alias Power)*, respectively.[29] Moreover, women often acted as executors or administrators of others, especially prior husbands. About 53 per cent of men's wills enrolled in the London Husting Court before 1500 mention a surviving wife who was to receive chattels (and/or real property), while a sample of sixteenth-century London wills has indicated that 89 per cent of male testators named their wife as sole or joint executor, and usually as sole recipient of the residue of the estate.[30] Also, as many as 57 per cent of young London widows re-married, often while still owed or owing debts contracted during a prior marital union by husbands for whom they were executors or administrators.[31] For example, in about 60 per cent (212 of 352) of the London-related debt, detinue and account cases involving a married female litigant sampled for this study (Table 6.1), the married woman was litigating as an executor or administrator of a prior husband.

These realities could lead women to be directly or indirectly – as an executor or administrator – in credit or indebted at the time of marriage. Additionally, the misconception that women litigated at Common Pleas overwhelmingly in actions relating to claims to lands, which formed only a small part of the court's business (see Table 6.1 and below), has the effect of redirecting the focus of historians of me-

28 Hawkes, '"[S]he Will ... Protect and Defend"', pp. 147, 149–50. This essay, while not responsible for the misconception, articulates and perpetuates it and is a common point of reference for historians writing on medieval women: e.g. J. Baker, *The Oxford History of the Laws of England, vol. VI: 1483–1558* (Oxford, 2003), p. 617; S. M. Butler, 'Law as a Weapon in Marital Disputes: Evidence from the Late Medieval Court of Chancery, 1424–1529', *Journal of British Studies* 43 (2004), 294; W. A. Matlock, '"A Long to Sue it is a Wery Thing": Legal Commentary in "The Assembly of Ladies"', *Studies in Philology* 101 (2004), 32; S. L. Forste-Grupp, '"For-Thi a Letter has he Dyght": Paradigms for Fourteenth-Century Literacy in "Sir Degrevant"', *Studies in Philology* 101 (2004), 131; Bardsley, *Women's Roles*, pp. 132–4; J. Loengard, 'What Is a Nice (Thirteenth-Century) English Woman Doing in the King's Courts?', *The Ties that Bind: Essays in Medieval British History in Honour of Barbara Hanawalt*, ed. L. E. Mitchell *et al.* (Farnham, 2011), pp. 55–6.

29 TNA, CP 40/688, rot. 479; CP 40/652, rot. 495.

30 B. A. Hanawalt, 'Remarriage as an Option for Urban and Rural Widows in Late Medieval England', *Wife and Widow in Medieval England*, ed. Walker, p. 146; J. Murray, 'Kinship and Friendship: The Perception of Family by Clergy and Laity in Late Medieval London', *Albion* 20 (1988), 376.

31 The given proportion of widows who re-married is based on records of widowed mothers of London wards, 1309–1458: Hanawalt, 'Remarriage as an Option', pp. 150–2.

dieval women to the much less voluminous records of the court of Chancery if they wish to study female litigants. For example, Sara Butler's discussion of recourse to law in marital disputes advises readers that 'women were significantly more likely to participate in legal activities in equity than in common law courts'.[32] Yet this statement does not make clear that while women formed a larger proportion of petitioners to Chancery than they did as litigants at Common Pleas (15 per cent as opposed to 5 per cent, respectively), the fifteenth-century Court of Common Pleas processed twenty to forty-five lawsuits for each one petition to Chancery.[33]

This is the historiographical context in which the present essay, using the London-related data discussed above, seeks to interpret common law actions involving female co-litigants, be they plaintiffs or defendants, as an indicator of the economic standing and wealth of medieval women during at least their first years of marital union, irrespective of the application of coverture. It is essential, consequently, to establish as precisely as possible the frequency with which women were involved in 'land', as opposed to 'non-land', legal actions. That, in turn, entails an evaluation of the evidence for the prevailing view that women were involved mostly in land disputes. More specifically, does that evidence suggest that the litigation patterns of London women were in any way anomalous in a national context?

The first steps toward determining women's overall participation in legal actions at the royal common law courts were taken in 2000 by Emma Hawkes, in an article assessing women's knowledge of the law across the central judicial forums, including Common Pleas, King's Bench and the jurisdiction in conscience of the Court of Chancery.[34] In this article Hawkes sampled Court of Common Pleas 'actions brought by Yorkshire and Lincolnshire litigants [that is, laid in these counties] in [progress during] Trinity [terms] 1479, 1500 and 1520', and at any stage of pleading.[35] This influential article suggests that the Yorkshire and Lincolnshire evidence indicates that women's litigation at common law 'was mostly concerned with claims to land', and further that 'women were even more likely than men to be involved in cases concerned with land'.[36] These findings, based on around 170 Yorkshire and Lincolnshire lawsuits involving female litigants, are in stark contrast to the evidence from three-quarters of the 1,083 London-related cases involving female litigants which were brought on economically-orientated actions, as identified in Table 6.1. At first glance, this difference might be dismissed as regional variation, but a close reading of Hawkes's article suggests that her interpretation of the Yorkshire and Lincolnshire evidence has been distracted by older and narrower case studies focused especially on the records of the gentry.

Hawkes's assessment of Yorkshire and Lincolnshire litigants cites, as context, Susan Wright's survey of the fifteenth-century Derbyshire gentry and Charles Moreton's work on a Norfolk gentry family, the Townshends. The suggestion that

32 Butler, 'Law and a Weapon', p. 294, citing Hawkes, '"[S]he Will ... Protect and Defend"', p. 151.

33 For relative volumes of litigation, see above, n. 4 and accompanying text; Hawkes, '"[S]he Will ... Protect and Defend"', pp. 148, 151.

34 Hawkes, '"[S]he Will ... Protect and Defend"', pp. 145–61.

35 Ibid., p. 145.

36 Ibid., pp. 147, 149; also, see above, n. 28.

women's litigation at common law 'was mostly concerned with claims to land' is followed by a citation of Wright's work on law and order, in which she states that 'ambitious men busily acquiring land ... generated disputes', that 'quarrels over family, marriage settlements and inheritances ... were a regular part of the pattern of litigation' and that 'the [Derbyshire] gentry were much preoccupied with [this] litigation'.[37] These lines, at the beginning of Wright's discussion of law and order in Derbyshire, are taken by Hawkes to imply that litigation involving women overwhelmingly concerned disputes over land. But the body of Wright's work makes no specific reference to the Court of Common Pleas, and a survey of Wright's notation suggests that her research made no use of the Common Plea rolls. The context for interpreting the Yorkshire and Lincolnshire evidence, that 'women were even more likely than men to be involved in cases concerned with land', is followed by a citation of Moreton.[38] This seems to be based on Moreton's discussion of the Townshends' five major land disputes of the later fifteenth century, four of which involved a woman as a litigant or petitioner to Chancery.[39] However, Moreton's work, while based on a few dozen lawsuits, stresses both the success of the Townshends in avoiding land disputes and their tendency to 'use the Common Pleas as a debt-collecting agency'.[40] Moreton further emphasizes the manner in which Eleanor Townshend 'used the law on a regular basis against debtors', with at least eighteen debt suits in progress in the last year of her life.[41]

The misconception that women most commonly litigated over land, and the notion that they were even more likely to do so than men, arises from a reality manifest in Moreton's work and illustrated in Table 6.1 above. The misconception arises from the much higher proportion of lawsuits concerning land, particularly actions of disseisin, which involved female litigants compared with other types of lawsuits (for example, in 60 per cent of disseisin cases a female litigant was involved). However, in absolute numbers – if not in relative terms – women in London-related lawsuits, like men, were much more frequently involved in the economically-orientated actions of debt, detinue and account; and in all actions, they were less likely than men to appear as litigants.[42]

Such misconceptions that exaggerate women's participation in pleas regarding land, though inconsistent with the data of London-related cases, are perhaps understandable in the absence of an overview of the records of Common Pleas. More importantly, they are evident in Hawkes's assessment of Yorkshire and Lincolnshire cases of Trinity terms 1479, 1500 and 1520. For example, when noting that less than a quarter of all lawsuits in progress in Trinity term 1479 involved either actions of disseisin or other actions likely to relate to land dis-

37 Hawkes, '"[S]he Will ... Protect and Defend"', pp. 147, 149; S. M. Wright, *Derbyshire Gentry in the Fifteenth Century: Derbyshire Record Society VIII* (Chesterfield, 1983), p. 120.

38 Hawkes, '"[S]he Will ... Protect and Defend"', p. 149.

39 C. E. Moreton, *The Townshends and Their World: Gentry, Law and Land in Norfolk, c. 1450–1551* (Oxford, 1992), pp. 83–5, 91–106.

40 Ibid., pp. 104–11.

41 Ibid., p. 107.

42 Hawkes, '"[S]he Will ... Protect and Defend"', pp. 147, 149.

putes, Hawkes commented that in 'the figures for 1479 ... [t]he numbers of female claims to land were out of line' with figures from 1500 and 1520, which better fitted her proposed pattern of women being involved primarily in land disputes.[43] Also significant is Hawkes's methodology in determining the number of 'claims to lands' involving female litigants, whereby she grouped together actions of disseisin and actions of trespass for illegal entry *vi et armis* (that is, by force and arms), and waste (that is, damages to properties, or the value of properties, held for a term of life or years). Inclusion of trespass actions claiming illegal entry is entirely appropriate as property disputes were, in the fifteenth century, increasingly brought before the court in this manner in order to convert the tortuous real action of disseisin into a potentially more efficient personal action.[44] Less clear-cut is Hawkes's inclusion of actions of waste as 'claims to lands'. Plaintiffs in actions of waste sought compensation, awardable as treble damages, for the devaluation of estates in which they had a vested interest, and which were held by the defendant for a term of years or for life.[45] In instances of deliberate waste as determined by a jury, the plaintiff could recover seisin (that is, lawful possession), but normally seisin only of the specific part(s) of the property which had been wasted (for example, as little as a single house or a secondary messuage on a manor).[46] Within a judicial framework where lawsuits were rarely prosecuted to their conclusion and the usual mode of termination was an extra-curial arrangement, the exceptional leverage and potential monetary reward of treble damages offered plaintiffs with a viable claim of waste strong economic inducements to sue, and offered defendants a good reason to settle. By comparison, a partial recovery of seisin could well have been inconvenient, and potentially unworkable, from the point of view of both parties. This is to say that actions of waste were, if not plainly economic disputes, then at least not always lawsuits brought with the intent of recovering seisin. Nevertheless, for the purpose of comparing the London-related data to that of other localities, even if all of London-related trespass cases recorded in Table 6.1 concerned land – whereas in fact they relate to a variety of dispute types – trespass and disseisin cases involving female litigants would only have amounted to a quarter of all London-related cases (259 of 1,083) with a female litigant. In the context of London-related cases, Hawkes's conclusion that a quarter of Yorkshire and Lincolnshire cases on the Trinity plea roll of 1479 concerned disseisin or trespass, accounting for only a minority of lawsuits involving female litigants, would not be 'out of line'.[47]

43 Ibid., pp. 148–9.

44 Ibid., pp. 148–9. The standard work on disseisin is D.W. Sutherland, *The Assize of Novel Disseisin* (Oxford, 1973). An approachable summary of Sutherland's work concerning the development cited here is J. S. Beckerman, 'Review: *The Assize of Novel Disseisin*. By Donald W. Sutherland', *The Yale Law Journal* 83 (1974), 634–6.

45 Treble damages were allowed in actions of waste by the Statute of Gloucester, 1278: S. S. Walker, 'The Action of Waste in the Early Common Law', *Legal Records and the Historian*, ed. J. H. Baker (London, 1978), pp. 189–90.

46 Ibid., p. 203.

47 Hawkes, '"[S]he Will ... Protect and Defend"', p. 149.

Table 6.2. Women's Lawsuits Involving Land
(London, Yorkshire and Lincolnshire)

			Women's claims to land			Womens economically-orientated actions	
	All lawsuits	Women's lawsuits	Disseisin	Trespass, illegal entry	All land-related cases	Debt, detinue and account cases	Married female litigants
London 1399–1500	6321	1083 (17%)	41	42	83 (8%)	810 (75%)	352
Yorkshire and Lincolnshire 1500	252	40 (16%)	11	6	17 (43%)	16 (40%)	7

Source: as in Table 6.1 and TNA, CP 40/953.

A more detailed reappraisal of the evidence for Trinity term 1500, regarding Yorkshire and Lincolnshire, for comparison with the data of London-related pleaded cases, is also fruitful (Table 6.2); it undermines the notion that most actions involving female litigants concerned claims to land.[48] Surveying all Yorkshire and Lincolnshire lawsuits recorded on the Trinity 1500 plea roll and including both mesne process (that is, records of efforts to secure a defendant's initial appearance before the court) and pleaded cases, it is calculated that 16 per cent (40 of 252) of these lawsuits involved female litigants; this is comparable to the 17 per cent of London-related pleaded cases which involved female litigants.[49] Excluding one action of waste, eleven of the Yorkshire and Lincolnshire cases were land disputes brought on writs of disseisin, directly disputing land ownership. A further six Yorkshire and Lincolnshire cases noted on the Trinity term 1500 plea roll were brought on writs of trespass with force and arms alleging forced entry, and are likely to indicate underlying real property disputes. In total, these land disputes, brought on writs of disseisin or trespass, account for 43 per cent (17 of 40) of cases involving female litigants, and reflect the activities of 48 per cent (21 of 44) of Yorkshire and Lincolnshire female litigants.[50]

48 No comparative London-related data have been compiled for the years after 1500. Also, confusingly, the 'Trinity term ... 1520' roll studied by Hawkes is referred to as TNA, CP 40/1025, which call number refers to the Trinity term 1519 roll.

49 Hawkes counted 253 cases on this roll, rather than 252 cases, a discrepancy probably arising from the double counting of a case with more than one related entry. This present survey, like Hawkes's, has included cases laid in the cities of York and Lincoln.

50 Cases involving female litigants may be found on TNA, CP 40/953 (debt) rots 2, 11d., 20d.(x2), 82(x2), 82d., 85, 85d., 203d., 206d., 214, 214d., 269d., 290d.; (detinue) 2d.; (disseisin) rots 2, 22, 83, 84d., 85, 216(x2), 218, 270d., 306, 341; (trespass, land) rots 76 (& 85d.), 213, 214d., 225d., 290, 291; (trespass, other) rots 2d., 20, 20d., 85d., 216, 269d.; (waste) 86. Hawkes also bundles with 'land' actions claims of 'waste', which seek compensation for damages to property held by 'cour-

The 43 per cent of Yorkshire and Lincolnshire lawsuits (Table 6.2) which involved female litigants in claims to land in 1500 is markedly higher than the 8 per cent of London-related lawsuits which might have concerned female litigants in similar disputes across the fifteenth century. The reasons for this disparity are more complex than the rural and urban concerns of non-London and London litigants – although the mercantile pre-eminence of London must not be wholly discounted.[51] While Yorkshire and Lincolnshire were large rural counties, the urban centres of York and Lincoln (whose cases are included here) were significant hubs of commercial activity. Likewise, the London-related pleaded cases considered include disputes arising from Londoners' diverse landed interests beyond the city, as well as non-Londoners' disputes arising from property transactions which took place in the city and so required lawsuits laid in London. The smaller proportion of Yorkshire and Lincolnshire lawsuits which involved women in debt disputes, relative to London-related cases, is likely due in part to the less intense use of the Court of Common Pleas by Yorkshire and Lincolnshire litigants. Across the fifteenth century, more than four times as many lawsuits were brought in Common Pleas by Londoners as by Yorkshire or Lincolnshire litigants, per head of population, due in part at least to the frequency with which Londoners traded with non-Londoners, and so litigated against them in England's national judicial tribunals.[52] At the same time, the smaller proportion of London-related cases which involved women in land disputes, relative to the Yorkshire and Lincolnshire cases, is likely to be due in large part to the London custom which reserved disputes between citizens to the city's own courts.[53]

Nevertheless, despite the differing litigation patterns of disputants in London-related lawsuits as opposed to those in Yorkshire and Lincolnshire lawsuits, there is no reason to believe that legal actions from either locality demonstrate other than that only a minority of lawsuits involving women were land disputes. Contrary to Hawkes's assessment of Yorkshire and Lincolnshire lawsuits in Trinity term 1500, women were not most frequently litigants at the Court of Common Pleas in land disputes. As with the London-related lawsuits, the most common single type of action to involve female Yorkshire and Lincolnshire litigants in 1500 was – in fifteen instances – an action of debt.[54] Neither this sample of non-London cases from 1500, nor the London-related evidence presented in Table 6.1, can speak for all parts of fifteenth-century England; much more extensive research is needed to explore regional patterns in the use of the central law courts. But the

tesy of England'; such lawsuits are also likely to have been economic in nature. Even were claims of waste counted as 'land' disputes, women's cases involving land would still be in the minority.

51 See D. Keene, 'Medieval London and Its Region', *London Journal* 14 (1989), 99–111.

52 Stevens, 'Londoners and the Court of Common Pleas', pp. 224–7, table 12.2.

53 P. Tucker, 'Relationships between London's Courts and the Westminster Courts in the Reign of Edward IV', *Courts, Counties and the Capital in the Later Middle Ages*, ed. D. E. S. Dunn (Stroud, 1996), p. 117. Small numbers of London citizens did choose to break the city's prohibition by employing the Court of Common Pleas against one another in the fifteenth century, but they did so overwhelmingly in personal actions: Stevens, 'Londoners and the Court of Common Pleas', pp. 231–2.

54 See n. 50 above.

data strongly indicate that the economic standing and wealth of later medieval women, both in Yorkshire and Lincolnshire c.1500 and in fifteenth-century London, were most commonly tested at the Court of Common Pleas in actions of debt. In London in particular, women – whether married or unmarried – were by a wide margin most commonly involved in economically-orientated suits of debt, detinue and account (Table 6.1).

Conclusion: Women in London-related Cases, New Directions for Study

Having sought to dispel the myth that as a by-product of coverture women were most likely to be litigants at Common Pleas in claims to land, it is appropriate to ask how the participation of so many single and, in particular, married women in economically-orientated pleas can inform the historian about the economic standing and wealth of medieval women. Medieval women have long been viewed, with respect to their roles in land disputes, as little more than conduits through which men might lay claim to lands. Does challenging the misconception that women were mostly involved in land disputes do anything more than suggest that women were conduits through which men might lay claims to debts? In short, can records of married women's debts tell us more about female agency and activities than land disputes?

These questions are too broad-ranging to be adequately explored here, but they may be answered tentatively in the affirmative. As discussed above, a married woman could appear in a debt case with her husband when the debt concerned had been owed to, or owed by, the wife from a time before her most recent marriage. The form of the lawsuits in the rolls of Common Pleas consistently notes if, and to whom, the woman may previously have been married since the debt was contracted. For example, in the debt suit of *Toller and Toller v. Barbour*, the plaintiffs' pleading expressly stated that, 'although often requested', the £10 arrears in question had not been paid by Richard Barbour, neither 'to Margaret while a single woman, nor to John le Toller and Margaret since their marriage'.[55] In this way, the debt disputes of married women – particularly when they were not acting as an executor or administrator to a prior husband or other deceased party – offer a window onto the lives of unmarried women, a sense of their financial fortunes on entering marriage and an indication of how marriage affected their use of the court. Referring again to the case of *Toller and Toller v. Barbour*, it is evident that Margaret had lent Richard Barbour the significant sum of £10 when she was a single woman, some nineteen years before and while likely quite young; the wording of the lawsuit suggests that she had not been married prior to her union with John le Toller.[56] It also suggests that she had only attempted to resolve the debt through an alleged arbitration after her marriage, some fifteen years subsequent to the accounting by which the arrears were determined. Lawsuits involving London wives

55 TNA, CP 40/568, rot. 479; see n. 2 above for Latin transcription.

56 Ibid.

who were creditors were frequently brought by married couples shortly after their nuptials (Table 6.3).[57] The historian might fruitfully speculate that Margaret Toller's marriage, far from debilitating her through the application of *coverture*, offered her the assistance she needed, in a patriarchal world, to attempt to recover the debt.

Table 6.3. Sample of Debts of Married Women (Neither Executors Nor Administrators) in Pleaded London-related Cases, 1399–1500, Median and Mode Values.

	No of debts*	Median debt value	Mode debt value(s)	Median time in arrears	Mode time in arrears
Wives as creditors	45	£11 6*s* 8*d*	£11 6*s* 8*d*	4 yr.	2 yr.
Wives as debtors	42	£10	£7 10*s*	5.5 yr.	4 yr.

Source: as in Table 6.1.
* This column reflects only debts, most often secured by bonds,

In a similar vein, quantitative analysis of the debts of married women who appeared before Common Pleas as litigants has the potential to shed light on the participation of women in the credit market and offers insights into the ways in which female indebtedness affected the credit market. Again, this is particularly relevant when the married woman was not acting as an executor or administrator to a prior husband, but instead when the woman herself contracted the debts in question as a single woman. For example, Table 6.3 shows the median and mode values of debts owed to and by female creditors and debtors, and the duration of time those debts had been in arrears at the time of pleading, in London-related cases involving a wife as a co-litigant, where that wife was acting as neither an executor nor an administrator.[58]

The data in Table 6.3, regarding debts owed to or by wives from a time before their marriage, suggest that unmarried women, as creditors, were likely to extend substantially more credit to individual debtors than they themselves were likely to receive as debtors. More speculatively, if the period of time during which a debt was in arrears before a case was pleaded at Common Pleas is used as a rough indicator of how long a female creditor or debtor remained unmarried, the data in Table 6.3 suggest that creditors married more quickly than debtors. Could this be because female creditors were subject to the attentions of grasping suitors, wishing to use coverture as a means by which to attain their unrealized assets? Or, in light of the prominence of coverture, could single female creditors have felt that they needed male assistance to use the courts effectively to recover outstanding

57 E.g. *Yorke v. Bedell and Bedell*. Compare with married-women debtors (Table 6.3); cases usually required several law terms, often amounting to years, to reach the stage of pleading. See Hastings, *Court of Common Pleas*, 'XV Delays and Hindrances to Justice', pp. 211–36.

58 As simple averages are easily skewed by large 'outlier' sums, median and mode values can be more useful. A median value is a 'middle value' in an ordered list, i.e. low to high. A mode value is the most frequently occurring value in a list.

debts, making difficulty in pursuing debts and recalcitrant debtors motivations to marry? Considering these data, it is perhaps worth recalling Blackstone's words that, in the eyes of the law, when a man took a bride he 'adopted her and her circumstances together'.[59] Nearly twenty years ago, Barbara Hanawalt's study, 'Remarriage as an Option for Urban and Rural Widows in Late Medieval England', pointed out that 'crass economic factors may have motivated new husbands'; there is little reason to believe that similar factors would not have motivated new wives as well.[60]

Little more can be done here than to point the way for future investigations of the experiences of medieval women as reflected in the Court of Common Pleas and other common law courts. The convention of coverture left ample scope for married women to appear before the court as party to litigation of an overtly economic nature, not directly related to claims to land. The evidence of women in London-related cases pleaded before the fifteenth-century court is dominated by female litigants' economically-orientated actions of debt, detinue and account. While the present orthodoxy about married women and the law, based on narrowly conceived studies, suggests that women were mostly named in common law actions where a husband claimed lands in right of his wife, there is in truth little evidence to sustain this argument. A thorough, comparative re-evaluation of Yorkshire and Lincolnshire cases from Trinity term 1500 suggests that land disputes may have been more common among female litigants' lawsuits from non-London localities. However, the notion that women at common law were involved predominantly in land disputes, based on the belief that coverture overwhelmingly precluded married women from participating in economically-orientated lawsuits, may prove to be no more than a myth.

59 Blackstone, *Commentaries*, pp. 340–1.

60 Hanawalt, 'Remarriage as an Option', p. 153.

7

MARRIED WOMEN, CONTRACTS AND COVERTURE IN LATE MEDIEVAL ENGLAND

Cordelia Beattie

> It is a wyues ocupacyon ... to go or ryde to the markette: to sell butter / chese / mylke / egges / chekens / capons / hennes / pygges / gees / and all maner of cornes. And also to bye all maner of necessarie thynges / belonging to housholde: and to make a trewe rekenynge and accompt to her husbande / what she hath receyued and what she hath payed.
>
> John Fitzherbert, *Book of Husbandry* (1523)[1]

Fitzherbert's picture of a woman buying and selling at market seems unremarkable. Craig Muldrew comments that, 'In any print or painting of marketplaces in the early modern period, women are always present', while Amy Erickson adds, 'In all of the illustrations that I have seen women actually predominate in the market both as buyers and as sellers.'[2] But what if we imagine a situation in which the goods that a wife wants to buy cost more than the goods that she has sold? Would anyone extend credit to this married woman? If so, who would be liable for the debt if she did not honour it? Would it matter if she bought luxuries rather than necessities, or if the goods were for her own trade?

Two scholars have recently argued, based in part on eighteenth-century legal treatises, that a 'law of necessaries' or 'law of agency' gave married women in England c.1660–1860 some relief from the strictures of coverture, the common law doctrine which meant wives were under the guardianship of their husband, had no legal possessions of their own, and could not enter into economic contracts in

1 J. Fitzherbert, *Here begynneth a newe tracte or treatyse moost profytable for all husbandmen and very frutefull for all other persons to rede* (London, 1523), fol. 50, accessed via Early English Books Online (hereafter cited as EEBO). I am grateful to Judith Bennett, Anthony Musson, Steve Rigby and Matthew Stevens for comments on previous drafts of this essay.

2 C. Muldrew, '"A Mutual Assent of her Mind"? Women, Debt, Litigation and Contract in Early Modern England', *History Workshop Journal* 55 (2003), 47–71, p. 49; A. L. Erickson, 'Coverture and Capitalism', *History Workshop Journal* 59 (2005), 1–16, p. 9.

their own right. Margot Finn describes the 'law of necessaries' as allowing wives 'to make contracts on their own behalf for necessaries, as agents of their husbands'.[3] *The Laws Respecting Women* (1777), for example, states that 'while they cohabit, the husband shall answer all contracts of hers for necessaries, for his assent shall be presumed to all necessary contracts ... unless the contrary appear'; 'necessaries' are defined here as 'meat, drink, clothing, physic, &c. suitable to his rank and fortune'.[4] The right to make purchases using her husband's credit still applied if a husband 'turns her away' (or if the wife was forced to leave because of her husband's cruel behaviour), but not if she 'runs away' from him or if he paid maintenance.[5] Finn and Joanne Bailey argue that, while the law of necessaries looks of limited application, in practice it enabled wives to make contracts for a range of goods, including luxuries, to secure a degree of independence from unsuccessful marriages, and to have a sense of ownership of property.[6] This is perhaps why Bailey prefers the term 'law of agency'. Bailey herself notes that, 'Agency was a broad concept in common law, under which one man gave another individual the authority to act on his behalf without gaining any rights or benefits.'[7] Thus a married woman acting as her husband's agent could do much more than merely enter into contracts for the household's meat, drink, clothing, and medicine. However, we should note that this definition of agency entails the husband giving his wife express permission to enter into contracts, whereas the law of necessaries, outlined in *The Laws Respecting Women*, states that 'his assent shall be presumed', unless otherwise proven.

When did this law of necessaries come into being? The legal treatise *Baron and Feme: A Treatise of Law and Equity Concerning Husbands and Wives*, in its third edition (1738), drew on a late medieval precedent when discussing what acts done, or contracts made, by the wife shall bind the husband: 'in 11 H. 6. 30 it is the Opinion of *Martin*, that if a Woman buy Things suitable to the Degree of her Husband, he shall be bound by it'.[8] This is a reference to a comment by Justice Martin, which was recorded in a year book for 1433.[9] This and other similar late medieval year book discussions were cited during a famous legal case from 1663, *Manby v. Scott*, about whether Scott was liable for goods sold to his wife who

3 M. Finn, 'Women, Consumption and Coverture in England, c. 1760–1860', *The Historical Journal* 39 (1996), 703–22, esp. p. 707.

4 Anon., *The Laws Respecting Women, as They Regard Their Natural Rights or Their Connections and Conduct* (London, 1777), pp. 68, 66.

5 Anon., *The Laws Respecting Women*, pp. 66–70.

6 Finn, 'Women', pp. 709–15; J. Bailey, 'Favoured or Oppressed? Married Women, Property and "Coverture" in England, 1660–1800', *Continuity and Change* 17 (2002), 351–72, esp. pp. 356–61.

7 Bailey, 'Favoured or Oppressed?', p. 359. See also Muldrew, '"A Mutual Assent"', pp. 47–8.

8 Anon., *Baron and Feme: A Treatise of Law and Equity, Concerning Husbands and Wives* (London, 1738), p. 274. Anon., *The Laws Respecting Women* references '11 Hen. VI c. 50' in its discussion of maintenance of a wife (p. 66, n. l) and it seems likely that it was referring to the same case. Year book cases are often referenced by date (year of a king's reign, sometimes preceded by the term, e.g. Michaelmas or Trinity) and then a folio or plea number.

9 Anon., *De termino Michaelis anno xj. Regni regis Henrici sexti* (London, 1582), fols 30–30v (accessed via EEBO).

had lived separate from him for twelve years.[10] Yet those interested in medieval women's history, rather than in legal history, have largely overlooked evidence of a law of necessaries, perhaps because our clearest evidence for it is contained in the year books, which record legal arguments. Ruth Kittel argued that 'the yearbooks are of more interest to the legal historian than the social historian'.[11] This essay contends that technical legal sources can still be of value to social history in that the law was, as Anthony Musson has maintained, 'an integral part of the way in which social relations were actually lived out and experienced'.[12]

For legal historians the law of necessaries is largely bound up with a married woman's ability to act as her husband's agent in the Middle Ages. Frederic William Maitland summarized the fully developed common law position as follows:

> During the marriage the wife can not contract on her own behalf. She can contract as her husband's agent, and has a certain power of pledging his credit in the purchase of necessaries. At the end of the middle ages it is very doubtful how far this power is to be explained by an 'implied agency'.[13]

He also commented that, 'The little that we can read about this [pledging a husband's credit for necessaries] in our oldest reports [c.1306] suggests that the lawyers were already regarding it as a matter of agency.'[14] But, as the above reference to 'implied agency' signals, by c.1500 a married woman would need her husband's *express* consent even if she was buying 'necessaries', which is different from the position in the eighteenth-century treatise, *The Laws Respecting Women*. A summary in J. H. Baker's *An Introduction to English Legal History* reinforces this view:

> as an agent of her own husband, the wife could sometimes make contracts on his behalf. Thus, it was settled by 1300 that she could bind her husband to a sale of goods which came to his use or profit. But by 1500 it was clear that the husband was bound in such a case

10 M. A. Robertson and G. Ellis, eds, *The English Reports*, 83 (Edinburgh, 1908), pp. 816–17. See also J. W. Smith, *A Selection of Leading Cases on Various Branches of the Law*, 13th edn by Sir T. W. Chitty *et al.*, 2 vols (London, 1929), II, pp. 417–46; Muldrew, '"A Mutual Assent"', pp. 60–3. For Maitland this case 'shows that the middle ages left behind them little law about this matter': F. Pollock and F. W. Maitland, *The History of English Law before the Time of Edward I*, 2 vols, 2nd edn (Cambridge, 1911), II, p. 435, n. 5.

11 R. Kittel, 'Women under the Law in Medieval England 1066–1485', *The Women of England from Anglo-Saxon Times to the Present: Interpretive Bibliographical Essays*, ed. B. Kanner (London, 1980), p. 129.

12 A. Musson, *Medieval Law in Context: The Growth of Legal Consciousness from Magna Carta to the Peasants' Revolt* (Manchester, 2001), p. 2.

13 Pollock and Maitland, *History of English Law*, II, p. 405.

14 Pollock and Maitland, *History of English Law*, II, p. 435. They cite Fitzherbert's reference to a report dated 'Mich. 34 Edw. I' and suggest that this might relate to the following case: A. J. Horwood, ed., *Year Books of the Reign of King Edward the First: Years XXXIII to XXXV (1305–1307)*, Rolls Series no. 31, part A, vol. 5 (London, 1879), p. 312. This case just says that a married woman could not own chattels. A more likely fit is the case I discuss from c.1306 below.

> only if he had either given his wife prior authority to act for him, or subsequently ratified a contract for his benefit.[15]

These brief summaries of the medieval legal position suggest not only that there was a medieval understanding of a law of necessaries, which was bound up with what we might call a law of wifely agency, but that married women's ability to make use of it actually declined over the late medieval period.

Evidence of a medieval law of necessaries or agency seems particularly significant in light of Marjorie McIntosh's reappraisal of the borough custom which enabled some married women to trade as *femmes soles*, that is, subject to the same legal rights and responsibilities as unmarried women. Early twentieth-century scholars, such as Mary Bateson, Annie Abram and Alice Clark, contrasted the 'freedom and autonomy enjoyed by *femme sole* traders with the limited opportunities available to wives who remained *femme couvertes de baron* ("covered" by their husbands)'.[16] More recently, Caroline Barron argued that *femmes soles* were among those who enjoyed a relative 'golden age' in the period after the Black Death of 1348–9. While others (such as Judith Bennett) have suggested that the custom's significance has been over-emphasized, being applicable 'to only a small group of atypical urban businesswomen', McIntosh goes further.[17] From a study of London's court records in the period 1300–1630, she concludes that the *femme sole* status for married women conveyed fewer economic and legal benefits, and was used much less actively, than previous historians had assumed. She argues that while it might have been in the husband's interest to require a financially unstable wife to register as *femme sole*, wives perhaps felt that it was more advantageous to remain as *femmes couvertes*, even if trading separately, as they would then have the husband's economic backing, his participation in the event of legal action, and a chance to manipulate their ambivalent status in the courts. McIntosh points out that scholars of the sixteenth, seventeenth and early eighteenth centuries have not made as much of the *femme sole* custom and sees this as reflective of the custom's decline by the mid-sixteenth century.[18] Bailey, for example, questions whether married women engaged in extensive buying and selling were doing this under local custom (as *femmes soles*) or whether they were 'simply acting at their husbands' direction, within the legitimate bounds of coverture'.[19] The latter was also Finn's understanding of why small claims courts in the eighteenth and nineteenth centuries 'recognized and accepted the evidence of married women as their husbands' agents'.[20]

Perhaps a law of necessaries or agency was a solution in common law to some of

15 J. H. Baker, *An Introduction to English Legal History*, 3rd edn (London, 1990), pp. 555–6. This view is repeated in J. Loengard, 'Common Law for Margery: Separate But Not Equal', *Women in Medieval Western European Culture*, ed. L. E. Mitchell (New York, 1999), p. 123.

16 M. K. McIntosh, 'The Benefits and Drawbacks of *Femme Sole* Status in England, 1300–1630', *Journal of British Studies* 44 (2005), 410–38, pp. 410–11.

17 See McIntosh, 'Benefits and Drawbacks', pp. 411–12, quotation at p. 412.

18 McIntosh, 'Benefits and Drawbacks', esp. pp. 412, 425, 427, 430.

19 Bailey, 'Favoured or Oppressed?', p. 359.

20 Finn, 'Women', p. 715.

the problems posed by married women's activities in the marketplace, in a similar fashion to the custom of *femme sole* in borough law. Indeed, if uptake of the latter custom – which anyway only existed in a few urban centres – was always small (even in its suggested peak period of the late fourteenth and fifteenth centuries), then our attention might be better placed exploring married women's ability to act as their husbands' agents rather than their use of the custom. This essay will first examine relevant year book reports, which record legal arguments, in order to delve deeper into the matter of married women's ability to make contracts under common law. Then it will discuss the relationship between the common law understanding that married women could buy and sell as agents of their husbands, or on behalf of their households, and the borough custom of *femme sole*.

Year Book Evidence for a Medieval Law of Necessaries or Agency

What we now refer to as 'Year Books' are abridged reports of legal arguments in specific pleas, including remarks attributed to judges, which came before the common law courts of Common Pleas (or the 'Common Bench') and King's Bench, at Westminster, and the general Eyres from the late thirteenth century onwards.[21] Although their purpose has been the subject of a great deal of debate over the years, the main motive for producing them seems to have been the recording, circulation and preservation of 'the intellectual aspect of litigation ... the possible moves in the recondite games of legal chess played by the pleaders in open court', for the benefit of both students and practising lawyers.[22] Indeed, the decisions of such cases were often not recorded. Although the year books did not seek to set legal precedents, E. W. Ives has argued that they did establish models of how to argue and that they were seen as the written memory of the profession.[23] Given the small number of legal treatises written in late medieval England, the year books are our principal source for the development of common law doctrines, concepts, and methods, which in itself is suggestive of how the common law was evolving (being 'tied more closely to the life of courtroom practice than to expository writing', as Baker puts it).[24]

The year books are largely written in Law French and their authorship is unknown. It is likely that they were not individual compilations but initially resulted from the exchange of notes generated at law school, which would help explain how very different reports of the same case can sometimes be found in different manuscripts.[25] William Craddock Bolland suggests that these notes would have

21 On their origins see P. Brand, 'The Beginnings of English Law Reporting', *Law Reporting in Britain: Proceedings of the Eleventh British Legal History Conference*, ed. C. Stebbings (London, 1995), pp. 1–14.

22 Baker, *Introduction*, p. 205. See also T. F. T. Plucknett, *Early English Legal Literature* (Cambridge, 1958), pp. 102–4.

23 E. W. Ives, 'The Purpose and Making of the Later Year Books', *Law Quarterly Review* 89 (1973), 64–86, pp. 67–71.

24 Baker, *Introduction*, p. 202.

25 Baker, *Introduction*, p. 205.

been handed in at a scriptorium to be written up into a text. He argues that this method of composition might explain why some cases are incorrectly written into the texts for different years.[26] (The books are generally ordered by law terms at Westminster, although in the late thirteenth century some are reports of particular Eyre sessions.)

For the modern scholar, there are editions which collate all or some of the known manuscripts for the reign of Edward I, the years 1–13 Edward II, and for the reign of Richard II, published by the Rolls Series, Selden Society and Ames Foundation. More recently, David Seipp compiled a searchable database which indexes all year book reports printed in the chronological series (1268–1535) and many of those printed only in abridgements, and cross-references the modern editions.[27] The canon of printed year books began c.1481 when the firm Lettou and Machlinia published the *Year Books 33–37 Henry VI*. By 1558 the canon of printed year books was held to be complete – ending with Michaelmas term 27 Henry VIII (1535) – but many years, including all those of Edward I and Edward II, more than ten years of Edward III, and the entire reign of Richard II, were omitted altogether.[28] Using the database in conjunction with references from later legal sources, I have found six examples which debate what married women could and could not do regarding contracts, spanning the period 1300–1500 (viz. c.1306, 1310, 1433, 1442, c.1499 and 1535). While it is possible that there are other relevant reports among the surviving manuscripts, discussion of these six reports enables elaboration on the brief summaries provided by Maitland and Baker, and – while each report is a comment on a specific case – the fact that many are referenced in later legal texts is suggestive of their impact.

Contrary to Baker's assertion that 'it was settled', the two reports from the early fourteenth century reveal it was unlikely that there was a single position on married women's ability to make contracts under common law c.1300. Both cases concern actions for debt, one brought against a married couple, one against a man for his late wife's debt. The first example probably dates from 1306, although it is found in the year books dated 1312 and 1313–14.[29] Here, Roger Peyntoun de-

26 W. C. Bolland *et al.*, eds, *Year Books of Edward II, Vol. VII, The Eyre of Kent 6 & 7 Edward II. A.D. 1313–1314*, II, Selden Society 27 (London, 1912), pp. xxxvii–xlii. See also Plucknett, *Early English Legal Literature*, pp. 107–9. For the argument that the later year books were also collective, informal compilations, see Ives, 'Purpose', pp. 64–86; J. H. Baker, ed., *The Reports of John Spelman*, 2 vols, Selden Society 93–4 (1976–7; London, 1977–8), II, pp. 165–6.

27 D. Seipp, 'An Index and Paraphrase of Printed Year Book Reports, 1268–1535', online at http://www.bu.edu/law/seipp/ (accessed July 2011). More than 22,000 cases have been printed and so only those from 1399–1535 (6,901) have been fully indexed and paraphrased in this database. I searched for 'coverture' in all fields, which gave 285 cases, but I also found other relevant cases through following the database's cross-referencing, as well as from references from later legal sources. Cases discussed will be referenced by their 'Seipp Number'.

28 Plucknett, *Early English Legal Literature*, p. 112; Baker, *Introduction*, pp. 207–8. The view of Maitland *et al.* that the printed year books are a 'hopeless mass of corruption' which could be corrected by a study of the manuscripts has been challenged by subsequent studies of the later year books. See W. C. Bolland, *A Manual of Year Book Studies* (Cambridge, 1925), pp. xii, 3–4; Ives, 'Purpose', pp. 74–8.

29 Seipp 1312.220ss and 1313.454ss. See P. Vinogradoff and L. Ehrlich, eds, *Year Books of Edward*

manded payment for a debt from William Musket, by reason of a contract entered into by William's late wife, Alice, during their marriage. Alice had purchased two quarters of wheat but failed to pay the 7s. agreed upon. Serjeant Asshele argued that the debt was the wife's and that 'no contract that the wife made while she was covert could place a charge upon her husband'.[30] Serjeant Tilton disagreed, first arguing that 'The deed of the wife is in such a case the deed of the husband, for they are as one person, and consequently the husband ought to answer for the wife's contract.'[31] In response to Asshele's argument that the husband only represents his own person, Tilton then contended that the wife's incapacity to make a contract ought to lead to a transfer of liability to her husband, as in the case of a removable prior of a religious house whose act would bind his successor *if* he had benefited from the money.[32] Whether the husband had benefited from the goods turned out to be the crucial point. The initial charge only stated that the wife had received the goods, not that she had received them for her husband's profit, and so the plaint failed. A note at the end of the case comments, 'if he had counted that this same William had received, by Alice his wife, so much to his profit, he would have recovered the debt'.[33]

Our second example – a case heard before the Court of Common Pleas in 1310 although its report is also included in the year book for the Eyre of Kent 1313–14 – had a quite different outcome. The case was brought by two executors, Adam de Middelton and John de Middleton, against Mauger Vavassur and his wife Alice, regarding a debt on a loan of 40 marks.[34] The husband alone responded and Justice Stanton stated that this was valid as 'The wife has no property; so he who has the property shall make the law [fra la ley].'[35] 'Make the law' is a reference to com-

II, Vol. XIII, 6 Edward II. A.D. 1312–1313, Selden Society 34 (1917; London, 1918), no. 41, pp. 153–6. The editors comment that that case 'seems misplaced from an earlier term' and believe that it corresponds with Fitzherbert's *Dette*, 163 (Mich. 34 Edw. I), which seems likely as the latter also names the wife as Alice: ibid., p. xlix; Anthony Fitzherbert, [La graunde abridgement] (London, 1516), *Dette*, 163 (accessed via EEBO); cf. n.14 above. Seipp also comments that Serjeant Tilton, who appears in this case, stopped appearing in the rolls after 1306. The same case is included in the report for the Eyre of Kent 1313–14, which illustrates the earlier arguments about how the year books were compiled: see Bolland *et al.*, eds, *Eyre of Kent, 6 & 7 Edward II. 1313–1314*, pp. 45–7.

30 Vinogradoff and Ehrlich, eds, *Year Books, 6 Edward II, 1312–13*, p. 155. See also Bolland *et al.*, eds, *Eyre of Kent, 6 & 7 Edward II. 1313–1314*, p. 46. For the role of serjeants at law, see Baker, *Introduction*, pp. 179–81.

31 Vinogradoff and Ehrlich, eds, *Year Books, 6 Edward II, 1312–13*, pp. 153–4. See also Bolland *et al.*, eds, *Eyre of Kent, 6 & 7 Edward II. 1313–1314*, p. 45. For a similar assertion, from a 1306 *cui in vita* case, see Horwood (ed.), *Year Books ... Edward the First (1305–1307)*, p. 330: 'we think that if she was coverte when you entered, anything that she did in that case was not her own act, but the act of her husband'.

32 Vinogradoff and Ehrlich, eds, *Year Books, 6 Edward II, 1312–13*, p. 156. See also Bolland *et al.*, eds, *Eyre of Kent, 6 & 7 Edward II. 1313–1314*, p. 47.

33 Ibid.

34 Seipp 1310.039ss and 1313.455ss. For the editions see F. W. Maitland, ed., *Year Books of Edward II, Vol. III, 3 Edward II. A.D. 1309–1310*, Selden Society 20 (London, 1905), 4A–C, pp. 67–8; Bolland *et al.*, eds, *Eyre of Kent, 6 & 7 Edward II. 1313–1314*, p. 48.

35 Maitland, ed., *Year Books of Edward II, 1309–1310*, 4B, p. 67.

purgation and one of the issues in this case was whether it was sufficient for the husband to do this alone or whether he should be joined by his wife. In another of the year book manuscripts for 1310 (as well as in the version written up under the Eyre of 1313–14) we are told that the defendant, through his lawyer, argued 'if any contract were made by our wife, it was against our will and pleasure, and we do not think that the husband is bound to answer to contracts made by her during the coverture'.[36] The justices clearly agreed with this argument, although the plaintiff's lawyer asked them to reconsider as otherwise they would have no remedy for the debt. Chief Justice Bereford told him to know better another time or, in Bolland's translation, 'You should have thought of all that before you lent your money [to a married woman].'[37]

On this evidence it seems unlikely that, as Baker has claimed, 'it was settled by 1300 that she [a wife] could bind her husband to a sale of goods which came to his use or profit'. The report for the c.1306 case does note that a plaint alleging that the husband had profited would have been successful. In the second example this argument was not raised and the winning one was that a married woman's contract ought not to bind her husband. Further, the defendant in this case made a point of arguing that any contract 'was against our will and pleasure' ('fut encounter nostre gree et nostre volunté'), which already has shades of Baker's argument that by 1500 the husband was bound 'only if he had either given his wife prior authority to act for him, or subsequently ratified a contract for his benefit'.[38]

Our next pertinent example is from a century or so later: the 1433 year book report cited in *Baron and Feme* and *Manby v. Scott*. The report discusses the buying of necessities, although the case was actually an action of debt brought against a monastery.[39] It raises the respective positions of monks and married women under the law, as do a number of year book reports (we saw above that the husband's liability for his wife in the c.1306 case was compared to that of a prior taking over a religious house from another prior).[40] One William Scot brought an action of debt before the Court of Common Pleas against Fountains Abbey. The central issue was whether the original debtor, a monk called Roger, had the power and authority to buy necessities for the House, as he was alleged to have borrowed twenty pounds with which to buy wheat 'for the use and profit of the Abbey'. The defence claimed that he was never the abbot (as the plaintiff's writ had named him), nor was he an officer of the House, a cellarer, a cook, or another officer, who might have had that power and authority; he was just a monk, a dead person under the law, and the debt could not be pursued. It was at this juncture that Justice Martin intervened:

36 Maitland, ed., *Year Books of Edward II, 1309–1310*, 4C, p. 68. See also Bolland *et al.*, eds, *Eyre of Kent, 6 & 7 Edward II. 1313–1314*, p. 48.

37 Maitland, ed., *Year Books of Edward II, 1309–1310*, 4C, p. 68, n. 1; Bolland *et al.*, eds, *Eyre of Kent, 6 & 7 Edward II. 1313–1314*, p. 48.

38 Maitland, ed., *Year Books of Edward II, 1309–1310*, p. 68. See also Bolland *et al.*, eds, *Eyre of Kent, 6 & 7 Edward II. 1313–1314*, p. 48 (where the Law French spelling differs slightly).

39 See Seipp 1433.038.

40 See also Seipp 1424.008; 1425.002; 1426.050; 1440.007; 1456.097; 1464.49; 1469.117; 1475.034; and 1535.067.

> If my wife borrows from one, and clothe herself better than belongs to my estate, I will not be charged to pay back this loan, even though it came to the use and profit of the husband, because his [my] wife must 'of necessity' be clothed, but because she went above her estate, the husband will not be charged, thus it seems that it will be accounted his [the plaintiff's] folly that he made this contract with a co-monk who was no officer of the Abbey.[41]

For Martin, it does not matter *who* used and profited from the goods (a community, a husband) if the person doing the purchasing acted beyond her/his status, either by buying better clothes or by taking on a role that was not his in the abbey. The reading that the anonymous author of *Baron and Feme* took from this report of a case – about whether a monk, who did not hold an office in Fountains Abbey, could bind the House to a contract he made – was Martin's implication that if a wife borrowed to clothe herself according to her husband's, and therefore her, estate then the husband would be charged because she 'of necessity' must be clothed. This is our first example of what we might call a law of necessaries and it seems telling that the case was not actually about a married woman. This suggests that Martin thought his point about what a married woman could (and could not) do was sufficiently commonplace by 1433 that it could be used as an analogy in a case about a monastic debt, which perhaps compensates for the long interval between the reports discussed here.

Our fourth example is a report from 1442, cited in the *Manby v. Scott* case.[42] It also concerned an action against a monk, and an analogy to a married woman was again made, although here the point about the husband's liability was challenged. In a case for debt brought before the Court of Common Pleas, the plaintiff was alleged to have loaned twenty pounds to the defendant abbot's predecessor, who had obliged himself to pay by a written bond. The plaintiff claimed that the sum was converted to the use of the defendant abbot's House and thus the defendant, as its current abbot, should honour it. The defence (Serjeant Markham) sought to argue that the plaintiff's action was invalid because it pertained to two matters rather than one: one of a contract arising from the loan, and the other of the written obligation. Thus Markham actually argued for the defendant's liability for the contract, with analogy to a wife's purchase of something that came to her husband's use:

> in several cases even if a contract be not valid to have an action against me, yet by a thing done afterwards it will be valid; because I put that your wife buy something from me, now you will not be

41 'si ma feme apprompte d'un, & luy array meliour que attient a mon estat, jeo ne sera charge a paier cest appromptage, coment que il devient al' oeps & profit le baron, pur ceo que sa feme covient "de necessitate" estre arraye: mes pur ceo que ele passe son estat, le baron ne sera charge: issint semble que il sera recte son folie que il aver fait cest contract ove le Commoine que ne fuit nul officer del' Abbey': Seipp 1433.038 (the Law French and the English have been amended, following checking of the Vulgate Year Books reprint, accessed via Seipp).

42 Robertson and Ellis, eds, *The English Reports*, 83, p. 817 (cited here as '22 H. 6, 20').

> charged for this against me, but if afterwards this *comes to your use*, now you will be charged; and it will be the same law if your servant buy anything, etc.; thus here even though the contract that the predecessor made was not of such force at first that the successor will be bound by this, yet when the predecessor converted the sum to the use of the House, this made the contract effectual to bind the House [my italics].[43]

Markham's argument that – as the original debt had been put to the use of the House – the current abbot should be liable for his predecessor's debt, rests on an assumption that a wife could bind her husband to a sale of goods that came into his possession. Not everyone agreed; Chief Justice Newton argued that it was 'not law' that a person was liable for something if it simply came to his use, and he used the example of a gift:

> because on this it would ensue that if after such purchase made by the servant and the same servant wanted to give the thing thus bought to the master, by this the master will be charged in an action, which is not law; it must be, if the husband or the master will be charged for a purchase made by the wife, or servant, that this buying be done *to the use* of the husband or the master, and then it will befall that the husband or the master come to have the thing afterward, he will be charged by this agreement [my italics].[44]

Thus Newton's position is that, for the contract to be binding on the husband, it needed to be done *on his behalf* and then the goods come into his possession. This suggests prior consent on the part of the husband, whether express or implied. The position has something in common with Martin's argument of 1433: a contract for something that came to the use and profit of the husband was not necessarily binding. Nevertheless, it is of note that in this report from 1442 – again concerning a monastic debt – Markham assumed that a married woman *could* bind her spouse to a sale of goods which simply came to his use or profit, as was suggested by the c.1306 case. The debate in this legal action continued into a subsequent proceeding.[45]

Our fifth example is from a year book report dated 1505, but perhaps actually originating from a case heard in 1499.[46] It explicitly concerns a married woman's

43 Seipp 1442.019.

44 My italics. Seipp 1442.019 (the English has been amended).

45 See Seipp 1442.095 (Trinity term).

46 The serjeant quoted in the case, Yaxley, died 19 July 1505 so it must have predated that: Seipp 1505.064. Baker argues that the printed text for 21 Henry VII contains cases of 11–19 and 22 Henry VII and that many seem to have been extracted from Fitzherbert's *Graunde abridgement* and relate to Trinity term 14 Henry VII: Baker, ed., *Reports of John Spelman*, II, p. 168. It is dated T. 4 H. 7 (1489) in the 1516 edition of Fitzherbert's abridgement but M. 21 H. 7 40 (1505) and T. 14 H. 7 (1499) in the 1577 edition: Fitzherbert, [*La graunde abridgement*] (1516), *Dette*, 160; Anthony Fitzherbert, *La graunde abridgement* ... ([London], 1577), *Dette*, 160 (accessed via EEBO).

contract and raises further distinctions: between a married woman making a necessary purchase (which did not bind the husband to the debt) and the husband *agreeing afterwards* with her necessary purchase or *commanding* the wife to make a necessary purchase (which might have bound him). A case had been brought before King's Bench for trespass. The plaintiff alleged that he had sold to a married woman certain goods for twenty pounds and that the husband had then paid him and taken the goods. He was now suing the husband for trespass (for taking the goods), and Serjeant Yaxley – who was pleading his case – claimed that the sale was void because a *femme couverte* could not make a contract. Justice Rede was the first to disagree, asserting that if a married woman bought clothing ('draps') and the husband agreed to it afterwards, that was a valid contract and so it was in this case. Chief Justice Fyneux also maintained that the plaintiff should accept this argument but elaborated on what should and should not bind a husband:

> a married woman [feme covert] cannot do anything that redounds to the prejudice or charge of her husband by contract, but she is 'able' to do things by which her husband will have advantage; because if I give goods to a married woman, this is good, and the husband can agree to this, but if a married woman makes a contract, or buys something in a market, this is void, because it can be that this will be a charge to the husband; but my wife can buy a thing to my use, and I can agree to this, and so if I command my wife to buy a necessary thing, if she buys these, I will be bound by this [purchase] by this general command; and if my wife buys a thing to keep my 'household', such as bread, etc. and I have no knowledge of this, even though it be expended in my household, I will not be charged for these.[47]

For Fyneux the key issue was that the wife's actions should not prejudice the husband.[48] Thus the husband could agree to her actions subsequently and make her purchase valid but if he did not know about a purchase – even if it was bread for the household, which the household consumed – he would not be liable for it.[49] Fyneux's argument thus differs from Martin's position in 1433 that a wife could

47 'femme couverte ne puit faire chose que tourne son baron en prejudice ou charge per son contract; mes ele est "able" de faire chose, pur quel son baron aura avantage. Car si jeo donne bien a femme couverte, ceo est bon, & le baron puit agreer a ceo: mes si femme couverte fait contract, ou achete chose en marche, ceo est voide, pur ceo que puit estre que ceo serra charge al' baron. Mes ma femme puit achete chose a mon use, & jeo puis agreer a ceo: & issint si jeo commande ma femme de acheter chose necessaire, si ele achete ceux, jeo serai lie per ceo per cest commandement general. Et si ma femme achete chose a garde mon "houshold", come pain, &c. & jeo n'ay conusance de ceo, coment que il soit expende en mon "houshold", jeo ne serai charge pur ceux': Seipp 1505.064 (the Law French and the English have been amended).

48 For another case in which it is argued that the wife cannot do something to the damage of the husband, see Seipp 1439.010 (Sjt Fulthorpe; but cf. Sjt Portyngton).

49 Cf. Loengard, 'Common Law for Margery', p. 123: 'Obviously if a woman ordered a leg of lamb and her husband ate it for dinner, the case would seem fairly clear.'

buy necessities without any prior command or subsequent agreement as long as they were in keeping with her and her husband's estate. Fyneux did allow, though, for a husband to issue a 'general command' to his wife to buy 'a necessary thing'. This report lends support to Baker's statement that 'by 1500 it was clear that the husband was bound in such a case only if he had either given his wife prior authority to act for him, or subsequently ratified a contract for his benefit'.

Our sixth example is from a year book report of 1535, which concerned John Holygrave's plaint before King's Bench that Henry Knightsbridge owed him £6 15s. The original debt had been owed by Oliver Tateham whom Holygrave had had imprisoned in the Bread Street Compter. Knightsbridge had asked Holygrave's wife, in her husband's absence, to let Tateham go free in exchange for him (Knightsbridge) undertaking the debt (in legal parlance, *assumpsit*).[50] She agreed but Knightsbridge now denied that he had taken on the debt, arguing – through his lawyer – that the evidence was not good and that the *assumpsit* was void because it was made with a married woman without prior command from her husband and because a wife could not do any act that would be to the prejudice of her husband (which had been Fyneux's starting point in the previous example).[51] However, all the justices agreed that the undertaking was good because the husband had agreed to it afterwards. One of the justices, Spelman, took the opportunity to say more about what things a wife was legally 'able' to do:

> Sir, a wife is 'able' to do acts that will be to the advantage of her husband, and to his disadvantage also, and these will be good by the husband's agreement. To his advantage she can; as if an obligation be made to her, or a feoffment, or a gift of goods, if the husband agrees, this is good. So can she disadvantage the husband, as if she disseises a man, and then the husband agrees, now the husband is disseisor *ab initio*, and this agreement will have relation to the time of the disseisin. So it is if a married woman [feme coverte] sells goods, or gives away goods, and then the husband agrees to this, these are made perfect sales, and gifts, and the cause is, the agreement afterwards makes them profit, and the reasoning, as has been said, is because a married woman does not have any will, but the will of the husband is her will, and so when the husband agrees to an act done by his wife, this agreement makes this the act of the husband. As the case where the wife [femme] gives away the husband's goods, or sells them, and afterwards the husband agrees; now by this agreement this is the gift or sale of the husband, and the husband will be bound by this agreement.[52]

50 See Baker, *Introduction*, pp. 360, 375, 446–7.

51 Seipp 1535.067. The wife's involvement is not mentioned in the King's Bench record nor in Spelman's reports: see J. H. Baker and S. F. C. Milsom, *Sources of English Legal History: Private Law to 1750*, 2nd edn (London, 2010), p. 454 (*Holygrave v. Knightsbridge*); Baker, ed., *Reports of John Spelman*, I, pp. 7–8.

52 'Sir, une feme est *able* de faire actes que sera al' avantage de son baron, & a s' disadvantage auxy,

Although the case was about whether Knightsbridge taking on Tateham's debt was valid or not (because the agreement had been made with Holygrave's wife), rather than about a married woman buying goods, it is nevertheless instructive that Spelman argues that the same principle applies to a whole range of actions: subsequent agreement to a wife's act makes it the husband's act. He argues – in contrast to Fyneux – that a wife could act to the disadvantage of her husband.[53]

We have seen that justices did not always agree as to what a married woman could do, both within a particular case and over the course of the late Middle Ages. If we were to look for a general pattern, though, it seems from the reports discussed that over the course of the fifteenth century there was greater restriction on married women's ability to make valid contracts *for necessities*. In 1433 Martin argued by implication that a wife could expect her husband to honour a loan if she had used it to buy clothing suitable to her estate because that was a necessity. In 1442 Newton countered that a husband could not be held liable for things that simply came to his use; instead his wife must have bought the things *for his use*, implying the purchase was done at his behest, with his subsequent possession of them signifying his agreement. Then c.1499 Rede noted that a wife's purchase of clothing was made valid if her husband agreed to it afterwards, and Fyneux went further in stating that a husband should not even be charged for bread that his household consumed if he had not issued a command – whether specific or general – for his wife to buy such necessities.

If we track a law of (wifely) agency, then there is a different and more complex trajectory than the long-term trend towards restriction which we find in the law of necessities. The c.1306 case ruled that a husband should be liable for a wife's contract if he profited from it, whereas the 1310 case concluded that the husband should not be held liable for contracts made during coverture. Fyneux argued c.1499 that a married woman could 'do things by which her husband will have advantage' but 'cannot do anything that redounds to the prejudice or charge of her husband by contract'. However, Spelman in 1535 argued that 'a wife is "able" to do acts that will be to the advantage of her husband and to his disadvantage also'. The acts are broader than the purchasing of 'necessities' but in most of the examples discussed – whether they relate to a law of necessaries or a law of wifely agency – the husband was required to give his consent, implicitly or explicitly, either before or afterwards.

& ceux sera bonne per l' agrement le baron. A s' avantage ele poit; come si une obligation soit fait a luy, ou feffement, ou donne des biens, si le baron agre, ceo est bon. Issint poit ele disavantager le baron; come si ele disseisist un home, & puis le baron agre, or le baron est disseisor *ab initio*, & cest agrement aura relacion al' temps del' disseisin. Issint est si feme coverte vende biens, ou donne biens, & puis le baron agre a ceo, ceux sont parfait vende, & donne: & la cause est, la agrement apres fist eux profit, & la reason come ad este dit, est pur ceo que une femme covertte n'ad ascun volonte, mes la volonte del' baron est s' volonte; & donq quand le baron agre a un acte fait per sa femme, cest agrement fait cest l'acte le baron. Come le cas ou la femme donne biens le baron, ou vende eux, & apres le baron agre; or per cest agrement ceo est le donne ou vendicion del' baron, & le baron sera lie per cest agrement': Seipp 1535.067 (the Law French and the English have been amended).

53 See also Seipp 1410.028 (CJ Gascoigne: 'for a wife's default will be adjudged her husband's default, because to his will she is amenable').

We now need to consider the extent to which other legal jurisdictions – such as those of borough courts and Chancery's court of conscience – stepped in to clarify or arbitrate what common law had left open regarding married women's contracts.

Beyond Common Law

For Janet Loengard, the borough custom of *femme sole* was 'a more effective way of permitting some [married] women to function in the commercial world' than the common law supposition that a wife might be acting under her husband's 'general authority'.[54] However, as discussed earlier, McIntosh has disputed how commonly that custom was used by married women. In this section we will consider what borough custom had to say concerning married women and contracts, but the focus will be deliberately indirect – on two Chancery cases in which London's customs about married women and trade are raised and disputed – with the intention of offering a perspective which prioritizes the actual practice of the time rather than legal theory. While there are undoubtedly risks in putting too much weight on a few suggestive examples, the advantage of this approach is that – by considering evidence from a court which did not rely on common law principles – we can obtain a better sense of how the doctrine of coverture was modified and adapted to suit households' needs. Further, without forgetting that the year book discussions related to actual court cases, and Chancery petitions, responses and depositions are clearly the products of lawyers and a legal system, the latter were composed with the intention of reflecting the point of view of the lay participants.[55]

We are concerned here with the 'English' side of Chancery, the Chancellor's jurisdiction to deal with bills of complaint, so called because its records are predominantly in Middle English.[56] The key aspect of the 'English' side is that it did not operate according to the principles of common law. Although some scholars prefer to call the late medieval Chancery a 'court of conscience' rather than of equity, the important point is that the Chancellor decided cases according to some notion of what was fair or just as opposed to strict rules of evidence.[57] In order for

54 Loengard, 'Common Law for Margery', p. 124.

55 See T. S. Haskett, 'County Lawyers? The Composers of English Chancery Bills', *The Life of the Law: Proceedings of the Tenth British Legal History Conference, Oxford, 1991*, ed. P. Birks (London, 1993), p. 11; T. S. Haskett, 'The Presentation of Cases in Medieval Chancery Bills', *Legal History in the Making: Proceedings of the Ninth British Legal History Conference, Glasgow, 1989*, ed. W. M. Gordon and T. D. Fergus (London, 1991), pp. 11–28.

56 Baker, *Introduction*, pp. 117–18. Before the reign of Henry VI (1422–61), the petitions were written in French, with a few in Latin. See J. H. Fisher, *The Emergence of Standard English* (Lexington, 1996), p. 54.

57 See T. S. Haskett, 'The Medieval English Court of Chancery', *Law and History Review* 14 (1996), 245–313, pp. 249–80; P. Tucker, 'The Early History of the Court of Chancery: A Comparative Study', *English Historical Review* 115 (2000), 791–811, p. 795. London's Mayor's Court also judged some cases according to conscience: P. Tucker, *Law Courts and Lawyers in the City of*

a case to fall under the remit of the 'English' side, the petitioner had to claim that she or he would not receive justice in another jurisdiction, for example, because the case was not actionable under common law, there was a lack of supporting documentation, the petitioner was too poor to afford legal counsel, or the opponent was so powerful that a trial in another jurisdiction would be unfair. Compared with common law procedure, bringing a case to Chancery was a less formal process and so could be swifter and cheaper.[58]

The first petition in which London's customs about married women and trade are raised concerns a married woman denying that she was a 'soul marchaunt', a term that the late fifteenth-century petitions use rather than *femme sole*.[59] Anne Davell, wife of John Davell, a London citizen and draper, had been found by a jury in London's Sheriffs' Court to be 'soul marchaunt' and to owe Christine Baxter, a single woman, 18s. In Anne's petition to Chancery in 1486, it is claimed that she 'never was soul marchaunt nor wist [knew] what that terme ment unto this tyme that necessitie ticheth hir, but was ever continually covert baron'.[60] Was this just a legal ploy to avoid paying the 18s., or might there be some truth to Anne's claim?

The wider context to the accusation was that Christine had first sued Anne's husband, John Davell, for 18s. – also in London's Sheriffs' Court – but this action had lapsed. However, John was still committed to Ludgate prison because he owed diverse sums of money to a number of people. Christine then pursued Anne for the same amount, by way of a trespass charge.[61] According to Anne's petition, this was just opportunistic and due to Christine's 'pure malice and evil will'.[62] In the course of her defence, Anne's petition does imply that she had been involved in buying and selling, but also claims that she had only done so under the protection of coverture:

> she never aught hir [Christine] peny nor never bought nor sold with hir nor with noon' othre creature the daies of hir life but undre the commaundement authoritie privilege and libertie of hir said husband as many other pour' women doon'.[63]

London, 1300–1550 (Cambridge, 2007), pp. 113–18.

58 For more on the court of Chancery, its process and its records, see C. Beattie, 'Single Women, Work and Family: The Chancery Dispute of Jane Wynde and Margaret Clerk', *Voices from the Bench: The Narratives of Lesser Folk in Medieval Trials*, ed. M. Goodich (New York, 2006), pp. 179–82.

59 E.g. see The National Archives, Kew (hereafter TNA), Early Chancery Proceedings, C 1/47/91 (1472–3 or 1475), C 1/64/434, C 1/64/883, C 1/66/229 (all 1475–80 or 1483–5), C 1/73/119 (1386–1486), C 1/110/125 (1486–93), C 1/201/32 (1493–1500); I discuss the last two petitions in C. Beattie, '"Living as a single person": Marital Status, Performance and the Law in Late Medieval England', *Women's History Review* 17 (2008), 327–40, p. 335. Petitions are undated but references to specific Chancellors in the bills' addresses set date limits in the absence of other information.

60 TNA, C 1/80/12 (1486).

61 The 18s. in this action being 'damages' for an unspecified offence.

62 TNA, C 1/80/12; this is formulaic language.

63 TNA, C 1/80/12.

The reference to acting under her husband's 'commandment, authority, privilege and liberty' suggests that she operated as her husband's agent. Anne's petition also claims that this is something 'many other poor women do'. We might want to be wary of putting too much weight on the adjective 'poor' as this was a term frequently used in Chancery petitions, both to get the Chancellor's sympathy and to ensure that the petition met one of the requirements for moving a case to this legal jurisdiction (that the petitioner was too poor to get justice in another court).[64] The Davells had clearly fallen on hard times, as John had been imprisoned for debt, but prior to this he was a citizen and draper and thus presumably part of London's mercantile elite. So we are left with the claim that Anne bought and sold under the commandment and authority of her husband 'as many other women do'. This claim is important in two respects: it counters the accusation that Anne was really a 'sole marchaunt' by casting her as her husband's agent and it asserts that this was a common practice.

Anne's claim in her Chancery petition of 1486 can be usefully compared with the closest year book example. Chief Justice Fyneux, with reference to the c.1499 case, argued that if a husband commanded his wife 'to buy a necessary thing' he would 'be bound by this general command'. Necessaries were usually defined as food, drink, clothing and medicine. While Anne was certainly responsible for such purchases, it is likely that her economic activities went well beyond this. According to Anne's own petition, since her husband's imprisonment, she had nothing from which 'to fynde him mete and drinke during his beeing in prisone save onely the daily labour and hand crafte of your said beedwoman [petitioner] havyng iij children upon' hir hand at hir daily birdyn' and charge'.[65] Thus Anne's conception of agency went beyond that of the justices in the king's courts; Bailey, from her eighteenth-century material, had suggested that this broader understanding of agency might have been how the law of necessaries was used in practice.

Our next Chancery petition goes further in its suggestion that London custom allowed married women a greater degree of agency than that granted to them under the common law. It is also from the late fifteenth century and relates to a case brought by a London vintner, William Lovell, and his wife, Elene, against William Hull, a mason, concerning silk bought from Elene by William Hull's late wife, Agnes. We have a number of surviving documents relating to this dispute: three petitions (two from the married couple, one from William Lovell alone after Elene's death), answers from Hull to two of the petitions, two replications from the petitioners (the first from Lovell and his wife, the second from Lovell alone), and the statements of three witnesses.[66] From these, we learn that the Hulls had allegedly agreed to seal and deliver a bond as security for the cost of the silk but had failed to do so and, when the Lovells took actions against them in the city of

64 E.g. see C. Beattie, *Medieval Single Women: The Politics of Social Classification in Late Medieval England* (Oxford, 2007), p. 30.

65 TNA, C 1/80/12.

66 See TNA, C 1 31/476 (1465–71), C 1/43/291–4 (1467–72), C 1/43/158–60 (1467–72). The silk had been allegedly purchased in September 1463.

London, the Hulls contested the charges by waging their law (that is, swearing an oath, together with eleven supporters) that they owed the Lovells nothing. In the Chancery case, William Hull went as far as to claim that he had no knowledge of Agnes buying the silk. Of particular interest here is the petition from William Lovell alone in which he paints a picture of how, during the frequent absences of mercantile husbands, their wives would take over the running of their households and all that this entailed. There is little surprising in this general picture.[67] However, Lovell goes further and says that:

> the comune gise [custom] within the saide citee is and of longe tyme hath been that the wyfes of men of worship and thrifte infraunchised in the same citee have by the sufferaunce of their husbands in thabsence of them used to by and selle all' manere of marchaundise towardes thencreece [the increase] and lyving of them and their household' the dutees of alle whiche bargaines comming or growing hath alwey ben contente by suche wifes or for nowne paiement of them by their husbondes.[68]

It has been assumed that Lovell was referring to London's custom of allowing married women to trade as if *femmes soles*.[69] I disagree and will first show how the two 'customs' differ, before arguing that the 'gise' Lovell refers to actually shares more with common law thinking on married women as agents than with the borough custom of *femme sole*, while also surpassing the common law position.

London's custom of allowing married women to trade as if *femmes soles* was copied into the city's *Liber Albus* in 1419:

> And where a woman coverte de baron follows any craft within the said city by herself apart [apar luy soule], with which the husband in no way interferes [dount le baroun se melle rienz], such a woman shall be bound as a single woman as to all that concerns her said craft [soun dit craft]. And if the husband and the wife are impleaded, in such case, the wife shall plead as a single woman in a Court of Record, and she shall have her law and other advantages by way of plea just as a single woman. And if she is condemned, she shall be committed to prison until she shall have made satisfac-

67 E.g. see A. F. Sutton, 'The Shop-floor of the London Mercery Trade, *c.* 1200 – *c.* 1500: The Marginalisation of the Artisan, the Itinerant Mercer and the Shopholder', *Nottingham Medieval Studies* 45 (2001), 12–50, esp. p. 22; C. Beattie, 'Economy', *A Cultural History of Childhood and Family in the Early Modern Age*, ed. S. Cavallo and S. Evangelisti (Oxford, 2010), p. 57.

68 TNA, C 1/43/293.

69 This was an audience reaction to my discussion of this case: C. Beattie, 'Women and the Law in Fifteenth-Century England', paper given at 'The Fifteenth Century Conference 2009', University of St Andrews, 3 September 2009. Kay Lacey gives this impression by referring to the case in close proximity to the London customs on *femme sole*: K. E. Lacey, 'Women and Work in Fourteenth and Fifteenth Century London', *Women and Work in Pre-industrial England*, ed. L. Charles and L. Duffin (London, 1985), pp. 43–4.

> tion; and neither the husband nor his goods shall in such case be charged or impeached.[70]

The custom concerns women who worked separately from their husbands and in a different trade from their husbands ('follows any craft ... by herself apart, with which the husband in no way interferes'). The Chancery case revolved around the buying and selling of silk, but William Lovell was described as a vintner, which suggests that husband and wife were operating in different trades. However, the custom is primarily about removing responsibility for a wife's debts from her husband, whereas Lovell's petition says that husbands would honour their wives' debts if their wives did not pay them. The petition also refers to wives working 'towards thencreece [the increase] and lyving of them and their household', and the 'them' on the previous line quite clearly referred to the husbands ('in thabsence of them'). Indeed, Lovell's point seems to be that wives had to take on their husbands' roles in their absence. Further, Lovell's petition is at pains to suggest that his wife's actions were by his 'sufferaunce', that is, he had given permission for her to buy and sell.[71] This term 'sufferaunce' is not only used with reference to the custom but also when Lovell's petition goes on to set out the precise circumstances behind the debt:

> nowe late Elyne wife of your said besecher in his absence *by his sufferaunce* sold unto Agneys late wife of William Hull of London mason *by his sufferaunce* in his absence for cause and in fourme aforesaid asmoche silke as amounted by bargayne betwixt them accorded to the some and value of xxij. li [my italics].[72]

The emphasis is on both husbands agreeing to the buying and selling and being absent, with the implication being that the wives were acting as their agents.[73]

What is the 'gise' or custom to which Lovell's petition refers? A custom relating to debt in *Liber Albus* does mention wives acting on behalf of their husbands:

> where plaint of debt is made against the husband, and the plaintiff declares that the husband made the contract with the plaintiff by the hand of the wife of such defendant [parmy la meyn la femme le defendaunt], in such case, the said defendant shall have the aid of his wife, and shall have a day until the next Court, for taking counsel with his wife.[74]

70 H. T. Riley, ed., *Munimenta Gildhallæ Londiniensis; Liber Albus, Liber Custumarum et Liber Horn*, 3 vols (London, 1859–62), I, pp. 204–5, III, p. 38 (for the translation). The other two recorded *femme sole* customs referred to the hiring of houses and answering pleas of trespass: ibid., I, p. 205, III, p. 39.

71 See *Middle English Dictionary* (hereafter *MED*), online at http://quod.lib.umich.edu/m/med/, sufferaunce (n.), 5(b) permission, leave.

72 TNA, C 1/43/293.

73 There is a further reference to Hull's absence and agreement towards the end of the petition: 'this said wyf in his absence by his sufferaunce bought the said silke' (TNA, C 1/43/293).

74 Riley, ed., *Munimenta Gildhallæ Londiniensis*, I, p. 206, III, pp. 39–40 (for the translation).

The central element here is that the husband can consult his wife in a debt case brought against him only.[75] For our purposes it is telling that the wife's involvement in the contracting of the debt, acting as her husband's agent, appears commonplace, but it does not amount to a legal custom to that effect. It is possible that Lovell was referring to something less formal by his use of the word 'gise', such as a common practice.[76] We should not confuse the writing down of customs with their origins. Thus while the first known record of London's *femme sole* customs was in the now lost Darcy's custumal of the 1330s and 1340s, the practice may actually have dated back to the early thirteenth century.[77]

It is plausible to suppose that urban jurisdictions, which would have experienced the greatest volume of wives buying and selling goods, might step in to clarify what common law had left debatable. A custom from Norwich c.1340 is one such example:

> In the case where the wife of any one without her husband's knowledge [preter scienciam viri sui] has accepted a loan from her neighbour, a citizen of this city, with or without gage, the husband must answer for the loan made to his wife in his absence, so long as the man and wife are on good terms, to wit so long as the wife of the said man is cohabiting with her husband at the time when the debt was made, or living separate by his assent and goodwill, so long as there is common knowledge of the said wife's good conduct, and that she does not (without being harshly and cruelly expelled by her husband's malice for no fault or demerit of hers) deceitfully or wrongfully separate herself from her husband by her own wilfulness, and that she does not separate herself to make mischief; for in such case if any of these things can be proved, the husband is not bound to restore the loans thus taken. And creditors should be warned that without the husband's consent they lend to a wife, separating herself thus wrongfully from her husband, only at their own risk.[78]

The custumal is mostly concerned with who was liable for the debts of wives who lived separately from their husbands. It is stated that the husband was still liable if he had made her leave or if he had assented to her leaving and was only not liable for her debts if she had left without his consent. This last exemption not-

75 Stevens has found examples of this custom being enacted in the Sheriffs' Court of 1320: M. F. Stevens, 'London Women, the Courts and the "Golden Age": A Quantitative Analysis of Female Litigants in the Fourteenth and Fifteenth Centuries', *London Journal* 37 (2012), 67–88, p. 76.

76 *MED*, gise (n.), 1(b) the practice of a particular time or place, custom.

77 C. M. Barron, 'The "Golden Age" of Women in Medieval London', *Reading Medieval Studies* 15 (1989), 35–58, pp. 39–40; cf. McIntosh, 'Benefits and Drawbacks', pp. 414–15, which suggests that the formal definition of the custom went hand in hand with its practice. Even when the custom had been formalized, parties found that they could not always successfully plead cases in the city's courts if there was no written record of the women formally registering as *femme sole*. See Beattie, '"Living as a single person"', p. 335.

78 M. Bateson (ed.), *Borough Customs*, Selden Society 18 (London, 1904), pp. 224–5.

withstanding, the custumal generally assumes that a husband was liable for his wife's debts, even if she acted without his knowledge, which is further than the justices of the year book discussions were prepared to go. This position is closer to that of *The Laws Respecting Women* (1777), which states that 'while they cohabit, the husband shall answer all contracts of hers for necessaries, for his assent shall be presumed to all necessary contracts, upon the account of co-habiting'.[79] If the assumption in Norwich in the mid-fourteenth century was that husbands were liable for contracts made by their wives in their absence, then this could have been a more widely held view.[80]

Whether Lovell, in his petition to Chancery, was referring to a formal custom or to a common practice that had not been codified, William Hull challenged the petition's claim by asserting that he knows of no such custom in the city of London. As discussed above with Davell's petition, there could have been some truth to this, or it could just have been an expedient claim. Hull's response does not rest on this one issue, though, since he also claims that he had no knowledge of his own wife's actions:

> the seid William Hull seyth that his wyffe bought never the seid silk nor no parcel therof to hys knowing ... nor never understood nor knewe that his wife ever any such silk had in hir life nor she any such silk bought by his consent will nor knowing.[81]

Hull's legal strategy was clearly to deny liability by asserting that his wife did not have his consent and that he had no knowledge of any such actions. Hull wanted the case to be judged under common law. As we have seen in the year book reports, the husband's lack of initial consent and certainly the lack of subsequent agreement could be a successful argument under common law. However, the examination of three silkwomen as part of this case damages his claims as they not only depose that Agnes bought and sold silk with them and diverse men and women, including Elene, wife of William Lovell, but that Hull had honoured some of his wife's debts after her death and sought to collect others.[82]

Clearly both William Lovell and William Hull used the arguments (and tried to use the jurisdictions) that would best serve their purposes, whether to have the debt honoured or to avoid it. But for both men the crucial issues were whether they had given their wives permission to buy and sell and whether they had knowledge of their wives' actions, both key elements in the common law debates.

79 Anon., *The Laws Respecting Women*, p. 68.

80 On the economic activities of fourteenth-century wives in Norwich, see E. Rutledge, 'Norwich before the Black Death', *Medieval Norwich*, ed. C. Rawcliffe and R. Wilson (London, 2004), pp. 181–3; P. Dunn, 'Trade', in ibid., p. 227.

81 TNA, C 1/43/294.

82 TNA, C 1/43/291. Margaret Duram said that the debt was paid 'by cohercion of the lawe' as there were obligations made between William Hull and his wife and William Duram and his wife for silk Agnes had purchased from Margaret. Elizabeth Stokton said that William Hull had partially repaid her after his wife's death. Emme Stokes said that William Hull sent an apprentice to tell her she now owed him for silk she had received from his late wife Agnes.

The case clearly reveals that the two wives had been involved in buying and selling, as had other married women, with all three of the female deponents being described as wives.[83] Although Agnes is referred to by two of the deponents as a silk throwster, there are no references to any of the women acting as *femmes soles*, with Margaret Duram deposing that her transactions with Agnes were supported by obligations made between William Hull and his wife Agnes on the one hand and William Duram and his wife Margaret on the other.[84] This lends support to the claim in Lovell's petition that it was a common custom in London for wives of citizens to buy and sell all manner of merchandise with the permission of their husbands, and also backs up the claim in Anne Davell's petition that she bought and sold under the authority of her husband 'as many other ... women doon'.

It is also worth spelling out that, although the buying and selling of silk by women like Elene Lovell and Agnes Hull would have been of benefit to their households, it clearly related to their own work and not that of their husbands, as was the case with Anne Davell's economic activities discussed earlier.[85] In these examples it would seem that some understanding of a 'law of agency' – even if it was understood more as 'a common gise' beyond the pale of common law jurisdiction – enabled them to make contracts. As Bailey has argued for a later period, in practice a law of agency might have been of use for wives' own occupations as well as the buying of household necessities. Such evidence, of married women acting as agents, might help explain the suggested low uptake of the custom of *femme sole* in late medieval London. It might also explain why scholars of late medieval England have not found evidence of the latter custom beyond a few urban centres. Thus there is a need for more research on this important issue.

Conclusion

The arguments heard in a number of late medieval English courts – whether they were advanced by the serjeants and justices in Common Pleas or King's Bench or the parties in Chancery cases – suggest that there were ways around the doctrine of coverture, especially when the managing of households was at stake. For common law, this took the form of what has been called a law of necessaries or a law of agency, but there was no clear-cut position as to when these applied. We have seen that over the course of the fifteenth century there was greater restriction on married women's ability to make valid contracts for necessities. The husband's consent, implicit or explicit, before or after the purchase, was needed – in contrast with the position outlined in *The Laws Respecting Women* (1777), where assent is presumed. The need for consent was also the case for women acting as their husbands' agents, although here there are some indications that the range of actions

83 TNA, C 1/43/291: Elizabeth Stokton, wife of John Stokton; Margaret Duram, wife of William Duram; Emme Stokes, wife of John Stokes.

84 TNA, C 1/43/291: Examinations of Margaret Duram and Emme Stokes.

85 See Sutton, 'The Shop-floor', p. 50, for the argument that silkwomen often brought in 'the, often essential, second income of the average household'.

considered valid by the justices increased over the period c.1306 to 1535.

It also seems likely that borough custom went even further and this area would repay further investigation. For example, the Norwich custom of c.1340 assumes that a husband is liable for his wife's debts, even if she acted without his knowledge. Also, in William Lovell's late fifteenth-century Chancery petition, it is claimed that it was a common 'gise' for the wives of London citizens to be given permission to buy and sell all manner of goods in their husbands' absence, and these debts would be honoured by the husbands, if not settled by the wives. We can compare this with Chief Justice Fyneux's argument in King's Bench c.1499 that a husband could command his wife to buy a necessary thing, such as food, and he would be bound by this 'general command', but that otherwise her contracts for purchases at the market, including bread consumed in his household, would be considered invalid if he had no knowledge of them. Thus, common law – which seems more geared towards the running of private, non-mercantile households than mercantile ones – allowed wives to make contracts, but all purchases were subject to review and approval (or potential veto) by the husbands, who could therefore refuse to honour deals they did not like. In contrast, Lovell's petition suggests that the London custom was that wives of citizens enjoyed advance blanket approval from their spouses to buy and sell various goods (not just purchase household necessities) and that the husbands were bound by those bargains, even if they disliked them, which would seem to be a necessary position in an urban market. That Hull tried to get the case moved to a common law court is indicative that common law was more restrictive than borough custom on this matter, needing consent to be clearly given and proven rather than assumed.

While restrictions were clearly still in place, it is evident that married women's ability to make valid contracts was not entirely hampered by coverture nor only alleviated by the borough custom allowing them to register and trade as *femmes soles*. These findings validate the use of technical legal sources to explore the social history questions with which this essay started.

8

PROPERTY, FAMILY AND PARTNERSHIP: MARRIED WOMEN AND LEGAL CAPABILITY IN LATE MEDIEVAL GHENT

Shennan Hutton

Three days after Christmas, 1357, Perneele, the wife of Willem Baillluz, went to the court of the aldermen of the *Keure* in Ghent to perform a legal act – paying part of a debt owed by her daughter.[1] Perneele was the surety, rather like a modern co-signer, for a debt that her daughter had contracted. When her daughter could not pay the debt, Perneele became legally responsible for paying the creditor. While the brief act recorded in the aldermen's register does not explain why Perneele acted as a surety for her daughter, there are two likely scenarios. The most likely is that Perneele was a remarried widow, and she had legally obligated herself as a surety for her daughter during her widowhood. A second possibility is that Perneele was married at the time that she obligated herself alone, without her husband, to be her daughter's surety. Since Perneele owned personal property coming from her family of origin, she could pledge her property, rather than the couple's community property, to secure a debt.[2] It is not likely that the clerk omitted Willem's name if he was a joint surety along with his wife, because the aldermen's clerks typically wrote down exactly who the debtor and surety or sureties were, and the clerks noted if one spouse paid for another.[3] But this clerk did not explain why a married woman could be legally responsible for a debt, or act legally without her husband. He did not record that Perneele had her husband's permission, even though in a few other acts clerks wrote out clauses indicating that the wife was acting as her husband's

1 Stadsarchief Gent [City Archives of Ghent; hereafter SAG], series 301, no. 1, fol. 167v, no. 6, 28 December 1357: 'Perneele Willem sBailluz wijf heeft betaelt her Diederick den Moenc IX s. II d. gro. min, in minder van XXVI s. gro. ende VI d. gro., daer af so borghe ward vor harer dochter Jans Smets wedewe. Actum XXVIII die decembris.'

2 I use the term 'community property' as the most direct translation of the Dutch term *ghemeenen goeden*. It should not be confused with the English common law or the modern Anglo-American legal category of 'community property', because the husband controlled the community property during the marriage.

3 It is impossible to know if this practice was universal, however. For examples, see SAG, series 301, no. 1, fol. 60v, act no. 7, 1350; series 330, no. 1, fol. 129r, act no. 1, 30 August 1351.

representative or with his permission.[4] Instead, the clerk merely stated that Perneele owed the money as surety for her daughter, and that she had paid part of that sum to the creditor. A married woman thus performed a legal act by herself before the highest officials in Ghent, without any expression of her husband's permission or special explanation of the circumstances. Perneele had some legal capability even though she was a married woman.[5]

The aldermen of the *Keure* were the highest legal authorities in Ghent, a city that was semi-autonomous from its titular overlord, the count of Flanders, and governed itself by an unwritten customary law.[6] According to that customary law, Perneele was 'under the power' of her husband, but at the same time the aldermen recognized that married women had rights and obligations arising from their ownership of personal property from their families of origin and from the actions that they had taken as single women or widows.[7] The clerk identified Perneele as a married woman (Perneele, Willem Bailluz's wife) but clearly indicated that Willem was not a surety and not present in the aldermen's court. None of the parties – the aldermen, their clerks, or the creditors – was worried about Willem later repudiating Perneele's act. How could such a casual approach to a married woman's legal capability stand up in court?

Since the customary law systems of the Low Countries, like English common law, subsumed the identity of a married woman under the coverture of her husband, it is usually argued that medieval married women had at best a very limited legal identity.[8] By contrast, I shall argue that in the mid-fourteenth century, al-

4 For example, SAG, series 301, no. 1, fol. 168v, act no. 1, 8 January 1358; fol. 254v, act no. 4, 22 July 1361.

5 This chapter is based on research undertaken at the Stadsarchief Gent, partially financed by a Fulbright Grant. The author wishes to thank both institutions.

6 J. Decavele, 'Bestuursinstellingen van de stad Gent (einde 11de eeuw – 1795)', *De gewestelijke en lokale overheidsinstellingen in Vlaanderen tot 1795*, ed. Walter Prevenier and Beatrijs Augustyn, Algemeen Rijksarchief en Rijksarchief in de Provinciën, Studia 72 (Brussels, 1997), pp. 277–321; P. Godding, *Le Droit privé dans les Pays-Bas méridionaux du 12e au 18e siècle*, Académie Royale de Belgique, Mémoires de la classe des lettres, Collection in -4°, -2° série, vol. 14 (Brussels, 1987), pp. 265–9; H. Van Werveke, *De Gentsche stadsfinanciën in de middeleeuwen*, Académie royale de Belgique, Classe des lettres et des sciences morales et politiques, Mémoires, collection in 8°, deuxième série, 34 (Brussels, 1934), p. 34. The custom of Ghent redacted in the sixteenth century is published in A. E. Gheldolf, A. Du Bois and L. De Hondt, eds, *Coutume de la ville de Gand*, 2 vols, *Coutumes des pays et comté du Flandre. Quartier de Gand*, Commission royale pour la publication des anciennes lois et ordonnances de la Belgique (Brussels, 1868–87) [hereafter: *Coutume Gand*].

7 *Coutume Gand*, rubric 20, no. 2, p. 86.

8 D. Nicholas, *The Domestic Life of a Medieval City: Women, Children, and the Family in Fourteenth-Century Ghent* (Lincoln, 1985); M. C. Howell, *The Marriage Exchange: Property, Social Place, and Gender in Cities of the Low Countries, 1300–1550* (Chicago, 1998), pp. 27–34, 197–211; M. Carlier and T. Soens, eds, *The Household in Late Medieval Cities: Italy and Northwestern Europe Compared: Proceedings of the International Conference Ghent 21st–22nd January 2000*, Studies in Urban Social, Economic and Political History of the Medieval and Early Modern Low Countries, no. 12 (Leuven-Apeldoorn, 2001); M. Boone, T. De Hemptinne and W. Prevenier, 'Gender and Early Emancipation in the Low Countries in the Late Middle Ages and Early Modern Period', *Gender, Power and Privilege in Early Modern Europe*, ed. J. Munns and P. Richards (Harlow and London, 2003), pp. 21–39; J. Gilissen, 'Le Statut de la femme dans l'ancien droit belge', *Recueil de la société Jean Bodin, 12: La Femme, 2*, ed. A. Gouthier (Brussels, 1962), pp. 254–62, 277–85,

though married women in Ghent were subject to patriarchal restrictions, they had more access to legal economic acts and more *de facto* legal capability than they enjoyed in later centuries. Ghent's married women were subject to their husbands, but they were not yet legally incapable. Their legal capability in actual practice derived from the property they inherited from their families of origin, Ghent's marital community property custom, and widespread acceptance of women's public performance of property management, both with and without their husbands.[9] Although it was becoming common by the mid-fourteenth century for important legal acts to be recorded, the original and legally binding act was a public performance, as people swore before witnesses, and often before the aldermen or other authorities, that they would secure a debt, for example, as Perneele did.[10] In the mid-fourteenth century, married women routinely performed legal acts which in later centuries would not be legally binding. This essay will analyse the evidence of married women's legal capability in the acts and contracts from the earliest surviving aldermen's registers, from 1339 to 1362, and conclude with a discussion of the similarities and differences in married women's legal capability between Ghent and other cities of the Low Countries.

This study juxtaposes two bodies of sources: the Ghent custom (redacted in 1563) and the acts from the oldest annual registers of the aldermen of the *Keure* (from the 1330s to the 1360s). In addition to the two-century time difference, the custom is a prescriptive source, while the contracts, lawsuit settlements and judgment records in the aldermen's registers are sources of actual practice. By the mid-fourteenth century, there were written records of certain provisions of the customary law, but much remained oral.[11] As a result, the redacted version of the Ghent custom from 1563 is our most complete source for the customary law. Because of its accessibility, it and other written customs from the Low Countries (mostly redacted in the sixteenth century) are the most popular sources used by modern scholars to understand the Low Countries' medieval gender norms.[12] Indeed, for most of the Low Countries, there are few records of actual practice surviving before the sixteenth century. Scholars have often been forced to rely on the redacted customs whenever the surviving sources from earlier centuries are silent. However, one of the features of unwritten customary law is its mutability. Before

306–18 [255–321]; M. Danneel, 'Gender and the Life Course in the Late Medieval Flemish Town', *Secretum Scriptorum: Liber alumnorum Walter Prevenier*, ed. W. Blockmans, M. Boone and T. de Hemptinne (Leuven-Apeldoorn, 1999), pp. 235–58.

9 For public performance, see E. E. Kittell, 'Women, Audience, and Public Acts in Medieval Flanders', *Journal of Women's History* 10:3 (1998), 76–7 [74–96].

10 M. Danneel, *Weduwen en wezen in het laat-middeleeuwse Gent*, Studies in Urban Social, Economic and Political History of the Medieval and Modern Low Countries, no. 3 (Leuven-Apeldoorn, 1995), pp. 282, 296; J. M. Murray, *Notarial Instruments in Flanders between 1280 and 1452* (Brussels, 1995), pp. 94–5; R. C. Van Caenegem, *Geschiedenis van het strafprocesrecht in Vlaanderen van de XIe tot de XIVe eeuw* (Brussels, 1956), pp. 87–8.

11 E. M. Meijers, *Het Oost-Vlaamsche erfrecht*, vol. 3 of *Het Ligurische erfrecht in de Nederlanden* (Haarlem, 1936); Godding, *Le Droit privé*, p. 269.

12 Most do this cautiously, however. Godding, *Le Droit privé*, pp. 77–81; Gilissen, 'Le Statut', pp. 254–62.

1563, the aldermen and their clerks could interpret customs in different ways as Ghent society changed. Ghentenars could change unwritten customs gradually, and still think that they were acting from tradition. For this reason, historians have cautioned against applying a rule of the redacted custom to previous centuries if there is no evidence of it in actual practice from the earlier time.[13] As a result, the sixteenth-century redacted custom has limited usefulness as a source for understanding legal capability in fourteenth-century practice.

The second body of sources for this study is the contracts and lawsuit adjudications recorded in the first surviving annual registers of the aldermen of the *Keure* in Ghent. Chosen from the city's elite groups (patricians and guild elites), this board of thirteen aldermen issued ordinances, judged civil and criminal cases, and punished offenders.[14] They also validated private contracts (for sales, loans, and other agreements) by witnessing an oral performance of the contract by the principals. The aldermen's clerk would record a terse account of the contract or agreement in duplicate on parchment, and then cut the parchment into two separate pieces, known as chirographes. He would then attach a clay blob with an imprint of the aldermen's seal to the bottom of each chirograph. These chirographes were the official legal proof of the acts, such as the one that Perneele had performed before the aldermen. For extra insurance, and an extra payment, the clerk recorded the legal act into the aldermen's annual register. Although few of the chirographes survive today, some of the aldermen's registers have been more fortunate. The first register (from 1339 to 1361) contains 1,580 contracts and lawsuit settlements relating to economic matters.[15] Although the acts in these registers are predominantly from the wealthier citizens and represent only a small fraction of the total economic acts in this large city, they involve the ordinary acts of thousands of people. Almost one-quarter of those acts included at least one woman acting in her own name, without male representation or supervision.[16] These judgments of the aldermen, contracts and other legal documents reveal how people understood the unwritten custom at that given moment. The acts are brief and highly formulaic, but the use of different formulas and the changes in the wording of formulas reveal the underlying discourses which informed these acts.[17] They preserve the names of the most important legal actors, the relation-

13 J. Gilissen, *La Coutume*, Typologie des sources du moyen âge occidental, fasc. 41 (Turnhout, 1982), pp. 24–7.

14 The aldermen came from three elite groups: patricians, leaders of the weavers' guild and leaders of the small guilds and, before 1361, leaders of the fullers' guild. A second board of aldermen of the *Gedele* supervised inheritance customs, guardianship of orphans, and reconciliation agreements. Decavele, 'Bestuursinstellingen', pp. 280–3; D. Nicholas, *Town and Countryside: Social, Economic and Political Tensions in Fourteenth-Century Flanders* (Bruges, 1971), pp. 60–1, 71.

15 SAG, series 301, no. 1.

16 From a total of 1,580 economic acts in the first annual register, 844 include men only; 375 feature women in their own names; 148 wives with husbands; 61 women represented by men; 51 adult women under guardianship; and 101 include women in more than one category.

17 Howell, *Marriage Exchange*, p. 14. A. Nevejans, '*Aldus staet in scepenen bouc ...* De Registers van de Gentse schepenen van de keure in de 14de eeuw', *Handelingen der Maatschappij voor Geschiedenis en Oudheidkunde te Gent* 56 (2002), 53–64.

ships among them, and sometimes their marital or social status. The formulas reveal what the aldermen and their clerks thought must be included to make the acts legal and binding, and, taken collectively, the acts show which provisions of the written custom were actually in force in the 1360s. In the following comparison, it will become evident that while the 1563 redacted custom was quite clear about married women's legal incapability, the 1362 oral custom was considerably less so. In some areas, such as the inheritance and marital property customs, there was continuity between the fourteenth and sixteenth centuries, but the customs on married women's legal capability and coverture changed dramatically over the same time period.

Major Provisions of the Customary Law

One clear area of continuity was the inheritance custom which gave women ownership and responsibility for property. Inheritance in Ghent was completely partible – that is, sons and daughters inherited equal shares of their parents' property (and that of other relatives), without regard for birth order.[18] The only exception was land held in fief, which went to the oldest son. Either when she married or at the death of her parents, every middling or wealthy Ghent woman received property from her family of origin. There were no dowries, and every woman from a wealthy family was an heiress.[19]

The marital property custom of Ghent also changed little between the fourteenth and sixteenth centuries. When two people married, all of their movable property (houses, life-rent annuities, furniture, possessions, valuables, coins) became community or joint property, a 'community of goods' (Middle Dutch: *ghemeenen goeden*; Modern Dutch: *gemeenschap*), owned by both, but managed by the husband during the marriage. The immovable property (rural land, city lots, and hereditary annuities) was not put into the 'community of goods'. Instead each spouse held it as personal property (*eigen goed*). If the couple bought or otherwise acquired property of any kind during the marriage, it became community property. Any property inherited from either spouse's family of origin, however, was divided between community property (for the movable items) and that spouse's personal property (for land and immovable annuities). These rules for ownership and division of property did undergo one change by 1563. In response to the increasingly fluid property market, authorities changed the classification of city lots from immovable to movable property.[20] Because movable property went into the community property, which was under the husband's control, this change decreased a wife's personal property. It may have had more far-reaching consequences as well, as Martha Howell argues that changes in ideas about property

18 Godding, *Le Droit privé*, pp. 162, 291, 333.

19 *Coutume Gand*, rubric 20, no. 20, p. 92; Godding, *Le Droit privé*, pp. 292–3, 311–12; Danneel, *Weduwen*, pp. 254–6, 271–2.

20 Godding, *Le Droit privé*, pp. 268–9, 273–4

played a major role in the emergence of companionate marriage.[21] However, the marital property custom of Ghent did not undergo a major shift in Ghent as it did in Douai.[22] Over time, the basic structure remained intact.

In contrast, the rules about management of property show distinct differences. The sixteenth-century written custom stated that the husband had complete charge over community property, while the wife could only manage property or perform legal acts with his explicit permission.[23] The husband was also to manage his wife's personal property, but he could not sell it without her consent. As I explain below, the aldermen did not apply these principles universally in the fourteenth century. Some husbands managed their wives' personal property without their wives' explicit consent, but some married women managed both personal and community property without official permission from their husbands.

The 1563 redacted custom and mid-fourteenth-century actual practice differed greatly in the area of coverture, the legally incapable status of a married woman. The redacted custom forbade married women to enter into contracts or agreements without the knowledge and consent of their husbands, unless they were 'female public merchants' (*openbare coopwijven*) 'concerning their own business and nothing else'.[24] Like the custom of *femme sole* adopted in some English towns, the Ghent female public merchant was legally capable, but only for economic activities totally separated from her husband's business. Unless they were female public merchants, married women needed the permission of their husbands to sell or encumber their personal property, or to sue or answer a lawsuit.[25] There were also some protections for the wife and her extended family, her 'side' (*zijde*), as contemporary clerks put it. Her husband could not sell or pledge her personal property without her consent, and she was shielded from responsibility for his debts while he was still alive.[26] In the 1350s, none of the rules were hard and fast. The terms '*openbare coopwijf*' or '*marchande publique*' do not appear in any of the surviving fourteenth-century ordinances or the acts from the annual registers of the aldermen of the *Keure* in Ghent, although they can be found in fourteenth-century documents from other cities in the southern Low Countries, such as Tournai, Liège and Brussels.[27] While the Ghent aldermen and their clerks probably knew the term, they did not qualify a married woman's ability to act legally by explaining that she was conducting an independent business as a female public merchant.

In contrast, both the 1350s oral custom and the 1563 written custom agreed on the rights and responsibilities of the survivor after one of the spouses died. There

21 M. C. Howell, 'The Gender of Europe's Commercial Economy, 1200–1700', *Gender and History* 20 (2008), 532 [519–38]; and 'From Land to Love: Commerce and Marriage in Northern Europe during the Late Middle Ages', *Jaarboek voor Middeleeuwse Geschiedenis* 10 (2007), 232, 241–2 [216–53]

22 Howell, *Marriage Exchange*.

23 *Coutume Gand*, rubric 20, nos. 1, 5 and 6, pp. 86–8.

24 *Coutume Gand*, rubric 20, no. 2, p. 86.

25 *Coutume Gand*, rubric 20, nos. 7 and 18, pp. 88 and 92.

26 *Coutume Gand*, nos. 6 and 8, p. 88.

27 Gilissen, 'Le Statut', p. 296.

was no distinction between the rights and responsibilities of the surviving husband or wife, except for fiefs. The surviving spouse inherited one-half of the community property, and could sell it freely, or take it into a second marriage.[28] The remainder of the community property went to the heirs, either the children of the couple or, if there were no children, the closest relatives in the deceased's family. Widows and widowers could not 'flee the estate' (refuse the inheritance because the deceased's debts exceeded his or her assets), but the heirs had this option. Widows could not claim some of the estate as a dower before the debts were paid.[29] The widow or widower had the right to usufruct (lifetime use) of half of the heirs' half of the community property, but she or he could not alienate it. Full use of that property returned to the heirs when the widow or widower died. The surviving spouse also received usufruct of one-half of the deceased's personal property under the same terms. But the deceased's personal property ultimately went to the children or to family heirs, not to the surviving spouse. As a result, the widow or widower would control three-quarters of the entire wealth of the couple for her or his lifetime, and, by remarrying, could convey half of the community property to a new family. But the custom also ensured that if there were no children, all the deceased's personal property and half of the community property would go back to the deceased's family. It also placed equal responsibility on widows and widowers, in rules that remained largely unchanged from the fourteenth to the sixteenth century. Overall, there were strong continuities in the marital property and inheritance customary law as it evolved from the mid-fourteenth-century oral custom to the 1563 redacted custom, but the 1563 custom defined and restricted married women's legal capability more sharply than early oral custom had.

Moreover, analysis of the rules the earlier oral and later written custom held in common suggests that family interests were a major reason for married women's legal capability in fourteenth-century actual practice. The custom balanced the tension between the rights of the household and the rights of the extended family.[30] By awarding a large portion to the surviving spouse and children, the custom provided for the continuation of the household. By reserving the deceased's personal property for family heirs, the custom saved land, fiefs and city lots for the extended family. This solution was quite workable, as long as Ghentenars considered the extended family as cognatic or bilateral (connected through both male and female lines) rather than patrilineal (connected through a single male line).[31]

In the mid-fourteenth century, Ghentenars probably believed in the basic principles that married women needed to submit to their husbands and husbands

28 *Coutume Gand*, rubric 20, nos. 19 and 20, p. 92; Godding, *Le Droit privé*, pp. 295–6, 304–6; Danneel, *Weduwen*, p. 263.

29 This is a significant difference from both Douai, where a widow could flee her late husband's estate (but only if the couple had a marriage contract that gave them that right), and Bruges, where creditors were paid only after the widow was given her portion of the community property. Howell, *Marriage Exchange*, pp. 29–36; J. M. Murray, 'Family, Marriage and Moneychanging in Medieval Bruges', *Journal of Medieval History* 14 (1988), 115–25.

30 Godding, *Le Droit Privé*, pp. 268–74.

31 D. Herlihy, *Medieval Households* (Cambridge, MA, 1985), pp. 82–6.

should control the household, although neither is directly stated in any of the early city charters or ordinances. However, oral custom placed large amounts of property in the hands of women, which meant that families had to rely on women to preserve that property for family heirs. Centuries of family reliance on women to manage property for the benefit of the family led many fourteenth-century Ghentenars to regard women as potentially helpful and useful in public performance of property management, particularly for humdrum, unimportant legal acts, such as payment of debts or standing as surety for the small debts, of a family member. Although no one would have questioned patriarchal control, the principles surrounding ownership of property and family rights were just as strongly rooted in Ghent custom. Ownership of property from their families of origin and the emphasis on rights of property ownership in Ghent custom gave some married women *de facto* legal capability in the mid-fourteenth century.

Married Women in the Acts from the Aldermen's Registers

In contrast to the 1563 custom's restrictions on married women's public performance of legal acts, the sources of actual practice from the mid-fourteenth century reveal married women performing legal acts in their own names without written permission or consent of their husbands. When a woman performed a legal act by herself without male representation or supervision, she was acting 'in her own name'. Fourteenth-century clerks used the husbands' names to identify married women acting in their own names, but the husbands were not present with their wives in the aldermen's court. In the number of married women who acted in their own names, I do not include women who were owners of property but did not perform any action, or wives who appeared together with their husbands. My analysis shows that of the 491 women who performed legal acts in their own names before the aldermen of the *Keure* between 1339 and 1361, eighty-one were married women.[32] Married women loaned and borrowed money, bought and sold property, and brought and answered lawsuits. Except for identifying married women by their husbands' names, the clerks used exactly the same legal formulas and language to record the acts of married women in their own names and acts performed by men.

Occasionally, the clerk's record of the contract or legal performance indicates that the wife had her husband's permission, or that he consented to her act.[33] But, in the overwhelming majority of these cases, there is no permission clause and no special

[32] For this period, there are four complete annual registers (for 1349–50, 1353–4, 1357–8 and 1360–1) and several partial registers (for 1339, 1343–4 and 1346) surviving. In total, there are 1,580 acts (contracts and lawsuit adjudications) which are economic in nature. There were 491 women acting in their own names (that is, without male representation and/or unaccompanied by husbands) in those acts. Eighty-one of these women (17 per cent) were married women. S. Hutton, *Women and Economic Activities in Late Medieval Ghent* (New York, 2011), pp. 42–57.

[33] For example, SAG, series 301, no. 1, fol. 70r, act no. 3, 1 June 1350; fol. 240r, act no. 1, 6 March 1361.

explanation of why the wife was performing the legal act. Instead, married women simply appeared acting as solely responsible, as this sales contract from 1362 shows:

> Be it known that Jan Haerkin, Gillis's son, has legally bought ... from Ver Mergriete, wife of Heinric Vriend, a house ... for the sum of 30 s. groot, which she maintains she has been paid.[34]

Later in the document, Jan promised to compensate Heinric for payment of annuities secured by the property, a clear indication that Heinric was still alive and that Mergriete was not actually a widow. Houses were movable and thus community property, which, according to the 1563 custom, was supposed to be under Heinric's control. While Mergriete may have been a *coopwijf* conducting a business other than that of her husband, there is no indication in the act itself that distinguishes that status. There is no special explanation of why Mergriete performed this legal act alone. Married women also borrowed money and secured it with their personal property as collateral, rather than community property. For example, in 1360, Mergriete, the wife of Heinric Gheleins, swore that she owed Willem van Eeke five pounds groot, secured 'on herself and all her property (*up hare ende al thare*)'.[35] There are no additional clauses explaining her actions, or expressing her husband's consent or permission.

In interpreting these acts, I considered certain possibilities. The first is that these married women were actually widows. To investigate this possibility, I used prosopographical analysis to ascertain if the husbands appeared in acts dated after the woman's appearance. In half of the twenty-six acts with married women from 1349–50, the husband was still alive, and there was no evidence that any of the husbands had died. Given the fragmentary nature of the evidence surviving from this period, the fact that half of the twenty-six married women from 1349–50 were definitely married women with living husbands strongly suggests that the clerks had correctly identified the rest as married women.[36]

A second possibility is that the assumption of a husband's authority over his wife was so ingrained in the custom and practice of Ghent that the aldermen and their clerks did not think it was necessary to record that the husband had actually

34 SAG, series 301, no. 1, fol. 178r, act no. 1, 6 March 1362: 'Kenlic sij etc. dat Jan Haerkin Gillis zone was ser Maeghelins heeft ghecocht ende ghecreghen wel ende redenlike tseghen ver Mergrieten Heinrix Vriends wijf een huus ... omme ene somme van XXX s. gro. tor., daer af dat hare ver Mergriete vors. kende wel betaelt ende al ghenough ghedaen.... Ende mids den redenen dat Heinric vors. vortijts sette sine erve te pande over de vors. XXIX s. par., so heeft Jan Herkin vors. ghelooft up hem ende al tsinen Heinricke voreghenoomt te haudene daer af costeloes ende al scadeloes, ende van al den andren toter tijt dat hij dese XXIX s. par. wel versekert zal hebben.'

35 SAG, series 301, no. 1, fol. 216v, act no. 1, 20 October 1360: 'Mergriete Heinrix Gheleins wijf heeft verkent ende verlijt dat soe sculdich es wel ende redenleec up hare ende up al thare Willeme van Eeke vijf lb. gr. tor.' This act was performed before the *erfachtige lieden* (hereditary people), an older institution of landowners who authorized acts, and later recorded in the aldermen's register. See also fol. 237r, act no. 5.

36 S. Hutton, '"On Herself and All Her Property": Women's Economic Activities in Late Medieval Ghent', *Continuity and Change* 20:3 (2005), 337–8 [325–49].

appeared to act for his wife, or had given her permission. However, the registers also contain fifty-one cases of husbands exercising guardianship over their wives and/or managing property owned by their wives.[37] The clerks often signalled the husband's authority by the phrase 'husband and guardian (*man ende voogd*)', to indicate that he was acting for his legally incapable wife. Even if the wife was in court with her husband, the act makes clear that he was authorizing her action. For example:

> Be it known that *Joncvrouw* Lijsbette, daughter of the deceased Heinric Gruter, wife of Gherem Borluut, has come before the aldermen ... with Gherem Borluut her husband and guardian ... [and] has legally sold a hereditary annuity with the consent and by the will of her legal husband and guardian.[38]

In this case, Lijsbette's name appeared first because the immovable property – a hereditary annuity – came from her father's estate. However, the clerk emphasized that Gherem, her husband, was with her and guiding her actions. There are even cases in which one married woman was acting in her own name and another married woman was under the guardianship of her husband:

> Be it known that Jan de Wulslagher and Gheraerd de Wulslagher ... came before the aldermen ... [and] said that they had sold *Joncvrouw* Kateline van Axpoele, wife of Jan van den Wallekine, half of a city lot and one-quarter of a house ... for a sum of money which Jan and Gheraerd say they have been paid ... *Joncvrouw* Kateline, their [Jan's and Gheraerd's] sister, wife of Godeverd van Zele, and Godeverd van Zele, her legal husband and guardian, give up any rights that they may have in the half city lot ... and *Joncvrouw* Kateline, wife of Jan van den Wallekine, is put into ownership of it as her purchased property.[39]

37 Hutton, *Women and Economic Activities*, pp. 45–7.

38 SAG, series 301, no. 1, fol. 187r, act no. 1: 'Kenlic zij etc. dat commen es vor scepenen vander kuere in Ghend, Jacop Willebaerde ende Janne den Amman ser Ghelnoets sone, Joncvr. Lijsbette bi wijlen Heinric Gruters dochter was Gherem Borluuts wetteleec wijf met Gherems Borluute haren wetteliken vocht, de welke heeft vercocht wel ende wettelike bi consente ende willen van Gheremme vors. haren wettelken man ende vocht.' See also fol. 12r, act no. 1, 19 January 1344. The title *Joncvrouw* indicates that Lijsbette came from an elite or middling social group, not that she was a young woman or unmarried.

39 SAG, series 301, no. 1, fol. 122v, act no. 1, 1353: 'Kenlic zij etc. dat Jan de Wulslagher ende Gheraerd de Wulslagher ghebroeden Jans Wulslaghers kindren waren, siin commen vor scepenen vander kuere in Ghend, Boudin van Swijnaerde ende Jacob Parisijs, de welke kenden ende verlijeden dat zij hadden vercocht wel ende redenlike Joncvr. Kateline van Axpoele, Jans wijf van den Wallekine, half de herve ende tvierendeel vander huus ... ende al dierghelike zo ghinghen ute Joncvr. Katelinen haerer zuster Godeverds wijf van Zele ende Godeverd vors. haer wettelike man ende vocht van al den rechte dat zij an dese vors. halve herve ende vierendeel van den huusinghen ... Ende Joncvr. Kateline Jans wijf van den Wallekine vors. ward der in gheeerft [*sic*] ende der toe ghedaen alse in haer wettelike coepgoet.'

The Kateline who was buying the property was a married woman acting in her own name.[40] But the Kateline who was the sister of the sellers appeared with her husband, who acted as her husband and guardian. If the property came from Kateline's family, Jan van den Wallekine may have left it up to her to buy up parts from her relatives.[41] By contrast, Godeverd van Zele accompanied his wife and acted for her. This act and many others like it show the mixing of traditional legal formulas with the awareness that in other courts, outside the city of Ghent, Godeverd van Zele might be able to claim that he had not consented to his wife's renunciation of her rights. Through concern to protect family interests against a lawsuit from a son-in-law, Kateline's brothers may have insisted that the clerk use that exact formula.[42] Although the clerk did not explain the reasons for the difference, the appearance of both a legally capable and a legally incapable married woman in the same act shows that the aldermen's clerks were well aware of the distinction and expressed it clearly.

The use of these legal formulas undercuts the argument that coverture or guardianship over married women was so automatic in fourteenth-century Ghent that it was not explicitly mentioned.[43] The aldermen's clerks knew and used formulas that expressed the subordination of married women to their husbands.[44] When the clerks did not use those formulas, married women were acting in their own names. In the Ghent aldermen's registers from 1339 to 1361, fifty-one acts include formulas expressing the legal incapability of married women, while in eighty-one cases, married women acted in their own names. Furthermore, the apparent contradiction did not seem to concern the Ghent aldermen or their clerks, who were prepared to validate contracts and witness performance of legal acts of both legally capable women and husbands acting for legally incapable married women.

It is also possible that the aldermen verified orally that each married woman was conducting her own business, or asked her to swear that she had her husband's permission, but the clerks did not consider that important enough to include in the written act.[45] Although there is no evidence to prove this, I think

40 Jan van den Wallekine appears in an act written into the registers right before his wife's act, which is unfortunately only dated by the year 1353 (meaning the aldermen's official year from 15 August 1353 to 14 August 1354. Jan's act is dated 14 February 1354; an act from 14 July 1354 identifies Kateline as a widow. SAG, series 301, no. 1, fol. 122r, act no. 4, 14 February 1354; fol. 122v, act no. 1; 1, 1353–4; fol. 137v, act no. 3, 14 July 1354.

41 All of these people were likely closely related to each other, because they are dealing with parts of city lots and houses, divisions which occurred when several children or other family heirs inherited parts of one piece of property from a parent or relative.

42 For more on multiple legal jurisdictions and use of patrimonial language to protect family interests, see Hutton, *Women and Economic Activities*, pp. 139–42.

43 Nicholas, *Domestic Life*, pp. 70–106; E. E. Kittell, 'Guardianship over Women in Medieval Flanders: A Reappraisal', *Journal of Social History* 31:4 (1998), 896–930.

44 Godding, *Le Droit privé*, pp. 77–9. For the development of comital feudal courts, see Dirk Heirbaut, 'Weduwen, erfgenamen en lenen: De evolutie van het feodale erf- en huwelijksvermogensrecht in Vlaanderen (1000–1300)', *Jaarboek voor Middeleeuwse Geschiedenis* 1 (1998), 16–18 [7–26]

45 For an act which does contain a statement of the husband's consent to his wife's actions, see SAG,

that the aldermen ascertained in some way that the woman's husband would not object before they allowed married women to act in their own names. Special circumstances, such as the husband's absence or illness, or the need for a remarried widow to fulfil obligations she had taken on during her widowhood, might have been involved. However, the fact that the fourteenth-century clerks omitted this information shows that rules restricting the legal capability of married women were not as stringent and significant as they later became. It was much more common in later centuries for clerks to include permission clauses.[46]

Another clue that the rules were not as strict comes from the clerks' recording (or lack thereof) of a woman's marital status to indicate her legal capability. In the registers from 1339 to 1361, the aldermen's clerks omitted the marital status and name of a male relative for almost half of the 491 women who acted in their own names.[47] Instead, the woman's own name sufficed to justify her legal capability. Reporting marital status to verify legal capability was not a priority of the aldermen or their clerks. The point is not that married women were defying their husbands and able to do what they wished, but that the aldermen and their clerks exhibit a lack of attention and a flexibility about married women's legal capability which contrasts sharply with the precision they devoted to the ownership of property. Later, the clerks had to spell out the husband's authority, but in the fourteenth century a casual understanding that the wife was acting with her husband's consent sufficed.

The aldermen and their clerks do not display any concern for separating a wife's business from that of her husband, or enforcing the rule from the 1563 custom that a wife could not perform legal acts in her own name involving her husband's business. The clerks did not use the phrase 'female public merchant' in the 1350s, or make any discernible attempt to divide the business activities of the wife from the husband. To be sure, the clerks did not explain the reasons for debts, and most of the acts are terse and uninformative. One unusually detailed record, a property inventory from a couple who died suddenly in 1361 (probably from the plague which raged that year), included testimony of witnesses about the debts the couple owed. The clerk listed the reasons for many of the debts, which were all connected to the production of wool cloth (Ghent's major industry). The couple,

series 301, no. 1, fol. 240r, act no. 1, 6 March 1361.

46 In the 1420–1 register, for example, there are nine acts with married women. Five have empowerment or permission clauses from the husband. Three explain that the married woman is 'haer zelfs wijf', literally her own woman, which may have been the equivalent of public female merchant, or indicate that the woman is separated from her husband (which is mentioned in one of these three acts). The phrase 'haer zelfs wijf' never appears in the mid-fourteenth-century registers. In only one 1420 act, the purchase of a bed on credit, is there no reason given for a married woman to be acting in her own name. SAG, series 301, vol. 26, no. 1, fol. 3v, act no. 1; fol. 10v, act no. 12; fol. 12r, act nos. 4 and 5; fol. 13r, act no. 11; fol. 13v, act no. 9; fol. 14r, act no. 6, and fol. 14v, act no. 6.

47 The 491 women who acted in their own names have the following marital status categories: 63 were single (identified by their fathers' or brothers' names); 81 were married; 109 were widows; 12 were religious (10 nuns and 2 beguines), 9 had mixed status (for example, married in one act; widowed in a later act). The remainder – 217 women – were identified by their own names alone, not by marital status or the name of a male relative.

Wouter and Aechte van Vinderhoute, contracted six debts together, but Aechte, by herself, contracted two debts, one of which was for warp-winding (measuring and winding warp threads on a loom).[48] There is no explanation of how a wife could legally contract debts alone for a business she shared with her husband, nor any indication that Aechte's acts were exceptional.

Between the two extremes of married women acting in their own names and legally incapable married women represented by their husbands was a third category of married women who appeared together with their husbands without any language of subordination. This group was larger; in 148 cases, married couples appeared before the aldermen to perform legal acts together. The clerks recorded these joint performances by listing the husbands' and wives' names together every time they were mentioned. In the following act, both the buyers and the sellers of this city lot and house were husbands and wives acting together:

> Be it known that Ghiselbrecht van Coudenhove and *Joncvrouw* Mergriete his legal wife came before the aldermen ... [and] related that they had sold all the rights that they had in a house and city lot ... to Wasseline van den Pitte and *Joncvrouw* Kateline his legal wife ... And this is for a certain sum of money that Ghiselbrecht and *Joncvrouw* Mergriete maintain that they have been paid by Wasseline and *Joncvrouw* Kateline ... and Ghiselbrecht and *Joncvrouw* Mergriete give up all the rights ... and do everything they are supposed to do ... [to transfer the property] to Wasseline and *Joncvrouw* Kateline.[49]

The sale of a city lot required a public performance of the sale and transfer of ownership, and both couples performed the act together. In the act, the clerk stated the wives' names immediately following the husbands' names eight times, and used the pronouns 'they' (*zij, sij*) and 'theirs' (*haerlieder*) consistently. This identification of husbands and wives performing acts together offers proof of economic partnership in marriage. The wife was not merely consenting to the sale or purchase of the property, but engaging in every aspect of the act.

48 SAG, series 330, no. 1, fol. 215.1, 21 August 1360

49 SAG, series 301, no. 2, fol. 5r, act no. 2, 4 October 1362: 'Kenlic zij etc. dat cam vor scepenen vander cuere in Ghend, her Lievine van den Hole, heer Ogiere tSuule, heer Lievine den Bosschere ende andren haren ghesellen, Ghiselbrecht van Coudenhove ende Joncvr. Mergriete ziin wettelic wijf, de welke kende ende verlijeden dat zij vercocht hadden wel ende redenlic Wasseline vanden Pitte ende Joncvr. Katelinen zinen wettelic wive al dat recht dat sij hadden an huus ende herve ... Ende dat omme eener zekere somme van ghelde van der welker hem de vors. Ghiselbrecht ende Joncvr. Mergriete hilden betaelt, vergolden ende al ghenouch ghedaen van Wasseline ende Joncvr. Kateline vors. Ende de vors. Ghiselbrecht ende Joncvr. Mergriete ghinghe ute ende te buten van al den rechte van huuse, van herven, ende van den loeven vors., ende worpene ende deden daer toe al dat zij doen mochten of sculdech waren te doene omme hem der af tonthuusene, tonthervene ende tontgoede ende Wasselin ende Joncvr. Kateline vors. waren dertoe ghedaen der inne ghehuust, gheherft, ende ghegoed als in haerlieder ghecochte goed.'

This sense of partnership is heightened in cases in which the wife's action cannot be interpreted as consent required by custom. There was no legal requirement for wives to consent to loans or debt contracts their husbands made involving community property, and yet husbands and wives often appeared together loaning and borrowing money, as in this act from 1362:

> Be it known that Godin de Wayere and Verghine his legal wife have said that they legally owe 12 lb. groot to Martin Berde, [payable] on themselves and all their property with no exceptions wherever it lies inside Ghent or outside.[50]

According to the redacted custom of 1563, husbands completely controlled the community property without any requirement for their wives' consent. However, it is quite common in the mid-fourteenth-century registers for husbands and wives to appear together swearing to pay debts. This suggests that the preference of fourteenth-century creditors was to have both spouses perform the legal act (and thus share the liability), even though, as we will see, the aldermen held widows and widowers responsible for debts contracted by their spouses. Husband-and-wife economic partnerships, appearing in nine per cent of all acts performed before the aldermen, offer further evidence of widespread acceptance of married women's performance of certain legal acts.

Factors Giving Married Women Some Legal Capability

Although a number of political, economic and social factors contributed to the *de facto* legal capability of some married women in mid-fourteenth-century Ghent, this essay focuses on the legal factors alone.[51] The first legal factor was the emphasis the aldermen placed on ownership of property, particularly in contrast to the lack of emphasis they placed on marital status. Almost every economic act in the registers clearly indicates who owned the property and how the principals in the act were related to the property. In the fourteenth century, if the property in question came from the wife's side of the family, the clerks listed her name first, and sometimes only her name. For example, in 1350, a clerk recorded an arbitration agreement in an inheritance dispute over household goods. The clerk introduced the two parties as 'Hughe van der Most' and 'Mergriete Pollepels and her husband', but never again referred to Mergriete's husband.[52] Instead, the clerk recorded Mer-

50 SAG, series 301, no. 2, fol. 13r, no. 2, 15 May 1362: 'Kenlic si etc. dat Godin de Wayere ende Verghinen siin wettel. wijf hebben verkend ende verlijt dat sij sculdich siin wel ende wettel. up hemlieden ende up al thare niet ute ghesteken ware dat ghestaen ofte gheleghen es eist binnen Ghend ofte der buten Martine Berde XII lb. g. t.'

51 Ghent was engaged in war and rebellions in this period, which may have distracted the attention of men and offered women more opportunity. In addition, structural changes in the wool cloth industry and rampant unemployment were also important elements. Hutton, *Women and Economic Activities*, pp. 17–29.

52 SAG, series 301, no. 1, fol. 68r, act no. 2, 24 May 1350. If the surviving spouse and the heirs could

griete's name alone ten times in the list of items decided by the arbiters, even though all but one of the items were movable property, belonging to the community property of the couple rather than to Mergriete's personal property. However, the arbiters, the clerk and the aldermen indicated that she was the most important party because the inheritance came from her family. They were not concerned enough about her husband's agreement to record it to prevent a future lawsuit, probably because he never objected and the goods in question were fairly inexpensive. If a married woman was managing property that came from her family of origin, the aldermen and their clerks seem to have considered her legally capable.

The aldermen's casual grant of legal capability to married women may also have arisen from two other situations: the acts of a remarried widow dealing with the affairs of her first family; and business deals conducted by women (with men and other women). Since the clerks seldom recorded reasons for debts, it is impossible to be sure of this. However, some acts, such as the following from early 1361, suggest either a family relationship or business dealings among the three women:

> The *Joncvrouw* wife of Gillis van der Boengaerde was ordered to pay [as a settlement] *Joncvrouw* Aechte Brunsch and her sister, the wife of Pieter Coninc, 28 shillings groot within the next fourteen nights.[53]

In this case, the clerk did not even record the first names of the married women, an indication that their identities were primarily as married women. There are two likely explanations for this settlement: it was either an inheritance dispute, in which case the three women were relatives; or the three women were involved in a business deal which led to the lawsuit. The clerk recorded the debt as owed and payable to the married women themselves, not to their husbands, even though the money was community property.

Partible inheritance and the view that women and their descendants were legitimate and responsible members of the extended family also helped give married women *de facto* legal capability. Parents usually gave some movable and some immovable property to their daughters when the girls married.[54] For example, in 1362, Margriete, the widow of William de Lange, gave her daughter a hereditary annuity as a wedding gift, probably along with movable property. The hereditary annuity gave the daughter, Ysabelle, thirty pounds per year, guaranteed by fiefs belonging to the mother. This annuity was Ysabelle's personal property, which her new husband, Robbrecht, could not sell without her consent. If Ysabelle died

not reach a settlement on the division of the estate, the aldermen of the *Gedele* asked each to nominate two arbiters. Those arbiters then tried to reach a compromise. Only if that failed would the aldermen themselves decide the division.

53 SAG, series 301, no. 1, fol. 231r, act no. 5, 20 January 1361: 'Der Joncvr. Gillis wijf vander Boengaerde was ghewijst dat zoe vermoeden soude Joncvr. Aechten Brunsch ende haren zuster Pieters Coninx wijf van XXVIII s. gro. binnen XIIII nachten naest commende.'

54 SAG, series 301, no. 2, fol. 1r, act no. 2, 9 June 1359. See also fol. 225r, act no. 1, 1360–1.

without children, the annuity would return to her mother and family heirs. The property was preserved for the family because Ysabelle's children would be family members and, if she had none, Robbrecht would not inherit the annuity. However, giving children personal, immovable property also meant that families had to rely on married sons and daughters, as holders of part of the family's 'patrimony', not to consent to the sale or risk of their personal property. It was in the interest of families to train daughters to be wise managers of property and empower married women to have a voice in decision-making about property. In addition, because husbands and wives were responsible for each other's debts, wealthy families had to be concerned that the personal property held by their sons and daughters might have to be sold to pay the debts of an insolvent daughter- or son-in-law.

There was no protection of a widow's property from the debts of her husband, or a widower from the debts of his late wife.[55] Ghent's succession custom was built on the idea that community property would be divided between the surviving spouse, on one side, and the 'heirs', on the other side. Rather than assigning an executor, the surviving spouse and the heirs had joint responsibility for carrying out a series of procedures for dividing the estate, satisfying the creditors, and distributing the bequests.[56] The widow or widower and the heirs had to split the debts, unless the heirs fled the estate, in which case the surviving spouse had to pay all the debts. Even though the redacted custom of 1563 allowed husbands to claim that they had not consented to debts owed by their late wives (thereby repudiating the debt), in fourteenth-century actual practice, the aldermen did not allow this. When married women borrowed money, their husbands could not later repudiate the debt. For example, in 1361, the mercer Lisbette van den Conkele sued Jan Bollaerd because Bollaerd's deceased wife owed her thirty shillings groot. Bollaerd protested to the aldermen that he did not know about the debt. The aldermen listened to testimony from witnesses on both sides, including the information that the wife's heirs had fled the estate. But in the end, the aldermen ordered Bollaerd to pay the thirty shillings, thus holding a husband responsible for debts contracted by his wife without his express permission.[57]

The aldermen were also strict with widows who claimed lack of knowledge. Just eighteen days after they ordered Jan Bollaerd to pay Lisbette van den Conkele, the

55 *Coutume Gand*, rubric 20, no. 19, p. 82.

56 The surviving spouse inherited half of the community property, and he or she had the right to do whatever she wished with it, including selling it or carrying it into a second marriage. All of the deceased spouse's personal property and the other half of the community property went to his or her heirs, the children, or if there were no children, to relatives from the deceased's natal family. The surviving spouse was entitled to a lifetime usufruct, called a *bijleving*, of one-half of the heir's half of the community property and one-half of the profits from the deceased's personal property and fiefs. The widow or widower had to draw an inventory of the estate, called a *deelbrief*. If he or she forgot to record a debt, the heirs had no later responsibility for it. All the debts the deceased owed had to be paid before the estate was divided. The heirs had to pay the bequests, the surviving spouse had to pay compensation for services already rendered, and they all had to split the costs of the funeral. Godding, *Le Droit privé*, pp. 273–4, 299–300, 311–12; Danneel, *Weduwen*, pp. 266–9.

57 SAG, series 301, no. 1, fol. 223v, act no. 3, 5 December 1360.

aldermen judged a lawsuit brought by a cleric, Brother Jan Inghele, against Kateline, the widow of Jacob van Smettelede. Inghele claimed that Jacob had borrowed twenty shillings groot from him and demanded repayment. The widow countered that 'she had not known or heard of the debt during the life of her husband Jacob'.[58] The aldermen reduced the amount she had to pay to twelve shillings, but ordered the widow to pay. Although there were undoubtedly many other factors that went into the aldermen's decisions (notably the testimony of witnesses, which was not recorded), these cases show that the aldermen held spouses responsible for debts with little consideration for gender differences. This meant that creditors could make loans to married women without the fear that their husbands would repudiate the debt. This made all women more credit-worthy, because changes in their marital status would not affect their liability.

The final factor contributing to this *de facto* legal capability for married women was the relative lack of importance of these legal acts. The dispute between Hughe van der Most and Mergriete Pollepels, two wealthy patricians, centred on household goods, not on vast tracts of property. All the male parties – the husbands, arbiters, aldermen and clerks – treated the participation of married women in these rather unimportant legal acts in a routine, non-controversial manner. The aldermen emphasized enforcing the terms of debt contracts and following the customs for rightful ownership of property much more strenuously than issues of married women's legal capability. There were many legal acts that married women did not perform, those concerning large business deals, international trade, guild leadership, and political activities, which means that married women were only legally capable within a very limited realm. Within those constraints, however, in act after act with married women acting in their own names or alongside their husbands, there is no evidence of controversy, no explanation, and no hint that the act is anything outside of routine, ordinary practice. In the 1350s, elite men did not seem to be concerned about these married women's activities as a threat to male authority.

Some men seem to have accepted the right of a married woman to be involved in household decisions and, especially, in decisions about property from her side of the family. Many married women who acted in their own names were actually carrying out a joint strategy of the couple in economic partnership. Symoen de Necker and Lijsbette van Sotteghem offer a good example. Symoen, a former alderman of the *Keure*, and his wife Lijsbette went before the aldermen on 28 June 1350 to settle a dispute with another woman over a house which had come from Lijsbette's side of the family.[59] On 2 July, Lijsbette van Sotteghem went back alone to the aldermen to perform a related act – the transfer of ownership of the house. The aldermen transferred ownership of the house (community property) to Lijsbette alone, not to Symoen and Lijsbette together.[60] There can be little ques-

58 SAG, series 301, no. 1, fol. 227r, act no. 1, 23 December 1360: 'Kateline vors. dede toeghen ende zecghen dat zoe van diere scult niet en wiste no ghehordten hadde binnen den levene van Jacoppe haren man vors., met meer redenen ende worden die zoe daer toe dede zegghen.'

59 SAG, series 301, no. 1, fol. 80r, act no. 1, 28 June 1350.

60 SAG, series 301, no. 1, f. 88v, act no. 6, 2 July 1350: 'ver Lijsbetten van Sotteghem, ser Symoens

tion that Symoen agreed with his wife's activity, but he did not think it necessary to accompany her to court. Lijsbette went to the aldermen to carry out the strategy of the married couple. Although Lijsbette's action broke numerous rules from the 1563 redacted custom, such as the lack of explicit permission from the husband and the wife's management of community property, neither the aldermen nor their clerks thought that was unusual enough to require explanation. Nor did they include any permission or consent clauses in the second act.

The question of whether the limited legal capability that Ghent married women enjoyed prevailed throughout the Low Countries is difficult to answer. Every city and locality in the Low Countries had its own customary law, and although there are broad similarities, such as partible inheritance, there are also important differences, which have always made it difficult to make accurate generalizations about the customary law throughout this exceptionally decentralized region. The marital property custom of Ghent was followed in areas of northern France, such as Artois, Brabant and Hainault, but not in Bruges or Douai, which followed the custom of the universal community.[61] Although marriage contracts were not allowed in Ghent, they were central to family strategies in Douai.[62] The Ghent rule that husbands and wives had to pay each other's debts and could not flee the estate played a significant role in making married women legally capable on occasion. However, in Bruges, Douai and other areas, widows had more flexibility and protection from creditors.[63] Where there are no surviving records of actual practice before the sixteenth century, the extent to which married women had *de facto* legal capability must remain an open question.

Reliance on the rules of the sixteenth-century redacted customs of all these areas to explain the medieval legal position of married women in the Low Countries would be a grave mistake, nevertheless. Ghent evidence of actual practice from the middle of the fourteenth century indicates that customary practices, such as partible inheritance, bilateral family structures, and community marital property systems heavily mitigated the general legal principle that married women were covered by their husbands. In 1350, there is little evidence of most of the detailed rules in the sixteenth-century custom restricting married women's activity, such as permission clauses, or separation of a wife's activities into *coopwijf* status. Instead, fourteenth-century actual practice was more fluid and flexible, emphasizing property over patriarchy, and tolerating ambiguities that would later be impossible.

wijf sNeckers, ende Lente Moelgies vors. quam voer scepenen mids pais faisant [ende] onthuucie hare van desen huse ende dedere ver Lijsbetten toe.'

61 Godding, *Le Droit privé*, pp. 270–80, 196, 303, 569.

62 Howell, *Marriage Exchange*, pp. 29–36.

63 *Coutume Gand*, rubric 20, nos. 19 and 20, p. 92; Godding, *Le Droit privé*, pp. 295–6, 304–6; Danneel, *Weduwen*, p. 263; Howell, *Marriage Exchange*, pp. 29–36; Murray, 'Family', 115–25.

9

'FOR HIS INTEREST'? WOMEN, DEBT AND COVERTURE IN EARLY MODERN SCOTLAND

Cathryn Spence

On 24 February 1629, George Reid and Isabel King, his wife, were ordered by the Burgh Court of Edinburgh to pay £6 10s. to James Graham and his wife, Agnes Johnston, for cloth.[1] While this case is largely unremarkable – in that it is just one of hundreds of debt cases entered into the burgh's Register of Decreets for 1629 – it does highlight an important aspect of the networks of debt and credit that existed in Edinburgh in the early modern period. Specifically, it highlights the role that wives played in these networks, for while Isabel's and Agnes's husbands are both named in the case and presumably appeared with their wives in court, the reason for the debt is identified as being for the complete payment of six quarters of lint bought by *Isabel* from *Agnes* a year and a half prior to the two couples' appearance in court. Theoretically, upon her marriage, a wife's legal identity was subsumed by her husband's, and she could no longer contract debts without her husband's permission. Yet, in this case we have one wife acting as a creditor and another acting as a debtor without the explicit permission of their husbands, although tacit permission can be assumed as both husbands are named in the case with their wives. Nor is this case exceptional when considering the tens of thousands of debt cases that were entered into the court records of Edinburgh, Haddington and Linlithgow between 1560 and 1640. Rather, numerous examples exist in the debt litigation for all three towns that show wives as active participants in the economy of debt and credit in early modern Scotland.

The presence of wives in debt litigation raises a number of questions. First, to what extent was the doctrine of coverture actively practised in early modern Scotland? Second, how did it affect the role of wives in debt transactions? Third, what economic roles were available to wives in Scotland, as elucidated through debt cases? This essay will demonstrate, quantitatively and qualitatively, that wives were active participants in both household and business debt transactions. Moreover, they appeared in great numbers and are sometimes specified as the prime movers in

1 Edinburgh City Archives (ECA), SL234/1/11. Upon her marriage in medieval and early modern Scotland, a woman did not take the surname of her husband. Rather, she kept her maiden name. However, any children born as a result of the marriage would assume the surname of the husband. I am grateful to the editors, especially Cordelia Beattie, for their helpful comments on previous drafts of this essay.

these debt transactions, as both creditors and debtors. This was particularly true in the city of Edinburgh, where opportunities to engage in credit and debt relationships were numerous. But, as will be shown, women account for more than 30 per cent of litigants in the debt records of three Scottish towns – those of Edinburgh, Haddington and Linlithgow, between 1560 and 1640. Moreover, women identified as wives form the majority of these female litigants. These debt cases indicate a number of economic opportunities which were open to married women and in which they engaged. A selection of these roles, including those as importers and sellers of cloth, wine and beer, and as money-lenders, will be considered towards the end of this essay and will serve to demonstrate how debt litigation in these communities can do much to bring to light the economic roles played by wives.

Women and Debt Litigation in Early Modern Scottish Towns

Edinburgh was, in this period, the largest, busiest and most influential town in Scotland, and its population grew from an estimated 12,000 people in 1560 to over 25,000 by 1640.[2] Edinburgh was twice the size of Dundee or Aberdeen, the next largest towns in Scotland during this period, and slightly larger than the Irish capital, Dublin, and the major English provincial centres of Norwich and Bristol.[3] Haddington and Linlithgow were smaller centres situated within reach of Edinburgh. Haddington lies thirty-two kilometres (twenty miles) to the east of Edinburgh, while Linlithgow is located thirty-two kilometres to the west of Edinburgh. While smaller than Edinburgh, Haddington and Linlithgow were nevertheless significant market centres for the still smaller communities which surrounded them. Much as Edinburgh served as a draw for people from communities like Haddington and Linlithgow, Haddington and Linlithgow in turn attracted people from their own hinterlands. Importantly, all three communities held markets and acted as trading points and each of these three communities has extant burgh court records dealing with debt.

In total, this essay draws upon over 50,000 court records including the Register of Decreets for Edinburgh, the Register of Deeds for Edinburgh and the Burgh Court Registers of Haddington and Linlithgow.[4] All three courts were attended by members of the immediate community, who could use the court to sue their neighbours or those from other communities. These courts were mainly concerned with determining the legal responsibility of individuals for debts, but also dealt with cases of slander, relations between landlords and tenants, transactions involving property, and marriage contracts. The Register of Deeds for Edinburgh exists for the entire eighty years under study, 1560 to 1640. The Register of Decreets for Edinburgh is somewhat less continuous, surviving from 1581 to 1583 and 1589 to 1592, and then becoming continuous from 1598. Although a note in the first volume of the decreets

2 L. Stewart, 'Politics and Government in the Scottish Burghs, 1603–1638', *Sixteenth-Century Scotland: Essays in Honour of Michael Lynch*, ed. J. Goodare and A. MacDonald (Leiden, 2008), p. 431.

3 Stewart, 'Politics and Government', pp. 431–2.

4 ECA, SL234/1/3–16; Nation Records of Scotland (NRS), B22/8/1–31; NRS, B30/10/3–13; NRS, B48/8/1–11.

describes it as a 'narrative of imprisonment', the court only ordered debtors to pay their creditors, with further actions, such as punishments, beyond the remit of the court. Similarly, the majority of entries in the burgh court records of Haddington and Linlithgow are debt-related, with some additional entries concerning matrimonial contracts and crime. Haddington's court records are extant from 1571, while Linlithgow's are extant from 1580. Debts recorded in all three communities ranged from only a few shillings to hundreds of pounds. Debts were most often incurred for the sale of drink and food, the rental of property, or the loan of money.

The recording of debt litigation in these records is both terse and fairly formulaic. The majority of cases deal with successful actions (the debtor is ordered by the bailies, or officers, of the court to pay the creditor a certain amount of money), but some cases in which a defendant was absolved of a debt were also recorded. In the Register of Decreets for Edinburgh, and the court registers for Haddington and Linlithgow, the reason for the debt then concludes the decreet. Men are typically identified by their profession or trade. When women appear in these records, they are typically identified by their marital status, as a wife or widow, by a relational status, as a mother, daughter or sister to another (normally a man), or as a servant. The fact that the clerk of the court habitually, but not always, noted if a woman was a wife, widow or servant allows for a comparison between these three groups of women. However, whether designated as a wife, widow or servant, these records show women of all social statuses suing and being sued, albeit for different causes and for differing sums.

Women, when considered as a whole, maintained a strong presence as both creditors and debtors in Edinburgh, Haddington and Linlithgow between the late sixteenth and mid-seventeenth centuries (see Table 9.1). In fact, the percentage of cases that name married women in each of these three Scottish communities is higher than that found in any other study of Britain or northern Europe for the medieval and early modern periods.[5] Within these communities, it was the women in Edinburgh who were most active – or recorded as being most active – as debtors and creditors. One reason for this is that Edinburgh women simply contracted debts more often. Edinburgh's position as Scotland's premier town offered greater opportunities to purchase, sell, or rent goods and services. Edinburgh's larger size and population, as well as its appeal to immigrants and frequent turnover of population, relative to Haddington and Linlithgow, might also have necessitated a more

5 See, e.g., E. Clark, 'Debt Litigation in a Late Medieval Vill', *Pathways to Peasants*, ed. J. A. Raftis (Toronto, 1981), p. 252; J. M. Bennett, *Women in the Medieval English Countryside: Gender and Household in Brigstock before the Plague* (Oxford, 1987), pp. 194–5; C. Briggs, *Credit and Village Society in Fourteenth-Century England* (Oxford, 2009), p. 114; M. K. McIntosh, *Working Women in English Society, 1300–1620* (Cambridge, 2005), pp. 86–90; M. K. McIntosh, 'Women, Credit and Family Relationships in England, 1300–1620', *Journal of Family History* 30:2 (2005), pp. 143–63; C. Muldrew, 'A Mutual Assent of Her Mind? Women, Debt, Litigation and Contract in Early Modern England', *History Workshop Journal* 55 (2003), 55; D. Nicholas, *The Domestic Life of a Medieval City: Women, Children, and the Family in Fourteenth-Century Ghent* (Lincoln, 1985), pp. 85–6; K. L. Reyerson, 'Women in Business in Medieval Montpellier', *Women and Work in Preindustrial Europe*, ed. B. A. Hanawalt (Bloomington, 1986), p. 132; S. Hutton, '"On Herself and All Her Property": Women's Economic Activities in Late-Medieval Ghent', *Continuity and Change* 20 (2005), 330.

stringent process for the recording of small debts, rather than a simple agreement between friends or neighbours, to ensure that those debts were repaid.

Table 9.1. Cases with Female Creditors and Debtors in Edinburgh, Haddington, and Linlithgow, 1560-1640

	All Creditors (A)	Female Creditors (B)	B as a % of A	All Debtors (C)	Female Debtors (D)	D as a % of C
Edinburgh	37,537	13,434	35.8%	37,537	12,768	34.0%
Haddington	6,953	1,356	19.5%	6,953	1,412	20.3%
Linlithgow	5,042	767	15.2%	5,042	741	14.7%

Source: ECA, SL234/1/2, 4-12, 14, 16, ECA, Register of Diets, 1606-22; NRS, B22/8/1-31; NRS, B30/10/3-13; NRS, B48/8/1-11.

While the percentages in Table 9.1 clearly show that women were participating in these economies, more information can be gleaned by breaking down these percentages into different classifications of women. This allows the differing legal statuses of wives, widows and servants to be taken into consideration. A fourth category, designated as 'Other', acts as a catch-all category for those women featured in the records who were identified by another designation or by no designation at all. It is possible, and even likely, that some women entered into this category were wives, widows or servants, but this cannot be proven. Table 9.2 thus illustrates that wives were, on average, the most common group of women to appear as creditors and debtors in court in Edinburgh and Haddington. (In Linlithgow, women in the 'Other' category were the most common, highlighting what was likely a difference in the record keeping for Linlithgow, whereby clerks were less likely to record the marital or occupational status of those who appeared in court.) The presence of so many wives acting as litigants in Edinburgh and Haddington is striking because, as we will see, the doctrine of coverture made the recording of wives theoretically unnecessary in litigation cases.

Table 9.2. Number and Percentage of Cases Featuring Female Creditors or Debtors in Edinburgh, Haddington and Linlithgow, 1560-1640

Town	Total Cases	Wives	Widows	Servants	Other
Edinburgh	37,537	14,569	4,922	1,333	6,623
	100%	38.8%	13.1%	35%	17.6%
Haddington	6,953	1,448	473	22	804
	100%	20.8%	6.8%	0.3%	11.6%
Linlithgow	5,042	583	168	7	685
	100%	11.6%	3.3%	0.1%	13.4%

Source: ECA, SL234/1/2, 4-12, 14, 16; ECA, Register of Diets, 1606-22; NRS, B22/8/1-31; NRS, B30/10/3-13; NRS, B48/8/1-11.

The Application of Coverture in Early Modern Scotland

To date, no studies have focused upon coverture in pre-modern Scotland and relatively few works have discussed women's roles in Scottish debt and credit networks. Further, the majority of those studies that do discuss the activities of women in debt and credit networks do not approach the topic quantitatively. They have, however, demonstrated that women were involved in these networks.[6] Most recently, an examination of the Aberdeen Baillie Court (which was the type of court that succeeded the burgh courts after the mid-seventeenth century) found that, in the late seventeenth century, single and widowed women participated in at least one-fifth of recorded cases and that, more surprisingly, married women were routinely named in debt cases. In fact, 34 per cent of cases examined by Gordon Desbrisay and Karen Sander Thomson featured at least one married woman.[7] They attribute this high figure to the Baillie Court's convention of naming wives both when they contracted debts on their own and when they acted with their husbands.

The reason that the numbers from both Aberdeen and this study are surprising is that upon her marriage in early modern Scotland, a woman gave up her independent legal persona.[8] Due to this loss of persona, wives could not act legally without their husband's consent, whether contracting or pursuing a debt, acting as a cautioner, or making a testament (although married women were allowed to retain control of their personal items, typically identified in a testament as a woman's 'ornaments and abulzements').[9] The ability of a woman to engage freely in debt litigation was thus theoretically dependent upon her stage in the lifecycle, and specifically whether or not she was married. Sir James Balfour, a sixteenth-century Scottish judge and politician, noted in his *Practicks* under 'Materis concerning the husband and the wife':

6 See, e.g., I. D. Whyte and K. A. Whyte, 'Debt and Credit, Poverty and Prosperity in a Seventeenth-Century Scottish Rural Community', *Economy and Society in Scotland and Ireland, 1500–1939*, ed. R. Mitchison and P. Roebuck (Edinburgh, 1988), pp. 70–80; L. Ewan, 'Debtors, Imprisonment, and the Privilege of Girth', *Perspectives in Scottish Social History: Essays in Honour of Rosalind Mitchison*, ed. L. Leneman (Aberdeen, 1988), p. 54; E. Ewan, '"For Whatever Ales Ye": Women as Consumers and Producers in Late Medieval Scottish Towns', *Women in Scotland, c.1100–c.1750*, ed. E. Ewan and M. Meikle (Edinburgh, 1999), p. 127; M. H. B. Sanderson, *A Kindly Place? Living in Sixteenth-Century Scotland* (East Linton, 2002), pp. 106–7.

7 G. Desbrisay and K. Sander Thomson, 'Crediting Wives: Married Women and Debt Litigation in the Seventeenth Century', *Finding the Family in Medieval and Early Modern Scotland*, ed. E. Ewan and J. Nugent (Aldershot, 2008), pp. 92–4.

8 P. G. B. McNeill, ed., *The Practicks of Sir James Balfour of Pittendreich*, vol. 1 (Edinburgh, 1962), p. 216; G. C. H. Paton, 'Husband and Wife: Property Rights and Relationships', *An Introduction to Scottish Legal History* (Alva, 1958), pp. 100–1; A. D. M. Forte, 'Some Aspects of the Law of Marriage in Scotland: 1500–1700', *Marriage and Property*, ed. E. M. Craik (Aberdeen, 1984), pp. 107, 109–10; W. Coutts, *Business of the College of Justice in 1600: How It Reflects the Economic and Social Life of Scots Men and Women* (Edinburgh, 2004), p. 139.

9 Forte, 'Some Aspects of the Law of Marriage', p. 111; Coutts, *Business of the College of Justice*, pp. 138–9.

> Ane woman beand cled with ane husband may not be callit, nor persewit in judgment, in ony civil action or cause, except hir husband in likewayis be callit and persewit to fortifie, assist and authorize hir ... In like maner scho may not persew in ony action or cause without hir husbandis consent.[10]

Wives could thus not pursue actions without the consent of their husbands, and were required to appear in court (if an obligation reached the point where it required legal intervention) with their husbands. Further, Balfour notes that 'Gif divers and sindrie persounis persew conjunctlie ony summondis or cause, and ane of thame be a woman cled with ane husband, and the summondis be not intendit and persewit at his instance, *for his interes*, scho may not persew the samin without avise of hir husband' (my italics).[11] It was thus imperative that a wife either had the consent of her husband, or that he stand up in court with her.

While coverture curtailed certain legal freedoms, it did arguably benefit wives in some ways. A husband was responsible for his wife's debts, even those that had been contracted prior to the marriage, and for any misdemeanours committed by her.[12] A wife was also entitled to be supported by her husband until death or divorce.[13] Sir James Dalrymple, a seventeenth-century Scottish lawyer and judge, noted that 'the aliment or furnishing of the wife is a debt of her husband's (not only for what is given by merchants and others *hoc homine* in the husband's life, but even her mournings after his death)'.[14]

Although Scottish law in this period did not allow wives to sue or be sued independently of their husbands, Scottish legal custom did allow wives to be named in debt cases. As was the case in England, particular Scottish burghs had distinct customary laws that governed a number of issues raised in their courts in matters such as debt litigation. These customary laws could recognize the necessity that wives be able to make certain transactions without the explicit permission of their husbands. Unlike England, there is no evidence that customary law in Scotland went so far as bestowing a designation similar to *femme sole* to denote married women who had received special permission to trade under their own names, rather than under the cover of their husbands.[15] Still, Scottish wives were not completely prevented from engaging with networks of debt and credit. Instead, a wife, 'in her domestic role as the person in charge of her master's establishment, was said to be *praepositura negottus domesticis*', which allowed her to pledge her

10 J. Balfour, *Practicks: or, a system of the more ancient law of Scotland* (Edinburgh, 1764), p. 93.

11 Balfour, *Practicks*, p. 93.

12 Forte, 'Some Aspects of the Law of Marriage', p. 110.

13 Coutts, *Business of the College of Justice*, p. 140.

14 J. Dalrymple, Viscount of Stair, *The institutions of the law of Scotland, deduced from its originals, and collated with the civil, and feudal-laws, and with the customs of neighbouring nations, In four books* (Edinburgh, 1759), p. 29.

15 For a discussion of what it meant to be a *femme sole* see M. K. McIntosh, 'The Benefits and Drawbacks of Femme Sole Status in England, 1300–1630', *Journal of British Studies* 44:3 (2005), pp. 410–38.

husband's credit for 'household necessities suitable to his station'.[16] However, this designation is only infrequently invoked in the records. One such rare occasion was on 13 April 1616, when Elizabeth Nicolson, the widow of John Aslowane, a merchant, was ordered to pay to David Junkin, a merchant, £47 7s. 4d. in complete payment of merchandise bought by Elizabeth from David as 'praesposita negottus mariti sui'.[17] This indicates that John was still alive when the merchandise was bought, but Elizabeth was permitted to make the purchase. In this, a Scottish wife's access to her husband's credit seems to have functioned in a similar manner to the so-called 'law of necessaries' in England. This 'law of necessaries' or 'law of agency', as it is variously known, has been used by Margot Finn and Joanne Bailey in their studies of women in England c.1660–1860 to argue that wives were not totally constrained by coverture and could (and did) engage in a range of economic activities.[18] For example, Finn argues that the small claim courts that form the basis for her study 'traditionally recognized and accepted the evidence of married women as their husband's agents'.[19]

In the Scottish burgh courts examined for this essay, husbands were invariably named alongside their wives in debt cases, although it is possible that the husband appeared in name only and was not physically present with his wife in court.[20] Although women identified as wives are never recorded as appearing without their husbands, men known to be husbands (often because they have elsewhere appeared in a case with their wife, or their wife has been named in the explanation for the debt) did act in cases without their wives. This suggests that when wives are named in cases with their husbands there is more to their presence than simply identifying another debtor who can be pursued in the event of the death, disappearance or other defaulting of the husband.

When a wife appears with her husband in court, it is important to look closely at the explanation for the debt to determine who exactly it was that contracted the debt and whether the wife was active in the transaction, complicit with her husband, or if the husband was the active party and the wife merely present. Most commonly, both partners acted together to contract the debt, and thus both partners are named in the explanation for the debt. An example of this is a case concerning Thomas Scott, a beer brewer, and Marjorie White, his spouse, who on 20 July 1622 were ordered to pay to John Bourdone, a merchant, and Margaret Lowes, his spouse, £7 7s. 2d. in complete payment of merchandise bought by one couple from the other.[21] There

16 Coutts, *Business of the College of Justice*, p. 139; Paton, 'Husband and Wife', pp. 105–6. The definition of 'praepositura negottus domesticis' can be found in John Erskine, *An institute of the law of Scotland, In four books, In the order of Sir George Mackenzie's Institutions of that law* (Edinburgh, 1773), p. 96.

17 ECA, Register of Diets, 1615–19, 13 April 1616.

18 J. Bailey, 'Favoured or Oppressed? Married Women, Property and "Coverture" in England, 1660–1800', *Continuity and Change* 17 (2002), 351–72; M. Finn, 'Women, Consumption and Coverture in England, c. 1760–1860', *The Historical Journal* 39 (1996), 703–22. See also Beattie's essay in this volume.

19 Finn, 'Women, Consumption and Coverture', p. 715.

20 Desbrisay and Sander Thomson, 'Crediting Wives', p. 89.

21 ECA, SL234/1/10.

are also examples in the records where a husband and wife appear together in a debt case, and the next debt case following directly after features only the husband, obviously acting without his wife. In the vast majority of cases where only one partner is named in the explanation for a debt that has been transacted by a married couple, it is the wife whose role as the principal actor in the debt is stated; only very rarely is the husband identified as the principal actor in a debt case that names both a husband and a wife. For example, when John Wilkie of Haddington was ordered to pay George Blackburn and Helen Johnston, spouses, £5 5s. on 21 July 1635, the reason for the debt was given as for clothing bought by *him* from *her* at the previous feast of Michaelmas.[22] Thus, when the Scottish records explicitly state that it was the wife alone who acted as a creditor or debtor, or as a buyer or seller, it seems reasonable to assume that the wife was acting alone, but had (or was assumed to have had) the explicit or tacit permission of her husband.

Desbrisay and Sander Thomson have found that, in the Baillie Court of Aberdeen in the late seventeenth century, decreets involving a wife included not only the name of the husband, but also the phrase 'for his interest', a stock phrase, 'signaling both the nominality of the husband's role in the transaction and his legal responsibility for it'.[23] They argue that readers of a debt case in which it appears can infer that a husband, although named, was not actively a part of the deal. However, while the phrase 'for his interest' was common in debt records for Aberdeen, this was not the case for debt records recorded in Edinburgh, Haddington or Linlithgow earlier in the seventeenth century. In the debt cases analysed for this essay, very few used the phrase 'for his interest', but neither was there any indication as to why some scribes chose to employ this phrase and others did not. Further, rather than being a phrase which was employed only by husbands appearing in court with their wives, there are also instances in the Edinburgh debt records of a woman being named 'for *her* interest' in a case. Isabel Drew, a widow, appeared in a case 'for her interest', in which she was owed money by another widow. Helen Scarlett owed Isabel £36. However, Isabel, in turn, owed George Duncan, a merchant burgess, £170.[24] In such cases, where a debt was owed by one person to another, and that creditor in turn owed a debt to a third party, 'for his interest' or 'for her interest' was often employed when identifying the first party to whom money was owed and who was also a debtor him- or herself, whether the two debts involved three men, three women, or a combination of men and women. 'For his interest' or 'for her interest' therefore denoted legal responsibility for a debt, but not solely between husbands and wives. Rather, this responsibility and burden of awareness also existed between other debtors and creditors.

This does not mean that cases which did not use the phrase 'for his interest' involved wives who were engaging passively, rather than actively, in these debts. In many cases that did not use this phrase, wives had clearly initiated the debts for which they would later appear in court with their husbands. This is borne out in

22 NRS, B30/10/13.

23 Coutts, *Business of the College of Justice*, p. 139; Desbrisay and Sander Thomson, 'Crediting Wives', p. 89.

24 ECA, Register of Diets, 1615–19, 7 March 1618.

numerous examples, such as a case from 1600 which featured Steven Bannatyne and Agnes Clavie, his spouse, as the debtors, and Elspeth Howson and Alexander Wardlaw, her spouse, as the creditors. The debtors were ordered to pay the creditors £19 10s. in remuneration for money paid by Elspeth for Steven (at his command) to another man, Alexander Livingston, for four barrels of beer bought by Steven from Alexander at the feast of the previous Martinmas.[25] The case does not explain why Steven requested Elspeth pay for his beer, nor why Elspeth complied, but it is clear by whom and to whom the money was owed. It is also clear that despite the fact that Elspeth's husband was named he was not part of the deal.

In numerous cases, the explanation for the debt case specifically indicates that the debt referred to goods or services prepared and provided by the wife alone. In two cases that appeared before the court on 12 October 1613, couples were ordered separately to pay money to Janet Liberton, wife of a locksmith, for ale.[26] Although Janet's husband was a locksmith, and therefore presumably had no part in the transaction, the phrase 'for his interest' does not appear. Similarly, on 21 January 1613, David Granger was ordered to pay £5 16s. 8d. to Bessie Darling, wife to Alexander Borthwick, in complete payment of nine and a half quarters of green cloth which he had bought from her. In another case, entered in the Edinburgh Register of Decreets on 6 June 1622, Adam Rea, one of the Edinburgh town guard, was ordered to pay to Eupham Mark and John Kers, her spouse, £3 3s. 'in complete payment of ale and lent money furnished and lent by her to him two years ago'.[27] The wording of the explanation for both debts, as well as the fact that John, Eupham's husband, is identified in the case as an officer, makes it clear that it was Bessie who sold the cloth and Eupham who was engaged in the practice of making ale and lending money, both independently of their husbands. That so many wives appeared in transactions with their husbands indicates that it was routine practice for wives to contract debts on their own and then act with their husbands in debt litigation. The presence of these wives did not require a special explanation in the records.

Shennan Hutton demonstrates that it was quite common in fourteenth-century Ghent for husbands and wives to appear together in court swearing to pay debts, as does Matthew Stevens for early fourteenth-century London.[28] Hutton suggests that creditors preferred to have both spouses perform the legal act and thus share the liability. The same may have been true in Scottish burgh courts, given the number of wives recorded. The naming of a wife must have sometimes been a form of insurance on the part of the creditor. If a debtor died while still owing a debt, the debt died with him or her, and the creditor could not pursue the debtor's executors through court if the deceased's debts outweighed their credits.[29]

25 ECA, SL234/1/4.

26 ECA, Register of Diets, 1612–15.

27 ECA, SL234/1/10.

28 See Hutton's essay in this volume; M. F. Stevens, 'London Women, the Courts and the "Golden Age": A Quantitative Analysis of Female Litigants in the Fourteenth and Fifteenth Centuries', *London Journal* 37 (2012), 67–88.

29 J. H. Baker, *An Introduction to English Legal History*, 3rd edn (London, 1990), p. 371.

Conversely, by naming both a husband and wife in a debt as creditors, the crediting party was assured that either party could continue to pursue a debt in the event the other died. Otherwise, under customary law, a person could not appear in court on behalf of another. While a husband could make his wife his 'cessioner and assignory', which allowed her to continue to pursue his debts after his death, this was a much more formal and all-encompassing arrangement.[30] Day-to-day debt transactions did not use it.

One final indication as to which half of the marital partnership had contracted the debt can be found in the margins of the court book. There, the surnames of the principal actors in the case were recorded for ease of reference. Desbrisay and Sander Thomson found in their investigation of debts entered into the Aberdeen Baillie Court in the 1680s that such marginalia tended to only include the wife's name when the debt had been contracted by her alone.[31] Evidence from the debt litigation consulted for this study indicates that, while the surnames of both spouses appeared in the marginalia, in cases where the wife was the principal actor her name tended to appear first, above her husband's. Some examples of only the wife's surname appearing in the margins do exist, but these are infrequent.

The Scottish records are also careful to record when a debt was contracted by a widow or single woman prior to a subsequent marriage, as in the case of the debt for £6 owed by Marion Bannatyne, a widow who had remarried, to Henry Bannatyne, a lawyer. The case made clear that Marion was a widow at the time the debt had been contracted but that her new husband was aware of it and accepted responsibility for it. He appeared in the case 'for his interest', as did another man, whom Marion had recruited as her 'cautioner' for the debt.[32] Similarly, Christian Furd and James Sinclair, 'now her spouse', appeared in the court because Christian owed £16 to a merchant for the maill (rent) of a house occupied by Janet Henryson. The explanation for the debt stated that Christian had, in June 1612 when she was still a widow, become surety for the debt of maill owed by Janet to the merchant. In these cases, wives were not acting without their husbands, but had committed these actions before they had married. While their husbands had taken on the legal responsibilities for the couples' finances, these wives still appeared in court to answer for their debts.[33]

Wives' Economic Roles

Now that it has been established that a close reading of the debt records of Edinburgh, Haddington and Linlithgow can often indicate which debts were contracted by wives, it is possible to explore the economic roles these women played. Moreover, the number of cases that name wives provide an impressive sample size, despite the informality of small-scale lending and the veil of coverture. As

30 Balfour, *Practicks*, pp. 93–4.

31 Desbrisay and Sander Thomson, 'Crediting Wives', p. 90.

32 ECA, Register of Diets, 1619–22, 6 May 1619.

33 For a discussion of this in relation to fifteenth-century London, see Stevens's essay in this volume.

Table 9.2 illustrated, wives were named in over one-third of the more than 37,500 debt cases entered into the records for Edinburgh-based courts between 1590 and 1640, one-fifth of the cases entered into the records for Haddington between 1570 and 1640, and one-tenth of the cases entered into the records for Linlithgow between 1580 and 1640. Many of these debt cases feature wives provisioning their households, but others saw them directly involved in large-scale enterprises.

Debts were typically pursued by creditors identified as wives for six distinct reasons, which were, in order of prevalence, drink, food, house rent (maill), lent money, cloth and merchandise, or a combination of two or more of these. The first of these, drink, includes all types of alcoholic beverages (ale, beer, wine, and aqua vitae), non-alcoholic beverages (milk), and those items which were used in the preparation of alcoholic beverages (malt, which was necessary for brewing ale, and draff, which was a by-product of brewing ale). Food consists of all types of food stuffs, including bread products, grain products and animal products. Maill refers to all amounts of money due for the rentals of houses, shops, chambers or beds. Lent money includes all amounts of money identified as being borrowed or lent by one person to another. Cloth refers to all amounts and types of cloth bought by one person from another, whether that cloth was simply an amount of cloth, or had been turned into clothing. Finally, merchandise might have been entered into debt cases specifically as 'merchandise' or as a certain type of merchandise, including tobacco, tar, apothecary wares and cramery wares,[34] which were bought less frequently than other items and due to their scarcity in the records can be dealt with under the catch-all term 'merchandise'. Some of the smaller-value debts incurred by married women resulted from provisioning the household. In these debts, while the husband was named with his wife in the case, it was certainly a form of clerical convention, rather than indicating that small amounts of food, drink and cloth were purchased jointly by husband and wife. The negotiation of these everyday debts seems to fall under something akin to the English 'law of necessaries', as previously discussed. Additionally, debts were contracted for unspecified 'necessaries' and 'furnishings', as well as for the provision of services, including work done by tailors, schoolmasters, washerwomen, and various people in the 'burding [boarding] and entertainment' of children.[35] Some of these debts were for significant amounts of money, indicating the participation of wives across the socio-economic spectrum.

Whether wives were appearing in these cases as debtors or creditors in these transactions is an important factor in understanding their specific roles. As Table

34 Cramery wares refer to merchandise sold by a stallholder or peddler.

35 See, e.g., the debt of 5 merks owed by Robert Cairns and Elspeth Thomson, his spouse, to James Muir, a tailor, for 'furnishings and workmanship of the tailor craft wrought by him to them', entered into the records on 17 May 1631; or the debt of £7 2s. owed by Katherine Henryson and Andrew Naper, her spouse, to Katherine Ker, a widow, for 'the making, dressing and washing of linen cloths pertaining to them, made and dressed by the said Katherine to them at their command within these two years last', entered into the record on 22 March 1631. Magdalene Craw and Andrew Ross, her spouse, were discerned to owe William Lock £5 'in complete payment of £26 for fostering and entertainment in bed and board during the space of a year of Jean Douglas, daughter to the said Magdalene', on 8 July 1634. (ECA, SL234/1/12)

9.3 illustrates for Edinburgh, wives were slightly more likely to appear as creditors rather than debtors. However, this did not hold true for all women; widows were more likely to appear as debtors. This was perhaps because wives might be named as creditors in transactions both for items produced by themselves and for those produced by their husbands. Thus, while wives and widows incurred similar debts in provisioning their households, widows had fewer opportunities to act as creditors. At the least, the presence of wives in these records shows wives, regardless of their legal position, demonstrating a vested interest in their families' economic dealings and sufficient agency to warrant a place in the courts. However, many of these cases show wives actively participating in these transactions as the primary creditors or debtors. As creditors, they sold a variety of items, including cloth, wine and books. As debtors, they purchased materials for home consumption or to use in a variety of businesses.

A large number of these cases, like the case presented at the beginning of this essay, named one couple as owing another couple. However, the reasons for these debts often identify the wives as those who were active in the case. It is thus likely that Scottish wives played a more important role in these economic activities than these relatively reticent entries suggest. A case involving two married couples in Haddington on 26 November 1588 ordered Katherine White and George Bathcat, her spouse, for his interest, to pay to Beatrix Mayne and George Ayton, her spouse, for his interest, £3 17s. of the rest of the cost of six firlottes of malt (used in ale production) bought by Katherine from Beatrix.[36] This case thus shows one wife, Katherine, involved in procuring goods, while at the same time it shows that Beatrix was the one responsible for the actual sale of these goods. Both economic roles are clearly visible.

Table 9.3. Women's Roles as Creditors and Debtors in Edinburgh, 1589-92, 1598-1640

	Wives	Widows	Servants	Other	Total Women
Creditors	7,585	2,088	1,149	3,524	14,346
Debtors	6,984	2,834	184	3,099	13,101

Source: ECA, SL234/1/2, 4-12, 14, 16; ECA, Register of Diets, 1606-22; NAS, B22/8/1-31.

The involvement of wives in the purchase and sale of cloth, wine and ale, as well as the practice of money-lending, is particularly evident from debt litigation.[37] These activities go well beyond the law of necessaries. Instead, they are clearly indicative of fields of work in which these wives were engaged. We will address each of these economic endeavours in turn. The first of these creditor activities, the sale of cloth, could be a lucrative one. Katherine Culan and James Haliburton, her spouse, were found to owe £87 to Frances Irving on 25 May 1605 in complete

36 NRS, B30/10/6.

37 See C. Spence, '"To Content and Pay": Women's Economic Roles in Edinburgh, Haddington and Linlithgow, 1560–1640', unpublished Ph.D. thesis, University of Edinburgh, 2010, chs 2, 4–5.

payment of £687 for English cloth bought in May 1603 and a further £127 worth of cloth bought in February 1604.[38] Elizabeth Stevenson, who died in December 1569, was obviously quite extensively involved in the cloth industry with her husband, Alexander Park, who was himself one of Edinburgh's leading merchants in the latter half of the sixteenth century.[39] The inventory of Elizabeth's testament contains a long list of various amounts and types of cloth, including serge, red and black velvet, black and purple satin, and red, green, yellow and purple taffeta. All together, the inventory of her goods was valued to the amount of £3,310 14s. 5d. This sum jumped to an impressive £12,263 16s. 6d. when the debts owing to her – which included a variety of debts owed by tailors who had likely purchased the cloth Elizabeth and her husband were bringing to Edinburgh – were factored in.[40] Elizabeth's inventory therefore indicates that she was very much involved in the import and export of cloth during this period, and, in general, the women who were most extensively involved in the import of cloth and imported the greatest volumes and varieties of luxury cloth into Scotland also tended to be those who were married to the richest and most prominent merchant burgesses in the burgh. That these women produced such detailed testaments and were able, in some cases, to bequeath the tools of their business (for example, the share of a ship) to their children indicates the active roles they played in the import and export of cloth, both in concert with their spouses and independently.[41]

The import and sale of wine was another area in which wives were actively engaged. Andrew Lawson and Isabel Tailpheir, his spouse, were found to owe Isabel Cockburn and Alexander Bains, her husband, who was also a skipper in Leith, £50 in 1609 for a puncheon of wine.[42] Bains's position as a skipper may indicate that he was engaged in overseas trade. As his wife, Isabel may have controlled the sale of the items, including wine, he imported. In 1612, James Nisbet and Marion Arnot, his spouse, were owed £46 10s. by George Waldy, £280 10s. by William Fleabairn, a merchant, and £247 12s. by John Lamb, also a merchant, in complete payment of wine. That James and Marion sold large amounts of wine to other merchants indicates that they too were involved in the importation of wine and sold it wholesale to others.[43] On 3 April 1634 William Somervell, a merchant, was determined to owe Hector Purves, also a merchant, and Isabel Adair, his spouse, and William Brown, their sub-factor, £215 for wine bought by William from Isabel half a year previously.[44] The sale of the wine specifically by Isabel to William, as well as the mention of a factor, indicates that Hector was an overseas merchant who may not have been in Edinburgh when the wine was sold and may have trusted

38 ECA, SL234/1/6.

39 M. Lynch, *Edinburgh and the Reformation* (Edinburgh, 1981), p. 373. Alexander Park was discerned to pay £60 in the tax roll of 1565. The average contribution made by merchants was £11 6s., so Park's contribution of £60 is notable.

40 NRS, CC8/8/1/708–13.

41 See Spence, '"To Content and Pay"', pp. 107–8.

42 ECA, Register of Diets, 1609–12 (20 June 1609).

43 ECA, Register of Diets, 1609–12 (4 February 1612, 14 April 1612, and 11 July 1612).

44 ECA, SL234/1/14.

its sale (and perhaps other sales also contracted during his absence) to his wife.[45] Thus, while women may not have been active in the importation of wine as individuals, they nevertheless participated in its control and sale with their merchant husbands once it arrived in port. These husbands and wives were responsible for, in turn, selling wine to a number of other married couples and widows. Many of those who purchased wine from these importers then sold or provided this wine to servants, who in turn sold it in smaller measures to customers in taverns and in the streets.[46]

The role of wives in the sale of wine can also be examined through their roles as debtors. Isabel Talipher, with her husband appearing 'for his interest', owed Alexander Pearson, a merchant, £130 for wine bought by her from him.[47] George Ker, a tailor, and Marion Nemo, his wife, owed Archibald Tod, a merchant, £200 for a tun of wine.[48] Large debts for large amounts of wine (barrels, casks, tuns, pipes, barykins, puncheons and butts) indicate that the individual or couple purchasing the wine intended to resell it.[49] This resale was often done through servants, as the case concerning Janet Dickson illustrates. Janet was a servant to Andrew Naper and Katherine Henryson, his wife, in 1631. She owed the couple £210 17s. 4d. when the cost of the wine and beer they had provided to her to sell in their service was totted up.[50]

When it came to the sale of ale and beer, which could be produced locally, wives often appeared as debtors in transactions concerned with the raw material, particularly malt or malted barley, and as creditors in transactions concerning the sale of the finished product. Wives were the group of women most likely to appear as debtors in a debt for malt, indicating that they were the women most likely to be involved in producing ale with that malt. Janet Trimble, who appeared in court with her husband on 10 December 1607 and was ordered to pay £9 10s. for a mask of malt bought by her from a Robert Brown, was likely the same Janet

45 It is possible that Isabel acted in a manner similar to Magdalena Paumgartner, a wife who lived in Nuremburg, Germany in the late sixteenth century. She never accompanied her merchant husband, Balthasar, on his trips to Lucca and Frankfurt, yet she acted as his 'virtual agent' at home, informing relatives, friends and clients of the state of their orders, and receiving, storing and distributing merchandise as it arrived. She also, when necessary, negotiated with clients and suppliers over payment of goods. See S. Osment, ed., *Magdalena and Balthasar: An Intimate Portrait of Life in 16th Century Europe Revealed in the Letters of a Nuremburg Husband and Wife* (New Haven, 1989), p. 17.

46 Spence, '"To Content and Pay"', pp. 118–19.

47 ECA, Register of Diets, 1609–12

48 ECA, SL234/1/16.

49 'Tun', 'pipe', 'butt', and 'puncheon' were all words for 'barrel' or 'cask', although these terms were also used to describe amounts of wine. Elizabeth Gemmill and Nicholas Mayhew use Rogers, *A History of Agriculture and Prices in England*, I, p. 619, to argue that there were 252 gallons to a tun of wine, and 126 gallons to a pipe, although they later suggest there may have been 111 gallons in a pipe: E. Gemmill and N. Mayhew, *Changing Values in Medieval Scotland: A Study of Prices, Money, and Weights and Measures* (Cambridge, 1995), pp. 399, 408. In terms of puncheons, Gemmill and Mayhew suggest that the ratio fluctuated between 2.67 puncheons to one tun, and four puncheons to one tun.

50 ECA, SL234/1/12.

Trimble who later appeared acting alone (perhaps she was then a widow) and as a creditor in debts for ale.[51]

The first step in making ale was to malt the grain (the beir) that would be brewed with the water. In late medieval and early modern England, the production and sale of malt was usually performed by men who would then use most of the malt in commercial brewing establishments and sell some to women who were brewing on a smaller scale.[52] The same seems to have been true for Scotland in the medieval period, as the demands of time and space involved in malting required that it be pursued on a professional, rather than a piecemeal, basis.[53] Edinburgh, for example, leased out common lands for large-scale malting operations from 1508.[54] The practice of professional maltmen selling malt to large- and small-scale ale producers was likely still in place in Edinburgh, Haddington and Linlithgow in the late sixteenth and early seventeenth centuries, as the majority of debts for malt which were entered into the records feature a married couple owing money to a man identified in the debt records as a 'maltman'.

Wives in all three communities were the most likely group of women to be engaged in the production of ale in the period under consideration. Again and again in the records, individual debt cases specifically identify the wife as the active creditor in cases concerning debts for ale and beer, even though her husband appears with her. Two cases entered into the Edinburgh Register of Decreets, one in 1599 and the other in 1606, help to illustrate this. In the first, Robert McClellan and Deborah Dalzell, his spouse, are discerned to owe Marion Porteous and John Hamilton, her spouse, forty-six merks for 'ale furnished by Porteous to them at diverse times within these three years last'.[55] In other words, Marion specifically furnished ale to Robert and Deborah not once but several times. In the second case, Agnes Lawson, the widow of Gilbert Skene, was discerned to owe Robert Thomson, a goldsmith, £60 for ale furnished by 'Robert and Susanna Ferguson, his spouse, to the said [deceased] Gilbert and Agnes at diverse times since Martinmas last'.[56] In this second case, Robert, the husband, is identified as a goldsmith.[57] It is unlikely that he was also producing ale, and so it is logical to assume that Robert's wife, Susanna, was the ale producer.

A number of factors contributed to this trend. Wives – and the wives of burgesses in particular – were considered by town authorities to be the most desirable type of women to engage in brewing. Married to members of the community of good standing, wives were perceived as less likely to engage in 'unchaste' behaviours, or to tolerate in their employ women who engaged in such behaviours. This went hand-in-hand with similar desires and attempts to limit the employment op-

51 ECA, Register of Diets, 1606–9, 10 December 1607, then 11 February 1608 and 13 February 1608.
52 McIntosh, *Working Women*, p. 145.
53 Ewan, '"For Whatever Ales Ye"', p. 128.
54 Ewan, '"For Whatever Ales Ye"', p. 132.
55 ECA, SL234/1/6.
56 ECA, SL234/1/5.
57 Robert attained the 'freedom' of the goldsmith craft on 13 November 1589: J. Munro, trans., and H. Fotheringham, ed., *Edinburgh Goldsmiths' Minutes, 1525–1700* (Edinburgh, 2006), p. 35.

tions open to widows, female servants, and other 'masterless' women who, if they were able to brew and sell ale, might be more likely to live independently, rather than in acceptable, male-headed households. Furthermore, wives – particularly those of elevated social standing – were in a better position to produce ale because they were able to hire servants to help them produce and disseminate it. A significant difference in the production of ale between Edinburgh and Haddington and Linlithgow, however, seems to have had little to do with marital status, and more to do with location. Wives were still the most active group of women engaged in the production of ale in Edinburgh, but it seems clear that women in Haddington and Linlithgow were more engaged with the production of ale for a longer period in time, thanks to evidence concerning not only the proportion of debts involving the sale of ale in these communities, but also the purchase of malt and beir, which were integral to the production, and the sale in these communities of draff, one of the by-products of the production of ale. Indeed, it seems clear that in Haddington and Linlithgow women were more likely than women in Edinburgh to be involved in the production of ale in the late sixteenth and early seventeenth centuries, but that women in Edinburgh were more involved in the sale of ale.

This involvement was not immune to change over time. As the commercialization of ale progressed in the early seventeenth century, the role of wives in the sale of ale in Edinburgh changed. Whereas women had previously acted as the producers of ale for their families and communities, by producing ale for their families and selling the excess, with the introduction of hops into Scotland ale could be produced on a larger, more commercial scale because it could be stored for longer. The majority of this large-scale production fell to men, and women were pushed out of ale production. In Edinburgh, in particular, the production of ale was controlled by the Society of Ale and Beer Brewers of the Burgh of Edinburgh, a public company established in 1596 for the purpose of making ale and beer on a large scale for the entirety of the burgh.[58] Upon the establishment of this society, no other fellowship or society which brewed ale or beer was allowed to be established within the burgh, and no one except the members of the society were allowed to sell or buy the ale and beer produced by the society. Also, freemen and their wives were forbidden to sell ale or beer in quantities larger than a pint or a quart, under pain of a fine of £5.[59] Given how completely women had dominated the brewing trades in the early part of the sixteenth century, the establishment of this society certainly had an impact on brewing carried out by women in Edinburgh. Michael Lynch has argued that 'it probably did more than any single other act to undermine the economic status of women'.[60] However, for a variety of reasons, the most pressing of which seems to have been the lack of profits for the sellers, the society was officially dissolved

58 William Moir Bryce, 'The Fellowship and Society of Brewers of Ale and Beer in Edinburgh', *The Book of the Old Edinburgh Club*, 10 (Edinburgh, 1918), p. 228.

59 Bryce, 'The Fellowship and Society of Brewers', p. 233.

60 Michael Lynch, 'Continuity and Change in Urban Society, 1500–1700', *Scottish Society, 1500–1800*, ed. R. A. Houston and I. D. Whyte (Cambridge, 1989), p. 109.

in 1619 and its lands returned to the common good.[61] The society's buildings were then leased to William Binny and Robert Livingston, maltmen, for seven years. In 1622, the lease was assigned to William Dick, who renewed the lease in 1632.[62] Increasingly, throughout the late 1620s and into the 1630s, wives purchased large amounts of ale from William Dick and his factor, presumably for resale. One of these women was Helen Brown, who was evidently running an alehouse out of her home. On 16 July 1630, Helen, who was the wife of Robert Wilson, a wright, was, alone, determined to owe £257 15s. 8d. to John Monro (factor to William Dick) for the cost of certain barrels of ale and beer:

> bought and received by *me and my servants* in *my* name at *my* command furth of the said society [of Edinburgh] and laid in by their workmen within *my* cellar and publicly vented there *by me and my servants* in name of my said spouse and me at diverse sundry times preceding the date hereof [my italics].[63]

Helen and her servants were explicitly identified as both the purchasers, and the resellers, of the ale and beer bought from the Society of Ale and Beer Brewers. Helen promised to pay the cost of the ale and beer by 11 November, together with 10 merks of annual rent for every 100 merks of the principal sum, along with the sum of 40 merks for expenses in case she failed to pay the said sum by the agreed day. Further, she presented herself as principal and David Brown, a saddler burgess, as her cautioner. It is clear that Helen's husband had no role in this deal beyond establishing that Helen was a married woman.

The records also show that money-lending was one of the most common endeavours in which wives engaged.[64] Debts categorized as 'borrowed money', 'lent money', 'borrowed silver' and 'lent silver' can be found throughout the records for this period. Sometimes these amounts were borrowed 'on obligation' or 'by bond', while others presented no such designation but did include a provision for the payment of a penalty if the repayment of the debt was late, or simply in addition to the original sum. On 5 October 1630, for example, John Craig, a stabler, was identified as owing to Margaret Puill, the wife of Peter Watt, the sum of £30, with no further information entered with the case. John promised to repay the sum to Margaret by 1 May 1631, with 10 merks of 'liquidate expenses', or penalty, indicating that this case did involve a loan of money.[65] In 1639, Isabel Denholme,

61 Bryce, 'The Fellowship and Society of Brewers', p. 236.

62 Bryce, 'The Fellowship and Society of Brewers', p. 238. For more information concerning William Dick of Braid, see L. A. M. Stewart, 'Dick, Sir William, of Braid (d. 1655)', *Oxford Dictionary of National Biography* (Oxford, 2004).

63 NRS, B22/8/26, fols 231v–232r.

64 Spence, '"To Content and Pay"', p. 179.

65 NRS, B22/8/26, fol. 257r. Most bonds and contracts involving lent money named an amount of 'liquidate expenses' which functioned as a penalty for non-payment of the original debt. This penalty does not appear to have been assessed at a fixed rate, and could vary from 2.5 to 65 per cent of the original debt. The amount was agreed upon by the two parties involved in the debt and in some cases was paid only if the repayment of the original debt was late. In other cases, it was a required part of

the wife of Andrew Oswald, a merchant, was owed £26 13s. 4d. by one man for the annual rent on a loan of 1,000 merks, and £40 by another man for the annual rent on a loan of £1,000, indicating an interest rate on each loan of between 8 and 9 per cent and 4 per cent respectively.[66] Debts for money-lending made up approximately 30 per cent of all debts which wives in Edinburgh pursued or for which they themselves were pursued. Wives tended to act with their husbands when loaning out large amounts of money of £100 or more, and by themselves (although their husbands were named with them in the debt cases) when loaning out smaller amounts of money, as the explanations for many debts make clear.

Conclusion

Whether considering money-lending, brewing, the cloth trade, or the provisioning of households, wives are clearly visible in the debt records of the burgh courts for Edinburgh, Linlithgow and Haddington between 1560 and 1640. As per the legal requirement, their husbands are always named alongside them. However, it is evident in the examples shown and in many other cases that wives appeared in court either as active partners with their husbands or because it was the wife who had actually incurred the debt. Additionally, the proportion of cases that name married women in these records is among the highest thus far noted for Britain or northern Europe in the pre-modern period. The simple clerical convention of naming wives in debt litigation allows us to see the economic visibility they enjoyed during this period. This is a visibility that is lost when consulting many similar records, but one that is evident for a broad range of economic activities in these three communities.

This notable presence of wives is reflective not only of their familial responsibilities, which required that they contract debts to purchase the necessities with which to provision their households, but also of their roles as producers and sellers of a variety of goods and services and perhaps as agents of their husbands. Within these roles, wives operated within court conventions to successfully negotiate their own economic endeavours. This implies a significant degree of agency in the lives of these women. Indeed, their economic activities extended far beyond the home, whether dealing with local markets or overseas merchants. While their status as women barred them from some lucrative economic roles in guilds and male-dominated industries, there were a number of economic spheres in which wives routinely operated, whether as individuals or in concert with their husbands. It is clear that, for the most part, marriage limited neither the actions nor the visibility of these women.

the bond and due, on the same date, with the original sum borrowed. It was not an annual rent or interest. See J. J. Brown, 'The Social, Political, and Economic Influences of the Edinburgh Merchant Elite, 1600–1638', unpublished Ph.D. thesis, University of Edinburgh, 1985, p. 238.

66 NRS, CC8/8/59/266.

10

THE WORTH OF MARRIED WOMEN IN THE ENGLISH CHURCH COURTS, C.1550–1730

Alexandra Shepard

When Joanna Remesbury and her husband Richard appeared as witnesses before the bishop of Salisbury's consistory court in 1599, they were both asked to provide an estimate of their net moveable estate. Richard, a shepherd, appears to have declared himself worth £20 in goods, 'every man being paid', before revising this estimate to the more modest sum of £10. Joanna, by contrast, responded that she did not know her worth 'bycause shee is a married woman & therefore during the life of her husband her goodes are at his disposing'. In response to a further question enquiring about how they got a living, they both declared simply that Richard had a copyhold worth £5 per annum in the nearby parish of Purton.[1] Joanna and Richard Remesbury were responding to questions routinely posed to witnesses in the church courts that were designed to test bias and to assess their creditworthiness both concerning the cause in dispute and more widely. As part of these efforts to assess the 'persons' of witnesses as well as their 'sayings', deponents were commonly asked for an account of their net worth in goods and how they maintained themselves.[2] Such questions were usually asked indiscriminately of all witnesses appearing on behalf of a particular litigant, so that when posed to married women they contravened common law conventions that wives possessed no moveable property and that they should be maintained by their husbands.

Joanna Remesbury's answer typifies the ambiguities associated with the operation of coverture in early modern England that have been highlighted by recent research into the practical realities of marital property relations. While dutifully rehearsing her husband's rights to dispose of any goods she brought to or acquired within marriage, Joanna's response also suggests that she nonetheless retained a sense of possession regarding '*her* goodes' which, in her mind at the very least, remained distinct as if on temporary loan during her husband's lifetime. It is possible that she was among those 'ordinary' women documented by Amy Erickson, at least 10 per cent of whom made marriage settlements to protect their property

1 Wiltshire and Swindon Archives [WSA], Chippenham, D1/42/16, fols 194r-v. I am grateful to the Leverhulme Trust for a research fellowship during which this essay was completed, and to Amy Erickson and the editors of this volume for their comments on earlier drafts of this essay.

2 H. Conset, *The Practice of the Spirituall or Ecclesiastical Courts* (London, 1685), pp. 114–15.

rights, mostly ensuring that the property they brought to a marriage would remain theirs or their children's after it.[3] Even in the absence of any such formal arrangements, Erickson has argued that married women 'must ... have regarded property in their possession as belonging to them even when it was not legally theirs'.[4] Whether or not protected by a formal marriage settlement, Joanna Remesbury may well also have deemed the allocation of her goods to be of mutual or familial benefit as opposed to simply being to her husband's advantage. Indeed, in contrast to traditionally pessimistic accounts of the restrictions imposed on wives by coverture, Joanne Bailey has gone so far as to argue that married women's continued sense of possession of the moveable goods they brought to marriage, and shared perceptions that these assets were dedicated to familial use (rather than to a husband's ownership), were 'standard rather than exceptional'.[5] In other words, these were not merely mitigating factors in a legal culture of constraint, craftily contrived as a form of resistance by a few canny women, but reflected widely-held notions of community property if not separate estate surrounding the goods that wives contributed to the household economy.

Erickson has additionally argued that 'the marital partnership formed by the joining of assets extended in some households also to the skills that each partner brought to the marriage and the management of the household economy during marriage'.[6] Although neither Joanna Remesbury nor her husband referred to her contribution to the marital economy, it is unlikely that his occupation as a shepherd and a copyhold worth £5 per annum were sufficient to keep them both without some input from her, even if at the ages of fifty-eight and fifty they may not have had offspring to maintain. The skills women brought to marriage have remained masked in a historical record that privileged a woman's marital status over her social or occupational identity, but it is likely that dual efforts by couples to provide for themselves and their dependants constituted an even greater practical contradiction of the legal fiction that wives depended upon their husbands for their worth and maintenance. Informal claims on marital property, as well as wives' productive capabilities, in turn shaped the credit that married women could claim in their financial dealings, even when conducted under the legal shadow of coverture.[7]

These issues can be explored fruitfully with reference to the responses supplied by the many married women who, like Joanna Remesbury, were ques-

3 A. L. Erickson, *Women and Property in Early Modern England* (London, 1995), pp. 130, 143. See also A. L. Erickson, 'Common Law Versus Common Practice: The Use of Marriage Settlements in Early Modern England', *Economic History Review* 43 (1990), 21–39; and C. Churches, 'Women and Property in Early Modern England: A Case Study', *Social History* 23 (1998), 165–80.

4 A. L. Erickson, 'Possession – and the Other One-Tenth of the Law: Assessing Women's Ownership and Economic Roles in Early Modern England', *Women's History Review* 16 (2007), 369–85, p. 370.

5 J. Bailey, 'Favoured or Oppressed? Married Women, Property and "Coverture" in England, 1660–1800', *Continuity and Change* 17 (2002), 351–72, p. 368.

6 A. L. Erickson, 'Married Women's Occupations in Eighteenth-Century London', *Continuity and Change* 23 (2008), 267–307, p. 269.

7 M. K. McIntosh, 'Women, Credit, and Family Relationships in England, 1300–1620', *Journal of Family History* 30 (2005), 143–63.

tioned as witnesses in the church courts about what they were worth and how they maintained themselves. This essay will investigate, first, the varied terms in which wives represented their worth in court when, according to coverture at least, they were technically worthless. Secondly, it will explore the answers wives gave to the question of how they were maintained. The analysis is based on a selection of 13,696 witness responses to the question of their worth, drawn from a range of ecclesiastical jurisdictions between 1550 and 1728.[8] Female witnesses comprise almost a quarter (24 per cent) of this dataset, of whom over half (at least 55 per cent) were married – a total of 1,843 wives. Of these, 303 (16 per cent) additionally responded to enquiries about how they maintained themselves. While many of their answers echoed the conventions of coverture that married women possessed no moveable assets and depended on their husbands for a living, as many as half of wives' responses contained varying degrees of ambiguity if they did not explicitly flout these norms. The ways in which married women's answers departed from the letter of the law, even in this most conservative of settings, are suggestive of far more widely held attitudes to the marital economy based not necessarily on equality but at least on expectations of partnership and mutuality.

Worth

Witnesses providing an estimate of their worth in goods, taking into account all outstanding debts, gave brief statements rather than detailed reckonings, which were often highly formulaic. The most common type of response was a monetary estimate, usually expressed in round numbers, which quantitative measures also held qualitative associations.[9] Unsurprisingly, married women's answers to the question of their worth were only rarely expressed as a simple monetary estimate of the net value of their moveable estate. However, the degree of variation in wives' responses is nonetheless indicative of flexible attitudes towards the dictates of coverture that included claims to joint spousal and independent property ownership by women within marriage.

[8] Witness statements have been collected from the dioceses of Canterbury, Chester, Ely, London, Salisbury and York, the archdeaconries of Lewes and Richmond, and the Cambridge University Courts (which adopted a similar procedure to the church courts in relation to a wider range of business). This research was enabled by a grant from the Economic and Social Research Council (grant reference RES-000-23-1111), and the material gathered has been collated as a dataset deposited with the UK Data Archive entitled 'The "Worth" of Witnesses in the English Church Courts, 1550–1728'. I am deeply indebted to Dr Judith Spicksley for her assistance in creating this resource.

[9] For quantitative analysis of the monetary estimates provided by witnesses, see A. Shepard and J. Spicksley, 'Worth, Age, and Social Status in Early Modern England', *Economic History Review* 64 (2011), 493–530. For the qualitative associations of certain sums with poverty, see A. Shepard, 'Poverty, Labour and the Language of Social Description in Early Modern England', *Past & Present* 201 (2008), 51–95. The full range of qualitative associations will be discussed in A. Shepard, *Accounting for Oneself in Early Modern England* (Oxford, forthcoming 2014).

The extent of variation also suggests that, in spite of the laconic character of most responses, they were neither overly formulaic nor unduly shaped by scribal influence. Married women's worth statements can be coded as 101 variants, ranging from rehearsals of coverture (with varying degrees of ambiguity), through assessments of their husbands' means, through a series of evasions, to claims to community property or separate estate. Only two of these variants (several of which were expressed in a range of ways) comprised more than 10 per cent of wives' responses. Women's answers to the question of their worth were less likely than men's to be recorded solely in Latin (not least because they contained few straightforward monetary estimates), and the variation in the phrasing of responses by witnesses in the same case indicates that scribal input was limited. The elaboration of some responses, and deletions, suggest that wives' own formulations of their worth, when forthcoming, were recorded. Of course the forms of appraisal adopted would still have been shaped by the court setting which is likely to have encouraged conservative or evasive strategies of self-description, although it should be remembered that a working knowledge of a person's (and one's own) net assets would have been an everyday necessity beyond the courtroom for the assessment of rates and for brokering credit, and was critical to rites of passage surrounding marriage and death.[10] Given that married women's accounts of their worth in court may have been more cautiously expressed than the ways they represented themselves in other arenas, their answers spanned an impressive spectrum of possibilities many of which fell firmly outwith the dictates of coverture.

The great majority of wives (71 per cent) specifically referred to their marital status in response to the question of their worth, but they did so in a wide variety of ways. The most straightforward response in this vein was expressed as two main variants, either simply as 'she is married' or 'she is under covert baron'. Coverture was expressly mentioned in 12 per cent of wives' answers to the question of their worth. Even without explicit references to coverture, several women spelled out the implications of marital status on a wife's worth in compliance with common law expectations that she forfeited ownership of moveable property on marriage. A fifth of all wives responding to the question of their worth declared that they were either married or under covert baron and therefore worth nothing. In the 1630s, for example, Margaret Jancock (the wife of a gardener) declared that she was 'nothing worth in her proper goods, for she is a married woman, and under Coverture', while in York in 1671 a miller's wife claimed that 'she being a marryed woman hath nothing of her owne'.[11]

Several wives (6 per cent) simply claimed they were worth little or nothing without any reference to their marital status. It is possible that such responses denoted material hardship in addition to or even instead of their lack of legal en-

10 For a full assessment of the accuracy of witnesses' statements of worth, see Shepard and Spicksley, 'Worth, Age, and Social Status', pp. 502–11. For the operation of credit in the early modern economy, see C. Muldrew, *The Economy of Obligation. The Culture of Credit and Social Relations in Early Modern England* (Basingstoke, 1998).

11 Canterbury Cathedral Archives [CCA], Canterbury, DCb/PRC 39/39, fol. 211v; Borthwick Institute [BI], York, CP.H.2959.

titlement to goods, and in several instances this was made explicit when married women also referred to themselves as 'poor'. In 1620, for example, Joan Comage (married to a shoemaker) responded simply that she was 'a poore woman'.[12] In 1635 Ellen Frie alluded to both material hardship and coverture when she answered that 'her husband is a poore man & she of her selfe [is] nothing worth', and in 1697 a sawyer's wife similarly declared that 'she hath no estate of her owne and is but a poore woman'.[13] The extent to which wives who declared themselves worth little or nothing (without any direct reference to their marital status in response to the question) was a product of relative privation as opposed to coverture can be explored further in the causes when both spouses appeared as witnesses, allowing comparison of their worth statements. A few such wives were married to men of reasonable means. In 1618, for example, Agnes Batty simply declared herself worth nothing, while her yeoman husband estimated his worth at £100.[14] However, of all the wives claiming simply to be worth little or nothing (with no explicit reference to their marital status in response to the question of their worth) alongside husbands who gave a monetary account, their husbands enjoyed a median worth of £5, and a mean worth of nearly £21. This was below the overall median and mean worth for men which was £10 and £51.90 respectively, and nearly half of the husbands married to women declaring themselves worth little or nothing (without reference to their marital status in response to the question) were worth forty shillings or less, which was a significantly higher proportion than that for all of the men in the dataset.[15] In such cases coverture was at the very least compounded by poverty, if not rendered irrelevant by it, and it is possible that such responses either reflected an accurate assessment of limited means in the same terms adopted by many men, or tactically failed to attribute a lack of goods to hardship as opposed to coverture.

The fact that a relatively high proportion of wives (compared with other women and men) supplied no recorded response to the question can also be linked to assumptions that married women had no worth to account for.[16] Several wives also declared explicitly that the question did not concern them because they were married, such as Catherine Wannell (married to a London freemason), who responded in 1625 that 'she is a married woman and therefore it concerneth not her'.[17] Another London wife, married to a haberdasher, responded in similar terms in 1617 that the question did not concern her 'because she is a mans wief', despite also claiming (in contravention of the terms of coverture) that she maintained herself 'by taking Clothes to wash'.[18] A few wives simply referred to their husband's response to the same question, while others rebutted the question of their worth

12 WSA, D1/42/36, fol. 145v.

13 CCA, DCb/PRC 39/46, fol. 72v; DCb/PRC 38/1 1696, fol. 4.

14 West Sussex Record Office [WSRO], Chichester, Ep II/5/11, fols 98v–99.

15 Of all the men in the dataset, 10.4 per cent were worth 40 shillings or less. See Shepard, 'Poverty', p. 75.

16 Of married women witnesses, 16 per cent gave no response to the question of their worth, compared with 6 per cent of the overall dataset.

17 Guildhall Library [GL], London, 9065A/6.

18 GL, 9065A/5.

more robustly by suggesting they were not legally obliged to answer, such as Margaret Tirrell (married to a butcher), who declared in 1686 that she 'hath been a marryed wife for about 18 yeares & that she doth conceive she is not bound to give any further answer to this Interrogatory'.[19] In such cases, therefore, coverture may well have aided evasion strategies by which witnesses avoided providing an estimate of their means.

The guiding logic of coverture was also present in more conformist ways in responses from wives who claimed to be worth nothing but what they received from their husbands. In Cambridge in the 1590s, Parnell Algate, married to a barber, responded that she was 'a marryed wyef & under covert baron, & ys nothinge worth of hir selfe but what she hath of or from hir husband', while a carter's wife answered that she 'oweth nothinge nor hath nothinge but upon her husbands Courtesye'.[20] A husbandman's wife from Hindon (Wiltshire) likewise replied that 'what she hath is from her husband and att his benevolens'.[21] Such responses were in line with the law of necessaries – one of the mitigating aspects of coverture which allowed women to make purchases of essential goods appropriate to their husband's worth and status.[22] It is possible that this gave some wives a sense of their worth in terms of a particular credit limit, which may be what Miriam Mortimer (a gardener's wife) had in mind when she declared in 1600 that she was worth forty shillings in her own proper goods, everyone paid, 'with the permission of her husband'.[23]

Several wives (3 per cent) provided a slightly more ambiguous formulation of the impact of coverture by declaring that they were worth little or nothing *besides their clothes* – which had legal status as 'paraphernalia' comprising a wife's clothes, jewels, bed linens and plate. While a husband enjoyed the right to dispose of these goods during marriage, they automatically reverted to a wife on his death. When in 1561 Elizabeth Jurdeyn declared that she was 'worth a cople of russet peticotes and the rest is her husbands' she therefore presumed present as well as future ownership.[24] In the early seventeenth century, the 'spinster' Margaret Younge, already married at the relatively early age of twenty to a yeoman worth £40, similarly responded that she was 'under covert barne & not worth any thinge more then her apparell, so longe as her husband lyves', and Helen Chapman, working as a maid in Cambridge, declared that 'as she is a marryed wyfe she is worth nothing but her Clothes of her backe'.[25]

Other wives – like Joanna Remesbury in the example which began this essay – implied more general claims to the goods they had brought to marriage, even

19 CCA, DCb/J/X.11.21, fol. 76v.

20 Cambridge University Library [CUL], Cambridge, Cambridge University Archives [CUA], Comm.Ct.II.4, fol. 168v; CUL, EDR D/2/19, fol. 205v.

21 WSA, D1/42/24, fol. 87v.

22 Bailey, 'Favoured or Oppressed?' See also M. Finn, 'Women, Consumption and Coverture in England, *c.* 1760–1860', *Historical Journal* 39 (1996), 703–22.

23 '[V]alet in bonis suis propriis aere alieno ... deduct cum licentia mariti sui xl s'. CCA, DCb/PRC 39/23, fol. 114.

24 CCA, DCb/J/X.10.8, fol. 140v.

25 CCA, DCb/PRC 39/32, fol. 325; CUA, V.C.Ct.II.20, fol. 5v.

while ostensibly acknowledging the strictures of marital property law. Eustacia Parmafoy, married to a labourer, responded in 1575 that 'her husband is owner of that she hath'; a weaver's wife answered in 1596 that she was 'an other mans wife and all which she hath is her husbands & at his comanndment'; and Agnes Mershe declared in 1608 that she was 'worth nothing for that which shee hath it is her husbands & he is living'.[26] Such answers convey the impression that the women concerned retained a continued sense of possession, if not legal ownership, towards the goods they had brought to marriage.[27]

A number of married women placed the focus more squarely on their husband's worth, rather than speaking about their own estate, lack of it, or limited rights to it. Thirteen per cent of wives responded to the question of their worth by referring solely to their husband's substance, with no mention of their own. These responses ranged from assertions of their husband's worth to professions of ignorance about their husband's assets. Around 6 per cent of wives provided a monetary estimate of their husband's worth, speaking of their spouse's moveable estate in the same terms that the majority of all male witnesses used.[28] So a husbandman's wife answered in 1626 that 'her husband is worth xx li his debts paid, or thereabouts, as shee beleeveth', while Mary Wilkinson of Pontefract (Yorkshire) declared in 1622 that 'she is perswaded her husbands estate is better then C li in debtles goodes' – a verdict with which her husband (a gentleman) concurred in his claim to be worth £100 'and more'.[29] When women appeared alongside their husbands as witnesses in the same cause, it is possible to compare wives' estimates of their husband's worth with the account provided by their spouse. In ten out of fifteen such cases the estimates provided by spouses matched. Interestingly, in the remaining cases in which there was a mismatch between spousal accounts, four of the five wives provided a higher valuation of their husband's goods than that declared by their spouse. Agnes Fulbrooke, for example, claimed in 1604 that her husband was worth 'of his owne goods every body payd the som of lx li', in contrast to his estimate of £50.[30] Whether or not they were optimistically appraised, wives' accounts of their husband's worth suggest at the very least that such women assumed knowledge of their spouse's estate, dealings and credit, if not shared in it.

A few wives referred to their husband's means in qualitative terms, without specifying a monetary value but nonetheless conveying the impression of substance. Sarah Hauson, for example, married to a Halifax carrier, declared in 1663 that she had 'an husband liveing of a pritty competent estate'.[31] All such responses were from the northeast, and came from women married to clothiers, gentlemen and clergymen. Another way of asserting a man's worth was to refer to his inclusion in the subsidy books. A London armourer's wife stated simply in 1597 that 'her husband is a subsidie man', while Joanna Hamlyn responded with more detail

26 GL, 9065A/1a, fol. 162v; CCA, DCb/J/X.11.5, fol. 91v; DCb/PRC 39/29, fol. 259.

27 Erickson, 'Possession'.

28 See Shepard and Spicksley, 'Worth, Age, and Social Status'.

29 CCA, DCb/PRC 39/38, fol. 274; BI, CP.H.1499.

30 CUL, CUA, Comm.Ct.II.12, fols 100, 99.

31 BI, CP.H.2445.

in 1608, declaring that 'her husband is a husbandman, & rated at iii li in goods in the Subsidie book'.[32] It is hard to imagine that such claims to spousal worth were not shared in some way, even if only as a measure for the law of necessaries to operate whereby a wife's credit was gauged in relation to her husband's status.

Several wives (3 per cent) also detailed the *limits* of their husband's means, by declaring them to be worth little or nothing or poor. Some wives spoke of their husband's indebtedness, such as Dorothy Binge, whose husband kept a poor house in Chartham, Kent, who admitted in 1575 that 'if every man were payd her husband were lytle or nothing worthe', and a saddler's wife from Salisbury who responded in 1590 that her husband was 'a very poore mann but litle thing worth beyond his debts or rather nothing at all worth'.[33] Others emphasized their husband's limited earning capacity, like a weaver's wife who described her husband as 'a poore blindeman ... very little worth' in 1635, and a sawyer's wife who answered in 1634 that 'her husband is a poor man, & lives by his labour & hath nothing els to stick to'.[34] These responses were echoed by these women's husbands who, respectively, responded that 'being a blind man, he is faine to have releefe from the Towne where he dwells, having no estate or meanes els of his owne', and that 'he liveth by his hand labor, & is worth nothing more than what [he] earns'.[35] A few women, such as Christiana Goddin, a weaver's wife from Salisbury, simply stated that 'her husband is a poore man'. That the language of poverty was deployed selectively is suggested by Christiana Goddin's response to the same question when appearing as a witness in a related cause a few weeks previously, in which she declared more conventionally (and also more evasively) that 'she is another mans wife & therefore not much worthe of her selffe'.[36] In cases where women's estimates of their husband's worth can be compared with statements by their husbands, however, wives were more likely to use the adjective 'poor' in relation to their husbands than the husbands describing themselves, even when couples agreed that their means were limited, just as women were more likely than men to describe themselves as 'poor' more generally.[37] It may be that in such circumstances husbands' appraisals were more optimistic than their wives', or merely more defensively couched, although it cannot be known how many wives cloaked their relative poverty under a veil of coverture when facing enquiries about their worth in court. A deletion in the response of Elizabeth Baldocke in 1584 is suggestive of such a strategy. Having first declared that her husband was 'but a pore man', this was deleted in favour of 'she is a mans wiffe & not verie privie to her husbands welthe' – clearly a preferable response in terms of both spouses' credit.[38]

Around 5 per cent of wives claimed ignorance of their husband's worth in what may have been deliberately evasive strategies. Some such responses were framed

32 GL, 9065A/2, fol. 181v; WSA, D1/42/25, fol. 67v.

33 CCA, DCb/PRC 39/8, fol. 134; WSA, D1/42/11, fol. 69v.

34 WSRO, Ep II/5/16, fol. 31; CCA, DCb/PRC 39/42, fol. 246v.

35 CCA, DCb/PRC 39/46, fol. 94; DCb/PRC 39/42, fol. 246.

36 WSA, D1/42/28, fols 27, 6.

37 Shepard, 'Poverty', pp. 71–7.

38 CCA, DCb/PRC 39/10, fol. 241v.

explicitly as a consequence of coverture, while others were more ambiguous. Mary Rutty, married to a husbandman, stated in 1620 that 'she is a maried wife & knoweth not her husbands estate'; a London tanner's wife responded in 1630 that she was 'unacquainted with the value of her husbands estate'; while Agnes Gibbes, a farmer's wife, claimed in 1664 that 'shee is a wife and what her husband is worth shee doth not knowe'.[39] Of the seventeen wives claiming to be unaware of their husband's worth whose husbands also appeared in court, eleven of their spouses provided firm monetary estimates of their moveable wealth, suggesting a discrepancy between spouses in their attitudes towards property and the ability to account for it. However, some husbands also claimed ignorance of their own worth and it is possible that neither partner had a clear idea of their household's assets. In 1700, for example, a tailor and his wife responded respectively that 'he does not know what he is worth his debts paid' and 'she does not know what her husband is worth his debts paid'.[40] Of all the male witnesses asked what they were worth, a similar proportion (6 per cent) claimed they did not know, so it is likely that several wives' responses in this vein (if not deliberately evasive) reflected shared ignorance rather than gender divergence.

Some wives provided explanations for their ignorance that were less consonant with the formal constraints of coverture, suggesting their lack of knowledge was either a temporary state of affairs or the product of complex credit arrangements to which, in some cases, they were party. The wife of William Hazell, a tanner, replied that 'she ... beeing newly a marryed woman is not *yet* acquainted with her husbands Dealings but hopeth her husband beeing a tradesman is not much in debt [my italics]', adding that 'if hee bee [in debt] its not knowne to her'.[41] That she was described in the biographical preamble to her deposition as Mary Wescott alias Hazell is also indicative of her newlywed status, and her response conveys the expectation of future familiarity with her husband's commercial affairs. Other wives attributed their ignorance of their husband's worth to a lack of up-to-date knowledge rather than to their marital status. Denise Browneinge, married to a blacksmith, claimed in 1646 that 'she cannot tell what her husband is worth (by reason she knowes not what debtes hee owes) but beleeves that hee is worth five powndes of lawfull English money his debtes payd'.[42] A few other wives similarly declared ignorance of their husband's worth while also ascribing a minimal monetary value to it, such as the husbandman's wife who responded in 1627 that 'she is a wife and knoweth not her husbands estate but beleveth he is worth x li at least his debts paid'.[43] It is likely that many a wife declaring ignorance of her husband's *net* estate was unsure of the extent of his – and indeed her own – current credit and debt relations rather than entirely ignorant of his assets. And, significantly, that this could work both ways is suggested by Thomas Erlam's response in 1596

39 WSA, D1/42/36, fol. 102; GL, 9065A/6, 9 January 1629/30; WSA, D5/22/15, fol. 83.
40 GL, 9065A/9.
41 WSA, D5/22/18, fol. 29.
42 CCA, DCb/PRC 39/49, fol. 196v.
43 GL, 9189/2, fol. 120v.

that 'he knoweth not what money his wiefe oweth the malte man'.[44] Of the wives who declared ignorance of their husband's estate, a disproportionate number were married to craftsmen and tradesmen from urban centres – that is, couples whose credit networks were likely to be dense and highly fluid, making net assets difficult to estimate with any precision from day to day.

There was considerable room for ambiguity, therefore, even in the worth statements of wives that ostensibly conformed to the conventions of coverture. In addition, several responses provided by married women more openly contradicted the common law framework governing marital property relations either by stressing shared spousal worth, or by claiming independent means. A few wives declared joint marital assets in monetary terms. While stating in 1590 that she was 'subjecte to her husbande' (a miller), Margery Farnecombe also declared that '*they* have a howsse of their owne & somthinge else to the valew of v li [my italics]'.[45] A husbandman's wife from Hastings declared more simply in 1638 that 'shee & her husband are worth xx li theire debts payd', while in the same year Mildred Baker responded 'she ~~is~~ and her husband are worth 60 li of lawfull English money their debts paid' – the deleted 'is' suggesting that her original impulse had been simply to state this sum as her own worth without reference to her husband.[46] Other wives referred to more limited resources in shared terms, such as a brazier's wife who responded in 1641 that 'she beleiveth she this deponent & her husband are not worth anythinge', and Katherine Younge who confessed in 1612 that 'this respondent & her husband are poore people'.[47] Others explicitly professed a joint sense of worth even when declaring they did not know the value of their estate, such as a farmer's wife in 1704 who claimed that 'she does not know what her husb[and] & she are worth theire debts payd' – in contrast to her husband's admission that 'he is worth but little his debts payd'.[48]

Furthest removed from the expectations of coverture were the responses of the few wives who did express a positive sense of worth independent from their husbands. Eighteen married women (1 per cent of all wives asked about their worth) referred to assets of their own and provided a monetary valuation, albeit sometimes in ambiguous terms. Ann Prime, for example, while declaring herself 'under Covert baron' in 1620, rather contradictorily 'sayth she is worth 40s her debts payed'. Her husband had also declared himself worth forty shillings when appearing as a witness in the same cause, a sum apparently revised downwards from his initial (deleted) estimate of £5.[49] It is possible that in this case Ann Prime was assuming joint worth with her husband rather than referring to any separate estate. This may also have been true of the other wives who simply provided a monetary estimate of their net estate in response to the question of their worth without any mention of their marital status, such as Jane Haines (a sailor's wife)

44 Cheshire Record Office [CRO], EDC 5(1596)/25.

45 WSRO, Ep II/5/5, fol. 258.

46 WSRO, Ep II/5/16, fol. 105v; CCA, DCb/PRC 39/48, fol. 40.

47 CUL, CUA, Comm.Ct.II.22, fol. 48; WSA, D1/42/28, fol. 31.

48 LMA, DL/C/248, fols 185v, 184.

49 CUL, CUA, Comm.Ct.II.18, fols 80v, 79.

who in 1594 stated that 'she is worth v li every man paid', and Anne Williams who in 1637 claimed to be 'worth x li in debtles goods'.[50] However, they might just as well have been claiming independent means, as suggested by the octogenarian Ellen Blacoe who claimed in 1600 that 'shee doth live of her self & is worth xx li of debtles goods'.[51]

In a few such responses the women concerned appear to have laid claim to separate estate. The wife of a Yorkshire shepherd replied in 1666 that she was 'a marryed woman ... of a small estate of worth about x li', while Johan Blacklache, having maintained in 1587 that she was 'not privie to her husbands substance', also stated that 'she hath her dowry out of certaine lands of her late husbands wherwith & by her husbands & her owne travell she liveth'.[52] A waterman's wife, declaring in 1719 that 'shee followes noe employment & ... is maintained by her Mother & her Father in law', added that she 'has alsoe thirty five pounds a yeare now comeing in'.[53] Elizabeth Jones, married to a gentleman, similarly referred to her dependence for maintenance, claiming in 1710 that 'shee followes noe trade buisnesse or employement nore ever did that shee knowes [and] that ... before her marriage to her present husband was maintained by her owne fortune & since then by her husband'. However, she also declared herself 'worth of her owne estate her debts paid between two & three thousand pounds, which consisteth in money land securities & annuities in the Government', suggesting that 'her own fortune' nonetheless remained distinct from her husband's worth, which he estimated at 'above two thousand pounds his debts paid'.[54]

More than half (eleven out of eighteen) of the wives who provided monetary estimates of their own worth appeared as witnesses in London, but the fact that some had clearly been married more than once and that they were married to men whose occupations involved long absences may have been just as significant.[55] Two were married to sailors, one to a merchant, and one to a waterman, while another was married to a conductor to the train of artillery (although he was unemployed at the time of her appearance in court). One clearly ran an independent business, replying that her husband was 'Gardiner to the Lady Russell' while she 'keepes a publick house', adding that '*shee* payes to all publick rates & taxes & beleives herselfe worth an hundred pounds her debts paid [my italics]'.[56] Three others, however, were married to gardeners, one to a shepherd, one to a flaxdresser, one to a gentleman, and one to the chamber keeper to the queen's gentleman-waiters' pages, and the chronological incidence of their responses spanned the late sixteenth to the early eighteenth centuries, suggesting that such answers defy any single explanation. While exceptional in the context of the church courts, it

50 GL, 9065A/2, fol. 28; CRO, EDC 5(1637)/14.

51 Lancashire Record Office [LRO], DRCH 1, Blacoe.

52 BI, CP.H.5500, 4 January 1665/6; WSRO, Ep II/5/4, fols 58v–59.

53 LMA, DL/C/258, fol. 294.

54 LMA, DL/C/251, fols 285–6, 293v.

55 Wives from London make up 23 per cent of the total.

56 GL, 9065A/10, fol. 135v. Her husband responded similarly that he was worth £100 and that he 'now payes to all publick taxes & rates', fol. 127v.

is possible that such open rejection of the conventions of coverture was indicative of wider expectations – albeit tacit – that married women could claim credit in these terms.

Maintenance

An impression of joint or shared spousal worth, and sometimes of economic independence, was also conveyed by many married women's answers to the question of how they maintained themselves. Although wives responded less frequently than unmarried women to enquiries about what they did for a living, 56 per cent of those who did provide information about their working lives departed from expectations that they should be maintained by their husband.[57] Of these many spoke in general terms of living by their labour or industry without specifying what this involved, but 103 wives described the nature, if not the proportion, of their contribution to the marital economy, with some detailing multiple tasks. The vast majority (82 per cent) of these wives supplying details appeared as witnesses in London, and 74 per cent occurred between the 1660s and 1720s, suggesting that more specific responses were principally a feature of the metropolitan context and its rapidly diversifying economy.[58] However, although not providing the level of detail specified by London wives from the later seventeenth century, married women appearing as witnesses in other jurisdictions and earlier in the period also gave varied impressions of their productive roles and often spoke in similar terms to male witnesses. It should also be remembered that the details of many men's economic roles were masked by the convention of describing them by their rank (as gentlemen, yeomen or husbandmen) rather than specifying the particulars of how they sustained it.

As with their worth statements, many wives provided conventional answers such as a miller's wife who declared in 1623 that 'she is a wif, and therefore her meanes & liveinge is and depends solely of & from her husband', and Katherine Mayne who replied in 1664 that 'she is under covert baron & her husband maintayneth her'.[59] Others stated that they had no occupation or employment, while several simply named their husband's occupation as the source of their maintenance, such as Margaret Gilbert in 1588 who declared 'her husband getteth her living by his trade being a joyner'.[60] Of the 278 cases in which their husband's occupation was stated, disproportionate numbers of those married to gentlemen, yeomen and professional men (lawyers, merchants and physicians) responded in this vein, although such answers were not exclusive to wealthier social groups. All

57 Of married women witnesses, 16 per cent provided information about how they maintained themselves, compared with 47 per cent of single women and 37 per cent of widows.

58 For an analysis of London responses see P. Earle, 'The Female Labour Market in London in the Late Seventeenth and Early Eighteenth Centuries', *Economic History Review* 62 (1989), 328–53; and for a critique, Erickson, 'Married Women's Occupations'.

59 CCA DCb/PRC 39/36, fol. 90; WSA, D1/42/58, fol. 124v.

60 LMA, DL/C/213, fol. 303.

the wives of professional men responded that their husbands maintained them, 73 per cent of gentry wives, and 50 per cent of yeomen's wives, compared with an overall average of 42 per cent of wives whose husbands' occupations were stated. Of the wives of tradesmen and craftsmen, 48 per cent replied that they were maintained by or depended on their husbands, compared with 30 per cent of husbandmen's wives and 27 per cent of labourers' wives.

By contrast, evidence of wives' economic contribution was not restricted to particular social strata or social groups even if it increased down the social spectrum, as 27 per cent of gentry wives, 50 per cent of yeomen wives, 52 per cent of artisanal wives, 70 per cent of husbandmen's wives, and 73 per cent of labourers' wives claimed to provide at least some of their living. So, for example, despite declaring in 1609 that she was 'of noe occupacion', a farrier's wife nonetheless added that she 'liveth by her owne industrie and her husbonds labor together'.[61] A sense of joint effort – and even shared occupational identity – is conveyed by the many wives who responded that they and their husbands lived by their labour, such as the blacksmith's wife who claimed in 1625 that 'she and her husband be labouringe people and have nothinge but what they gett by their owne labor'.[62] Despite claiming that 'she is a wife and her husband is a poore man whose estate she knoweth nott', Alice Wheskyn (married to a 'mealeman') nonetheless declared in 1623 that 'she liveth par[t]ely by the meanes her husband getteth and partely by her owne honest labours'.[63] A husbandman's wife similarly claimed in 1605 to get 'parte of her livinge ... by her honest labour & paines taking' while declaring herself worth nothing because she was married and her husband still living.[64] Very occasionally, a wife's input was explicitly acknowledged by her spouse, such as when a septuagenarian husbandman responded in 1621 that he lived 'by the labor of himself & his wife'.[65] It is also likely that many of the wives claiming to be maintained by their husband's trade were actually active participants in it, as implied by Alice Dodridge who rather ambiguously stated in 1594 that 'she is a mans wife & livethe by his occupacion beinge a tailor without want she thancketh god'.[66] Some wives specified the proportion of their contribution, such as a tobacco pipe maker's wife who stated that 'she laboureth for >a parte of< her living, but for her maintenance she dependeth more on her husband than her owne labor'.[67] Others outlined a less attractive division of labour, such as a builder's wife who responded in 1625 that she had 'lived for theis two yeares last past by her labors for her husband hath bene absent from her for all that tyme', and a harness maker's wife who complained in 1623 that 'although she be a wife yett she is constrayned to get her lyving by anie lawfull meanes as she can to maintaine her by being a servant to other men'.[68]

61 WSRO, Ep III/5/1, fol. 26.

62 CCA, DCb/PRC 39/38, fol. 89v.

63 GL, 9189/1, fol. 75.

64 CCA, DCb/PRC 39/28, fol. 144v.

65 WSRO, Ep II/5/12, fol. 26v.

66 GL, 9065A/2, fol. 10v.

67 GL, 9065A/6, 24 October 1629.

68 GL, 9065A/6, 28 January 1624/5; 9189/1, fol. 146.

In this last case, the wife's complaint most likely betrayed expectations that she should be undertaking independent work once married (rather than remain in service), and not that she should be maintained by her husband.

The significance of wives' work to the household economy can also be gauged from the responses of the married women who claimed in general terms to get their living – wholly or partly – 'by their labour'. While married to men with a wide range of occupations, their proportions similarly increased as the social status of their husband decreased. Of those whose husband's occupation was stated, 36 per cent of labourers' wives claimed to live by their labour compared with 30 per cent of husbandmen's wives, 18 per cent of women married to crafts/tradesmen, and 10 per cent married to yeomen and gentlemen. These proportions followed a roughly similar pattern to those of male witnesses stating that they lived by their labour, with 83 per cent of labourers speaking of their maintenance in these terms, 48 per cent of husbandmen, 17 per cent of men occupied in crafts/trades, 5 per cent of yeomen and 2 per cent of gentlemen. Of all wives responding to the question of how they maintained themselves, 21 per cent claimed to live by their labour. Remarkably, this corresponds to the proportion of men responding in the same way to the question of their maintenance, which was 24 per cent. By contrast, only 12 per cent of single women claimed to live by their labour, compared with 28 per cent of widows, suggesting a greater divergence in the working identities of married women and their never-married counterparts than between married women and men of comparable status.

It would be misleading to conclude that all working wives were victims of poverty consigned to a life of drudgery. Nearly a quarter (24 per cent) of wives responding to the question of how they maintained themselves detailed specific forms of work, often without reference to their husband, suggesting not only independent employment but also in a few cases a distinct occupational identity. Besides speaking of their labour or industry, wives also referred to their trade, occupation and even 'profession' in relation to a variety of tasks ranging from service and charring to craft, retail, nursing and midwifery. Wives also undertook a much wider range of roles than single women (83 per cent of whom were in domestic service), detailing work patterns that were similar to those of widows.

Most commonly specified was nursing/medical care, with 20 per cent of wives who provided details about how they made a living looking after children or tending women in childbed, including Joan Charnon, married to a shoemaker, who stated in 1625 that 'she liveth by her profession of a midwife'.[69] Almost as many (19 per cent) were involved in selling goods, ranging from old clothes, butter, eggs, fish, fruit and herbs, to chandlery, books, fans and perfume, some at market or as street sellers, and others as shop keepers. Next came many forms of making and mending clothes (17 per cent), ranging from knitting to embroidery and plain work, and making caps, gloves, scarves, children's clothes, stays, and mantuas. While many professed simply to live by their needles, some detailed the training, skill and status involved, such as a painter's wife who declared in 1688 that

[69] GL, 9065A/6, 19 May 1625.

she had 'served 7 yeares as an apprentice to one Mrs Rirburensen to the Trade of Embroidery, by which she gets her liveing', and Mary Bellchamber, married to a shoemaker, who stated in 1719 that she got 'her livelyhood by working at the Taylors trade'.[70] Several (12 per cent) were involved in victualling and catering trades, with some keeping inns and public houses. Nearly 10 per cent maintained themselves by washing, starching, scrubbing or charring of some kind, including a woman who in 1624 claimed to be married to a gentleman while getting 'her lyving by starchinge of bands to shopps'.[71] Equal proportions (9 per cent) worked as domestic servants to those involved in textile manufacture, spinning, carding, and winding silk. One wife drove cattle, one carried water, another carried tubs, one taught children to sew, and in 1703 one claimed to maintain herself and her child as 'a journey woman to carry Tobacco Pipes'.[72] Some wives, deft at the economy of makeshifts, undertook more than one type of work, such as Anne Buck, who in 1709, 'worth litle', lived 'by her husbands pay as a seaman & her owne industry in innkeeping & doeing thread worke', and Misericordia Jeke, a butcher's wife, who at the age of 63 in 1724 'followes the buisnesse of Nursekeeping & when out of place sells fruite'.[73]

When witnesses providing details of their employment also specified their husband's occupation, it is possible to assess the extent to which they worked jointly with or independently from their spouse. Of the eighty-eight such cases listed in the appendix below, only twelve (14 per cent) wives worked alongside their husbands. Alice Dayly, for example, married to a fruiterer in the west end of London, responded that 'she helps to get her liveing as well as her Husband by selling fruit and Chandlery ware'.[74] These joint enterprises mostly involved victualling and catering, or making clothes – occupations that were also undertaken separately by both wives and husbands. Of the couples working in unrelated occupations, in some cases both spouses contributed wage work to the household economy, in other cases one partner earned wages in addition to the other's trade, while in a few cases a 'double business household' can be identified.[75] Catherine Jennings, for example, simply described herself as a mantua maker without responding to the question of her worth, while her husband declared that he was 'by trade a Glassegrinder ... worth about two hundred pounds his debts paid'.[76] In such cases marriage was clearly no bar to female commercial enterprise, and women's industry was not necessitated by financial hardship.[77]

A quarter of the wives providing details of their working lives claimed to be worth little or nothing or poor, or described their husbands in these terms. A

[70] LMA, DL/C/242, 10 February 1687/8; GL, 9065A/11, fol. 230v.

[71] GL, 9189/1, fol. 200v.

[72] LMA, DL/C/248, fol. 93.

[73] GL, 9065A/10, fol. 230v; 9065A/12, fol. 470v.

[74] LMA, DL/C/242, fol. 68.

[75] Erickson, 'Married Women's Occupations', p. 276.

[76] GL, 9065A/11, fols 347v, 349.

[77] For a detailed case study of gentlewomen's entrepreneurial activity both within and beyond marriage, see A. L. Erickson, 'Eleanor Mosley and Other Milliners in the City of London Companies 1700–1750', *History Workshop Journal* 71 (2011), 147–72.

further quarter did not respond to the question of their worth at all, while several maintained that the question either did not concern them or that they were not obliged to respond. A few referred to their husband's worth, if only to profess ignorance of it. Only one married woman who described what she did for a living also claimed independent means, and these were derived from 'an estate of thirty pound a yeare left her by her first husband' rather than from her work at cap making – an occupation she shared with her current husband.[78] For the majority of wives it appears that contributing to their livelihood made little impact on how they accounted for their worth, and in many cases it was a direct consequence of their relative poverty. In 1696, for example, Susan Kettey claimed to get her living 'by buying of old Cloths', declaring herself 'worth nothing she being forced to work to gett bread'.[79] However, it would clearly be wrong to conclude from such statements that married women's work was born of desperation any more than married men's work. What is evident from such women's statements about how they maintained themselves, if not always from how they described their worth, is the extent to which provisioning their households was approached as a joint undertaking between spouses, even if this was mostly unspoken and only very rarely admitted by their husbands. Robert Wheare was an exception to this rule when he responded in 1634 that 'he being a Taylor and his wyfe a midwyfe they doe maynteyne them selves by theire honest indevours'.[80]

Conclusion

A sceptical reading of the evidence presented here would place heavy emphasis on the many wives who responded simply that they were married, or, more explicitly in line with legal convention, that they were worth nothing because under covert baron and that they were maintained by their husbands. However, the exceptions were too many and too varied simply to constitute proof of such a rule, and a more nuanced reading would emphasize the ways in which wives both exploited the mitigating factors governing the operation of coverture such as the law of necessaries, and openly flouted expectations that they had no claims to moveable goods and that they depended upon their husbands. Between the extremes of dependence and independence lies an extensive grey area of considerable ambiguity, as well as the possibility of strategic self-fashioning in court to mask the level (and often the lack) of marital assets. Significant numbers (7 per cent) of wives speaking about their own or their husband's worth implied either jointly or independently held goods, and if those describing themselves and/or their husbands as worth little or nothing are included, the proportion of wives providing some sort of evaluation (albeit many in negative terms) rises to 51 per cent. In addition, over half of those who gave information about their maintenance departed from assumptions that this should be provided by their spouse, and some such

78 LMA, DL/C/258, fol. 238.

79 LMA, DL/C/245, fol. 299.

80 WSRO, Ep III/5/2, fol. 202v.

wives were clearly occupied in crafts, trade and retail as a matter of choice and in an entrepreneurial capacity rather than out of crude economic necessity. Of particular significance is the extent of overlap in the language deployed by men and women claiming to live 'by their labour', with similar proportions of men and married women responding in these terms. Amongst lower ranking people this was linked to a more profound divergence between married and single women than between men and their wives. It also suggests that marriage, rather than widowhood, was the stage at which women undertook more varied and independent forms of productive work. Even in the relatively conservative forum of the church courts, therefore, the majority of married women – and very occasionally even their spouses – acknowledged informal expectations of joint marital property, if not personal estate, and an active contribution of resources, labour, management and skill to the domestic economy.

APPENDIX: OCCUPATIONS OF MARRIED COUPLES APPEARING AS WITNESSES IN THE CHURCH COURTS, 1567–1726

Year	Jurisdiction	Husband's occupation	Wife's occupation	Husband's worth
Related Occupations				
1641	Chester	sells ale	sells ale with her husband	
1687	London	fruiterer	sells fruit and chandlery ware	
1687	London	glover	makes gloves	
1687	London	porter	she and her husband carry tubs and other such hard labour	very little
1705	London	keeps a victualling house and chandlers shop	keeps a victualling house and chandlers shop	
1713	London	drover	sometimes droving, sometimes nurse keeping	
1714	London	victualler	victualling	
1716	London	staymaker	assists her husband as a staymaker	
1719	London	velvet cap maker	cap making	
1720	London	baker	'she is a baker by trade'	
1723	London	watchmaker / keeps a wax chandlers shop	keeps a wax chandlers shop with her husband	
1724	London	victualler (formerly a clothworker)	keeps a public house	
Unrelated Occupations				
1567	Canterbury	tailor / featherbed maker	spinning and carding	more than 20s, less than 40s
1588	London	poulterer	dry nurse	
1595	Canterbury	labourer	knits	3s 4d
1607	Canterbury	butcher	victualling and selling beer	
1611	London	labourer	milk wife	
1614	London	bricklayer	keeps women in childbed	
1616	Canterbury	farrier	spinster	
1617	Chichester	clerk	teaches children to sew	
1621	London	chandler / chops marrow bones (described by his wife as a yeoman)	sells fish and other things as the season affords	worth little

Year	Jurisdiction	Husband's Occupation	Wife's occupation	Husband's worth
1621	London	chandler	nurses children and 'other work'	£10
1623	London	harness maker	servant	
1623	York	gentleman	household servant	£20
1624	London	gentleman	starches bands to shops	
1625	Canterbury	blacksmith / labourer	labourer	
1625	London	shoemaker	midwife	
1628	Canterbury	shoemaker	helps to wash for other folks	
1629	Canterbury	wheelwright	midwife	
1631	Salisbury	day labourer	servant	
1633	Canterbury	husbandman	nurse	
1637	London	needle maker	keeps women in childbed	£6 or £7
1637	London	marking stone / whetstone seller	carries water	nothing besides household stuff
1641	Chester	labourer	nurse	is poor
1666	Chester	soldier	baking and selling pies and puddings	is poor
1669	London	sailor (in prison for debt)	silk winding	
1671	London	butcher	attends women who lie in	
1676	London	labourer	carries milk	
1680	London	mariner	nurse keeping / silk winding	
1688	London	carpenter	washing / scouring	
1688	London	dyer	servant	
1688	London	horner	midwife	
1688	London	fringe weaver	keeps a herb stall	
1688	London	shoemaker	embroidery	
1688	London	painter	embroidery	
1697	London	husbandman	sells milk	
1697	London	drover	buying and selling old clothes	
1700	London	house carpenter	keeps a victualling house	
1702	London	sailor	silk winding	
1703	London	cowkeeper	nurses children / winds silk	
1703	London	mariner	journeywoman carrying tobacco pipes	
1704	London	labourer	milk woman	
1704	London	porter	sells butter, eggs and other things	

Year	Jurisdiction	Husband's occupation	Wife's occupation	Husband's worth
1705	London	vintner	makes mantuas and children's coats	
1705	London	haberdasher	servant	
1708	London	gardener	keeps a public house	£100
1708	London	gardener / lets houses	sometimes takes in children to nurse	£40
1709	London	seaman	innkeeping / threadwork	
1709	London	tailor	washer woman	
1710	London	shoemaker	any employment of washing / scouring or the like	not worth 5s his debts paid
1710	London	shoemaker	sometimes spins	
1710	London	staymaker	nurse keeping	
1710	London	gentleman	mantuamaker	
1710	London	broadsilk weaver	petty chapwoman	
1712	London	gentleman / pensioner to Chelsea / formerly stage door keeper to Drury Lane playhouse	nurse keeping and taking in clothes to wash	
1713	London	tinman	keeps a public house	
1713	London	mariner	silk winding	
1713	London	mason	servant	
1713	London	joiner	servant	
1713	London	mariner	servant	
1714	London	baker / works on board ship at the Customs House	makes scarves and mantuas	
1715	London	mariner	sells fruit	
1716	London	broker	nurse keeping and taking in children to nurse	
1716	London	shoemaker	starcher	
1716	London	hostler	washes gentlewomen's linen and plain work	
1716	London	grocer	plainwork / starching	
1719	London	gentleman/horseguardsman	cap making	
1720	London	carpenter	sells fruit and greens	
1720	London	mathematical instrument maker	nurse keeping	
1720	London	glass grinder	mantuamaker	£200
1720	London	coachman	keeps a chandlers shop	
1724	London	shoemaker / leather cutter	looks after a child	
1724	London	butcher	nurse keeping / sells fruit	

Year	Jurisdiction	Husband's occupation	Wife's occupation	Husband's worth
1724	London	porter	keeps a chandlers shop/ washes clothes	
1726	London	silversmith	mantuamaker	
1726	London	yeoman	book selling	

11

MARRIED WOMEN, WORK AND THE LAW: EVIDENCE FROM EARLY MODERN GERMANY

Sheilagh Ogilvie

Married women in early modern Germany were affected by the law in a wide variety of ways – so many, in fact, that a single essay cannot hope to cover them all. The special character of women's legal position in each German polity forces us, in fact, to pause and ask ourselves what we mean by concepts we have largely taken for granted – 'the law' itself and how it assigned different rights to people according to sex and marital status. In pre-Napoleonic Germany, this question is of immediately striking relevance. For one thing, the Holy Roman Empire of the German Nation contained a large number of sovereign territorial units – almost 2,500 when one includes the sovereign estate of Imperial Knights, and 384 even when these are excluded.[1] Moreover, these territories were widely heterogeneous on almost every conceivable axis of comparison including their legal systems. Furthermore, in German-speaking central Europe both the law itself and its concrete implementation in daily life were affected by the co-existence of various levels of authority in each society – empire, prince, community, guild, church – so the nature of the 'composite state' of the Empire raises questions about the legal system, which are not easy to fit into the framework which historians have devised for other early modern European societies with a closer resemblance to modern nation-states.[2] Germany is thus a good context for reflection on what we might mean by the effect of the law on the lives of married women, because it undermines so many of the ideas we have come to take for granted about what the law is, where it comes from, and how it functions.

We cannot proceed to study married women and the law in Germany until we understand much more concretely what 'the law' meant when it derived simultaneously from multiple levels of authority. Only by looking at how the law affected married women in practice, in specific spheres of activity in particular early modern German societies, will one begin to understand the complicated ramifications of what was meant by 'the law' for early modern women. In pur-

1 J. G. Gagliardo, *Germany under the Old Regime, 1600–1790* (London, 1991), pp. 2–3.

2 S. C. Ogilvie, 'The German State: A Non-Prussian View', *Rethinking Leviathan: The Eighteenth-Century State in Britain and Germany*, ed. E. Hellmuth and J. Brewer (Oxford, 1999), pp. 167–202.

suit of this goal, I will concentrate my examination here on married women in the Duchy of Württemberg, a middle-sized state in southwestern Germany. I will focus primarily on how the law affected married women in one broad sphere of their lives – their economic activities. Many of the details will be specific to Württemberg, and neither here nor elsewhere in early modern Europe did women live by bread alone. But I will show how the multiple ways in which the law affected how married women could earn bread for themselves and their families in this particular society help us understand more general principles about how the law mattered to married women's lives in early modern societies more widely.

A dominant theme in the history of married women and law is the question of their legal autonomy – in the English-speaking world the question of 'coverture', in the German-speaking world the issue of *Geschlechtsvormundschaft* ('gender guardianship'). This essay will argue that, important though legal autonomy was, it should not lead us to neglect other legal influences on married women. The case of early modern Germany throws into prominence two additional ways in which the law crucially circumscribed the economic options of married women, and thus their life chances and well-being: the legal privileges of guilds and other occupational associations; and the legal powers of local communities, including local church courts' jurisdiction over the conduct of married life.

The German Territory of Württemberg and the Legal Position of Married Women

The Duchy of Württemberg was a principality in southwestern Germany of about half a million inhabitants (450,000 in 1600, rising to 620,000 by 1790) – what has been called a 'German territory of the second rank'.[3] Although market-oriented in many ways, Württemberg had strong non-market institutions, which enjoyed extensive legal powers and imposed quite serious legal constraints on women.[4] For married women, three aspects of this legal framework were of particular importance in circumscribing their economic choices – the Württemberg version of 'gender guardianship'; the legal privileges of guilds and other professional associations; and the legal powers enjoyed by local communities and their officials.

3 J. A. Vann, *The Making of a State: Württemberg, 1593–1793* (Ithaca, 1984), p. 36; P. H. Wilson, *War, State and Society in Württemberg, 1677–1793* (Cambridge, 1995), pp. 42–6.

4 For a detailed examination of these constraints, see S. C. Ogilvie, *A Bitter Living: Women, Markets, and Social Capital in Early Modern Germany* (Oxford, 2003); S. C. Ogilvie, 'How Does Social Capital Affect Women? Guilds and Communities in Early Modern Germany', *American Historical Review* 109 (2004), 325–59; S. C. Ogilvie, 'Women and Labour Markets in Early Modern Germany', *Jahrbuch für Wirtschaftsgeschichte* 2004:2 (2004), 25–60; S. C. Ogilvie, 'Guilds, Efficiency and Social Capital: Evidence from German Proto-Industry', *Economic History Review* 57 (2004), 286–333; S. C. Ogilvie, *State Corporatism and Proto-Industry: The Württemberg Black Forest, 1580–1797* (Cambridge, 1997), pp. 45–57.

The first aspect of the law that affected married women was 'gender guardianship' (*Geschlechtsvormundschaft*). The legal system in Württemberg, as in other pre-industrial German societies, did not regard a married woman as a legal adult.[5] Instead, it placed her under the guardianship of an adult male called a *Kriegsvogt*. This term translates literally as 'war governor' or 'war overseer': 'Krieg' meant 'war' and 'Vogt' was an Old High German term for an overlord who exerted guardianship or military protection as well as secular justice over a particular territory or area of responsibility.[6] The obligation for a married woman to be under the legal guardianship of a *Kriegsvogt* meant that she did not have the legal right to sign enforceable contracts without this man's permission, let alone to engage independently in any other legal proceedings.

Every part of German-speaking Europe had some variant of gender guardianship in the early modern period and, as Figure 11.1 shows, most of them retained it until at least 1815. The medieval period had seen a limited legal emancipation of women in German legal thinking, especially with the so-called 'Reception' of Roman Law, overlaying (though not eradicating) the older German customary law. However, the legal emancipation of women under Roman Law had been largely resisted in Württemberg, whose *Erste Landrecht* (first national law-code) of 1555 subjected women to unlimited male guardianship. But Württemberg was by no means unique in this regard. Rather, it was part of a much more widespread pattern that characterized almost all the Swabian, Alemannian, and Franconian polities of German-speaking Europe, in which both unmarried and married women remained subject to unrestricted male guardianship.[7] A very similar degree of full gender guardianship for both unmarried and married women prevailed in those many parts of Germany subject to Saxon or Lübeck law, including Lübeck itself and the other great cities that used its legal system; much of Mecklenburg, Holstein, Pomerania, East Friesia, Schleswig, the Duchy of Prussia, and Prussian Poland; and a number of areas of Electoral Saxony, Lusatia, Thuringia, and Silesia.[8] Somewhat milder versions of gender guardianship appear to have prevailed in eighteenth-century Prussia, parts of Thuringia, Silesia, Anhalt, Halberstadt, Magdeburg, Lauenburg, Holstein, Lower Saxony, Westphalia, Electoral Palatinate, Tirol, and most of the south German Imperial Cities.[9] However, the legal status of women varied so much from one early modern German territory – or town – to the next that even the modern expert on the German law of gender guardianship, Ernst Holthöfer, concludes that many more monographs based on much deeper archival research would be

5 E. Holthöfer, 'Die Geschlechtsvormundschaft. Ein Überblick von der Antike bis ins 19. Jahrhundert', *Frauen in der Geschichte des Rechts: von der frühen Neuzeit bis zur Gegenwart*, ed. U. Gerhard (Munich, 1997), pp. 390–451; C. Ulbrich, *Shulamit und Margarete: Macht, Geschlecht und Religion in einer ländlichen Gesellschaft des 18. Jahrhunderts* (Vienna, 1999), pp. 32–3 with n. 117.

6 For a discussion of the institution and meaning of the office of the 'Vogt' in the territories of late medieval German-speaking central Europe, see F. Reichert, *Landesherrschaft, Adel, und Vogtei: Zur Vorgeschichte des spätmittelalterlichen Ständestaates im Herzogtum Österreich* (Cologne and Vienna, 1985).

7 Holthöfer, 'Geschlechtsvormundschaft', pp. 419–20.

8 Holthöfer, 'Geschlechtsvormundschaft', pp. 420–3.

9 Holthöfer, 'Geschlechtsvormundschaft', pp. 423–4.

Figure 11.1: Geographical Distribution of Gender Guardianship in German-Speaking Europe, c. 1815

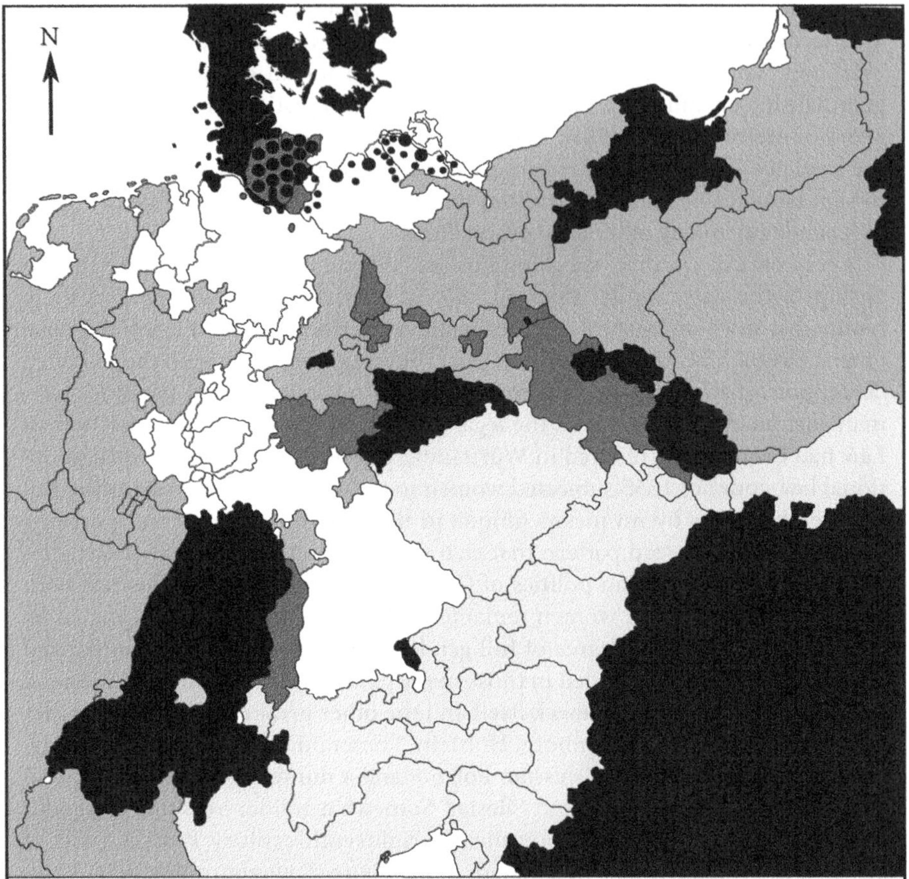

- All women autonomus (women's legal position set by common law)
- All women autonomous, married women subject to subsidiary power of representation by husband (limited *cura maritalis*; women's legal position set by Austrian law)
- Unmarried women autonomous, married women non-autonomous (full *cura maritalis*; women's legal position set by French and Prussian law)
- Unmarried women autonomus but cannot conduct legal proceedings, married women non-autonomous (limited *cura sexus*; women's legal position set by Saxon law)
- All women non-autonomous (full *cura sexus*, full *cura maritalis*; women's legal position set by particular law
- ●• These towns have women's legal position set by Lübeck law (full *cura sexus*, full *cura maritalis*)
- ●●● All these towns have women's legal position set by Lübeck law
- ●• These towns have women's legal position set by Saxon law (limited *cura sexus*, ful *cura maritalis*)

Source: Holyhöfer, 'Die Geschlechtsvormundschaft', pp. 436–7

necessary to clarify the heterogeneous and blurred picture of the legal situation of women in German-speaking Europe around 1800.[10]

The legal position of married women only began gradually to become more standardized across German-speaking Europe in the course of the great legal codifications that took place at the end of the 'natural law' period – the 1794 *Allgemeine Landrecht* in Prussia, the 1804 *Code Civil* in France (important for those German territories occupied by France during the Napoleonic period), and the 1811 *Allgemeine Bürgerliche Gesetzbuch* in Austria. As late as 1815, there was still enormous variation among the different polities of German-speaking Europe, which fell into five main zones and a range of sub-variants. First, at the most liberal end, a small number of territories in the centre of German-speaking central Europe (those shaded white in Figure 11.1) allowed full legal autonomy to both unmarried and married women. Second, and slightly less liberal, came the newly codified Austrian system, under which, although all women were legally autonomous, a married woman was still subject to power of representation by her husband. Third, with only an intermediate degree of female legal autonomy, came those German polities subject to the French and Prussian codes, according to which unmarried women were legally autonomous but married women were not. A fourth group of Germany polities, in which a more severe situation prevailed, were those subject to Saxon law, where unmarried women were autonomous except for not being allowed to engage independently in legal proceedings, but married women still enjoyed no legal autonomy. The fifth group, characterized by the most severe legal restrictions on women, consisted of those territories – including Württemberg – where the 'particular law' of that specific territory's legal system, as handed down from the medieval and early modern period, continued to prevail, and both unmarried and married women continued to be subject to a completely non-autonomous legal status well into the nineteenth century (in the case of Württemberg until 1828).[11]

What did gender guardianship actually mean for married women? Some interpretations of the German law of gender guardianship regard it as having existed mainly to shield the property of a married woman from the control of her husband, and especially to protect her from his possible prodigality or coercion. This view was put forward by many German legal commentators in the later eighteenth century, when female legal emancipation began to be debated more widely in German-speaking Europe.[12] However, it is also accepted by some modern historians of pre-industrial Germany. In the context of early modern Württemberg, for instance, David Sabean has emphasized the beneficial role of gender guardianship in

10 See the survey of the law of gender guardianship in early modern Germany in Holthöfer, 'Geschlechtsvormundschaft', pp. 419–26. Cf. on this D. W. Sabean, 'Allianzen und Listen: Die Geschlechtsvormundschaft im 18. und 19. Jahrhundert', *Frauen in der Geschichte des Rechts*, ed. Gerhard, pp. 460–479, here p. 463, according to which gender guardianship in early modern Germany had become quite standardized by the late seventeenth century. This is contradicted by the map in Holthöfer, 'Geschlechtsvormundschaft', pp. 436–7.

11 Holthöfer, 'Geschlechtsvormundschaft', pp. 427–32.

12 See, e.g., C. L. C. Röslin, *Abhandlung von besondern weiblichen Rechten* (Stuttgart, 1775).

protecting wives against exploitative husbands and their kinship groups.[13] On the other hand, by the later eighteenth century there was a strand of thought within German jurisprudence which advocated the abolition of gender guardianship on the grounds that there was no 'natural' difference in intelligence between the sexes and that gender guardianship was often manipulated by both sexes in ways that inhibited the efficient functioning of the economy.[14] A number of modern historians have also discovered that in practice gender guardianship often operated in such a way as to protect male producers against competition by entrepreneurial females, since it restricted women's ability to operate independently in agriculture, crafts, proto-industry or commerce, all of which required the ability to sign enforceable contracts relating to real estate, labour, credit, and output.[15]

This essay will show that neither of these extremes accurately reflects how gender guardianship worked for early modern German women. Instead, it argues, we should recognize that gender guardianship was used by different people in early modern German societies for different purposes. Some women were able to use it to their own benefit, either by pitting their guardians against abusive husbands or by claiming legal incapacity in order to escape from the consequences of disadvantageous contracts. But men were also able to manipulate gender guardianship in ways that circumscribed women's economic options and reduced their well-being. Husbands themselves were often able to block their wives from either appointing guardians to begin with or using those guardians to protect their economic interests within marriage. Furthermore, men who regarded married and widowed women as dangerously entrepreneurial used the regulations governing gender guardianship to claim that married women were not autonomous legal agents, could not enter into binding contracts, and thus could not carry out all the activities needed to conduct an independent business – particularly one that competed with their own.

Gender guardianship, though important, was not the only aspect of the law that affected married women in early modern German society. A second major set of legal prescriptions that constrained the economic choices of married women in Württemberg, as in almost all other German societies in the early modern period, were the legal privileges of guilds and guild-like merchant associations. As in many other parts of German-speaking Europe, in Württemberg guilds existed not just in traditional handicrafts, but in export-oriented proto-industries, in tertiary activities such as shop-keeping and merchant trading, and even in some primary activities such as fishing, sheep-herding, or wine-growing.[16] Guilds regulated economic activities not only in large cities but in the smallest towns. Moreover, in Württemberg and many areas of central, southern and eastern Germany, guilds even extended their controls

13 Sabean, 'Allianzen'; D. W. Sabean, *Property, Production and Family in Neckarhausen, 1700–1870* (Cambridge, 1990), pp. 208–14.

14 See, e.g., A. S. P. Semler, 'Über die Entbehrlichkeit und Abschaffung der Geschlechtscuratel in Deutschland überhaupt', *Archiv für die theoretische und practische Rechtsgelehrsamkeit* 6 (1792), 30–85.

15 See, e.g., A. Ryter, 'Die Geschlechtsvormundschaft in der Schweiz: Das Beispiel der Kantone Basel-Landschaft und Basel-Stadt', *Frauen in der Geschichte des Rechts*, ed. Gerhard, pp. 494–508.

16 See Ogilvie, *State Corporatism*, pp. 72–9.

out into the village workshops in the countryside. In addition, guild-like merchant associations monopolized many sectors of commerce, including the proto-industrial export trades.[17] As late as 1793, one traveller's account remarked that industry and commerce in Württemberg 'is constantly made more difficult by the form which it has taken for a long time. The greatest share of trade and manufactures are in the hands of closed and for the most part privileged companies.'[18] Where guilds retained their legal privileges, they regulated who could engage in particular economic activities, whom they could employ, the wages they could pay workers, the amount they could produce, the prices they could charge customers, which of their family members could participate, who was allowed to buy and sell particular goods, and what equipment and techniques could be used. It was 1864 before guilds in Württemberg were abolished.[19] In earlier publications I have discussed how guilds in early modern Württemberg generated a rich 'social capital' of shared norms, information transmission, sanctions on deviance, and collective action, which enabled them to exercise intensive surveillance and control over their members as well as over non-members whose economic activities impinged on that sector.[20]

A third major component of the law that constrained the economic choices of married women in early modern Württemberg was the legal powers devolved to the local community. Württemberg – like many other parts of German-speaking central Europe – had an institutional framework which gave very strong legal powers to local communities. People held legal citizenship rights in their community first and foremost, and in the nation only by virtue of their community membership.[21] The villages and tiny towns of rural Württemberg operated their own powerful community courts, appointed a myriad of community officials (about one-fifth of male household heads held some communal office), and met in annual face-to-face community assemblies (*Vogt-Rüg-Gerichte*), where the princely district officials asked each (male) citizen if he had anything to report. This 'social capital' enabled communities to exercise intense surveillance and control over crop choice, farming techniques, agricultural and industrial markets, citizenship, settlement, marriage, mobility, inheritance, residential arrangements, sexuality, education, diligence, leisure, and consumption.[22] Württemberg communities also maintained a strong symbiotic

17 W. Troeltsch, *Die Calwer Zeughandlungskompagnie und ihre Arbeiter. Studien zur Gewerbe- und Sozialgeschichte Altwürttembergs* (Jena, 1897); Ogilvie, *State Corporatism*, pp. 77–9, 106–11; H. Medick, *Weben und Überleben in Laichingen 1650–1900. Untersuchungen zur Sozial-, Kultur- und Wirtschaftsgeschichte aus der Perspektive einer lokalen Gesellschaft im frühneuzeitlichen Württemberg* (Göttingen, 1996), esp. pp. 65–140.

18 C. Meiners, 'Bemerkungen auf einer Herbstreise nach Schwaben. Geschrieben im November 1793', *Kleinere Länder- und Reisebeschreibungen*, ed. C. Meiners (Berlin, 1794), vol. 2, pp. 235–380, here p. 292.

19 Ogilvie, *State Corporatism*, pp. 72–9, 419–37.

20 Ogilvie, *A Bitter Living*; Ogilvie, 'How Does Social Capital Affect Women?'; Ogilvie, 'Women and Labour Markets'; Ogilvie, 'Guilds', esp. pp. 289–90, 297–8, 303–7, 312–13.

21 Ogilvie, *State Corporatism*, pp. 45–57.

22 S. C. Ogilvie, 'Coming of Age in a Corporate Society: Capitalism, Pietism and Family Authority in Rural Württemberg, 1590–1740', *Continuity and Change* 1 (1986), 279–331; Ogilvie, 'The German State', pp. 193–9; Ogilvie, *State Corporatism*, pp. 42–72; Ogilvie, *A Bitter Living*; Sabean, *Property*, pp. 106, 109, 148, 160–1.

relationship with the Lutheran state church, especially through the local church courts (*Kirchenkonvente*) which were established in the 1640s and remained active until c.1890. These local church courts had the power to impose fines and incarceration as well as religious penances, and their minutes show that they closely regulated work, consumption, sociability, sexuality, poor relief, and cultural practices.[23]

Information on women's economic activities in pre-industrial societies is extremely scarce, and is particularly hard to obtain for married women.[24] Statistical sources usually record only household heads, which means that they typically exclude all females except for widows (or deserted wives) who headed their own households. Censuses and parish registers provide information on the demographic behaviour and household status of other females, but no details of their economic activities. For information about the work of married women, we have to rely almost exclusively on scattered references in qualitative sources such as court records, petitions, and account-books. Württemberg is fortunate in possessing unusually detailed local archival sources, and this essay relies on a large database of observations of women (and men) working, compiled from such sources for the administrative district of Wildberg in the Nagold Valley in the Württemberg Black Forest. It uses this database both qualitatively, to examine the detailed context for women's market work, and quantitatively, to assess the relative importance of particular types of work for different women and men.

This quantitative database was created out of a legal source, the sixteen volumes (over 7,000 handwritten pages) of the church court records (*Kirchenkonventsprotokolle*) for two Württemberg communities – the small town of Wildberg (population c.1,300) and the village of Ebhausen (population c.900) – in the period 1646–1800. From these church court records, all observations of working activities by either females or males were extracted, transforming a qualitative source into a quantitative database. The records of the local church courts in Württemberg communities are well suited for investigating women's work because they regulated sexual and familial relationships, thereby opening a window into the domestic sphere, and because they legally required the reporting of all work performed at religiously forbidden times. In compiling the quantitative database, only references to *actual tasks being carried out* were enumerated. References to people earning a living from a certain occupation, serving a master of a certain occupation, or being apprenticed to a certain craft were excluded, on the grounds that they did not register actual working behaviour, and were also likely to be biased towards males, who were more likely than females to hold formal occupational designations but not necessarily more likely to engage in tasks relating to these occupations. Likewise, this church court work database excluded all references to individuals begging, being given money or food by their relatives, or receiving public poor relief, on the grounds that such references

23 Ogilvie, *A Bitter Living*.

24 On this, see R. Wall, 'The Contribution of Married Women to the Family Economy under Different Family Systems: Some Examples from the Mid-Nineteenth Century from the Work of Frédéric Le Play', *Socio-Economic Consequences of Sex-Ratios in Historical Perspective, 1500–1900: Proceedings, Eleventh International Economic History Congress Milan, September 1994*, ed. A. Fauve-Chamoux and S. Sogner (Milan, 1994), pp. 139–148, here p. 139.

did not register actual working behaviour, were likely to be biased towards widows and spinsters who were disproportionately represented among the poor, and were likely to overstate the importance of charity as a livelihood source.

This exercise yielded a database of 2,828 separate observations of individuals working, as Table 11.1 shows. It includes 397 observations of the work of married women, approximately proportionate to their share (43 per cent) in the female population over the age of eleven.[25] In the discussion that follows, this database, enhanced by references to married women's work in other sources, particularly petitions and the minute-books of other local law-courts, is used to provide a window onto the activities of a group of women about whose work the historiography has long contained more theoretical assumptions than empirical findings.[26]

Married Women in Agriculture

The most important sector of the pre-industrial European economy was agriculture, which means that it is particularly important to examine married women's ability to participate fully in that sector. As Table 11.1 shows, married women in early modern Württemberg were highly active in agriculture, which accounted for 20 per cent of their observed work in Wildberg and Ebhausen between 1646 and 1800. This was not as high as the share of agriculture in the work of unmarried daughters living at home with their parents (22 per cent), independent unmarried women (27 per cent), widows (33 per cent), or maidservants (40 per cent), but farm-work still made up a non-trivial proportion of married women's working activity. Although it was also much less than the share of agriculture in the observed work of unmarried men (50 per cent for male servants, 42 per cent for sons), it was not enormously lower than its share in the observed work of married men (29 per cent).

This finding from the quantitative database is borne out by a more detailed analysis of the qualitative evidence, which illuminates the wide variety of agricultural activities married women undertook. For one thing, land, the absolute prerequisite for all agricultural activities, was bought and sold in markets in which married women participated. Sometimes they did so without any involvement from their husbands, as in 1611 when the wives of two Wildberg men got into conflict in the community court over the sale of an arable field,[27] or in 1654 when a married woman from Effringen appeared in the Wildberg church court and successfully demanded right of prior purchase on a pasture and an arable field

25 See Ogilvie, *A Bitter Living*, p. 27 (table 1.3), for a detailed breakdown of contemporary censuses for this part of Württemberg showing that 43 per cent of females (and 55 per cent of males) over the age of eleven were 'currently married'.

26 For a detailed discussion of the compilation, composition and representativeness of this database, see Ogilvie, *A Bitter Living*, pp. 22–36.

27 Hauptstaatsarchiv Stuttgart (henceforth HStAS) A573 Bü. 25, 4.3.1611, unpag. ('Jeorg harders weib Clagt Ab Michel Brossen weib').

Table 11.1. Observed Work by Females and Males, According to Marital and Household Status, Wildberg, 1646-1800, and Ebhausen, 1677-1800

	Agricul-ture		Guilded craft		Guilded proto-industry		Unguil-ded craft (esp. spinning)		Mill		Tavern		Com-merce		Labour		Service		House-work		Care		Healing		Mar-ginal occupa-tions		Total	
	no.	%	no.	%	no.	%	no.	%	no.	%	no.	%	no.	%	no.	%	no.	%	no.	%	no.	%	no.	%	no.	%	no.	%
Daughters	30	22	2	1	3	2	30	22	0	0	0	0	2	1	4	3	2	1	16	12	13	10	0	0	34	25	136	100
Maids	43	40	0	0	2	2	10	9	2	2	0	0	1	1	0	0	0	0	19	18	15	14	0	0	15	14	107	100
Wives	81	20	17	4	9	2	34	9	10	3	18	5	12	3	7	2	4	1	111	28	43	11	8	2	43	11	397	100
Widows	58	33	3	2	11	6	16	9	11	6	5	3	5	3	8	5	5	3	25	14	17	10	6	3	4	2	174	100
Indep. unmarried women	34	27	0	0	0	0	42	33	0	0	0	0	2	2	5	4	7	6	8	6	14	11	1	1	13	10	126	100
Unknown status	0	0	0	0	0	0	0	0	0	0	0	0	1	50	0	0	0	0	1	50	0	0	0	0	0	0	2	100
Total females	**246**	**26**	**22**	**2**	**25**	**3**	**132**	**14**	**23**	**2**	**23**	**2**	**23**	**2**	**24**	**3**	**18**	**2**	**180**	**19**	**102**	**11**	**15**	**2**	**109**	**12**	**942**	**100**
Sons	88	42	26	12	12	6	4	2	12	6	2	1	3	1	7	3	7	3	6	3	3	1	0	0	42	20	212	100
Male servants	108	50	25	12	4	2	1	0	27	12	2	1	1	0	15	7	1	0	3	1	3	1	0	0	27	12	217	100
Husbands	405	29	198	14	170	12	8	1	119	8	54	4	56	4	75	5	63	4	58	4	25	2	26	2	146	10	1403	100
Widowers	6	33	0	0	2	11	0	0	4	22	0	0	0	0	0	0	0	0	3	17	3	17	0	0	0	0	18	100
Indep. unmarried men	4	15	1	4	1	4	3	12	1	4	0	0	1	4	1	4	0	0	0	0	1	4	0	0	13	50	26	100
Unknown status	1	10	0	0	0	0	1	10	0	0	0	0	0	0	0	0	5	50	2	20	0	0	1	10	0	0	10	100
Total males	**612**	**32**	**250**	**13**	**189**	**10**	**17**	**1**	**163**	**9**	**58**	**3**	**61**	**3**	**98**	**5**	**76**	**4**	**72**	**4**	**35**	**2**	**27**	**1**	**228**	**12**	**1886**	**100**
Total persons	**858**	**30**	**272**	**10**	**214**	**8**	**149**	**5**	**186**	**7**	**81**	**3**	**84**	**3**	**122**	**4**	**94**	**3**	**252**	**9**	**137**	**5**	**42**	**1**	**337**	**12**	**2828**	**100**

Source: PAW, Kirchenkonventsprotokolle (church court minutes), Bde. I-VII (1646-1800); PAE, Kirchenkonventsprotokolle (church court minutes), Bde. I-VII (1674-1800).

Notes:

Agriculture = all forms of farm-work, plus selling farm output.

Guilded craft = all guilded activities except for worsted-weaving.

Guilded proto-industry = making worsted textiles and selling them.

Unguilded craft = spinning, seamstressing, knitting, brewing, attending or holding spinning-bees.

Mill = operating mill, transporting materials to or from mill.

Tavern = operating or serving in tavern.

Commerce = as merchant, shopkeeper, peddler, or private person.

Labour = carting, day-labouring, building, repairing, military work.

Service = teaching, music, writing, magic, housekeeping, laundry, barbering, bathing, prostitution, miscellaneous service.

Housework = indoor and outdoor household chores, providing lodgings.

Care = child-minding, nursing, tending women in child-bed, and all other forms of paid and unpaid care for other persons.

Healing = as barber-surgeon, physician, *Feldscherer*, bathman, *Kleemeister*, shepherd, midwife, sworn woman, private person.

Marginal occupations = doing errands, gathering, stealing.

from an unrelated male.[28] Wives expressed strong views on their husbands' property transactions, as in 1613 when a Nagold man was forced to retreat from an agreed contract on the grounds that 'his wife simply did not like the sale',[29] or in 1767 when the wife of an Ebhausen weaver refused to co-sign a note for 70 *Gulden* because it would mean that 'their best lands would be pledged'.[30] Wives even sometimes took the initiative in land transactions, as in 1788 when an Ebhausen man described how 'it was his wife who first had the idea that the farm that had been sold ... should be brought back into their possession, and she herself consequently went to Nagold to consult with the public secretary there about how this might be initiated'.[31]

These examples of the economic initiative women were willing and able to manifest in land transactions, though, should not lead us to exaggerate their economic autonomy, which was constrained by several aspects of the legal arrangements discussed in the preceding section. We must, for example, consider the way in which the system of gender guardianship in practice operated to shape married women's position in agriculture by affecting their rights of disposition over land. Women were subjected to unrestricted gender guardianship in the Württemberg national law-code of 1555, and were not liberated from it until 1828.[32] However, gender guardianship does not appear to have been systematically enforced until around 1600, as shown by two civil cases of 1602 in the Wildberg community court. In one, explicit uncertainty about whether a married woman 'may go to law without her husband' was resolved when the court ordered the woman in question to withdraw from a civil case unless and until she could appear in court with her husband.[33] In the other, an unmarried man defended the validity of his purchase several years earlier of a field from his widowed mother despite her lack of a community-appointed *Kriegsvogt*, on the grounds that 'no guardian and *Kriegsvogt* were appointed because at that time this was not customary'. The exact date of the transaction in question was not stated in the court-minutes, but the unmarried status of the man suggests that it had probably been fairly recent since he must have himself reached his majority in order to engage in such a purchase, and the mean age at marriage for men in this society in the seventeenth century was twenty-six.[34]

28 Pfarrarchiv Wildberg (henceforth PAW), Kirchenkonventsprotokolle (henceforth KKP), Bd. I, fol. 112v, 14.6.1654.

29 HStAS A573 Bü. 15, fol. 141v, 11.3.1613.

30 Pfarrarchiv Ebhausen (henceforth PAE) KKP Vol. V, p. 230, 20.9.1767.

31 PAE KKP Vol. VII, fol. 74v, 22.1.1788.

32 On gender guardianship in Württemberg, see A. Kraut, *Die Stellung der Frau im württembergischen Privatrecht: eine Untersuchung über Geschlechtsvormundschaft und Interzessionsfrage* (Tübingen, 1934). For the relevant Württemberg laws, see 'Erstes Landrecht' (6.5.1555), *Sammlung Vollständige, historisch und kritisch bearbeitete Sammlung der württembergischen Gesetze*, ed. A. L. Reyscher, 19 vols (Stuttgart, 1828–51), here vol. 4, 95, referring to 'Zweites Landrecht' (1.7.1567), pp. 171–420, where differences between the 1555 and the 1567 version are recorded in the footnotes, here esp. p. 231; 'Pfandgesetz', *Regierungsblatt* (21.5.1828), pp. 361–3.

33 HStAS A573 Bü. 14, fol. 130r, 10.8.1602.

34 HStAS A573 Bü. 14, fol. 107r, 16.3.1602. On marriage ages in early modern Wildberg, see Ogilvie, *State Corporatism*, p. 244 (table 8.3).

Many eighteenth-century German jurists and some modern historians view gender guardianship as having operated to benefit married women. In support of this interpretation, they make four related claims, which I shall treat in turn in relation to early modern Württemberg.

First, they argue that the institution of gender guardianship in Germany in general and Württemberg in particular was directed 'solely and only against husbands', to prevent their abuse of wives' property rights.[35] Doubt is cast on this view by the fact that a *widow* was also required to have a *Kriegsvogt*, even though she did not have a husband against whom protection might have been required. Further doubt is cast on this notion by the fact that in practice, the local authorities in early modern Württemberg appear to have regarded a husband as an acceptable *Kriegsvogt* for his own wife. In August 1602, for instance, Appollonia Schelling from the Württemberg village of Ebhausen was ordered by the Wildberg district court to get her husband to appear in court with her 'as her *Ehevogt* and *Kriegsvogt*'.[36] ('Ehevogt' translates literally as 'marital governor' or 'marital overseer'.) A husband's position as *Ehevogt* meant that he had the right to carry out legal business on behalf of his wife as her representative and in her name, as well as to administer his wife's property, although he was not entitled to alienate it without her consent to cover his own liabilities.[37] When a married woman had a different man than her husband as a *Kriegsvogt*, then she had at least the formal legal possibility of giving expression to her own will, but if her *Kriegsvogt* was also her *Ehevogt* (that is, if both types of guardianship were combined in the person of the husband), as was the case for Appollonia Schelling, then obviously the institution of gender guardianship did not give her this advantage and instead only brought the constraint that she could not bring legal proceedings without his permission and participation.

Second, some defenders of gender guardianship maintain that it did not reflect any legal conception that women were inherently incapable of acting responsibly: 'no jurist regarded women as "weak" and "submissive" vis-à-vis persons who did not belong to their own families'.[38] But legal histories provide rich evidence that in German law, *Vormundschaft* (guardianship) was applied to adult persons who were regarded as incapable of acting responsibly.[39] This applied to all women, since females were viewed as inherently having this characteristic. It also applied to a small number of men, who were regarded by their community courts as having demonstrated by their behaviour that they were unable or unwilling to act responsibly, although in these cases it was sometimes justified in terms of inherent personal characteristics such as old age. To give just one example, in 1677 a Wild-

35 Sabean, 'Allianzen', p. 461.

36 HStAS A573 Bü. 14, fol. 130r, 10.8.1602.

37 Kraut, *Die Stellung der Frau*, pp. 295, 329, 392; J. B. Wiesner, *Das Vormundschaftsrecht sowol nach gemeinen deutschen, kanonischen und römischen als auch nach heutigen statutarischen vorzüglich nach Sächsischen, Schlesischen und übrigen Preussischen Rechten theoretisch und praktisch in systematischer Ordnung abgehandelt* (Halle, 1785), p. 209.

38 Sabean, 'Allianzen', 461.

39 Holthöfer, 'Geschlechtsvormundschaft', p. 392; S. Weber-Will, 'Geschlechtsvormundschaft und weibliche Rechtswohltaten im Privatrecht des preußischen Allgemeinen Landrechts von 1794', *Frauen in der Geschichte des Rechts*, ed. Gerhard, pp. 425–59, here esp. p. 453.

berg weaver who had applied for poor relief because 'he could no longer attend to his craft', and was finding it impossible to control his offspring, instead found the communal church court assigning him a *Kriegsvogt* 'because he is an old man'.[40] Cases such as this imply that early modern law-courts did regard the appointment of a *Kriegsvogt* as reflecting the conception that the person placed under such guardianship was inherently incapable of acting responsibly.

Third, proponents of gender guardianship have claimed that women voluntarily chose their own *Kriegsvögte*, and that although this choice had to be approved by the legal authorities it was a free choice on the part of the woman and there was no compulsion involved.[41] Doubt is cast on this claim by the many cases in early modern Württemberg community court-minutes in which a *Kriegsvogt* was not voluntarily chosen by a woman, but rather was imposed on her by the community, often in situations of conflict or coercion. In 1664, for instance, Catharina, widow of Gabriel Sahl, complained in the Wildberg church court that she had been defamed by Georg Berger and his wife and had been asked why she did not go back to Reutlingen where she came from. The communal church court fined Berger and his wife, but also compulsorily appointed Hannß Faißler as a *Kriegsvogt* for Catharina.[42] In 1712, likewise, when a married woman complained in the Ebhausen church court that she had been defamed by her father-in-law, the schoolmaster, who had accused her of frequenting taverns, she was sentenced to half a day in the 'Häuslin' (the women's lock-up in the village) and told that 'she shall have a *Kriegsvogt* set for her'.[43] Such cases show that the appointment of a *Kriegsvogt*, whether for a married woman or for a widow, was not necessarily a matter of voluntary choice; rather, it was regarded as a component of the penalties inflicted by the communal legal authorities when a woman was viewed as having misbehaved in some way.

Finally, certain eighteenth-century jurists and modern historians claim that gender guardianship did not affect women's dealings with other members of the kinship group or with outside individuals or institutions.[44] Doubt is cast on this view by the fact that in Württemberg after c.1600 a married woman had to be supported by a *Kriegsvogt* in all transactions, including those with persons outside their families.[45] Württemberg community authorities began in the early years of the seventeenth century to forbid married women and widows to litigate without *Kriegsvögte*, appealing to the national law-code to justify this policy.[46] In 1614, for instance, Hanß Großman refused in the Wildberg community court to answer a

40 PAW, KKP Vol. IV, fol. 102v–103r, 8.6.1677.

41 Sabean, 'Allianzen', p. 466.

42 PAW, KKP Vol. II, fol. 104r, 3.6.1664

43 PAE KKP Vol. II, fol. 98v, 4.11.1712.

44 Sabean, 'Allianzen', p. 461.

45 Cf. S. Sogner and H. Sandvik, 'Minors in Law, Partners in Work, Equals in Worth? Women in the Norwegian Economy in the 16th to the 18th Centuries', *La donna nell'economie secc. XIII–XVIII. Attit della 'Ventusima Settimana di Studi' 10–15 april 1989*, ed. S. Cavaciocchi (Prato, 1990), pp. 633–53, here pp. 634–5 with n. 5, on early modern Norway, where having a *Kriegsvogt* was a right, not an obligation.

46 For the law, see '2. Landrecht' (1567), in Reyscher, *Sammlung*, vol. 4, 231.

civil case brought by a married woman on an unpaid debt on the grounds that her son Martin Klaiß was not present to speak on her behalf, and the court accepted the argument.[47] We also find cases in which the community authorities put pressure on a *Kriegsvogt* to compel a woman to undertake an economic transaction against her will. In 1621 Jerg Müller from the village of Oberjettingen appeared in the Wildberg court to describe how he had been appointed as the *Kriegsvogt* of Jerg Küentz's wife and 'he had been commanded ... to sell the house, which the woman did not want to do'.[48] Ryter describes similar situations in Switzerland, where guardians were legally entitled to act against women's expressed desires in economic matters.[49]

Conversely, in situations when a married woman *did* wish to have a *Kriegsvogt*, the legal system often failed her, since it did not automatically appoint one for her and her husband was in an advantageous position to deter her from obtaining one. In 1708, for instance, a Wildberg butcher's wife testified in court that her husband had come to her in childbed and threatened to:

> deal with her in such a way that she would have to give her money to the doctor; he had heard that she was looking for a *Kriegsvogt* and a guardian for his children, he would set matters up in such a way that she would not get very much more from this bloody farm [that she had brought into the marriage], and would have to eke out the household with spinning.[50]

In situations such as this, for a wife to appeal to the community court could be worse than useless. In 1652, when an Effringen farmer used his wife's marriage portion to buy a small farm, which he then sold 'without her prior knowledge and consent', she first demanded an official inventory of their property, and when this failed walked out, taking some of her possessions; this finally spurred the community court to appoint a *Kriegsvogt* for her, but also to order her to move back home and 'recognize her own weakness, meet her husband with good words, and loyally do her part in the householding as best she knows how'.[51] In 1686, when a Wildberg tanner 'whipped his wife until her teeth rattled ... because she would not deliver her property as stated in the inventory', although he had been repeatedly warned and gaoled for 'bad householding' and wife-beating, and his wife had left him on at least one occasion, the community court ordered her to 'deliver up her property'.[52]

Even when a wife did get a *Kriegsvogt*, her husband could sell conjugal property without consulting him, as in 1775 when a woman in Ebhausen complained that 'only a few days ago [her husband] had put the house and lands on sale without

47 HStAS A573 Bü. 15, fol. 232r, 22.9.1614; ibid., fol. 248v, 9.2.1615.

48 HStAS A573 Bü. 15, fol. 545v, 25.8.1621.

49 Ryter, 'Geschlechtsvormundschaft', pp. 498–502.

50 PAW KKP Vol. IV, fol. 265r–266v, 15.6.1708.

51 PAW KKP Vol. I, fol. 87r, 10.12.1652.

52 PAW KKP Vol. V, fol. 54v–55r, 12.3.1686.

in the least consulting his wife and her *Kriegsvogt*, and had sold some of them'.[53] In 1788, when an Ebhausen woman objected to her husband's prodigal dealings with her land (and his fornication with the maidservants), the church court told her 'that although she had a larger property than her husband, she should not regard him as a servant but rather as a husband, and not strive for unrestricted domination'.[54] Sabean's research on the Württemberg village of Neckarhausen also provides many examples of Württemberg husbands who dissipated their wives' property despite the fact that these wives had *Kriegsvögte*.[55]

As these examples illustrate, an important practical influence on how gender guardianship operated, and hence on the economic position of married women more generally, was the stance taken by community officials and community courts, which exercised considerable legal powers over spouses' behaviour both outside and inside the household. In Württemberg, as in most other pre-industrial European societies, community officials, from the town mayor or village headman down through the twelve members of the village council to the lowly field-wards, were all married (or occasionally widowed) males. Community assemblies invited each male household head in turn to report his concerns to his fellow citizens but did not invite the same expression of views from married women and even excluded the c.15 per cent of household heads who were widowed females.[56] Females were thus excluded from community assemblies, community council membership, and community offices. The interests of wives and daughters may have been represented by their husbands and fathers, but those of widows and independent unmarried women relied on more distant male relatives (if they were fortunate enough to possess any) – or on *Kriegsvögte* who were appointed by the community council and thus reflected its interests, as well as (sometimes instead of) those of the women. Community courts were widely recognized by contemporaries as not being impartial. They favoured the kin of the court members, as reflected in a 1717 complaint in Ebhausen 'that the church-court members, when their kin are examined in a case, have the custom of continuing to preside, which means that the latter's accusers are reluctant to testify properly'.[57]

When it came to marital conflict, too, community courts had their own priorities, high among which was the desire to sustain existing marriages at almost any cost, in order to ensure tax payments and prevent welfare burdens. Community courts were also made up of married men who had to deal with accused husbands as their fellow citizens and guild members in everyday transactions after the court-hearing was over, and who in any case explicitly held the view that wives should defer to husbands and husbands were entitled to discipline wives. In cases of marital conflict, this led them to inflict often risibly feeble penalties on erring husbands while ordering wives to defer to their husbands, even when these were feckless, alcoholic, violent, or deranged. As married males, commu-

53 PAE KKP Vol. VI, fol. 18r, 2.9.1775.

54 PAE KKP Vol. VII, fol. 75r, 23.1.1788.

55 Sabean, *Property*, pp. 214–22.

56 HStAS A573 Bü. 81–103 (1554–1801). Ulbrich, *Shulamit*, pp. 153–4.

57 PAE KKP, Vol. III, fol. 44, 21.12.1717; Sabean, *Property*, pp. 48–9 with n. 53.

nity council members tended to show understanding for the difficulties of other married males but little for those of married females. Thus in 1720 the Ebhausen court excused a man for physically abusing his pregnant wife on the grounds that 'his wife is unspeakably wicked [*bös*], which the court-members bear witness to'.[58] Although the law in principle provided protection for wives' property, a wife was vulnerable to her husband's physical coercion and to admonitions by community courts to 'recognize her own weakness', 'not strive for domination', and give way even to a prodigal husband.[59]

Community courts also had discretion to decide the conditions under which a deserted wife might be allowed to dispose freely of her land, and the married male members of communal courts tended to use this discretion in the interests of married males, not married females. Thus in 1784, the Liebelsberg village court refused a deserted wife the right to sell her lands, despite the husband's desertion having lasted the statutory seven years, and 'even though they knew well that the property standing in guardianship did solely belong to the deserted woman'. When she appealed to the district court, she was refused access to her land unless she set aside 90 *Gulden* to support her husband should he ever return – a clear case of the community court members placing the interests of a married male (not to mention themselves as contributors to the community poor-relief fund) ahead of the property rights of a married woman.[60] Such decisions made it hard for a married woman, even if she was deserted by her husband, to sell or mortgage land, which in turn constrained her ability to secure the agricultural micro-credit which kept Württemberg's small-scale farmers afloat from season to season.

On paper, therefore, the legal system might protect the property rights of married women, whether through gender guardianship or through the inheritance system. But in practice these legal rights were interpreted and enforced mainly through communal institutions which had wide-ranging legal powers and were manned by married (or occasionally widowed) men. The implementation of the law thus often functioned to limit married women's ability to protect their land or dispose of it freely, and thus constrained their ability to operate independently in agriculture, regardless of how economically active they were in the actual operation of the farm.

Married Women in Crafts and Proto-Industries

The legal system affected the economic options of married women somewhat differently in the industrial sector than it did in agriculture, since industrial activities

58 PAE KKP, Vol. III, fol. 87v, 25.7.1720.

59 For similar admonitions administered to wives by community courts in other parts of Germany, see L. Roper, *The Holy Household: Women and Morals in Reformation Augsburg* (Oxford, 1989), p. 174; R. Beck, 'Frauen in Krise: Eheleben und Ehescheidung in der ländlichen Gesellschaft Bayerns während des Ancien Régime', *Dynamik der Tradition. Studien zur historischen Kulturforschung*, ed. R. Van Dülmen (Frankfurt am Main, 1992), pp. 137–212, here pp. 179–80.

60 HStAS A573 Bü. 49, fol. 197v–199r, 27.10.1784.

were much less dependent on their practitioners, having secure property rights in land. In early modern Württemberg, as in many other parts of Europe, married women participated vigorously in industrial activities, in the form both of locally-oriented crafts and of export-oriented 'proto-industries'.[61] This can be seen quantitatively in the database of observed work (see Table 11.1).

Married women's participation in the core tasks of guilded crafts appears to have been quite limited: only 4 per cent of their observed work occurred in guilded crafts and 2 per cent in the regional worsted-weaving proto-industry, which was also guilded. By contrast, 9 per cent of married women's observed work occurred in *unguilded* industrial activities, particularly spinning, but also knitting, sewing and lace-making. Furthermore, married women also participated in the commercial side of craft activity, which accounted for another 3 per cent of their observed work. Finally, married women were active in operating mills, which accounted for another 3 per cent of their observed work. In combination, these variegated industrial activities accounted for 21 per cent of the observed work of married women – about the same proportion as for agriculture.

This is confirmed by qualitative sources, which show the wide array of industrial activities in which married women participated. For one thing, craft output was sold in markets in which we observe active selling by the wives of – to give just a few examples – shoemakers,[62] hat-makers,[63] bakers,[64] butchers,[65] and proto-industrial worsted-weavers.[66] Some married women were devious bargainers, as with a Sulz weaver's wife who was accused in 1661 of supplying short measure to a customer buying her woollen broadcloth.[67] Craftsmen's wives often emerge as relentless debt-collectors, as in 1617 when a worsted-weaver's wife tried to collect a 17-*Batzen* debt from a customer 'four times in a single day',[68] in 1706 when a shoemaker's wife threatened to report a customer to the district governor for a shoe-repair bill,[69] or in 1720 when a baker's wife collected debts around the town just before attending confession at the church.[70] Wives courted marital conflict by selling craft output independently, as in 1675 when a potter accused his wife of selling pottery in a way that he characterized as 'not fair',[71] in 1681 when a butcher's wife berated her husband for spending 'the 24 *Kreuzer* which ... the shoemaker paid her on a meat debt',[72] or in 1785 when an Ebhausen

61 C. Vanja, 'Zwischen Verdrängung und Expansion, Kontrolle und Befreiung. – Frauenarbeit im 18. Jahrhundert im deutschsprachigen Raum', *Vierteljahrschrift für Sozial- und Wirtschaftsgeschichte* 79 (1992), 457–82, here pp. 463, 472–3; M. E. Wiesner, *Working Women in Renaissance Germany* (New Brunswick, 1986), pp. 153–6; Ulbrich, *Shulamit*, p. 186.

62 HStAS, A573 Bü. 15, fol. 566r, 16.1. 1622.

63 HStAS, A573 Bü. 4395, Heftchen #1 (1636–42), unpag.

64 PAW, KKP, Bd. IV, fol. 68v, 1.8.1676; PAW, KKP, Bd. V, fol. 146r, 17.8.1694.

65 PAE, KKP, Bd. VII, fol. 50v, 5.12.1786.

66 HStAS, A573 Bü. 12, fol. 19.5r-v, 4.11.1591.

67 PAW, KKP, Bd. II, fol. 22r, 15.2.1661.

68 HStAS A573 Bü. 15, fol. 357v, 18.12.1617.

69 PAW, KKP, Bd. V, fol. 255r-v, 26.2.1706.

70 PAW, KKP, Bd. V, fol. 363r, 16.8.1720.

71 PAW, KKP, Bd. III, fol. 692–3, 15.1.1675.

72 PAW KKP Vol. IV, fol. 199r, 22.4.1681.

nail-smith's wife insisted on accompanying him to Berneck to sell nails 'because she knew well that he would gladly drink away the earnings'.[73]

Craftsmen's wives not only sold the output from the craft workshop but also took responsibility for securing raw material inputs through market transactions. Thus, for example, in 1595 a Wildberg woollen-broadcloth-weaver's wife was recorded buying raw wool from another married woman,[74] in 1636 a butcher's wife participated in a purchase of beef-cattle,[75] and in 1668 a worsted-weaver's wife complained that her husband was being prodigal with four and a half hundredweight of wool which they had purchased.[76] A craftsman's wife might be far readier to pursue a putting-out debt than her husband, as in 1622 when Jacob Klay loaned raw wool to Basti Mosapp on a promise of repayment in cloth and cash. Mosapp repaid the cloth but refused to pay the cash, so Klay 'regarded it as best to let these 9 *Batzen* fall, so that he might be spared further running around'. But Klay's wife 'would not permit him to do this, so he told her she should bring in these 9 *Batzen* herself'; she ultimately elicited repayment after repeated disagreeable confrontations and verbal abuse from Mosapp and his wife.[77] Many of these wives regarded themselves – rightly or wrongly – as better suited to business than their husbands.

Legal provisions still shaped and constrained the activities of married women in the industrial sector, just as they did in agriculture. In industry, however, the main aspect of the legal system affecting married women consisted of the legal privileges of guilds. According to the guild ordinances which regulated almost all crafts and proto-industries in Württemberg, as in most other parts of early modern Germany, the wife of the master was the only female allowed to carry out all tasks associated with the craft – but she could legally do so only in the particular occupation in which her husband held his mastership licence. Most guild ordinances were uncompromising. The master was allowed to work with male journeymen (too costly for most poor masters, and rationed by the guild), male apprentices (cheaper, but untrained and also rationed by the guild), male offspring (often non-existent or the wrong age), or his own wife. He was not allowed to use non-guild-trained servants or labourers (of either sex), or his own daughters, or other female relatives. This is reflected quantitatively in Table 11.1, where we see that more than half of all observations of guilded work (crafts, proto-industry and milling) recorded for females were by married women and another 36 per cent by widows: only 13 per cent (mostly running errands and operating mills) was carried out by daughters or maidservants, and none by independent unmarried women.

These guild restrictions on craft work created strong incentives for craftsmen's wives to participate in all aspects of the activities of the workshop, including the heaviest physical labour. Thus in 1592 a Wildberg mason's wife 'was making a wall'.[78]

73 PAE KKP Vol. VII, fol. 1r, 3.1.1785.

74 HStAS, A573 Bü. 12 , fol. 248r, 16.1.1595.

75 HStAS, A573 Bü. 17, fol. 401v–402r, 3.9.1640.

76 PAW, KKP, Bd. III, pp. 252–3, 2.4.1669.

77 HStAS A573 Bü. 15, fol. 608r, 19.12.1622.

78 HStAS A573 Bü. 12, fol. 87v, 22.6.1592.

In 1668 the wife of a fountain-master was repairing the Wildberg fountains.[79] In 1676 a Neubulach baker's wife was carrying bread long distances in hilly country when eight months pregnant.[80] In 1687 a Wildberg baker's wife was lifting heavy bales of flour when eight months pregnant.[81] In 1709 a Wildberg cooper's wife was carrying barrel-wood in from the forest.[82] In 1738 a smith's wife was helping him drag a heavy load of iron from Nagold to Altensteig in pouring rain.[83] In 1790 a twenty-four-year-old woman pregnant by a journeyman nail-smith described their intention of working together at a nail-smithy after they married.[84]

On the other hand, guild regulations absolutely *excluded* married women from work in any *other* occupation. Thus in 1624 the wife of a man who wove both traditional woollen broadcloths and new-style proto-industrial worsteds sought to purchase a share of a shipment of raw wool which was legally reserved for members of the woollen-broadcloth-weavers' guild. She was excluded on the grounds that her husband was a member of the worsted-weavers' rather than the woollen-weavers' guild.[85] In 1635, a woman whose woollen-broadcloth-weaver husband had just died was fined the equivalent of one-third of a maidservant's annual wage by the worsted-weavers' guild in Wildberg because 'she had taken it upon herself to practise the craft even though her husband had never been apprenticed to worsted-making'.[86] The only exceptions to this rule were activities such as mill-labouring, spinning, and working as a seamstress. The millers' guilds were unusually liberal in permitting the employment of unguilded general servants and labourers, with the result that some mill-labourers were married women, such as the donkey-driver's wife employed by an Ebhausen miller in 1736.[87]

Guilds also limited married women's work by prohibiting masters from paying employees above a particular maximum rate. A particularly severe example was the spinning piece-rate ceiling imposed by the guilds of the worsted-weavers and the merchant-dyers, and enshrined in law so that it could be enforced by state officials.[88] As the weavers' guild-ordinance put it, 'spinning a pound [of yarn] shall be paid at as high a wage as the [weavers'] craft agrees among its members, and the dyers as well as the worsted-weavers shall support this in all ways, and each master shall then infallibly stick to the agreed wage'.[89] We can observe these legal privileges of the male weaving-masters affecting married women's industrial work

79 HStAS A573 Bü. 92, fol. 6v, 1.12.1668.

80 PAW KKP Vol. IV, fol. 68v, 1.8.1676.

81 PAW KKP Vol. V, fol. 64r, 4.2.1687.

82 PAW KKP Vol. V, fol. 268v, 31.5.1709.

83 PAE KKP Vol. III, fol. 207r, 16.3.1738.

84 PAE KKP Vol. VII, fol. 194v, 20.5.1790.

85 HStAS A573 Bü. 16, fol. 79v, 19.8.1624.

86 HStAS A573 Bü. 810, 1635–6, unpag., 'Strafen'.

87 PAE, KKP, Bd. III, fol. 201v, 18.11.1736; for the occupations, see HStAS, A573 Bü. 6967, fol. 30r, 1736.

88 For a detailed discussion of these regulations, see Troeltsch, *Zeughandlungskompagnie*, pp. 125–31; Ogilvie, *State Corporatism*, pp. 353–5; Ogilvie, *A Bitter Living*, pp. 165, 298, 307–8, 318, 347.

89 Emendations dated 1654 to 'Engelsattweberordnung in A. 1608 [actually 1611] vfgerichtet', in Troeltsch, *Zeughandlungskompagnie*, 435–53, here article 21 (p. 446 n. 2).

in practice. In 1623, for instance, a married spinner from the village of Gültlingen fell foul of these guild piece-rate ceilings when she was reported to the district court for charging weavers higher prices for finishing work faster, in violation of the legal maximum rate she was allowed to charge.[90]

Even when guilds permitted married women to work and did not cap their earnings, there were other aspects of the law that constrained their work in the industrial sector. Here, again, gender guardianship can be seen in action as a way for male transaction partners to gain an advantage over a female seeking to conduct a business independently. In 1614–15, a woman called Anna Klaißin was operating as a broadcloth-weaver in Wildberg on the basis of the guild licence of her husband, who had either died or deserted her, leaving her to enjoy the legacy of his guild licence. However, Anna's ability to continue conducting the workshop was limited by the legal requirement, which had been introduced in Wildberg after about 1600, for a married or widowed female to be represented in transactions before the community court by a legal guardian. For five months in 1614–15 two of Anna's male customers managed to delay payment of a debt on cloths she had supplied – in the amount of 78 *Gulden*, equivalent to three-quarters of the value of an average house at the time – by refusing to answer her debt suit until she was represented in court by a male relative.[91]

The legal powers of the local community also affected married women's ability to earn a living in the secondary sector. Even when an industrial occupation was not regulated by a guild, it could require a licence from the community authorities, which they might prove extremely unwilling to grant to a married woman. In 1793, for instance, a male citizen of Wildberg complained at the annual communal assembly that a basket-maker called Kiefer was dwelling at the paper-mill in the nearby village of Gültlingen, 'and his wife, equipped with a slip of paper from [the paper-miller], but without any permit [*Patent*], is roaming around this district and neighbouring ones under the pretext of collecting rags'. The assembly responded by instructing the Gültlingen village headman 'no longer to permit this basket-maker to stay there, and to make known this prohibition against giving him shelter to the entirety of the inhabitants, and especially the paper-miller, on pain of a *Kleine Frevel* [3 *Gulden*] fine'.[92] Even an industrial occupation from which women were not debarred by any guild, such as collecting rags to make paper, was regarded as requiring a legal *Patent* (permit), and could prove impossible to pursue for a married woman who had not secured permission to do so from the local community.

Communal courts also constrained married women's work in industry, by systematically supporting husbands against wives in cases of marital conflict over the craft activity which provided the family's livelihood. In 1668, when a Wildberg worsted-weaver beat his wife for objecting to his drunkenness, gambling, and prodigality with their purchased store of raw wool, 'and now there was none left, and they still owed 12 *Gulden* down there in the purchasing-

90 HStAS, A573 Bü. 15, fol. 618r, 20.2.1623.

91 HStAS A573 Bü. 15, fol. 232r, 22.9.1614; ibid., fol. 248v, 9.2.1615.

92 HStAS A573 Bü. 100, fol. 28r-v, 1793.

house, and also had various other debts', the community court did gaol the husband briefly, but admonished the wife 'to show and conduct herself towards her husband peacefully and modestly, and loyally attend to the householding as befits an honourable wife, and not give him cause to give her trouble'.[93] In 1674, when a Wildberg butcher beat his wife, ejected her from the house, and threatened to murder her for not yielding up to him 30 *Kreuzer* which she had earned from selling meat ragout, the court regarded the situation as dangerous enough to send their child to foster-parents, but ordered the wife to return home to her husband, feebly admonishing both spouses to treat each other better in future.[94] In 1697, when the Ebhausen community court reproved (but did not punish) a miller for beating and abusing his wife 'wickedly and bestially', as well as for his 'tyranny and cruelty ... enmity and embittered moods', the wife was 'also, as a *Weib* [wife/woman], given the appropriate lesson, with illustrations of how she should not incite her husband with scornful, impertinent and wicked words or unpeaceful gestures to anger and beatings but rather much more greet him virtuously at all times and thus protect herself from misfortune'.[95] In 1778, when a Wöllhausen worsted-weaver threatened to kill his wife if she continued to criticize him for his perpetual bad householding, idleness, drinking and gambling, the court warned him to improve his behaviour, but concluded by ordering the wife to stay home, work diligently, and refrain from gossiping about her husband with her sisters, which he claimed had caused all the problems.[96]

Not surprisingly, husbands regarded their own decisions as sovereign, used physical violence to enforce them, and acted bemused when reproved by community courts.[97] In 1681, for instance, when a Wildberg butcher threatened his wife with a knife if she would not stop criticizing his prodigality with a sum of money collected from a customer, he evidently regarded such behaviour as normal, putting it to his fellow married men in the church court that, after all, 'one can easily imagine that sometimes trouble arises between married people'.[98] In 1785, when an Ebhausen nail-smith nearly throttled his wife on discovering that she had drawn up a list of his debts to send to the district authorities to prove his poor householding, and threatened to kill her when she insisted on accompanying him on a nail-selling expedition for fear he would drink away the proceeds, he defended himself to the community court in wondering tones: 'the money belongs to me, after all'.[99] In 1797, when an Ebhausen woollen-broadcloth-weaver subjected his wife to violent sexual assault after she objected to his gambling and criticized his conduct of the household economy, he answered that 'he had the choice, he did what he wanted, he didn't have to ask anyone ... it was nothing to

93 PAW KKP Vol. III, p. 254, 2.4.1669; ibid., pp. 256–7.

94 PAW KKP Vol. III, pp. 641–2, 12.6.1674.

95 PAE KKP Vol. I, fol. 82v–83r, 9.12.1697.

96 PAE KKP Vol. VI, fol. 41v–44r, 6.2.1778.

97 For similar acceptance, on the part of both husbands and communities, of violence against wives, see Roper, *Holy Household*, pp. 185–94; Ulbrich, *Shulamit*, pp. 78–9.

98 PAW KKP Vol. IV, fol. 199r-v, 22.4.1681.

99 PAE KKP Vol. VII, fol. 2v, 3.1.1785.

do with her, he didn't need to ask such a snot-nose as she, after all she doesn't have anything, he could give her (saving reverence) filth to her and then she could go wherever she wished'.[100]

Married women were both able and willing to participate in industrial activity. Neither physical weakness, domestic responsibility, nor lack of specialized training prevented them from doing so. What did constrain their participation in the secondary sector were legal rules – guild privileges, community powers, and gender guardianship – which, even if they were not deliberately devised to regulate the economy in the interests of male masters and male citizens, were interpreted in such a way as to give rise to this outcome in a large number of situations.[101]

Married Women in the Service Sector

The service sector was an important and growing part of most early modern European economies. Commerce, in particular, expanded greatly in the early modern period, and evidence from all over Europe testifies to married women's active engagement in trading and retailing. The same was true in Württemberg, in so far as this was not prevented by the complex network of legal privileges governing permission to participate in commercial activities. According to Württemberg law, farmers and craftsmen were the only people allowed to sell their own products. Middlemen (and -women) who traded in goods they had not themselves produced, and that were not on the list of legal 'merchants' wares', were defined as *Fürkäufer* (regraters), whose activities were illegal. To specialize in commerce legally, one had either to obtain admission to the guild of merchants and shopkeepers as a master, or to pay a fee to the guild in lieu of membership, or to obtain a special dispensation from the duke of Württemberg. Those trading under the latter two conditions were restricted to the specific goods named in their permits.[102] Trading in certain wares, specifically proto-industrial worsteds destined for export-markets, was after 1650 made the monopoly of an association of merchant-dyers whose legal charter explicitly excluded all women from trading, even their own members' wives and widows.[103]

Wives of men who possessed the required guild membership (or other special permit) did participate actively in commercial businesses, as shown by the 3 per cent of the observed work activities of married women in commerce in Table 11.1. In 1615, for instance, a Heilbronn merchant's wife sold a sack full of raw wool to a Wildberg worsted-weaver,[104] and in 1714 a Wildberg shopkeeper's wife was fined

100 PAE KKP Vol. VIII, p. 100, 10.4.1797.

101 For similar conclusions see Wiesner, *Working Women*, pp. 168–85.

102 See J. F. C. Weisser, *Das Recht der Handwerker nach allgemeinen Grundsätzen und insbesondere nach dem herzoglichen Wirtembergischen Gesezen entworfen* (Stuttgart, 1780), pp. 329–30; Ogilvie, *State Corporatism*, pp. 70–9; Sabean, *Property*, p. 160.

103 Troeltsch, *Zeughandlungskompagnie*, p. 67; on women's non-participation in other early modern merchant trading companies, see M. E. Wiesner, *Women and Gender in Early Modern Europe* (Cambridge, 2000), p. 107.

104 HStAS, A573 Bü. 15, fol. 282r, 7.9.1615.

for crying out wine for sale on the Sabbath.[105] Soldiers often got permits from the prince allowing their wives to run small shops in their absence, as in Balingen in 1711 when 'Conradt Götz, by profession a bird's-nester, got a ducal permit to conduct a business ... and (because he has not been here now for more than 3 years and is serving in the army) he conducts through his wife some little business selling tobacco cuttings',[106] or when Adam Achach in Dagersheim, 'a hussar and in the field ... obtained a ducal command dated 22 October 1697 ... permitting him to conduct a little shop with tobacco, and his wife thus runs this little shop'.[107]

But the legal privileges of the guilded shopkeepers – and of the masters of other guilds who had monopoly rights over retailing wares they regarded as appertaining to their craft – severely constrained married women's ability to pursue such commercial activities. In 1711, for instance, the guilded shopkeepers of Backnang sought to prevent married women from selling soap and other washing products at weekly markets 'without being able to show any permits to do so'.[108] In 1742 an Effringen soldier's wife was gaoled for 'dealing in foreign nails' after a complaint by the Wildberg nail-smith that this 'violates the nail-smiths' [guild] ordinance and damages him in his craft'.[109] In 1793 five male citizens separately made use of the *Vogt-Rüg-Gericht* – an assembly of all community citizens at which each (male) citizen in turn was asked if he had anything to report – to complain that 'in Liebelsberg and Schönbronn, lard is being bought up by a *Fürkaufferin* [female regrater] from Teinach, even outside shop-opening-hours'. The community officials immediately sent out written reminders to all communities in the district about the illegality of regrating, urged all citizens to report every case of regrating instantly, and wrote to the governor of the district in which this woman lived, 'warning her against further regrating and the penalties it involves'.[110]

Married women were active not just in commerce but also in other tertiary-sector activities such as music, teaching and healing. Pastors' wives worked as organists, as in 1720 when the new Ebhausen pastor applied for a yearly salary of 12 *Gulden* for his wife for playing the organ at church services, funerals and weddings, 'as she had in Bulach for 3 years and previously in Dettingen near Anhausen for 11 years'.[111] When the pastor's wife died in 1721, the village embarked on wearisome years of unsatisfactory contracts with male organists.[112] Schoolmasters' wives contributed actively to teaching, as reflected in legislation of 1654 and 1744 forbidding schoolmasters from leaving their pupils 'solely to their wives' while they themselves worked as clerks or tavern-keepers.[113] In 1764, the Wildberg church court appointed the sex-

105 PAW, KKP, vol. V, fol. 308r, 18.5.1714.

106 HStAS A228 Bü. 713, #8, fol. 2r, 15.9.171.

107 HStAS A228 Bü. 713, #11, fol. 6v, 14.9.1711.

108 HStAS A228 Bü. 713, #10, 7.10.1711.

109 HStAS A573 Bü. 95, fol. 6v, 25.1.1742.

110 HStAS A573 Bü. 100, fol. 37r, 1793.

111 PAE KKP, Vol. III, fol. 92r, 21.12.1720.

112 E.g. PAE KKP, Vol. III, fol. 96r, 26.10.1721.

113 'Cynosura Oeconomiae ecclesiasticae Wirtembergicae', in Reyscher, *Sammlung*, vol. 11, part 1, pp. 12–17, here p. 14; 'Gen. Syn. Reskript an die Gen. Superintendenten, betr. die Einführung eines ausführlichen Modus visitandi' (9.10.1744), in Reyscher, *Sammlung*, vol. 11, part 1, pp.

ton's wife over the heads of four male applicants as *Collaboratorin* to teach the mixed beginners' class in the town school, on the grounds that she 'desired no increase in the salary, and possesses sufficient capability for the vacant *Collaboratur* or teaching of the smallest children'.[114] Within five months, the ducal consistory was objecting to the appointment, but the sexton's wife declared that 'she would not step down voluntarily from the *Collaboratur* which she has been taking care of hitherto'.[115] It was not her lack of the requisite skills, but her not having pursued the formal professional training (something she could not do since Latin schooling was legally reserved for males) that ultimately prevented her from continuing to work as a schoolteacher.

A similar pattern can be observed in the healing professions. The only type of medical activity legally permitted to women was that of official midwife (*Hebamme* or *Wehemutter*) and her assistant 'sworn women'. This work was recognized to be skilled, but the occupation of midwife was also a formal office, requiring ratification by the community church court and the taking of an oath, and had regulatory as well as medical functions, here as elsewhere in early modern Germany.[116] Midwives and sworn women were expected to report signs of attempted abortion or infanticide,[117] testify to whether a birth was premature or indicated premarital 'fornication',[118] physically examine girls suspected of illegitimate pregnancies,[119] interrogate unmarried mothers during labour about the identity of the father,[120] and report superstitious practices surrounding childbirth.[121] Appointments of midwives and sworn women generated tension between communal religious authorities who emphasized moral stature, and expectant mothers who preferred medical skill. Even when the views of married women in the community were consulted, as in Ebhausen in 1710, they 'were warned beforehand to have an eye to piety'; ultimately they were only permitted to determine a field of four candidates, from which the members of the community court – all males – chose the most morally suitable (the schoolmaster's wife).[122] The implication was that, left to themselves, childbearing women would consider other traits than piety – perhaps not surprisingly, considering that they were choosing the woman on whose medical skills their lives might depend.

In practice, childbearing married women rejected the services of official midwives they did not trust, and sought to employ illegal midwives whose medical skills (or discretion) they preferred. Thus in 1603 the communal authorities fined and gaoled a Wildberg rope-maker's wife, who had 'driven out a premature child

25–30, here p. 26.

114 PAW KKP Vol. VI, fol. 142v–143r, 26.10.1764.

115 PAW KKP Vol. VI, fol. 146v–147r, 29.3.1765.

116 As discussed, e.g., in Vanja, 'Auf Geheiß', p. 82; Ulbrich, *Shulamit*, pp. 69–72.

117 E.g. PAW KKP Vol. III, p. 591, 25.9.1673. See also M. E. Wiesner, 'The Midwives of South Germany and the Public/Private Dichotomy', *The Art of Midwifery: Early Modern Midwives in Europe and North America*, ed. H. Marland (London, 1993), pp. 77–94, here p. 87.

118 E.g. PAW KKP Vol. IV, fol. 68v, 1.8.1676. See also Wiesner, 'Midwives', p. 87.

119 E.g. PAE KKP, Vol. III, fol. 214r, 17.9.1738. See also Wiesner, 'Midwives', p. 87.

120 E.g. HStAS A573 Bü. 15, fol. 16v, 19.7.1610; PAW KKP Vol. IV, fol. 4v, 17.9.1675. See also Wiesner, 'Midwives', p. 86.

121 E.g. PAE KKP Vol. I, fol. 69r–69v, 22.3.1696.

122 PAE KKP Vol. II, fol. 69v–70r, 5.12.1710, here 69v.

for Young Hans Göltling's wife'.[123] In 1654, Gültlingen was described as being 'ill-equipped with midwives, [since] the old one cannot properly be used any more on account of great age, and no-one else will take on this service', yet a baker's wife was reported to the communal church court for having helped another woman give birth, allegedly using superstitious practices.[124] In 1675 the Wildberg church court agreed to formalize the position of a worsted-weaver's wife who had 'stepped into the place of the deceased ... previous midwife'; her father had been a physician, which may have led expectant mothers to turn to her.[125] In 1691 a worsted-weaver's wife was gaoled because she 'allowed herself to be used as a midwife' despite not holding the office.[126] In 1723 a baker's wife was fined 'because she committed encroachment [*Eintrag*] upon the midwife'.[127] In 1773 the childbearing women of Wildberg and their husbands were threatened with fines if they continued to avoid the legally appointed new midwife and insist on employing the illegal old one.[128] The explicit use of the guild terminology, *Eintrag* ('encroachment'), to refer to unlicensed midwives illustrates how community authorities manipulated the corporate craft ethos against unlicensed female healers, concerned both to maintain monopoly rents for licensed midwives (by which the authorities secured midwives' loyalty as reproductive 'spies'), and to ensure that all sex-related activities were subject to official surveillance. It was not that unofficial midwives lacked skill or could not attract willing customers, but rather that the rationing of legal licences prevented them from practising more widely.

Married women were thus active in the service sector, but their ability to pursue these activities depended on the legal privileges of the guilds and professional associations that dominated service occupations, and on the legal powers of local communal institutions concerned to regulate the economy in the interests of their – male – citizens. Young females were legally excluded from apprenticeship and advanced schooling, but this did not mean that adult women were incapable of successfully working in skilled crafts and educated professions in later life – as long as they were legally entitled to do so. A married woman was legally permitted to practise a guilded occupation if she had married a man with the relevant guild licence, irrespective of her father's occupation or the length of her marriage, and qualitative evidence shows wives engaging in a wide array of skilled craft activities. Likewise, some married women managed to learn musical, pedagogical, and medical skills that they were allowed to practise, as long as they did so under the aegis of the legal entitlement of a pastor or sexton husband, or as official midwives licensed by the community. But these skills were in higher supply among married women than were the requisite official licences, suggesting that the binding constraint on married women's activity in these sectors was not lack of skills but legal barriers governing whether they were to be permitted to put those skills to practical use.

123 HStAS A573 Bü. 24, fol. 27v, 31.3.1603.

124 HStAS A281 Bü. 1585, fol. 4v–5r, 25.5.1654.

125 PAW KKP Vol. III, p. 740, 30.4.1675

126 PAW KKP Vol. V, fol. 100v, 24.3.1691.

127 PAW KKP Vol. V, fol. 391v, 26.11.1723.

128 PAW KKP Vol. VI, fol. 266r-v, 5.3.1773.

Conclusion

In pre-industrial Germany, as in most other societies in northwest Europe, married women participated in a wide range of economic activities. But their production decisions were comprehensively constrained by the operation of the law. Gender guardianship in theory protected married women from exploitative husbands, but in practice also exposed them to exploitation by guardians and limited their ability to conduct independent businesses as farmers, craftswomen, or shopkeepers because they were not legally entitled to enter autonomously into the requisite contracts. Guilds limited married women's work in manufacturing and commerce unless this work was carried out in the workshop of a husband with a licence to operate as a master in that specific occupation – whether it was a locally-oriented craft, an export-oriented proto-industry, or a retail business. Local communities limited married women's work when it threatened marital harmony or was carried out without the requisite legal licence. Exclusion from full legal rights in these fundamental social networks of pre-industrial German societies not only excluded married women from full enjoyment of any social capital such networks may have generated, but also enabled this social capital to be manipulated by male members of these networks to constrain married women's production and consumption decisions.

Despite these legal restrictions imposed by gender guardianship, community regulations, and guild privileges, married women enjoyed much wider economic opportunities in most early modern German economies than did unmarried or widowed females. But these opportunities were dependent on the approval of their husbands, who alone enjoyed full membership of the fundamental social networks which governed so many aspects of economic life in pre-industrial society. These social networks, particularly the guild and the local community, compelled wives to submit to husbands' decisions, however ill-judged, about how they should allocate their time and what they should produce. It seems likely that this led both to deprivation for many married women and to inefficient allocation of resources for the economy as a whole.

INDEX

Printed and bound by CPI Group (UK) Ltd, Croydon, CR0 4YY

13/09/2026

14960995-0003